Evaluating the Reliability of Macro-economic Models

Evaluating the Reliability of Macro-economic Models

Edited by

GREGORY C. CHOW
Princeton University

and

PAOLO CORSI
Centro Scientifico IBM, Pisa

A Wiley–Interscience Publication

175 YEARS OF PUBLISHING
1807 1982

JOHN WILEY & SONS
Chichester · New York · Brisbane · Toronto · Singapore

Library of Congress Cataloging in Publication Data:
Main entry under title:

Evaluating the reliability of macro-economic models.
Papers presented at the International Symposium on Criteria for Evaluating the Reliability of Macro-economic Models, held Dec. 16–18, Pisa, Italy, organized by the IBM Scientific Center of Pisa and sponsored by the University of Pisa. Includes index.
1. Econometrics — Congresses. 2. Macroeconomics — Mathematical models — Evaluation — Congresses. 3. Economics — Mathematical models — Evaluation — Congresses. I. Chow, Gregory C., 1929–000 II. Corsi, Paolo 1941–000 III. International Symposium on Criteria for Evaluating the Reliability of Macro-economic Models (1980: Pisa, Italy) IV. Università di Pisa.
HB141.E89 339′.0724 81-19766
ISBN 0 471 10150 8 AACR2

British Library Cataloguing in Publication Data:
Evaluating the reliability of macro-economic models.
1. Macroeconomics — Congresses 2. Econometrics — Congresses
I. Chow, Gregory C. II. Corsi, Paolo
339′.0724 HB171.5

ISBN 0 471 10150 8 ✓10|1

Produced in Great Britain by Speedlith Ltd., 76 Great Bridgewater Street, Manchester M1 5JY.
Printed by Pitman Press Ltd., Bath, Avon

Contents

Preface

On December 16 to 18, 1980, the IBM Scientific Center in Pisa, under the directorship of Dr Renzo Marconi, organized an International Symposium on Criteria for Evaluating the Reliability of Macro-economic Models, with the University of Pisa serving as sponsor. Approximately 260 people attended. The Symposium, held in the Centro Studi Cassa di Rispaxmio di Pisa, was an exciting experience because of the important subject matter and the distinguished participants.

Although the use of macro-economic models is widespread around the world, how to evaluate the reliability of these models is by no means a simple matter. Many approaches should be taken to perform this difficult task. The Symposium has provided a forum for the presentation and discussion of some of the most important approaches. The papers presented and the accompanying discussion are now collected in this volume. The material is extremely useful for anyone who wishes to formulate an informed opinion concerning a macro-economic model or who wishes to improve the reliability of one. Certainly, no simple magic formula can be expected to do the job, but an understanding of the concepts and tools presented in this volume will enable a reader with patience and ingenuity to evaluate and improve the reliability of econometric models.

We owe a special debt to Professor Edwin Kuh of MIT who contributed significantly to the planning of the Symposium and was to serve as its chairman, but could not attend because of an untimely illness. This volume would not be possible without the enthusiastic cooperation of every author and discussant. To them, our sincere thanks. The first editor would also like to acknowledge financial support from the National Science Foundation for his work in editing this volume and for the preparation of Chapters 1 and 8.

GREGORY C. CHOW
PAOLO CORSI

Evaluating the Reliability of Macro-economic Models
Edited by G. C. Chow and P. Corsi

CHAPTER 1

Introduction

G. C. CHOW
Princeton University

P. CORSI
Centro Scientifico IBM, Pisa

How does one evaluate an econometric model? This is not a simple question to answer. Most econometric textbooks concentrate on presenting formal procedures for the identification and estimation of econometric models, but the presentation of procedures for evaluating and validating them is much more limited and less systematic. We believe that this volume will provide some useful answers to this important question.

As the following chapters will show, the evaluation of an econometric model can and should be approached in different ways, and the different approaches complement one another. There does not exist a simple way to evaluate an entity as complex as an econometric model. In practice, when a model is specified, its parameters are estimated, passing the tests of correctness in sign and statistical significance at reasonable levels, and the residuals are not obviously correlated, then it is often considered a completed model. What can and should be done to evaluate the model consists of a variety of tasks, some of which are discussed in this volume. First, one should appeal to economic theory to judge the reasonableness of model specifications. In fact, as the chapters by Klein and Deaton show, economic theory can effectively guide the specification of econometric models. Secondly, one can compare the model (or certain parts of it) with alternative formulations, using appropriate statistical criteria for choosing among them. This is the theme of the chapters by Deaton and by Godfrey and Wickens. This theme encompasses the decision as to whether an ARMA structure should be used to model the residuals. Thirdly, one can test whether the exogenous variables used are indeed exogenous and decide how to model accordingly, as discussed in the chapter by Richard.

Fourthly, besides the usual significance tests, there are methods for detecting unduly influential data points and for limiting their undue influence, and methods for pinpointing the parameters and exogenous variables which are most influential in determining the behaviour of a model, as expounded in the chapter by Kuh and Neese. Fifthly, methods based on stochastic control theory are also available for uncovering the trade-off relationships implicit in a model, for measuring the importance of each policy variable (as a generalization of the multiplier concept), and for performing comparative dynamic analysis for the model when a policy rule or a behavioural relation changes, as pointed out in the chapter by Chow. Sixthly, there are tests of the stability of model parameters, as exemplified by the work of Corsi, Pollock, and Prakken.

Seventhly, one may devise measures of the degree of model misspecification, as Fair has done. Eighthly, one can use the accuracy of forecasts to evaluate a model, a topic treated in the chapters by Salmon and Wallis and by Bianchi and Calzolari. Finally, the use of a model for policy analysis and formulation, as exemplified by the work reported by Gauron, Guillaume, Maurice, and Milleron, will help detect model inadequacies and eventually lead to more reliable econometric models. The above listing is by no means complete, but it does represent a very substantial portion of the tools available for the evaluation of econometric models. With this list in mind, we will now give a preview of each of the chapters. The reader will also gain a perspective of the subject from the remarks in Chapter 2 by Mario Sarcinelli and in Chapter 3 by Alvin Karchere and Edwin Kuh, which were prepared for the opening of the Symposium.

In Chapter 4, Lawrence Klein has argued forcefully that economic theory is useful in the construction of econometric models. From the viewpoint of judging the validity of a model, its theoretical content should be an important element, but how well economic theory has been incorporated in a model is partly a matter of subjective judgment. There is no escape from the fact that knowledge of economics is required to judge the validity of an econometric model, in addition to the statistical criteria which will occupy most of the remainder of this volume. Klein's chapter is valuable as it is based upon experiences from the building of econometric models in over three decades, for which the author was awarded the Nobel Prize in Economics in 1980.

In Chapter 5, Angus Deaton has presented an interesting approach to testing non-nested hypotheses. In essence, when there are two non-nested hypotheses explaining the same dependent variable $\mathbf{y}$, this approach takes each hypothesis in turn as the true hypothesis to compute the expectation of the maximum likelihood estimator of the parameters of the remaining hypothesis, and compares this expectation with the above maximum likelihood estimate itself. In the case of comparing two linear regression models with $\boldsymbol{X}$ and $\boldsymbol{Z}$ as alternative explanatory variables, the method reduces to forming an artificially nested regression model with both $\boldsymbol{X}$ and $\boldsymbol{Z}$ as explanatory variables, assumes the true explanatory variables to be $\boldsymbol{X}$ (or $\boldsymbol{Z}$) alone, and tests the hypothesis that the coefficients of $\boldsymbol{Z}$ (or $\boldsymbol{X}$) are zero using the standard F statistic. This method was used in Chow (1957, p. 65) to answer the question whether automobile purchase y was better explained by permanent income X or by a pair of variables Z

consisting of current income and the stock of automobiles. Using this approach, the econometrician may find that if $\boldsymbol{X}$ is the true set of explanatory variables, the coefficients of $\boldsymbol{Z}$ are significantly different from zero, and *vice versa*. This was what Deaton found when he generalized this method to compare two models of consumer demand, one with a free choice of the number of working hours and the other with the number of working hours rationed.

In the regression example, having found that each set of variables $\boldsymbol{X}$ and $\boldsymbol{Z}$ has significant coefficients given the presence of the other set in the composite regression, one may ask which set has better explanatory power. This question can be answered by testing the hypothesis that the residual variances of the two regressions are equal. This test was suggested by Chow (1980) as a generalization of a test of Hotelling (1940) which applies when both $\boldsymbol{X}$ and $\boldsymbol{Z}$ consist of a single explanatory variable. Deaton's chapter is interesting for at least two reasons. First, it demonstrates the power of economic theory in the formulation of econometric hypotheses, a theme stressed in Klein's chapter. Secondly, it suggests an interesting methodology for comparing non-nested hypotheses. As readers will realize, the comparison of non-nested hypotheses has remained an important subject of research, and many approaches are available for the applied econometrician to consider.

The chapter by Leslie Godfrey and Michael Wickens is concerned with testing the null hypothesis that a subset $\boldsymbol{\theta}_2$ of the parameters $\boldsymbol{\theta} = (\boldsymbol{\theta}_1, \boldsymbol{\theta}_2)$ of a nonlinear model $\mathbf{f}_t(\boldsymbol{\theta})$ is zero using the Lagrange multiplier test statistic:

$$s = -[\partial L_T(\hat{\boldsymbol{\theta}})/\partial\boldsymbol{\theta}]'[\partial^2 L_T(\hat{\boldsymbol{\theta}})/\partial\boldsymbol{\theta}\,\partial\boldsymbol{\theta}']^{-1}[\partial L_T(\hat{\boldsymbol{\theta}})/\partial\boldsymbol{\theta}]$$

where $L_T(\boldsymbol{\theta}) = \sum_t l_t(\boldsymbol{\theta})$ denotes the log likelihood function based on a sample of T observations and $\hat{\boldsymbol{\theta}}' = (\hat{\boldsymbol{\theta}}'_1, \mathbf{0})$ maximizes $L_T(\boldsymbol{\theta})$ subject to $H_0 : \boldsymbol{\theta}_2 = \mathbf{0}$, or using an asymptotically equivalent statistic:

$$s^* = \left[\sum_{t=1}^{T} \partial l_t(\hat{\boldsymbol{\theta}})/\partial\boldsymbol{\theta}\right]'\left[\sum_{t=1}^{T} (\partial l_t(\hat{\boldsymbol{\theta}})/\partial\boldsymbol{\theta})(\partial l_t(\hat{\boldsymbol{\theta}})/\partial\boldsymbol{\theta}')\right]^{-1}\left[\sum_{t=1}^{T} \partial l_t(\hat{\boldsymbol{\theta}})/\partial\boldsymbol{\theta}\right].$$

The basic idea is to replace the alternative model $\mathbf{f}_t(\boldsymbol{\theta})$ by the following locally equivalent alternative (LEA) models:

$$\mathbf{f}_t^*(\boldsymbol{\theta}) = \mathbf{f}_t(\boldsymbol{\theta}_1, \mathbf{0}) + [\partial \mathbf{f}_t(\boldsymbol{\theta}_1, \mathbf{0})/\partial\boldsymbol{\theta}_2]\boldsymbol{\theta}_2$$

and

$$\mathbf{f}_t^+(\boldsymbol{\theta}) = \mathbf{f}_t(\boldsymbol{\theta}_1, \mathbf{0}) + [\partial \mathbf{f}_t(\hat{\boldsymbol{\theta}}_1, \mathbf{0})/\partial\boldsymbol{\theta}_2]\boldsymbol{\theta}_2.$$

The use of $\mathbf{f}_t^+(\boldsymbol{\theta})$ instead of $\mathbf{f}_t(\boldsymbol{\theta})$ will often lead to s and s^* statistics which are asymptotically equivalent but computationally much simpler. The authors apply this approach to testing serial independence and homoskedasticity in the residuals of a linear or nonlinear regression model, and of the structural equations in a linear simultaneous-equations model. In reporting on these tests for choosing among nested econometric models one should perhaps mention another approach based on the information criterion, as set forth in Chow (1981a, b).

The chapter by J.-F. Richard summarizes a paper of the same title by Robert Engle, David Hendry, and Jean-François Richard. It provides definitions of weak and strong exogeneity in terms of the distribution of the observable variables in an econometric model, attempts to relate the concept of exogeneity to the invariance of certain structural parameters, and discusses some statistical tests of exogeneity. Weak exogeneity is defined only with reference to certain parameters of interest. A variable $\mathbf{z}_t$ is said to be weakly exogenous for a set of parameters ψ if inference on ψ conditional on $\mathbf{z}_t$ involves no loss of sample information. Let the variables in the model be $\mathbf{x}_t = (\mathbf{y}_t, \mathbf{z}_t)$ and let X_t denote a matrix consisting of $\ldots, \mathbf{x}_0, \mathbf{x}_1, \ldots, \mathbf{x}_t$. The joint density of $\mathbf{x}_t$ can be factorized as

$$D(\mathbf{x}_t | X_{t-1}, \lambda) = D(\mathbf{y}_t | \mathbf{z}_t, X_{t-1}, \lambda_1) D(\mathbf{z}_t | X_{t-1}, \lambda_2)$$

$\mathbf{z}_t$ is weakly exogenous for ψ if and only if ψ is a function of λ_1 only and $(\lambda_1, \lambda_2) \in \Lambda_1 \times \Lambda_2$, Λ_i being the set of admissible values of λ_i. $\mathbf{z}_t$ is strongly exogenous if it is weakly exogenous and is not Granger-caused by the endogenous variables, which, according to the authors, is equivalent to

$$D(\mathbf{z}_t | X_{t-1}, \lambda_2) \equiv D(\mathbf{z}_t | Z_{t-1}, Y_0, \lambda_2).$$

Strong exogeneity permits the use of a separate model for the explanation of $\mathbf{z}_t$ and the disregard of this model for inferences concerning the parameters ψ in the model explaining $\mathbf{y}_t$ alone. Arnold Zellner's excellent discussion has raised a number of theoretical and practical issues and provides a useful supplement to this chapter.

Chapter 8 by Edwin Kuh and John Neese suggests three kinds of diagnostic tools for studying the characteristics of econometric models. The first aims at providing coefficient estimates which will not be greatly influenced by uncharacteristic data. This is done by diagnostics to detect data points which have undue influence and by estimation methods which give less weight to the uncharacteristic data points. A more thorough discussion of these topics can be found in Belsley, Kuh, and Welsch (1980). The second measures the sensitivities of model behaviour to particular parameters, thus providing guidance on where to concentrate our estimation effort. The third is based on the study of the dynamic characteristics of a linearized version of the model using the characteristic roots of the linear system and tracing the effects (measured in terms of elasticities) of exogenous variables and of parameter values on the important roots. The tools of linear analysis are applied to uncover the most important exogenous variables and the crucial parameters in the Michigan Quarterly Econometric Model.

Also in the spirit of detecting certain important characteristics of an econometric model as an aid to its evaluation, the chapter by Gregory Chow brings to bear the methods of optimal control. After briefly explaining the methods of optimal control as applied to nonlinear simultaneous-equations models, the author discusses four applications. The first is the derivation of important trade-off relationships, as between inflation and unemployment or between consumption and defence, implicit in an econometric model. The second is the use of a value function which measures the effect of each control variable on the expected multiperiod loss generated by the model, given a quadratic loss function. This complements the linear analysis of Kuh and Neese for assessing the importance of certain exogenous variables. The third is the study of the effect of a policy rule on the stability characteristics of a model, as an extension of the method of comparative dynamics. The fourth is the study of the effect of a government policy rule on the parameters of other behavioural equations in the model which are the result of private economic agents' optimizing behaviour taking into account the policy rule of the government.

The chapter by Paolo Corsi, Ralph Pollock, and Joel Prakken studies the Chow test of the equality between the coefficients in two regressions when the residuals are serially correlated. It reports on results of Monte Carlo experiments generated by a simple regression model where the residual satisfies

$$u_t = \rho u_{t-1} + \varepsilon_t \qquad |\rho| < 1$$

and the explanatory variable satisfies

$$x_t = \phi x_{t-1} + \psi_t \qquad |\phi| < 1$$

with ε_t and ψ_t normal and independent, the sample size being 50. It was found that when ϕ is zero, the right tail 0.05 and 0.01 probabilities given by the F distribution are reasonable approximations for a wide range of ρ between -0.8 and $+0.6$. However, when ϕ and ρ are both large in absolute value and have the same sign, the distribution of the test statistic has a much thicker right tail than the F distribution, leading to the rejection of the null hypothesis of regression stability with a much higher probability than specified. Some examples from the IBM Quarterly Econometric Model illustrate that when regressions with positively correlated residuals are re-estimated by using the Cochrane–Orcutt transformation, a highly significant F statistic based on the Chow test becomes insignificant. The Monte Carlo results should be compared with those obtained analytically by Isabella Consigliere (1981).

Chapter 11 by Ray Fair is an attempt to estimate the effect of model misspecification on forecasting errors. It is based on a method proposed by the author for decomposing the forecasting error into four components: (1) the residual error, (2) the error in estimating the coefficients, (3) the error in predicting the exogenous variables, and (4) the error in specifying the model. The method is applied to Fair's own model of the U.S. economy in order to study the effect of its possible misspecification. The decomposition suggested is interesting and appears to be useful. However, one should be cautious in interpreting the fourth component as measuring specification error. For example, take a multiple regression model with a correct forecast of the values of the exogenous variables, so that component (3) is absent. There is a well-known formula for the variance of the forecast error based on the variances and covariances of components (1) and (2). If the forecasts turn out to have variances larger than given by the above formula, it might not be due to misspecification in the sense of omission of explanatory variables, but to possible shifts in the regression coefficients. On the other hand, assuming that the model is indeed misspecified by omission of explanatory variables, the actual forecasting errors will have a variance close to the one given by the above formula based on components (1) and (2), provided that the covariance structures of the included and omitted explanatory variables are the same during the sample and forecast periods. In other words, detecting a fourth component does not imply detecting a specification error, and not detecting it does not insure the absence of specification error.

Although economists agree that forecasts should be used to evaluate an econometric model, how they should be used is by no means a simple matter to decide. It is therefore useful to have a systematic exposition of this topic by Mark Salmon and Kenneth Wallis who discuss three types of forecasting comparisons: (a) with actual outcomes, (b) with forecasts by purely statistical time-series models, and (c) with other macro-econometric models. The first comparison is based mainly on the covariance matrix of forecasting errors, which is related to the topic treated by Fair. The second comparison is treated by pointing out the relationships between econometric models and time-series models and some difficulties encountered in comparing the forecasts by the two types of models based on the same set of data. The third comparison also has many dimensions and raises interesting problems for the econometrician. Besides discussing the above three comparisons in terms of linear models, the authors point out the difficulties generated by nonlinear models and by possible changes in model structure.

While Fair's method decomposes forecasting errors into four components, Chapter 13 by Carlo Bianchi and Giorgio Calzolari is concerned with the second component, the errors in estimating the parameters of the model. It is also related to the first comparison as treated by Salmon and Wallis. It compares three methods for estimating the covariance matrix of forecasting errors generated by nonlinear simultaneous-equation models which are derived from the covariance matrix of the estimates of the structural parameters. These methods are due respectively to G. R. Schink, R. C. Fair, and the authors themselves. The last method is partly analytic, as it is based on a linear approximation of the vector $\mathbf{y}$ of endogenous variables as a function of the structural parameters using a first-order Taylor expansion. It can be regarded as a generalization of the method of Goldberger, Nagar, and Odeh to nonlinear simultaneous-equations models. These methods are applied to several macro-econometric models. Some lessons from these computations are reported.

The last chapter, by Andre′ Gauron, Henri Guillaume, Joel Maurice, and Jean Claude Milleron, is noteworthy because it describes how the I.N.S.E.E. model DMS was actually used to assist in the preparation of the VIIIth Plan of France for the years 1980–1985. The model is large, consisting of some 1500 equations. Optimization techniques were used to search for good policies. In fact, total employment was chosen as the objective to maximize, and linear programming was used for maximization subject to inequality constraints which set upper and lower bounds to a number of control and target variables. Not unexpectedly, the optimal solution entails setting most of these variables at either the upper or lower bounds. One should remark that, for the purpose at hand, optimal control techniques can be used instead of linear programming. For example, the rate of unemployment can be used as a target variable in the optimal control formulation, together with other endogenous variables and policy variables. A quadratic function of all these target variables can serve as the objective function. The desired rate for unemployment may be set equal to zero, or some low rate which is not achievable in practice. Instead of the somewhat artificial upper and lower bounds for the target variables (which include the control variables as well), one can use certain desired values for them and penalize the squared deviations from these desired values using a quadratic objective function. The solution values for these variables will no longer equal the bounds previously set, but there will be trade-offs among values of the different target variables to maximize the objective function.

We hope that the above comments will be useful as an introduction to this volume and may also supplement the thoughtful comments provided by the discussants following each chapter.

REFERENCES

Belsley, D. A., Kuh, E., and Welsch, R. E. (1980). *Regression Diagnostics*, Wiley, New York.

Chow, G. C. (1957) *Demand for Automobiles in the United States*, North-Holland, Amsterdam.

Chow, G. C. (1980). 'Selection of variates for use in prediction: A generalization of Hotelling's solution.' In L. R. Klein, M. Nerlove, and S. C. Tsiang (Eds), *Quantitative Economics and Development*, Academic Press, New York. pp. 105–114.

Chow, G. C. (1981a). A comparison of the information and posterior probability criteria for model selection. *Journal of Econometrics*, **16,** 21–33.

Chow, G. C. (1981b). 'Evaluation of econometric models by decomposition and aggregation.' In J. Kmenta and J. B. Ramsey (Eds), *Large-Scale Macro-Economic Models*, North-Holland, Amsterdam, pp. 423–444.

Consigliere, I. (1981). 'The Chow test with serially correlated errors.' *Rivista Internazionale di Scienze Sociali*, **LXXXIX,** 125–137.

Hotelling, H. (1940). 'Selection of variates for use in prediction with some comments on the general problem of nuisance parameters.' *Annals of Mathematical Statistics*, **11,** 271–283.

Evaluating the Reliability of Macro-economic Models
Edited by G. C. Chow and P. Corsi

CHAPTER 2

Policy-making and Macro-economic Models: a Symbiosis?

M. SARCINELLI
Banca d'Italia

What problems do macro-economic models present when used for economic policy purposes?

This was the first question I asked myself when I gladly accepted the invitation to address this Conference, and it is one of the main problems on which I hope to gain some enlightenment from our work.

Naturally, a policy-maker does not rely only on the use of models, nor opt for a single one, nor live by its simulations. He studies the results of a series of models, gathers together the views and estimates submitted or prepared by experts — and this is the activity that probably takes up most of his time — consults his staff and only then reaches a decision ... except when it is taken by default.

This course of action, which is the one usually followed, is certainly a cautious and sensible one. In practice, however, it means that a policy-maker uses an empirical and highly subjective criterion to weigh the sometimes conflicting indications provided by his sources of information. But although the use of this criterion has had a long and honoured tradition among central banks throughout the world, it cannot be considered adequate from a methodological point of view. If I may draw on my own experience and that of my Bank, I would say that there has, over time, been a considerable shift in the relative importance between the judgmental and the formal econometric elements as the Bank's staff have acquired analytical skills in the latter field.

As one would expect, a policy-maker cannot fail to be aware of the debate and competition, even regarding methodology, that exist among his sources of information and so is bound to be interested in the criteria proposed for the evaluation of models and methods, the results of which are brought to him daily.

This brings me to touch upon the heart of the theme of this conference, the examination of the criteria for evaluating the reliability of macro-economic models, which are the most widely known and used quantitative instruments of economic forecasting and analysis.

To begin, however, I should like to make a preliminary point concerning economic policy that is already implicit in the title of the Conference. We are about to hear a discussion on how to evaluate macro-economic models, which describe and forecast the formation of the main aggregates of the national accounts. Almost all the models used for this purpose nowadays are structural econometric models, often of large dimensions, although it is also true that an average European model is still much smaller than is usual in the United States.

I have often wondered how such a major change has come about, how models have grown from tens of equations to thousands and progressed from the experimental to the operative, in what seems to me a relatively short space of time, when I think of my own experience over the past fifteen years and even of my training as an economist.

The first reason, a technical one, is to be found in the assimilation of earlier techniques, such as informal GNP forecasting, and of various methods based on leading indicators or time series analysis, in the dynamic and error structure of the models currently in use. Hence, it seems to me that there is no longer any sharp contrast between informal methods and econometric methods: between traditionalists and empiricists on the one side, and innovators and mathematicians on the other. Model-builders have met with ever-growing success in incorporating into their procedures the knowledge and information acquired elsewhere.

This is fully confirmed by the experience of my Bank, where, in the first stage, a method of forecasting the financial aggregates prevailed based on a simplified scheme of flow-of-funds tables, filled in with econometric projections of single variables or values deduced from specific information, which relied on the balancing accounts constraint and implicitly on the consistency principle which goes with it. This instrument has progressively developed into a real model of the monetary and financial sector of our economy, in which the econometric element has played a large and growing role.

This leaves us with a question which I think will be covered in several interventions and which I would put as follows: how does one evaluate, at the policy-making level, the reliability of forecasts obtained from this or that model or by this or that research team if those forecasts have been obtained by partly formal and partly informal methods? In other words, should we put more trust in the methods used or in the personality and experience of the forecaster?

Going back to the rapid advance of econometric models, a second reason seems to be the emergence and then the extensive development of management and generalized access techniques for national information systems.

I have personal experience of this aspect since I was involved as an executive in setting up some important segments of the Bank of Italy's information systems. At present the new facility gives direct computerized access to the statements of accounts of all banks and to the central risk office's reports on multiple debt positions, as well as to the main series of economic data, in part through the use of interactive techniques.

These systems were created in answer to banking information and supervision requirements, but one can easily imagine their potential role in the building of models of the financial sectors of the economy and in the development of methods of credit control. This is a case in which the supply of statistical information far exceeds the demand justified by the state of development of existing models, which are more backward and less sophisticated in this field than those of the real economy.

In this connection, the tentative question I should like to raise is the following. Is the effort to set up and maintain ever-expanding data bases and collect more and more detailed information justified by the objective of greater accuracy and better understanding of the economic and social milieu, or is there a good chance that they will be fitted into macro-economic models? In other, blunter words, what are the prospects that the econometric profession will use micro-economic and disaggregated data for the validation of decision models of a macro-economic nature?

Finally, there is a third reason, which I understand and appreciate even more than the others — the increased complexity of the economy and its management. The difficulties of the international financial system and the crisis of raw material markets have imposed new and longer-lasting shocks. In general, the economy can be said to have become more vulnerable, not only to external events but also to the errors and delays of economic policy. Hence the need for more detailed study of the economy's structure and of the interaction between structural and institutional mechanisms.

Professor Klein, who has certainly contributed more than anyone else to the development and broader coverage of econometric models, has for some time now been warning us of the need to make our representation of the economy less sketchy. In his presidential address to the American Economic Association he argued that demand management alone is no longer sufficient and that it is necessary to tackle the problem of introducing fully the supply side. Since to face up to the complexity of the economy means to recognize that it is fundamentally characterized by a high degree of interdependence, a revisiting of the Walrasian general equilibrium theory represents a good point of departure for further advancement of economic thought in its three main avenues: the interpretation of social facts, the formalization of analytical models, and the definition of intervention criteria for policy-makers.

The main factor behind the more articulated macro-models we have today can be further analysed from at least three points of view. The large number of economic policy instruments to which it is necessary to make recourse multiply the equations that model the channels through which the sought-for effects take place. Moreover, different users may be interested in separate segments or aspects of the same model. Finally, the drive towards greater accuracy of analytical results may lead to the inclusion of a larger number of variables and equations in any given macro-model.

If there is no other road open to model-building theory, new questions arise. Since large systems, be they communications, welfare programs, national bureaucracies, or international corporations, can counteract the built-in tendency to degradation only through higher and higher maintenance costs, are we to believe that large models, which are themselves, *mutatis mutandis*, large systems, are also affected by the same type of difficulties? Apart from keeping the product quality unaltered in time, another question bewilders the policy-maker in his role as the end user (or victim) of this increased complexity of econometric models. What criteria should he adopt in order to assess the reliability of extremely complex models, the structure and, in a certain sense, the underlying theory of which he may not fully master? In other words, what is the relationship between the increase in the complexity and scope of models and their reliability for decision making?

This question, as I made clear at the beginning, is not meant to be a criticism of model building but rather a pragmatic request on the part of those who, in governments, public administrations, or universities, also have the task of promoting and financing research in this field, as well as making any possible use of its results. In fact, the greater size of models subjects the organization of research itself to management problems and limits that did not exist only a few years ago. Moreover, there is the risk that an excessive division of tasks and an overspecialized approach to model building procedures will result in the advantages of an overall view being lost. I am well aware that such a tendency is both necessary and natural, but I should also like to stress that the parallel between economics and the physical sciences, where this development has taken place, is not really all that close. In economics, the relationship between theory and application is much more dialectic.

At all events, the evolution of econometric models that we have witnesssed—from the first attempts to today's achievements which integrate the demand block of equations with the input–output representation of production and the flow-of-funds schemes on the financial side—represents a considerable intellectual success, the credit for which should go to an entire generation of economists and applied econometricians, which is widely and eminently represented at this gathering in Pisa.

Macro-models do provide an important part of the information upon which to base economic policy decisions: in particular, they can be credited with having made it possible to conduct detailed analyses of complex tax plans. Nonetheless, macro-models do not perform the whole task. There are many aspects of economic policy even in the real sector—such as manpower problems or the preparation of plans for industrial restructuring—in which modelling is still not very advanced.

Thus, from the more general point of view of policy making, there still appears to be a relatively limited area in which models can be used, compared with the overall complexity of the problem. This consideration tends, on the one hand, to cool down the debate regarding model building and, on the other, arouses the desire to push further ahead precisely in the direction of scientific research into the testing and reliability of models. In fact, it is primarily the advance of knowledge and methodologies in this field that will make it possible to understand how far econometric methods can be extended beyond aggregate models of the economy and applied to other vital areas of economic decision making.

In particular, I should like to point out that there is an element of economic policy activity that is keenly appreciated by those who do not want to or cannot limit themselves to managing the present structures even with the help of available models describing the existing framework. I would define this element as innovation. Faced, that is, with changes in circumstances or in the aims of the community, there is a desire, and often a need, to create new frameworks or to use old instruments for new purposes.

In fact, a crucial aspect of all research is the choice of the problem to be investigated or of the emphasis to be given to its various ramifications. In my opinion, this aspect can only superficially be considered, to use Schumpeter's terminology, 'pre-scientific' or pre-analytical. Amongst other things, it implies dissatisfaction with the approaches used in the past that derives from the analytical reconsideration of the causes of the failure of previous economic policy. Perhaps this choice of new problems to be tackled by models — which cannot and must not be considered as universal tools — is the stage of econometric research at which the policy-maker can make a specific contribution, particularly if this is based on previous experience in the use of models for economic policy purposes.

Such experience can also serve the policy maker in another field in which he is called upon to make a specific and creative contribution — the study of possible institutional changes designed to modify the structures of the economy that are reflected in the parameters of existing econometric models. Such models can provide important information with regard to both the sign and the size of the effects of parametric changes on the endogenous variables that are of the greatest interest, but the relationship between the institutional change and the new value of the corresponding quantitative parameter is left to the judgment and experience of the policy maker and to his knowledge of the internal workings of the institutions.

This is, of course, an extremely complex problem and it appears to be especially so in the field of financial structures. In the credit sector, in fact, the legal and institutional frameworks have a profound influence on the objective functions of operators, whose decisions — in the face of changes in these frameworks — are taken in conditions of considerable uncertainty on the basis of subjective assessments of the probabilities and risks involved.

The increased economic and financial instability and the stagflation of the last few years have made it necessary to have greater recourse to monetary policy with the use of new instruments, including some of an administrative nature. In Italy, for example, it was deemed necessary to impose limits on the growth of bank lending and to require the banks to hold a volume of bonds corresponding to a fixed proportion of their deposits. The repercussions of these measures on bank profits and, therefore, on the capital structures of individual banks have raised a problem which can only be partially solved on the basis of the past experience that is incorporated in econometric models. The problem is that of the search for an optimum mix of the various market and institutional instruments that can be used to strengthen the credit system: liability management, early warning, lending of last resort, deposit insurance, special intervention by the central bank, and so on.

The central banker stands even more alone when facing up to the unknown in an international situation like the present one. The Polish question has further increased the instability of world politics in the wake of the crises in Iran and Afghanistan. At the same time, the renewed need of the Soviet Union to import grain tends to affect its price and perhaps that of gold. On the monetary side, the picture is characterized by wide divergences in inflation rates and inflation control policies, which, together with large swings in the demand for money and in expectations, have brought about erratic movements in interest rates, exchange rates, and capital flows. A great deal of progress has been made with multi-country models in dealing with income and expenditure flows and balance-of-payments current accounts. On the other hand, they provide not only much less, but also much less reliable, information regarding the international links between the variables that are of the greatest interest for the harmonization of national monetary policies.

At the present moment there is much questioning about the determinants of the high levels of interest rates in the United States—which have come after fluctuations of as much as 100 per cent—and of the strong upward trend of the dollar. Western Germany finds it difficult to raise interest rates any further above their already high real level in order to counter the pressures on the Deutschmark at a time when GNP is falling at an annual rate of 3 per cent. The United Kingdom, on the other hand, could, and perhaps should, lower its rates from their present very high level, but the general stance of its economic policy does not as yet point clearly in that direction. All this suggests that there is a wide gap in our knowledge about the role played by the factors that are combining to cause the present inconsistencies among interest rates in the major countries and erratic capital movements.

In this state of affairs, some leading countries have undertaken or begun a reappraisal of their approach to monetary policy, as well as of their intervention techniques. In the United Kingdom the monetarist faith upon which the Government has pinned its hopes of both bringing down inflation and reviving long-term growth is not universally shared. In the United States the analysis of money markets is made more complex by the difficulty of assessing technical aspects of the Federal Reserve's new strategy with its emphasis on money supply rather than interest rate objectives. Besides, there has been uncertainty regarding the measurement and even the definition of the money supply, while the instability of the preference for liquidity has been particularly high.

To what extent this backward state of our knowledge is due to insurmountable difficulties of interpretation rather than to 'X-inefficiency' in specifying, estimating, selecting, and analysing econometric models is, I believe, a problem that can only be solved through in-field research. It will nonetheless be a subject for reflection at this Conference, and I am sure that both the papers and the ensuing debate will provide valuable indications in this connection.

Evaluating the Reliability of Macro-economic Models
Edited by G. C. Chow and P. Corsi

CHAPTER 3

Some Initial Thoughts about Model Reliability

A. J. KARCHERE
IBM Corporation
E. KUH
Massachusetts Institute of Technology

The subject of this symposium, *Criteria for Evaluating the Reliability of Macro-economic Models*, is one of principal interest to the econometricians in IBM's Scientific Center in Pisa, and, if your presence here is any indication, it is a subject of concern to a much wider audience. These comments, in two parts, reflect the combined interests of the second author who is concerned with methods of improving model reliability and the first author, whose daily concerns include economic forecasts and their presentation to corporate management.

3.1 AN ACADEMIC VIEW OF MODEL RELIABILITY

When in the mid- to late 1940's econometric modelling as we now know it had its genesis at the Cowles Foundation, it was a time of exuberant optimism. In my (Edwin Kuh's) opinion it is fair to say that the progenitors of modern econometrics believed that economic theory existed — or at the very least that the foundations were there to enable its successful evolution — to model reality well enough to encompass most if not all significant economic phenomena. Coupled with this strong faith in the power of economic theory was an equally optimistic belief in the power and adaptability of classical statistics to solve important problems posed by economic theory.

Thirty years later these early high hopes for econometrics are muted. Econometric models often fall short of expectations, despite major gains in knowledge and many notable theoretical and empirical accomplishments. Some of these concerns, which will be spelled out more below, are a direct consequence of growing aspirations rather than just unfounded optimism.

Once one becomes engaged in the modelling process, it becomes evident that economic theory is silent or incomplete on some central issues, not the least of plicit guidance about dynamic structure, the ch in turn is related to dynamics), and behaviour of rfect competition and what should be done in the al change. Even where economic theory is sufficiently ifficult to make meaningful distinctions among alternatives al inference. For example, production or consumption functions ifferent behavioural implications as a rule more often than not ie data equally well. It is also clear that statistical theory, whether c al or Bayesian, does not correspond closely to the processes of iterative model building we all use.

Some of the shortcomings alluded to have their origins in the nature of the data with which we must deal. In most instances the highly complex socio-economic processes whose essential nature we try to characterize are not amenable to controlled experimentation. Thus, basic assumptions about exogeneity are not subject to verification and the isolation and measurement of theoretically significant components, in the absence of fortuitous experiments generated by Nature, are often difficult or impossible to capture by regression analysis in its various forms. Thus, statistical paradigms which at least implicitly assume experimental control are often inadequate for their task.

If the preceding remarks are not too wide of the mark, it behoves modellers (of all methodological inclinations, not just econometricians) to make suitably modest claims for their progeny. We conduct our trade in circumstances where the most we can realistically hope to accomplish is an adequate approximation of reality. Even then, the quality of that approximation will diminish with time, often quite rapidly, while certain components will completely break down at times.

While experienced modellers know many limitations of their models, a verbal and written tradition of salesmanship has grown up which outsiders, including model clients, find hard to appraise. If we are smart and lucky at the same time, we can squeeze out some useful insights from models. At the same time, it is important to be explicit about the limitations of model analysis.

In an environment such as this, model assessment takes on increased importance. The development of procedures that measure the extent of model adequacy is badly needed if we are to make sensible claims about the information models can provide. Properly qualified, I am convinced that the benefits are both real and important.

Early on during the period surveyed, models were academic exercises: properly so since this art form was then in its infancy. Assessment consisted of peer review of the usual sort including exchanges in journals, conference proceedings, and the like. During this time models were treated as esoteric mysteries by business and government alike. Beginning in the 1960's, it is our impression that models have come to be used, and sometimes even taken quite seriously, in the policy processes of government. The business sector currently pays handsome sums for short and medium term forecasts from which we might infer that they also take models seriously. The use of models in policy is qualitatively different from the use of models to advance knowledge for its own sake. In particular, the notions of what constitutes acceptable performance have changed (slowly, as the culture changes only gradually), and become tougher in certain respects.

While the application of models to policy problems was rapidly expanding, model structures were becoming more sophisticated and complex. Abetted by dramatic reductions in computer costs, modellers have attempted to mimic reality more closely, address more detailed and intricate policy issues, and reduce aggregation biases. One major consequence of greater complexity has been the obscuring of the link between the user's intuition and model behaviour. A black box in the absence of powerful theory or strong intuitive comprehension does not inspire confidence. The commercialization of many models offers an institutional barrier, with similar impediments, to accessibility that permits peer review to function.

The overwhelming emphasis of model builders and users has been on the building and use of models, to the relative neglect of model evaluation. Users want answers yesterday for urgent matters and the model builders respond. Until model users insist on more than minimal evaluation, criteria and procedures for evaluation will continue to lag far behind.

For a host of reasons, including those already suggested, there has been growing scepticism and at times outright hostility to models. Given the nature of the social sciences, we should expect that models will continue to be inherently controversial. Appropriate model evaluation can lead to the articulation of explicit scientific standards for models and thus blunt some valid concerns about models in the policy process. When strengths and limitations have been realistically evaluated, models can offer useful insights into some policy issues more effectively than is now possible.

3.2 A PRACTICAL PERSPECTIVE ON MODEL RELIABILITY AND FORECASTING

My (Alvin Karchere's) perspective on model reliability is that of a forecaster. For many years I have been subject to the salutary experience of presenting a new forecast and explaining why it is different from the last one. It is an experience that teaches humility and instils a sincere, deep-seated interest in improving the reliability of econometric models. By reliability I mean conditional forecast accuracy consistent with sample period experience.

It is necessary at once to make a distinction between model forecast accuracy and the forecast accuracy of econometricians who use models to help them make their forecasts. When I refer to model reliability, I imply an interest in model forecast accuracy. The forecast accuracy of econometricians who use models is another question.

At this point I would like to make a distinction between applied econometrics, by which I mean the building and use of models for forecasting, and theoretical econometrics. The holy grail for both, it seems to me, should be identical—models that forecast accurately. The theoretical econometrician has the luxury of uncompromising pursuit of the holy grail. The applied econometrician, on the other hand, by the nature of his occupation, has a different priority. His primary objective has to be forecast accuracy. This difference in objective has from time to time produced some tension between applied and theoretical econometricians. This occurs because econometric models sometimes produce forecasts that applied econometricians can, or think they can, improve by judgmental rather than statistical techniques. To those econometricians who are dedicated to the unqualified pursuit of the holy grail this appears to be *ad hoc* heresy.

In the work in which I have been involved, the small models we use in forecasting demand for our products produce forecasts that usually are not subject to judgmental adjustment. The forecasts from our medium-sized income and expenditure models usually are. I think the reason this is so is that we have worked harder and devoted more time to the models of business demand than we have to the income and expenditure models. In particular we have focused more on attaining coefficient stability in the demand models than we have in the larger income and expenditure models.

Why is it that almost all econometricians who use income and expenditure models to forecast economic activity override at least part of their models' forecast by judgment? Most of them probably do as we do; we reserve eight quarters or more of the most recent data for systematically testing the accuracy of our stochastic functions beyond the period of fit each time we make a forecast. If the errors in any estimated function are not random in sign and consistent in size with those within the period of fit, we take this as an indication that the function is not behaving properly.

A catalogue of possible difficulties includes: data revisions, economic developments that involve variables not contained in the function, known cyclical bias in the function in the period fit, or instability of the coefficients for other reasons.

To avoid forecast error, action of some kind is necessary. The counsel of perfection is clear. Find the difficulty, re-specify, and estimate the function in such exemplary fashion that the offending out-of-sample residuals become well behaved.

Data revisions are easiest. If the function is a good one, the revised data will generally improve it. The problem is more difficult if some of the other difficulties are present: for example, a consumption function that does not have wealth as an argument in a period of rapidly rising home prices; or the forecaster may know that he has not got the cyclical turning points and amplitudes quite right in a given function and the economy is entering a cyclical downturn.

An applied econometrician labouring under the burden of an imminent forecast deadline, whose reputation depends on forecast accuracy, may find his quest for the holy grail is not an absolute. He does what is possible in the time that is available. That usually means a change in specification and re-estimation is not possible. Instead, he makes the judgments that the knowledge of his model and the data indicate are necessary and adjusts the model accordingly. When time allows, he returns to the quest for the holy grail.

If you assume that constant adjustments are frequently *a priori* evidence of defective stochastic functions, their prevalence in income expenditure model forecasts suggests that stochastic functions suffer from a high mortality rate. Given the pride that usually goes with creative work, and the unrealistic expectations that sometimes accompany model building, it is heartening that applied econometricians continue to maintain the level of enthusiasm that pursuit of the holy grail requires, although a number give up the quest.

Models are subject to failure for a number of reasons, but one is most important. The number of variables that influence economic behaviour are usually more than the statistical methods we use can deal with. For reasons of collinearity in the sample period we omit variables. Frequently the variables that are included suffer from collinearity. Most often there is no theoretical reason for believing that the correlation of the variables on the right-hand side of a function with each other, or with omitted variables, should be stable.

In these circumstances it is not surprising that model coefficients frequently become unstable when they are used for forecasting and that applied econometricians sometimes get tired and lose faith in the holy grail. Their forecasts become dominated by constant adjustments because the forecast accuracy of their models has decayed and the forecaster lacks the time, resources, and enthusiasm to re-specify and re-estimate his model before the next forecast is due.

Despite the predominance of judgmental forecasts made with econometic models, I think that it is too early to abandon the faith. I believe that there are fundamental difficulties that suggest that no one will ever build the perfect model that will remain perfect forever — by perfect I mean that the models' coefficients will remain stable and its forecasts will remain consistent with the experience of its sample period. But that does not mean that the models as they now exist are the end of the line.

Much remains to be done, not the least of which is to use what we know about model reliability, in a word apply, the established statistical tests and procedures that we know, to develop models with stable coefficients and to reject models that will forecast poorly. We also need new thinking as well as new emphasis on model reliability, and that is what this conference is about.

Evaluating the Reliability of Macro-economic Models
Edited by G. C. Chow and P. Corsi

CHAPTER 4

Economic Theoretic Restrictions in Econometrics

L. R. KLEIN
University of Pennsylvania

4.1 WHY A PRIORI RESTRICTIONS?

The sample data used in econometrics come from the living laboratory of actual economic life. They are not controlled, and this makes statistical inference in our subject especially difficult. Econometrics is not unique in this respect, but we do operate with a special branch of statistics. In this living laboratory everything depends on everything else. The economy, in Walrasian spirit, can be represented as a system of simultaneous equations. They are nonlinear, stochastic, and dynamic. But the equation systems of other disciplines may also have these characteristics.

How can we identify the equation systems of econometrics, not only of the economy as a whole but of partial systems as well? The late T. C. Liu argued forcefully that equation systems of econometrics are under-identified because of this high degree of mutual interdependence (Fisher, 1966; Liu, 1960). Econometricians have simplified, grouped effects of some variables on a practical basis, and used various techniques for overcoming difficulties of identification and statistical inference.

By a generous sprinkling of zero coefficients in linear systems or by grouping variables (such as 'all other prices') in more general systems, we have effectively made the equation systems distinctive, so that an economic system does not necessarily resemble an engineering, political, sociological, or other system in any precise sense. But identification problems are not the only issues. Cogent reasons for using *a priori* information are:

(i) small sample size;
(ii) multi-collinearity;
(iii) accounting balance.

(i) All behavioural information is not contained in statistical samples. It is surely advantageous to supplement statistical information with information from other sources. It eases the burden on data if assistance is provided by *a priori* information. In many cases, the *a priori* information may be more soundly based than the statistical information. By and large, in econometrics, we shall rely on statistical inference from samples of data, but there is no reason to regard that as the sole source.

If we are guided by the principle that everything depends on everything else, we shall find that equations contain many variables and unknown parameters. This will happen without being extreme, i.e. without having literally millions of explanatory variables and unknown parameters in each relation. But if the spectrum of interest rates is included in financial equations, there may well be 10–15 such explanatory variables. This number will frequently absorb an excessive number of degrees of freedom in relatively small samples. Frequently, econometric relationships have about 25 observations and sometimes exceed 100. In cross-section samples, we may have thousands of data points, but this is not typical of time series samples, which dominate the field.

What is true of the spectrum of interest rates in financial market equations is also true of demand and supply equations, when entire vectors of prices span the consumer's budget or the producer's range of price alternatives for products and factors. A large number of relative prices would quickly absorb many available degrees of freedom even if the decision process is layered or nested. Of course, *a priori* information is used in the layering and nesting themselves.

(ii) The spectrum of rates or the range of price variables raises complications beyond the absorption of degrees of freedom. Among rates or among prices it will usually be the case that separate variables are highly intercorrelated, though not perfectly intercorrelated: there is significant variance among prices and rates, but the intercorrelation is likely to be sufficiently large in small uncontrolled samples to obscure the underlying relationship. Rarely does an econometrician directly estimate an equation with ten or more unknown parameters and find that they are all statistically significant with appropriate directions of effect. It usually happens that *a priori* information will have to be introduced in order to make things work out satisfactorily.

Multi-collinearity is one of the most serious problems confronting good econometric results, and the use of *a priori* information is one way of meeting this problem head on. It is worthwhile doing so because the subrelationships implied by the sample intercorrelations are usually not basic and break down in extrapolations outside the sample—just when they are most needed. If purely statistical information is not enough to provide indication of future effect, the econometrician should be looking towards *a priori* information to get a start in the new situation outside the sample. As new observations build up under a situation of changing subrelationships, re-estimation can make use of added statistical information, but the *a priori* information often proves to be invaluable at the start.

(iii) An important branch of *a priori* information is provided through accounting balance. These implied relationships are part of the structure of economic theory, but they can be used independendently, as well. In large-scale models, hundreds or thousands of variables are being generated simultaneously, and it is important to force them to satisfy accounting balance. In world systems, total exports must equal total imports, overall and by commodity. National income must be reconciled, in single-country models, with national product. Wealth and budget identities must be satisfied. In long-range projections, from estimated models, the large number of variables can start to move astray unless they are held together in consistent accounting balance by the kinds of identities mentioned. A careful eye must be kept, too, on residual variables that are estimated directly from an identity. They could move into impossible economic regions unless they are monitored and restrained by *a priori* considerations. The large-scale computer becomes a 'black box', with many of the interim and subcalculations hidden from view. It is important (but not sufficient) to feel assured that the end results for different variables are, at least, mutually consistent.

4.2 A PRIORI ANALYSIS OF ECONOMIC SYSTEMS

Given that *a priori* information is useful and is going to be taken into account, what are the sources to look for? First of all, there is personal experience. We would like econometric modelling to be as objective and person-free as possible, but it is still true that an artistic element plays a prominent role in our science. The data are taken from life experiments; therefore it is not surprising that experience in observing economic life provides useful *a priori* information for econometric analysis. The average consumer or producer reaction, the typical time shape of delays in reaction, the tendencies towards market clearing, the average size of system multiplier response, and the average periodicity of a dynamic system are all properties or characteristics of different economies that give one intuitive impressions of what to expect. Econometrics needs to focus the numbers involved and their interacting total effects, yet it is no surprise that food demand is price inelastic, that residential housing is more interest elastic (in the U.S.A.) than is nonresidential investment, and so on. The practising econometrician carries a number of approximate parameter values around in his head, and draws on this inventory to good advantage when designing or interpreting results for a system. Many of the ε-values that appear as 'zeros' in the coefficient matrix of a linear system are based on experience.

Part of experience is knowing something about the institutional structure of an economy, or part of it. Institutionally-based equations compete with behaviourally-based equations in making up the structure of an economy. Some of the more prominent institutions are the

—tax system
—banking system

—system of foreign trade and exchange control
—judiciary control of production and consumption
—regulation of markets
—mechanism of wage bargaining.

There is no such thing as an anarchical system of completely free competition anywhere in the world. Most of the institutions listed above are governed by public authorities but some are motivated from the private side—cartels, quota systems, consumer groups. Knowledge of the functioning of these institutions is partly gained from experience in economic life but partly from being made aware of statutes, business practices, or voluntary agreements. It is a question of possessing the facts about the functioning of the economy in a purely descriptive sense and having the ability to translate this knowledge into design of econometric structure. It is valuable information for supplementing statistical estimation of coefficients.

Many of the facts of experience or institutional knowledge come from 'casual empiricism' or simply familiarity, but some come from systematic statistical observation. Knowledge of the periodicity of the U.S. economy may come from the reading of history books or from having lived through several cycles, but it is more likely to have come through the work of Mitchell, Burns, and Moore at the National Bureau of Economic Research (Burns and Mitchell, 1946; Mitchell, 1960; Moore, 1962). We know from their work that the average duration of American cycles is about 4.0 years. It was this systematic empirical finding that prompted Irma Adelman to look for this cyclical characteristic in the Klein–Goldberger model. Many other cyclical characteristics have been systematically observed in the National Bureau's long history of empirical investigations. Constancy of savings rates, the wage share of GNP, capital-output ratio, and many other empirical facts are known about the various economies of the world on the basis of pure empirical research, largely unguided by theoretical considerations. This led T. C. Koopmans to label the work of Burns and Mitchell as 'measurement without theory' (Koopmans, 1947). Using more mathematical methods than Mitchell, Burns, and Moore, time series analysts have been advocating approaches with a similar philosophical bent to try to measure the characteristics of the economy, or even to predict, without the guidance of economic theory. An intermediate position has been taken by Sims and Sargent in an attempt to build statistical models 'without very much theory', meaning economic theory (Klein, 1977; Sargent and Sims, 1977). Without going into the relative merits, at this stage, of measurement with or without theory, suffice it to say that systematic empirical measurement is a way of gathering important information that is useful for econometric specification and *a priori* estimation.

Restrictions on the specification of econometric models that are provided by experience, knowledge of institutions, or pure empirical research are made use of when found and on occasion. They are not always used at all; they are not always used in the same way. It may be said that they are used on a somewhat *ad hoc* basis, although this term should not be used in a perjorative sense, as it often is.

Another approach to statistical and econometric analysis that uses *a priori* information in a fixed way is Bayesian analysis. The classical formula of Bayes relates *a posteriori* distributions (information) to *a priori* distributions (information):

$$\begin{aligned} P(\mathbf{X}, \boldsymbol{\theta}) &= p(\boldsymbol{\theta})p(\mathbf{X}|\boldsymbol{\theta}) \\ &= p(\mathbf{X})p(\boldsymbol{\theta}|\mathbf{X}). \end{aligned}$$

These are simply two equivalent ways of expressing the joint distribution of sample vector ($\mathbf{X}$) and parameter vector ($\boldsymbol{\theta}$) as products of marginal and conditional distribution. It follows that

$$p(\boldsymbol{\theta}|\mathbf{X}) = \frac{p(\boldsymbol{\theta})p(\mathbf{X}|\boldsymbol{\theta})}{p(\mathbf{X})}$$

The *posteriori* density of the parameter vector, given the samples, is expressed in terms of $p(\boldsymbol{\theta})$, the prior distribution of $\boldsymbol{\theta}$, the likelihood function $p(\mathbf{X}|\boldsymbol{\theta})$, and a constant, $p(\mathbf{X})$, the marginal distribution of the sample.

The conventional methodology of econometrics is to assume that the parameters of the system are unknown constants, or are changing by fixed rules. The model is

$$\mathbf{F}(\mathbf{Y}'_t, \mathbf{Y}'_{t-1}, \ldots, \mathbf{X}'_t, \mathbf{X}'_{t-1}, \ldots, \boldsymbol{\theta}) = \mathbf{e}_t.$$

$\mathbf{F}$ is a vector of functions $f_1, \ldots, f_n$. The variables are row vectors

$$\begin{aligned} \mathbf{Y}'_t &= Y_{1t}, \ldots, Y_{nt} && \text{(endogenous variable)} \\ \mathbf{X}'_t &= X_{1t}, \ldots, X_{mt} && \text{(exogenous variable)} \\ \boldsymbol{\theta} &= \theta_1, \theta_2, \ldots, \theta_r. && \text{(parameters)} \end{aligned}$$

The random errors are a column vector, with each element being attached to one equation of the system. They are identically zero for definitions and accounting identities. Econometric methods of estimation are designed to obtain estimates of the fixed parameters, $\boldsymbol{\theta}$. In the Bayesian approach, it is assumed that the elements of $\boldsymbol{\theta}$ are generated according to an *a priori* probability distribution.

While prior information may be available about the values of ranges of values for some parameters, there is little information about the prior distribution of $\boldsymbol{\theta}$ in this model. A common procedure is to use a flat prior, implying equal information of the unknown. Posterior distributions and estimates of parameters can be obtained for different assumptions about prior distributions. Degrees of personal belief, expressed as probabilities, can be used for prior information about some parameter values.

The Bayesian approach has not been used extensively in any actual econometric investigations where the results are used for hard decision making. They are not used in any of the mainstream econometric models that are made available to businesses and public bodies. They are generally not used in any large-scale models that are regularly maintained. They are, however, used in small system and partial system investigations of a scholarly research nature.

Finally, in this brief review of *a priori* analysis, we come to the use of economic theory, meaning by that term received doctrine of many sources — neoclassical theory, Keynesian theory, classical theory, Marxian theory.

A structural equation in an econometric system can be placed in one of four types: (1) behavioural, (2) technological, (3) institutional, (4) definitional. Economic theory is applied principally to the specification of type (1). But if it is an integrated theory of a small subsystem, the accounting identities making up part of type (4) should be theoretically based. Budget and wealth identities are common equations in theoretical systems. Also, technological equations, although engineering based, are integrated into economic theory, particularly the theory of the firm. Some specific parametric forms are commonly used in this branch of theory.

The principal use of theory is to enable the econometrician to identify who is acting in the various behavioural equations of a system — consumers, producers, both together (in bargaining equations), or public authorities.

Neoclassical theory is generally based on an optimizing or market clearing principle. Optimization produces first- and second-order conditions, which become the behavioural equations of econometric systems. Optimization is carried out subject to constraints. For the second-order conditions to hold, constraints should introduce some convexity conditions, which will govern their parametric form.

Optimization is a great generator of implied relationships. Other branches of theory may proceed differently. Keynes' 'psychological law' used for specifying the aggregate consumption function in a macro system is based on a more intuitive type of theoretical reasoning. Marxian theory is based on principles of exploitation, class struggle, and capital accumulation. These, too, are not based on the deductive reasoning of neoclassical type. Yet, all varieties of theory generate hypotheses about economic behaviour. These hypotheses then appear in model structure.

The advantage of this approach is that each piece of an interrelated system has some separate meaning. When we adjust for technical progress, behavioural change, statutory change, and similar effects, we know where to enter the structural system and the specific kinds of changes that have to be made in a numerical way.

4.3 HOW MUCH CAN THEORY DO?

At a very minimum, theory will tell which variables enter which equations. General theory of the household indicates in the simple static model that consumer demand for the ith commodity (or service) in a budget depends on the vector of prices of different items and an income restraint.

$$X_i = f_i(P_1, \ldots, P_n, Y).$$

The accounting budget constraint indicates that Y (total household income) should be a variable in the functions, together with the whole set of prices, $P_1, P_2, \ldots, P_n$.

General theory provides two more pieces of *a priori* information, namely that the functions be homogeneous of degree zero in prices and income and that the whole set of demand functions should satisfy the adding-up constraint implied by the budget. These two properties are immediately evident from the economic conditions of optimization of utility subject to a budget constraint:

$$\frac{\partial \mu/\partial X_i}{\partial \mu/\partial X_j} = \frac{P_i}{P_j}$$

$$\sum_{i=1}^{n} P_i X_i = Y.$$

Among many alternative forms for satisfying the homogeneity conditions, we may write

$$X_i = f_i\left(\frac{P_1}{P_i}, \ldots, \frac{P_n}{P_i}, \frac{Y}{P_i}\right).$$

This reduces the number of explanatory variables by one. The adding-up constraint reduces the number of independent demand equations by one. Either the equations may be specified so as to satisfy adding-up automatically, or one item may be (arbitrarily) selected as a residual. The latter procedure generally produces unsatisfactory results for the residual items.

These contributions of theory may seem to be relatively light, yielding conclusions that may have been reached by application of some common-sense reasoning. In econometrics, however, every piece of information is important and useful; therefore, we must not disregard anything that might contribute something to the resolution of difficult problems. As we shall see in the next section, stronger assumptions together with the same theory produce even more restrictive results. These assumptions, in consumer theory, are placed on the subjective preference functions, and generate the more specific demand systems that are used to good advantage in much contemporary econometric analysis.

The general kinds of theory used for consumer optimization are also used for producer theory. In that case, we may have factor demand functions

$$l_i = g_i(w_1, \ldots, w_n, p)$$

depending on the whole price vector of factor costs (w_i for factor l_i) and output price (p), and the production function

$$x = f(l_1, l_2, \ldots, l_n).$$

As in the case of household theory the functions are homogeneous, because they are derived from

$$\frac{\partial f}{\partial l_i} = \frac{w_i}{p}$$

but there is no budget restraint in the pure theory of the competitive firm. There is, however, restrictive information in the sense that f must be convex.

Similar findings about the set of variables and accounting or other constraints apply to foreign trade relations, portfolio decisions in financial markets, demography, and other branches of the socio-economic system.

This approach has limitations, other than its lack of information for solving the problem completely. The limitations of pure theory are that it is atomistic, static, based on perfect assumptions, nonstochastic, and not unique. Optimizing theory in economic analysis rarely applies to groups or aggregates of economic agents; it applies more properly to individual households and to firms. To make use of theory properly we should aggregate over all decision units and sometimes over types of goods. This can lead to complicated formulae and to the inclusion of new variables, namely those describing the distribution of economic magnitudes such as their variance, concentration measures, or parameters of distribution functions. Economic theory as such does not have much to say about aggregation, other than to suggest some theorems that are nearly useless—goods whose prices move proportionally may be grouped into a single good. On the other hand, some strong assumptions about underlying micro relations and the relevant distribution functions can provide some highly interesting results (Houthakker, 1955). The assumptions are not so sweeping as to render the results trivial.

Just as economic theory tells us little about aggregation, so it also tells us little about dynamics. The main theoretical results used in the specification of relationships in econometric models refer to static theory. In this respect, they are better suited for specification of the steady-state and less for short-run dynamics. Many can be usefully superimposed on static results. This improves the working of econometric models but is not actually theory based and is somewhat *ad hoc*. It also adds to the already large list of variables. A typical dynamic specification is

$$X_t - X_{t-1} = \lambda(X_t^* - X_{t-1})$$

where

λ = speed of adjustment

X_t^* = value of X given by a theory-based static relationship.

There is nothing in theory to indicate that this is the appropriate specification of the size (sign) of λ. If the theory of the household or firm is cast in dynamic form at the start, the list of variables and wealth restraints becomes very large, almost so large as to be unmanageable.

While micro-economic theory has little dynamic content, macroeconomics appeals to stability conditions for parametric restrictions in dynamic systems. There is an assertion, rather than a deduced proposition, that macro dynamic systems have stable fluctuations. This produces useful parametric restrictions, but their theoretical soundness is dubious.

It is an accepted proposition that econometric systems are stochastic, but here again theory is not informative—not any more so than about dynamics. Additive error terms are introduced into structural equations of a model. Economic theory does not indicate additivity, but this form lends itself to statistical tractability. A convenient assumption about normality is also generally used. To the extent that the error term represents a multitude of small independent factors, the law of large numbers from statistical theory can be used for a normal specification. More complicated stochastic specifications are possible—non-normal and not necessarily additive. These must be based on considerations outside standard economic theory.

Theory is most frequently based on extreme assumptions about the economic environment. These involve perfect information, perfect mobility, and no imperfections in market performance. Actually, markets are significantly imperfect. If the theoretical doctrines of imperfect competition are substituted for those in the perfect model, the results are less elegant and simplified. Also, some new parameters will have to be introduced.

An idea that has been difficult to put across, in terms of theoretical specification, is that there is more than one way to specify a given model. The equations of the firm can be specified in terms of:

(i) production function and efficiency conditions

$$x = f(l_1, l_2, \ldots, l_n)$$

$$\frac{\partial f}{\partial l_i} = \frac{w_i}{p} \qquad i = 1, 2, \ldots, n$$

(ii) production and factor demand functions

$$x = f(l_1, l_2, \ldots, l_n)$$

$$l_i = g_i(w_1, w_2, \ldots, w_n, p) \qquad i = 1, 2, \ldots, n$$

(iii) supply functions

$$x = s(w_1, w_2, \ldots, w_n, p)$$

(iv) cost and revenue functions

$$x = f(l_1, l_2, \ldots, l_n)$$

$$\frac{\partial f/\partial l_i}{\partial f/\partial l_j} = \frac{w_i}{w_j} \qquad i \neq j = 1, 2, \ldots, n$$

$$\frac{\partial(px)}{\partial x} = \frac{\partial\left(\sum_{i=1}^{n} w_i l_i\right)}{\partial x}.$$

All these (and more) are possible ways of writing the equations of the theory of the firm. Similarly, there are different ways of expressing the equations of the household and other sectors of the economy. Also, there are different ways of combining these with the laws of market clearing. All have equal standing as far as the economic theory is concerned. Some reveal more parametric information than others; some have different data requirements; and some are more or less convenient. They all draw upon the same body of theory but use it differently.

The trouble with econometric reasoning is that it does not lend itself to a 'crucial' experiment. There is no body of data that will be so convincing that it absolutely excludes one theoretical hypothesis or another. It will always be possible for an adherent to argue that some factors were not controlled or that the sample was otherwise inadequate. Theory is used as a vehicle for suggesting fruitful hypotheses, and econometric methods can use these hypotheses for testing, estimation, and system building, but it will have a very difficult time excluding them.

Some economists look to *parsimonious* theory for the building of elegance and manageability into econometric systems. The rule of parsimony can be very misleading. It says: accept between any pair of competing hypotheses that specification that explains a given data set at least as well as the other but uses fewer parameters. This rule can be quite misleading in the interpretation of small samples of econometrics. It may lead us to accept a simple hypothesis that ignores the effects of some variables that have been quiescent during the sample period. In applications in new situations, the quiescent variables may have come to life, affected the economic situation greatly, and thrown off course the simple hypothesis. This, in my opinion, is what happened to the quantity theory equation used by monetarists in the late 1960's. It did not serve well in the 1970's. The true system was, in fact, more complicated than a parsimonious model suggested.

Parsimony appears to be at variance with the Walrasian concept that everything depends on everything else. To reach closer to the Walrasian ideal, we ought to be building more simultaneity into our models and going away, to the extent possible, from the simplistic systems of parsimonious reasoning.

4.4 SOME SPECIFIC EXAMPLES

Very general theory enabled us to make some small steps towards the introduction of manageable restraints. In the case of consumer theory $n + 1$ variables were reduced to n, and one equation was eliminated by imposing homogeneity and adding-up principles. The adding-up principle was not imposed automatically, but simply by determining one equation as a residual. If we go further and impose automatic adding-up, together with the second-order conditions of Slutsky, for optimization

$$\frac{\partial X_i}{\partial P_j} + X_j \frac{\partial X_i}{\partial Y} = \frac{\partial X_j}{\partial P_i} + X_i \frac{\partial X_j}{\partial Y}$$

we may get additional restrictions. These additional restrictions do not seem to help very much in an econometric sense unless they are placed in a more particular context. If we also require that the resulting system be linear in relative prices and real income then we obtain the linear expenditure system. This system was developed from just these considerations: find that linear system of demand functions that simultaneously satisfies homogeneity, adding-up, and Slutsky conditions (Klein and Rubin, 1947–1948). The resulting system

$$P_i X_i = \alpha_i P_i + \beta_i \left(Y - \sum_{j=1}^{n} \alpha_j P_j\right) \qquad i = 1, 2, \ldots, n$$

$$\sum_{i=1}^{n} \beta_i = 1$$

introduces an enormous reduction in the number of parameters—from $n(n - 1)$, where only homogeneity and adding-up are used, to $2n - 1$ in the linear expenditure system. If n were a modest 10 (categories in a household budget) the reduction would be from 90 to 19. In moderate size samples there will generally be enough degrees of freedom to estimate 19 parameters, while 90 requires a much larger data base.[1]

It is not only a degrees of freedom problem but also a multi-collinearity problem in obtaining reasonable statistical estimates of the parameters of a demand system in which all the different price variables have separate effects. Many plausible estimates have been obtained using the restrictions of the linear or other complete expenditure systems, but it is virtually impossible to have obtained similarly acceptable results from unconstrained regressions of the general form (Pollak and Wales, 1969; Stone, 1954)

$$X_i = f_i\left(\frac{P_1}{P_i}, \ldots, \frac{P_n}{P_i}, \frac{Y}{P_i}\right).$$

The linear expenditure system is linear in economic variables, relative prices, and real income, but it is not linear in parameters. Products of β_i and all α_j enter each equation. Given a stochastic specification, either for the nominal or real formulation of the system, and a method for dealing with nonlinear estimation, then it has proved to be possible to overcome the joint problems of collinearity and degrees of freedom. Also, the resulting numerical estimates can be obtained for dynamic as well as static versions.

The linear expenditure system satisfies integrability conditions. Accordingly, Samuelson and Geary showed, independently, that it can be generated from the utility function

$$U = \prod_{i=1}^{n} (X_i - \alpha_i)^{\beta_i}$$

a displaced Cobb–Douglas type (Geary, 1949–1950; Samuelson, 1947–1948). This immediately suggested another approach to consumer theory: construct well-known parametric specifications of utility functions and find the implied demand functions. Tractable results have been obtained for nested CES functions and translog functions (Brown and Heien, 1972; Christensen *et al.*, 1975). Thus, demand systems with theoretical restrictions on the parameters can readily be found and estimated, without undue trouble, from available data. The CES and translog systems have more parameters and add to explanatory power in this sense. Yet the parameters of these extended systems are capable of being estimated in spite of added requirements for degrees of freedom. They are not demonstrably superior to dynamic versions of the LES, but they certainly merit serious consideration. The important aspect of this theory-inspired approach to the econometrics of consumer demand is that it permits the simultaneous estimation of all the cross price effects. This has been an important achievement for interpretation of a new era of price relationships, in which energy, food, and other prices have had unusually wide movements. Having an estimate of a total expenditure system has enabled the econometrician to estimate the important secondary or indirect effects.

Tobin and Brainard have argued persuasively that asset-liability demand functions, making up a total portfolio, should reflect the existence of a total wealth constraint and the whole spectrum of interest rates (Brainard and Tobin, 1968). Saito (1976) has shown how the LES concept can be extended to portfolio choice and has estimated complete systems of asset–liability demand functions for various sectors of the economy, incorporating a complete spectrum of interest-rate effects. His estimates add automatically to total wealth.

The same methods that have worked in the theory of household behaviour work also in the theory of the firm, applied to a complete set of factor demands, together with a production function. The Cobb–Douglas, CES, translog, or other production function specifications have been used to produce optimization conditions that become very manageable equations for parameter estimation.

The Cobb–Douglas specification for cost-minimization is

$$\frac{l_i}{l_j} = \alpha_i \alpha_j \left(\frac{w_i}{w_j}\right)^{-1}$$

$$x = A \prod_{i=1}^{n} l_i^{\alpha_i}.$$

The other production function specifications are only slightly more difficult to estimate. As in consumer theory, stochastic and dynamic specification must be added. From the original researches of Cobb and Douglas, collinearity has been a serious problem. Now, meaningful estimates of all parameters of the system can be readily estimated using theory for guidance (Coen and Hickman, 1970; McCarthy, 1972). The benefits of this approach in system building should be obvious. Looking at the issues from a negative point of view, I would say that the samples of data that we have in econometrics are simply not going to provide sharp enough variations to pick out separate effects of all the individual variables that belong in each sector's relationships and that the use of theory provides the only workable alternative for including a wide set of explanatory variables. The use of side conditions of economic optimization are powerful ways to generate useful *a priori* restrictions. These restrictions are applicable to a wide range of processes in consumer and producer sectors, but they are equilibrium conditions.

We have noted that the linear expenditure system in demand analysis was designed partly to deal with the adding-up problem. In static form it satisfies the consumer budget restraint automatically. In a similar way, the systems of equations that are used in international trade modelling, covering the whole world, are designed to ensure that

$$\text{world exports} = \text{world imports}$$

apart from some valuation, reporting, or transit complications. Accordingly, exports are often estimated from relationships

$$\mathbf{X} = A\mathbf{M}$$

where

$$\begin{aligned} \mathbf{X} &= \text{export vector} \\ \mathbf{M} &= \text{import vector} \\ A &= \text{trade share matrix.} \end{aligned}$$

The elements of A are shipments (from i to j, for example) divided by total imports of j. As long as exports are computed from this relationship, where the column sums of A are unity, the world identity will be satisfied.

This formulation avoids the larger-scale problem of estimating bilateral trade relationships that are numerous and not well supported by data. It may be possible, eventually, to estimate all the bilateral elements of A directly, but until that time the use of the trade matrix relationship is a convenient specification that satisfies the world accounting identity.

The identity

$$\mathbf{X} = A\mathbf{M}$$

holds for simultaneous time periods for $\mathbf{X}$, A, and $\mathbf{M}$ respectively, but not in an exact sense if A is held steady at base period values—the world identity is satisfied as long as the columns of A sum to unity, but the export calculations are inexact.

Theories for the changing of A, over time, are the same for trade analyses as for production analyses of input–output systems. Theories that specify some particular production function or import relationships for columns of A can be used to project this matrix column by column, through time. One such theoretical specification based on a CES relationship

$$X_j = \left(\sum_{i=1}^{n} \delta_{ij} X_{ij}^{-\rho} \right)^{-1/\rho}$$

has been used where

X_i is either total production of sector j or total imports of j.
X_{ij} is either intermediate material from i used in sector j or imports from i to j.

Least cost materials bills or import bills are used to derive export or production equations that satisfy accounting identities (Hickman and Lau, 1973; Preston, 1975).

Consumers and producers are rarely in equilibrium. We do not have samples of equilibrium observations. This is where the approach of time series analysis and economic analysis can usefully join forces. Within the confines of a purely linear system, both in economic variables and in parameters, there is much to recommend the general lag distributions for each individual equation

$$\sum_{j=1}^{n_i} \alpha_j(L) Y_{jt} + \sum_{j=1}^{m_i} \beta_j(L) X_{jt} = \gamma_i(L) e_{it} \qquad i = 1, 2, \ldots, n.$$

The operators $\alpha_j(L)$, $\beta_j(L)$, and $\gamma_i(L)$ are polynomials in the displacement factor

$$L^K Y_{jt} = Y_{j,t-K}, \qquad L^0 \equiv 1.$$

This is a system in which every relation is potentially an autoregressive in a normalized dependent variable and a moving average in the other dependent variables, the independent variables, and the error term. From the point of view of time series analysis each of these is a useful forecasting equation, and from the point of view of Sargent and Sims (1977) it forms the basis for a whole system, devoid of theoretical specification. But from the point of view of mainstream econometrics it may be viewed as the dynamic representation of a steady-state or equilibrium system of relationships

$$\sum_{j=1}^{n_1} \alpha_j Y_j + \sum_{j=1}^{m_1} \beta_j X_j = \gamma_i e_i, \qquad i = 1, 2, \ldots, n.$$

The following procedure for system building is thus suggested:

(i) Use received theory to specify a complete equation system in steady-state equilibrium.
(ii) Transform every stochastic equation to an autoregressive moving average form (ARMA).

(iii) Find the best fitting ARMA equation system that isolates white noise residuals, $\hat{e}_{it}$, and also satisfies steady-state restrictions for the economic relationships.

4.5 THE CASE FOR THEORY

In the preceding sections, the argument has been made that economic theory is important for model specification in order to avoid problems of degrees of freedom and multi-collinearity. This is the only visible way, and the only way that has been seriously tried, for getting ever closer approximations to the Walrasian concept of the economy's being represented by the solution to a system of simultaneous equations with a high degree of interdependence. There are ways for superimposing dynamics, nonlinearities, and stochastic elements on the equations of an equilibrium system.

This is the way that economic theory is presently used in econometrics. It also adds to identifiability of economic relationships. The advantages of this approach are that it gives some content to economic theory and conveys structural knowledge to the practising econometrician.

Economic systems look different from other equation systems, once some theoretical structure is built into the system. This satisfies intuition that we do indeed have a distinctive subject. For more than 200 years, economists have built, block-by-block, a body of knowledge, and theory-based econometric models are devices for bringing some empirical content into that theory. Relative shapes and positions of economic relationships can be discerned from empirical systems that are designed and estimated with 'a great deal of theory'.

In the application of economic policy through the use of models and in pure forecasting, it is important to be able to get inside the equation system in order to make adjustments, amendments, and extensions. This cannot be done efficiently in reduced form systems or in anonymous equations. It is for these reasons that theory-based systems are so much more meaningful.

NOTE

[1] The number of degrees of freedom will be the number of data points times the number of independent stochastic equations less the number of estimated parameters.

REFERENCES

Brainard, W. C., and Tobin, J. (1968). 'Pitfalls in financial model building.' *American Economic Review*, **58,** 99–122.

Brown, M., and Heien, D. (1972). 'The S-branch utility tree: A generalization of the linear expenditure system.' *Econometrica*, **40,** 737–747.

Burns, A. F., and Mitchell, W. C. (1946). *Measuring Business Cycles*, National Bureau of Economic Research, New York.

Christensen, L. R., Jorgenson, D. W., and Lau, L. J. (1975). 'Transcendental logarithmic utility functions.' *American Economic Review*, **65**, 367–383.

Coen, R. M., and Hickman, B. G. (1970). 'Constrained joint estimation of factor demand and production functions.' *Review of Economics and Statistics*, **52**, 287–300.

Fisher, F. M. (1966). *The Identification Problem in Econometrics*, McGraw-Hill, New York.

Geary, R. C. (1949–1950). 'A note on "A constant utility index of the cost of living."' *Review of Economic Studies*, **18**, 65–66.

Hickman, B. G., and Lau, L. J. (1973). 'Elasticities of substitution and export demands in a world trade model.' *European Economic Review*, **4**, 347–380.

Houthakker, H. S. (1955). 'The Pareto distribution and the Cobb–Douglas production function in activity analysis.' *Review of Economic Studies*, **XXIII**, 27–31.

Klein, L. R. (1977). 'Comments on Sargent and Sims' "Business cycle modeling without pretending to have too much *a priori* economic theory."' In C. A. Sims (Ed.), *New Methods in Business Cycle Research*, Federal Reserve Bank of Minneapolis, Minneapolis, pp. 203–208.

Klein, L. R., and Rubin, H. (1947–1948). 'A constant–utility index of the cost of living.' *Review of Economic Studies*, **15**, 84–87.

Koopmans, T. C. (1947). 'Measurement without theory.' *Review of Economics and Statistics*, **XXIX**, 161–172.

Liu, T. C. (1960). 'Underidentification, structural estimation, and forecasting.' *Econometrica*, **28**, 855–865.

McCarthy, M. D. (1972). *The Wharton Quarterly Econometric Forecasting Model, Mark III*, University of Pennsylvania, Philadelphia. pp. 6–12.

Mitchell, W. C. (1960). *What Happens During Business Cycles*, National Bureau of Economic Research, New York.

Moore, G. H. (1962). 'Tested knowledge in business cycles.' *Forty-second Annual Report*, National Bureau of Economic Research, New York.

Pollak, R. A., and Wales, T. J. (1969). 'Estimation of the linear expenditure system.' *Econometrica*, **37**, 611–628.

Preston, R. S. (1975). 'The Wharton long-term model: Input–output within the context of a macro forecasting model.' *International Economic Review*, **16**, 3–19.

Saito, M. (1976). 'Household flow-of-funds equations.' *Journal of Money, Credit and Banking*, **I**, 1–19.

Samuelson, P. A. (1947–1948). 'Some implications of linearity.' *Review of Economic Studies*, **15**, 88–90.

Sargent, T. J. and Sims, C. A. (1977). 'Business cycle modeling without pretending to have too much *a priori* economic theory.' In C. A. Sims (Ed.), *New Methods in Business Cycle Research*, Federal Reserve Bank of Minneapolis, Minneapolis, pp. 45–109.

Stone, R. A. (1954). 'Linear expenditure system and demand analysis: An application to the pattern of British demand.' *Economic Journal*, **64**, 511–527.

Discussion

L. L. Pasinetti

Università Cattolica, Milano

Professor Klein has given us a long survey on the ways in which information may be used in econometric modelling. I shall try to offer a few comments.

Professor Klein's paper reminds me of an old discussion among econometricians, which goes back to the well-known article—'Measurement without theory'—written by Professor Koopmans more than 30 years ago. There has always been a kind of opposition between two conflicting souls in econometric work. There is the soul of the empiricist, who is looking for significant correlations and good fit, independently of any theory; and there is the soul of the economic theorist, who is always looking for logically consistent theoretical schemes, expressing relations which the econometrician is supposed to be able to quantify. I have tried to find which of the two souls is behind Professor Klein's paper. From the first part of the paper one gets a strong impression—which was a surprise to me—that Professor Klein is entirely on the side of the empiricists. From the second part of the paper it sometimes seems the other way round. But if this is so, it is not very clear to me how the two souls are going to be reconciled.

The approach which seems to be taken since the beginning of the paper is that the econometrician starts from the idea of overall interdependence, but is facing a number of difficulties. The idea of interdependence is related to the Walrasian system, in which everything depends on everything else. The difficulties that are mentioned are: multi-collinearity, and/or lack of degrees of freedom, and/or problems of identification, and so on. In order to overcome these difficulties, the econometrician must do something; and Professor Klein mentions a number of ways of doing something. He mentions statistical inference, experience in observing economic life, 'casual empiricism' and knowledge of institutions, some systematic empirical measurements, Bayesian models, and even the degree of personal beliefs. Finally, only finally, does Professor Klein mention economic theory, which thereby is simply introduced as one of the ways of avoiding econometric difficulties.

Some further elucidations appear at the very end of the paper, where Professor Klein says explicitly that, in econometric applications, 'economic theory is important for model specification in order to avoid problems of degrees of freedom and multi-collinearity'. One wonders: should one infer from this that if there were no problems of multi-collinearity and degrees of freedom there would be no need for any economic theory? Yet a few lines later Professor Klein adds that 'theory-based econometric models are devices for bringing some empirical content into...theory. Relative shapes and positions of economic relationships can be discerned from empirical systems that are designed and estimated with "a great deal of theory".' One wonders again: is this the other soul coming back? I find myself a bit baffled.

In any case, using economic theory in order to avoid econometric difficulties does not seem to me to imply 'getting ever closer approximations to the Walrasian concept of the economy's being represented by the solution to a system of simultaneous equations with a high degree of interdependence'. In fact, precisely the opposite would seem to me to be the case. I am thinking of another series of discussions, in the econometric literature, about the opposition between the interdependent systems of equations and what have been called the causal systems of equations, i.e. systems in which the sequence in which the variables are determined is governed by an asymmetrical chain of relations. On this subject Herbert Simon has written in the United States and Herman Wold in Europe. The message is that, in econometric work, and especially in estimation, causal systems entail by far fewer econometric difficulties than interdependent systems. So, it would seem to me that, if we were simply to aim at avoiding the econometric difficulties hinted at by Professor Klein, the causal systems would be much more appropriate than the interdependent systems.

At the same time, it seems to me that the Walrasian idea of the economy as an overall interdependent system of simultaneous equations should not be used as an excuse for the bad habit of throwing all possible available data into the computer with the hope that the computer may sort out some reasonable correlations, to be rationalized *ex-post* and presented as *the* result (sometimes even without mentioning all the other attempts which have failed). This would clearly be the worst method one could possibly think of. And yet the availability of computers on the one side—capable of carrying out an enormous amount of numerical computations—and the excuse offered by the Walrasian idea of overall interdependence on the other have rendered such a procedure much more widespread than many of us dare to admit.

Personally, I should like to see a stronger commitment to economic theory, and I should also like to stress in this connection that the Walrasian system of interdependent equations *is not* the only theoretical system we possess. Theoretical alternatives do exist and, where they do not exist, it should be our task to develop them.

Another important point which Professor Klein has made is the difficulty of finding in econometric works those crucial tests that may enable us to discriminate between theories. This, I think, has been one of the great failures of econometric models and of econometrics in general. Let me recall here the great enthusiasm among the founders of the Econometric Society, around 1930. One of their driving forces was the idea that by quantifying economic theory and by putting economic relations to the test of empirical observations, one should be able to discriminate between acceptable and unacceptable theories, in the same way as the natural scientists have done. Well, we have had great disappointments on this matter. Professor Klein mentioned before that perhaps we shall never be able to do this. Yet it seems to me that to say so is not enough. If it is impossible to use econometric work to discriminate between alternative theories, we should prove it, by a kind of impossibility theorem. Otherwise, we should go on investigating the matter. At present it is not even clear whose fault this is. Is it the fault of the economic theorists, who do not formulate their theories in an appropriate way? Or is it the fault of the econometricians? The fault is perhaps a bit on both sides. If the theorists are not sufficiently induced in the direction of specifying their theories in such a way as to make them empirically testable, the econometrician should be able to tell them how to proceed, or at least contribute to tell them how to proceed.

On the side of the theorists, I have myself become convinced that many theories which are sometimes proposed as alternative to each other in fact refer to different things, hence they are not exactly *alternative* theories. Economists use sometimes the same words; they seem to use the same concepts, but in fact they do not mean the same things. To give an example, the Walrasian conception of prices, to be determined as equilibrium points in a demand and supply context, and Sraffa's conception of relative prices, as determined by the conditions of production, refer in fact to quite different aspects of economic reality. It seems to me that this type of opposition ought to be brought out explicitly.

Finally, just in order to close on a note which is not completely negative, let me point out one particular aspect of the opposition between various theories which has struck me recently. It refers to the distinction between what is changing and what is not changing, in the real world and in the theories. I mean, if you like, the distinction between what is constant and what is variable. We have been told that in economics the trouble is that there is no constant; everything is variable (this is what Schumpeter used to say). Yet some variables are more variable than others and one has got to make a choice at a certain point. Now it seems to me that the way in which economic theory has historically developed — with priority given to micro-static economic theories—has accustomed us to make a kind of association between data and constants on the one side and unknowns and variables on the other.

Yet, at the very moment we step into dynamic analysis, we find that our 'data' are not constant — they vary all the time. And that our unknowns sometimes may not be variable — they may remain rather constant over long periods of time (even with short-run fluctuations). There is a kind of distortion here which has been introduced into our reasoning by the way in which traditional theory has accustomed us to look at the real world, namely the way connected with static analysis. Now, there is no reason why we should always rely on the traditional type of approach. We might well seek some alternative ones, much more appropriate to dynamic investigation. Of course there may be problems here. Many of the 'data' that are changing through time may have nothing to do with economic analysis — think of technical progress and of population movements in growth models, for example. And some of those magnitudes which in the long run seem to be rather constant are typical economic magnitudes, which have to be explained — think of the capital-output ratio and of the rate of profit. They clearly must be considered as 'unknowns', even if they remain constant. These are methodological problems, which are certainly not easy to solve. Yet they must be faced.

I shall leave this as a challenge to the audience, if I may, at the end of my comments, not without adding however that, personally, I have been fascinated by these problems (I may refer, for lack of time, to *Structural Change and Economic Growth.*[1]) Thank you.

NOTE

[1] Pasinetti, L. L. (1981). *Structural Change and Economic Growth*, Cambridge University Press, Cambridge.

Reply by L. L. Pasinetti to a question from a member of the audience, concerning the difficulty in the testing of economic theories:

I think the question which has been raised refers to the problem I mentioned at the end of my comment.

If the economic reality we observe contains magnitudes which the economic theorists consider as 'data', but which in fact vary very much, then the clear implication is that we cannot rely on economic theory alone. There is something here that constitutes a formidable obstacle to empirical testing of economic theories.

Most of our theories are some kind of logical schemes which consider many magnitudes as given — they are stated *coeteris paribus*. But if, in reality, the *coeteris* are not *paribus*, you cannot put the theories to empirical test. This is what always gives the theorist an easy way out. What happens is that you may well take a theoretical model and put it to the empirical test. If you get an unsatisfactory result, the theorist will simply come and say: of course! — some of the things that were supposed to be given have changed! Clearly, we shall never be able to test any theory when it is presented in this way. There is a very deep methodological problem here. My guess is that the relations themselves between the magnitudes which are dealt with by economic theory and all other elements that are relevant for a satisfactory empirical performance of the model will have to be specified explicitly when empirical applications are contemplated.

Evaluating the Reliability of Macro-economic Models
Edited by G. C. Chow and P. Corsi

CHAPTER 5

Model Selection Procedures, or, does the Consumption Function Exist?

A. S. DEATON
University of Bristol

5.1 INTRODUCTION

Virtually all conventional macro-econometric models are built around some form of consumption function. The details vary from model to model, and the literature of the last forty years contains no end of theories and empirical tests to lend support to one variant or another. Recently, however, there has come to the fore a body of macro-economic thought which dispenses altogether with this backbone of conventional analysis. This modern work, in contrast to analysis in the Keynesian tradition, describes the economy as a system which is essentially in equilibrium. In particular, wages and prices are such that employees are on their supply curves, employers on their demand curves, and labour markets clear. If this is so, commodity demands are a function of all prices including the wage rate, and the consumption function is at best unnecessary, at worst non-existent. There is a good deal of (perhaps superficial) evidence that labour markets in most developed economies do *not* clear, at least in the short-run, in which case the consumption function is both legitimate and necessary. But very little hard evidence is available one way or the other (largely because, to most economists, it seemed blatantly obvious that involuntary unemployment exists, or at least has existed). This paper is concerned with the methodology and testing of whether labour markets do or do not clear. Although I shall report some results which suggest, if anything, that clearing may explain my data better than nonclearing, the main interest at this point is methodological. There are a number of very difficult issues in conducting a satisfactory test; some are (partially) discussed below, others are stated but ignored.

The plan of the paper is as follows. Section 5.2 is concerned with the methodology of testing. Typically, equilibrium and disequilibrium theories will produce non-nested hypotheses and in Section 5.2 I propose a procedure, based loosely on the Cox test, which formalizes more closely the sort of calculations which would be typical in applied econometric work. Section 5.3 presents a model of consumer demand and labour supply which in principle allows a test of whether or not consumers are free to adjust their hours of work. Section 5.4 is a description of the data used and of the (largely unsolved) econometric problems of using them for the analysis of the model of Section 5.3. Section 5.5 contains tests of weak separability between leisure and goods; these are necessary because of the consequences of separability for the way in which disequilibrium in the labour market affects the demand for goods. In Section 5.6 I report the results of some first attempts to discriminate between the equilibrium and disequilibrium stories. The results are rather indecisive with the tests yielding little evidence against either model. On balance, however, the equilibrium model appears to yield a slightly more complete account of the data. Section 5.7 summarizes and re-emphasizes the many caveats and unsolved problems.

5.2 NON-NESTED TESTS FOR APPLIED ECONOMETRIC MODELS

There is now a very substantial literature on alternative methodologies for testing non-nested hypotheses. The test originally proposed by Cox (1961, 1962) and discussed in econometric contexts by Pesaran (1974) and Pesaran and Deaton (1978) is my starting point. However, there is clearly a large number of alternative procedures. In particular, I wish to bear in mind the idea of artificial nesting (i.e. constructing a general alternative containing both models as special cases) which has been emphasized particularly by Atkinson (1970), but see also Quandt (1974) and Davidson and MacKinnon (1981). The Cox test compares the actual likelihood ratio with its probability limit under each of the alternatives in turn. In regression models, this turns out to be equivalent to comparing the error variance (or generalized variance) of each model with an estimate of its probability limit under the other. Such a procedure is a very natural one and is clearly designed to yield powerful tests against the specific alternatives considered. This basic idea I wish to retain. However, in applied work, the error variances are not usually the parameters of interest so that a rejection of one or other model by the Cox test gives little immediate information about the nature of the problem. In such a situation, it is natural to turn to the regression coefficients and to inquire whether or not the estimates obtained for each of the models are consistent with expectations based on the truth of the other. Informally, this sort of exercise is standard in all applied econometrics; each estimated relationship is examined for possible inconsistency with the investigator's prior beliefs, independently of whether the relationship would itself have been suggested by those beliefs. The fact that one may believe that labour markets clear does not preclude one from predicting the results of estimating an econometric model in which they are assumed not to do so. Indeed, the current 'rational expectations' critique of Keynesian econometric models is precisely of this form.

I begin with a simple example illustrating the application of these ideas. The general formulae are given later in the section.

Let H_0 and H_1 be the two non-nested linear regression models

$$H_0 : \mathbf{y} = X\boldsymbol{\beta}_0 + \mathbf{u}_0 \tag{1}$$

$$H_1 : \mathbf{y} = Z\boldsymbol{\beta}_1 + \mathbf{u}_1 \tag{2}$$

where, for simplicity, X and Z are nonstochastic $(n \times k_0)$ and $(n \times k_1)$ matrices, and $\mathbf{u}_0$ and $\mathbf{u}_1$ are zero mean, constant variance and independent disturbances. I shall assume normality when necessary, but it is not required for much of the argument. Assuming H_0 and H_1 to be true in turn, the usual estimators for $\boldsymbol{\beta}_0$ and $\boldsymbol{\beta}_1$ are obtained, i.e.

$$\hat{\boldsymbol{\beta}}_0 = (X'X)^{-1}X'\mathbf{y} \tag{3}$$

$$\hat{\boldsymbol{\beta}}_1 = (Z'Z)^{-1}Z'\mathbf{y}. \tag{4}$$

I first test H_0: if the model is correct, $\boldsymbol{\beta}_1$ has no meaning, but the expectation under H_0 of $\hat{\boldsymbol{\beta}}_1$ is well-defined, viz:

$$E_0(\hat{\boldsymbol{\beta}}_1) = (Z'Z)^{-1}Z'X\boldsymbol{\beta}_0. \tag{5}$$

To test H_0, with power against H_1, $\hat{\boldsymbol{\beta}}_1$ is compared with its expectation under H_0 as given by (5). But (5) involves the unknown $\boldsymbol{\beta}_0$ which may be replaced by its estimate $\hat{\boldsymbol{\beta}}_0$ from (3). Hence, the test of H_0 is based on the difference $\hat{\boldsymbol{\beta}}_1 - \hat{E}_0(\hat{\boldsymbol{\beta}}_1)$, $\mathbf{t}_0$ say, given by

$$\begin{aligned}\mathbf{t}_0 = \hat{\boldsymbol{\beta}}_1 - \hat{E}_0(\hat{\boldsymbol{\beta}}_1) &= (Z'Z)^{-1}Z'\mathbf{y} - (Z'Z)^{-1}Z'X(X'X)^{-1}X'\mathbf{y} \\ &= (Z'Z)^{-1}Z'M_x\mathbf{y}\end{aligned} \tag{6}$$

where M_x is the idempotent matrix

$$M_x = I - X(X'X)^{-1}X'. \tag{7}$$

Now $\hat{E}_0(\hat{\boldsymbol{\beta}}_1)$ plays an essential part in the calculation of the Cox test since it is necessary input for the calculation of $\hat{E}_0(\hat{\sigma}_1{}^2)$, the comparison of which with $\hat{\sigma}_1{}^2$ is the basis of the test; see Pesaran (1974) for details. However $\mathbf{t}_0$ in (6) is of interest in its own right. It is the regression on Z of the OLS residuals from the regression of $\mathbf{y}$ on X. If H_0 is correct, $\mathbf{t}_0$ should be approximately zero, while if H_1 is correct, elements of $\mathbf{t}_0$ can be expected to be significantly different from zero. In applied work, inspection of $\mathbf{t}_0$ (and $\mathbf{t}_1$, the regression of $M_z\mathbf{y}$ on X) is likely to be directly informative since it identifies those aspects of the $\mathbf{y}$ and Z regression which are not explained by the truth of H_0. However, it is still of interest to form a composite test based on $\mathbf{t}_0$.

Under H_0, from (1),

$$\mathbf{t}_0 = (Z'Z)^{-1}Z'M_x\mathbf{u}_0 \tag{8}$$

so that, under normality of $\mathbf{u}_0$, $\mathbf{t}_0$ is normally distributed with zero mean and variance $\sigma^2(Z'Z)^{-1}Z'M_xZ(Z'Z)^{-1}$. Hence, the quantity

$$\tau_0 = \mathbf{y}'M_xZ(Z'M_xZ)^{-1}Z'M_x\mathbf{y}/\sigma^2 \tag{9}$$

is, under H_0, distributed as χ^2 with k_1 degrees of freedom. But this is familiar from another context. If we consider the composite artificially-nested model

$$\mathbf{y} = X\boldsymbol{\beta}_0{}^* + Z\boldsymbol{\beta}_1{}^* + \mathbf{u}^*, \tag{10}$$

then τ_0 is the LM or efficient score test of the hypothesis that $\boldsymbol{\beta}_1{}^* = 0$, i.e. of the restriction which reduces the nested model to H_0, and it can be estimated by noting that the numerator of (9) is the explained sum of squares from the regression of the residuals $M_x\mathbf{y}$ on both X and Z together; see Engle (1979). Note that expression (9) will only exist if none of the columns of Z are obtainable as linear combinations of the columns of X. In practice this involves no loss of generality since if, for example, one explanatory variable is common to H_0 and H_1, its corresponding $\mathbf{t}_0$-value provides no information as to the validity of H_0. Only the $\mathbf{t}_0$-values for the non-overlapping variables need therefore be considered. A fuller treatment of this issue is given by Dastoor (1981), who has independently proposed an essentially identical test.

In practice, τ_0 would not be used as a test criterion. The quantity σ^2 is unknown and replacing it by its estimate $\hat{\sigma}^2$ renders the χ^2 distribution only asymptotically valid. However, in this context, the small sample distribution of (9) with $\hat{\sigma}^2$ in place of σ^2 is known, and the corresponding exact test is the usual F-test for the joint insignificance of the Z variables in the compound regression (10). This is the methodology for non-nested testing put forward by Atkinson (1970). This result should not be very surprising given the close relationship between the current procedure and the Cox test and the asymptotic equivalence of the latter with Atkinson's test. However, the fact that the LM procedure has known optimality properties and that consideration of $\mathbf{t}_0$ leads to it suggests that testing the difference of $\hat{\boldsymbol{\beta}}_1$ and $\hat{E}_0(\hat{\boldsymbol{\beta}}_1)$ is likely to be useful in general. Note that Pesaran (1981) has shown that the F-test, i.e. the exact equivalent of (9), is asymptotically *less* powerful than the Cox test against a suitably defined sequence of local alternatives. Clearly this carries through to (9) so that, under Pesaran's alternatives, τ_0 and the square of the Cox test are, under H_1, each distributed as a noncentral χ^2 variate with identical noncentrality parameters but with the Cox test having one degree of freedom as opposed to k_1 for τ_0. But this extra power is obtained at a price. The Cox test of H_0 against H_1 assumes that H_1 is taken as a whole and that its specification is known to be correct (given that H_1 is). This is made very clear in the (asymptotically equivalent) variant of the Cox test proposed by Davidson and MacKinnon (1981) in which a t-test is performed on the significance of $Z\hat{\boldsymbol{\beta}}_1$ as a single variable in addition to X in the regression of (1). Clearly this is likely to be more powerful than putting all elements of Z into the regression as is implied by inspection of $\mathbf{t}_0$ and its associated F-test. But $\mathbf{t}_0$ (and the F-test) are more informative, at least in the situation where the structure of the alternative is uncertain. For clear-cut, well-specified alternative hypotheses, the Cox test would appear to be appropriate and the basis for its power justifiable. In less well-defined situations, the less powerful F-test is more likely to be useful.

Turning now to the general case, (1) and (2) can be replaced by the two competing densities $f(y_i, \boldsymbol{\beta}_0)$ and $g(y_i, \boldsymbol{\beta}_1)$, $i = 1, \ldots, n$. The two log likelihood functions can then be written

$$H_0 : L_0(\boldsymbol{\beta}_0, \mathbf{y}) = \Sigma \ln f(y_i, \boldsymbol{\beta}_0) \tag{11}$$

$$H_1 : L_1(\boldsymbol{\beta}_1, \mathbf{y}) = \Sigma \ln g(y_i, \boldsymbol{\beta}_1) \tag{12}$$

which are respectively maximized by MLE's $\hat{\boldsymbol{\beta}}_0$ and $\hat{\boldsymbol{\beta}}_1$. By symmetry, I can again concentrate on the investigation of H_0. Under fairly weak conditions, see White (1982) or Huber (1967), the probability limit of $\hat{\boldsymbol{\beta}}_1$ under H_0 exists; denote this $\boldsymbol{\beta}_{10}$, i.e.

$$\boldsymbol{\beta}_{10} = \boldsymbol{\beta}_{10}(\boldsymbol{\beta}_0) = \text{plim}_0\, \hat{\boldsymbol{\beta}}_1. \tag{13}$$

Alternatively, $\boldsymbol{\beta}_{10}$ can be defined by

$$\text{plim}_0 \left\{ \frac{1}{n} \frac{\partial L_1(\boldsymbol{\beta}_{10}, \mathbf{y})}{\partial \boldsymbol{\beta}_1} \right\} = 0, \tag{14}$$

as suggested by Cox (1961). The $\mathbf{t}_0$-test suggested above is then based on the comparison of $\hat{\boldsymbol{\beta}}_1$ with $\hat{\boldsymbol{\beta}}_{10} = \boldsymbol{\beta}_{10}(\hat{\boldsymbol{\beta}}_0)$. Expanding the formula for $\hat{\boldsymbol{\beta}}_{10}$ around $\boldsymbol{\beta}_{10}(\boldsymbol{\beta}_0)$ gives

$$\mathbf{t}_0 = (\hat{\boldsymbol{\beta}}_1 - \boldsymbol{\beta}_{10}) - \Sigma_k \frac{\partial \boldsymbol{\beta}_{10}}{\partial \boldsymbol{\beta}_{0k}} (\hat{\boldsymbol{\beta}}_{0k} - \boldsymbol{\beta}_{0k}). \tag{15}$$

Now Cox has shown that under H_0, $\hat{\boldsymbol{\beta}}_1$ and $\hat{\boldsymbol{\beta}}_0$ have an asymptotic joint normal distribution with means $\boldsymbol{\beta}_{10}$ and $\boldsymbol{\beta}_0$ and variances and covariances given by

$$V(\hat{\boldsymbol{\beta}}_0) = \boldsymbol{Q}_0^{-1} \tag{16}$$

$$V(\hat{\boldsymbol{\beta}}_0, \hat{\boldsymbol{\beta}}_{10}) = \boldsymbol{Q}_0^{-1} \boldsymbol{J} \tag{17}$$

$$V(\hat{\boldsymbol{\beta}}_{10}) = \boldsymbol{Q}_{10}^{-1} \boldsymbol{G}_{10} \boldsymbol{Q}_{10}^{-1} \tag{18}$$

where $\boldsymbol{Q}_0$ is the usual information matrix, i.e.

$$Q_{0ij} = E_0 \left\{ -\frac{\partial^2 L_0(\boldsymbol{\beta}_0)}{\partial \beta_{0i} \partial \beta_{0j}} \right\} \tag{19}$$

$\boldsymbol{J}$ is the $(k_1 \times k_0)$ matrix of derivatives of $\boldsymbol{\beta}_{10}(\boldsymbol{\beta}_0)$, i.e.

$$J_{ij} = \partial \beta_{10i} / \partial \beta_{0j} \tag{20}$$

$\boldsymbol{Q}_{10}$ is the 'crossed' information matrix

$$\boldsymbol{Q}_{10ij} = E_0 \left\{ -\frac{\partial^2 L_1(\boldsymbol{\beta}_{10})}{\partial \boldsymbol{\beta}_{1i} \partial \beta_{1j}} \right\} \tag{21}$$

and

$$G_{10ij} = E_0\left\{\frac{\partial L_1(\boldsymbol{\beta}_{10})}{\partial \beta_{1i}} \frac{\partial L_1(\boldsymbol{\beta}_{10})}{\partial \beta_{1j}}\right\}. \tag{22}$$

Hence, from (15),

$$V(\mathbf{t}_0) = \boldsymbol{Q}_{10}^{-1}\boldsymbol{G}_{10}\boldsymbol{Q}_{10}^{-1} - \boldsymbol{J}\boldsymbol{Q}_0^{-1}\boldsymbol{J}', \tag{23}$$

which can be used to define an asymptotically valid χ^2 test of $\mathbf{t}_0 = 0$.[1] I have not so far made any progress on possible relationships between this test and tests arising from artificial nesting of the densities f and g.

There are a number of parallels between this proposed procedure and the specification tests derived by Hausman (1978). In particular, both involve the comparison of two estimates of the same parameter vector (here $\hat{\boldsymbol{\beta}}_1$ and $\hat{\boldsymbol{\beta}}_{10}$) one of which is asymptotically efficient (in this case $\hat{\boldsymbol{\beta}}_{10}$, the MLE of $\text{plim}_0\hat{\boldsymbol{\beta}}_1$). Hausman's theorem on variances can thus be applied to the variance of $\mathbf{t}_0$. However, Hausman is working within a nested framework in which the parameters of the generalization are essentially nuisance parameters, whereas the lack of nesting is important in the current context. And even when the procedure given here is equivalent to a nested test (as in the example given above), it is not equivalent to a Hausman test. The latter, applied to (10), examines the effects on $\boldsymbol{\beta}_0$ of possible omission of the $\boldsymbol{Z}$ variables and does *not* lead to the LM test, see Holly (1980).

5.3 A MODEL FOR TESTING FOR LABOUR MARKET DISEQUILIBRIUM

The basic idea in what follows is to use consumer behaviour in commodity markets to make inferences about the state of the labour market. As is well-known, the imposition of quantity restrictions in one market has predictable consequences in other markets so that, in principle, the examination of these other markets can give us information about the market which may or may not be in disequilibrium. To fix ideas, utility u is defined over leisure q_0, and a vector of goods $\mathbf{q}$, i.e.

$$u = v(q_0, \mathbf{q}) \tag{24}$$

for direct utility function $v(.,.)$. The budget constraint for an unrestricted consumer is simply that

$$\omega q_0 + \mathbf{p}\,.\,\mathbf{q} = \omega T + \mu \tag{25}$$

for wage rate ω, price vector $\mathbf{p}$, time endowment T, and transfer income μ. Maximization of (24) subject to (25) yields the free, unrestricted demands. With a quantity constraint in the labour market, q_0 is fixed at z, say and the restricted demands for $\mathbf{q}$ result from adding this constraint to the previous problem. Substituting for q_0 in (25) gives the restricted budget constraint

$$\mathbf{p}\cdot\mathbf{q} = \omega(T - q_0) + \mu \tag{26}$$

and the right-hand side of this is *income*. In this case, individual commodities are a function of income, prices, and the leisure constraint z and a consumption function can be said to exist.

For much of this paper, I shall be concerned with the special case of separability between goods and leisure. This corresponds to (24) having the form $v(q_0, \phi(\mathbf{q}))$ for some function $\phi(.)$ with v increasing in its value. In this case, there exist subgroup demand functions for goods alone, so that the complete system of commodity leisure demands can be written in the recursive form

$$q_i = g_i\{\omega(T - q_0) + \mu, \mathbf{p}\} \tag{27}$$

$$q_0 = g_0\{\omega T + \mu, \omega, \mathbf{p}\} \tag{28}$$

where g_i, $i = 1, \ldots, n$, is independent of ω except via money income. Note that (27) and (28) hold even though labour supply is entirely under the consumer's control so that weak separability also guarantees the existence of a consumption function even without labour market disequilibrium. If q_0 is now restricted to z, equation (28) no longer holds, but equation (27) is virtually unaffected with only q_0 being replaced by z. There is no change of functional form for the unrationed goods. Hence, testing for rationing under weak separability is essentially a matter of testing for the exogeneity of q_0 in the commodity demands with the additional information that, if q_0 is endogenous, its functional form is given by (28) (which is, of course, determined from (27) given adding-up).

Without separability, the analysis is more complex, although testing for restrictions may well be easier in principle since they have more widespread effects on behaviour. Without restrictions, maximization of utility produces, say, for $i = 0, 1, \ldots, n$

$$q_i = f_i\{\omega T + \mu, \omega, \mathbf{p}\} \tag{29}$$

while, with q_0 restricted to z, the demands become, $i = 1, \ldots, n$,

$$q_i = f_i^*\{\omega(T - z) + \mu, z, \mathbf{p}\}. \tag{30}$$

The f_i^* contain different arguments from the f_i functions and there is no simple link between them as exists under separability. Efficient discrimination between the two requires the ability to proceed from one to the other and this analysis is provided in Deaton and Muellbauer (1980, pp. 109–114), Neary and Roberts (1980), and Deaton (1981). I shall not proceed further with it here since the tests reported later will be confined entirely to the separable case.

For practical analysis, specific functional forms are required. Here, I use Muellbauer's (1981) extension of the Gorman polar form which is defined by the (full) cost function

$$c(u, \omega, \mathbf{p}) = \{a(\mathbf{p})\}^{1-\delta}\omega^{\delta}u + b(\mathbf{p})\omega + d(\mathbf{p}) \tag{31}$$

where $\delta \in (0, 1)$ is a parameter, $a(\mathbf{p})$ and $d(\mathbf{p})$ are linearly homogeneous functions of goods prices $\mathbf{p}$, and $b(\mathbf{p})$ is homogeneous of degree zero. Application of Shephard's lemma gives, after some rearrangement, the commodity demand and 'income supply' functions

$$p_i q_i = \gamma_i + \beta_i \omega + \alpha_i \mu + u_i \tag{32}$$

$$\mu + \omega l = \gamma_0 + \beta_0 \omega + \alpha_0 \mu + u_0 \tag{33}$$

where $l \equiv (T - q_0)$ is hours worked (so that $\mu + \omega l$ is income) and, where subscripts denote partial differentiation, for $i = 1, \ldots, n$

$$\gamma_i = p_i d_i(\mathbf{p}) - \frac{p_i a_i(\mathbf{p})}{a(\mathbf{p})} d(\mathbf{p})\,(1 - \delta) \tag{34}$$

$$\beta_i = p_i b_i(\mathbf{p}) + \frac{p_i a_i(\mathbf{p})}{a(\mathbf{p})} \tau(1 - \delta) \tag{35}$$

$$\alpha_i = \frac{p_i a_i(\mathbf{p})}{a(\mathbf{p})}(1 - \delta) \tag{36}$$

$$\tau = T - b(\mathbf{p}), \tag{37}$$

and

$$\gamma_0 = \Sigma\gamma_i,\ \beta_0 = \Sigma\beta_i,\ \text{and}\ \alpha_0 = \Sigma\alpha_i. \tag{38}$$

The terms u_i and u_0, with $u_0 = \Sigma u_i$, are stochastic error terms reflecting variation in tastes over households. Although, in principle, all parameters of tastes could be allowed to vary over micro-units, it is particularly convenient to restrict variation to the γ-parameters. These will in any case be modelled as functions of specific household characteristics later in the analysis, see equation (48) below, and stochastic terms could equally well have been added there.

The cost function (31) represents the cost of minimal subsistence when $u = 0$; hence $b(\mathbf{p}) = \partial c/\partial p_0$ at $u = 0$ is minimal leisure requirements so that τ measures free time to be allocated to work or leisure. The coefficients α_i, β_i, and γ_i are functions of $\mathbf{p}$, but not of μ and ω, and since I shall be using cross-section data in which $\mathbf{p}$ is assumed to be the same for all data points, I have suppressed the $\mathbf{p}$ arguments. It is in this context that the Muellbauer form is of such great convenience since it generates the fully linear system (32) and (33).

In general, the imposition of $q_0 = z$ in the Muellbauer model gives rise to demand functions which look very different from (32); see Deaton and Muellbauer (1981) for a description. However, (31) has a weakly separable subcase so that, if separability is true, the simpler analytical apparatus can be used. Weak separability of $\mathbf{q}$ implies, and is implied by,

$$\frac{\partial^2 c}{\partial \omega \, \partial p_i} = \rho \frac{\partial^2 c}{\partial u \, \partial p_0}, \qquad i = 1, \ldots, n \tag{39}$$

for some quantity ρ not indexed on i; see Deaton and Muellbauer (1980, pp. 128–129). It is easily checked that, trivial cases apart, this holds if and only if $b(\mathbf{p})$ is a constant function. This implies that $b_i(\mathbf{p}) = 0$ so that, from (35) and (36)

$$\beta_i = \alpha_i \tau \qquad i = 1, \ldots, n \tag{40}$$

so that (32) and (33) become, in view of (38),

$$p_i q_i = \gamma_i + \alpha_i(\mu + \omega\tau) + u_i \tag{41}$$

$$\mu + \omega l = \gamma_0 + \alpha_0(\mu + \omega\tau) + u_0. \tag{42}$$

This specification, on a single cross-section, is indistinguishable from the linear expenditure system augmented for leisure as estimated, for example, by Abbot and Ashenfelter (1976), Phlips (1978), or Ashenfelter (1980).

From this restricted version of the model, the specific analogue of (27) and (28) can be calculated. Equation (42) is used to solve for $(\mu + \omega\tau)$ in terms of $(\mu + \omega l)$ and the result substituted in (41) to yield

$$p_i q_i = \left(\gamma_i - \frac{\alpha_i}{\alpha_0}\gamma_0\right) + \frac{\alpha_i}{\alpha_0}(\mu + \omega l) + \left(u_i - \frac{\alpha_i}{\alpha_0}u_0\right) \tag{43}$$

which is the specific form of (27) used below. Note, once again, that although these equations give expenditures as a function of income, income is endogenous to the consumer. Indeed, in view of the income supply function (42), the explanatory variable and the error in (43) are likely to be correlated in general, so that, with free choice, the equation is not by itself a suitable vehicle for estimation. If however, the consumer is rationed, (42) is false, $\mu + \omega l$ is exogenous, and there is no reason to expect anything other than consistent estimates from (43). Hence, an immediate test with rationing as the null would be a Wu (1973)-Hausman (1978) test for the exogeneity of $(\mu + \omega l)$ in (43) with $(\mu + \omega\tau)$ as an instrument (from (42)). That is rather close to what I shall do, although by exploiting the precise form of (41) and (42), the methodology of Section 5.2 is likely to be more powerful in discriminating between the two alternatives considered.

The procedure is then as follows. *At the first stage*, the free model given by (41) and (42) is estimated by full information maximum likelihood (FIML). The resulting parameter estimates of γ, α, τ and the variance–covariance matrix of the $\mathbf{u}$'s are consistent under the truth of the free model. These parameter estimates can then be used to calculate the parameters of (43) together with maximum likelihood estimates of the probability limits of the parameter estimates obtained by estimating (43) under the mistaken view (if the free model is true) that $(\mu + \omega l)$

is an exogenous variable. Calculating these probability limits is a straightforward exercise in simultaneous equations bias. To be specific, let $\boldsymbol{\Omega}$, typical element ω_{ij}, be the variance–covariance matrix of the u_i's, $i = 1, \ldots, n$, in (41), i.e.

$$E(u_{ih}, u_{jk}) = \delta_{hk}\omega_{ij} \tag{44}$$

for observations h and k. Then the bias in estimating (43) is determined by the covariances of $u + \omega l$ and $(u_i - \alpha_i u_0/\alpha_0)$. Elementary manipulation gives, for $i = 1, \ldots, n$,

$$\text{cov}\left\{\mu + \omega l,\ u_i - \frac{\alpha_i u_0}{\alpha_0}\right\} = \sum_{k=1}^{n} \omega_{ik} - \frac{\alpha_i}{\alpha_0}\sum_{j=1}^{n}\sum_{k=1}^{n} \omega_{jk}.$$

This formula can be used in the usual way (N.B. (43) is otherwise a set of n straightforward OLS regressions) to give estimates of what is expected from (43) under the truth of (41) and (42). The test of the free model is then a comparison of these estimates with what is given directly by the estimation of (43), these latter being, of course, the maximum likelihood estimates under the truth of the labour constrained model. Note that it is possible for the covariance to be zero if the following condition holds:

$$\frac{\alpha_i}{\alpha_0} = \frac{\sum_k \omega_{ik}}{\sum_k \sum_j \omega_{jk}} \tag{45}$$

and if this is true there will be no simultaneity bias. It is also not entirely implausible that (45) should hold. First, under Theil's (1971, 1975, pp. 56–90) theory of 'rational random behaviour', the variance–covariance matrix reflects the structure of substitution, so that, under separability, (45) can be shown to hold; see also Deaton (1975, pp. 161–168) for a closely related result. However, to the extent that the u_i's reflect omitted variables, errors of measurement, and such extra-model phenomena, it is not likely that the theory of rational random behaviour will apply. But there is a second possibility, that the effects of omitted variables on each demand are proportional to the corresponding income effects; this is a type of 'general' separability which is not entirely unlikely. Of course, if for whatever reason (45) does hold, it will be very difficult to distinguish the two models since, in effect, the truth of the free model implies that in all respects the constrained model will appear to be correct.

The *second stage* of the testing procedure is to assume the constrained model to be true and examine its predictions for the estimation of the free relations. This is always likely to be less powerful since, while the free model explains all the variables, the restricted model offers no explanation for determining hours worked. Even so, the actual testing is more straightforward this way round.

Denoting exogenous money income $\mu + \omega l$ by y, the labour-constrained model gives

$$p_i q_i = \psi_i + \theta_i y + v_i \tag{46}$$

in an obvious notation, with the error v_i independent of y. Under the free model, equation (41) is correct, i.e. $p_i q_i$ is determined by available full-income $\mu + \omega\tau$ and not by money income y. Hence we have the standard non-nested two-regressions case and, as argued in Section 5.2, the suggested methodology leads to a standard F-test for the significance of $\mu + \omega\tau$ in (46), i.e. the following regression is estimated:

$$p_i q_i = \psi_i^* + \theta_i^* y + \xi_i^*(\mu + \omega\tau) + w_i \tag{47}$$

and the test of the rationed model is carried out via the t-value of $\hat{\xi}_i^*$. Under the rationed model, this should be insignificantly small. Note carefully, however, that the possible significance of $\hat{\theta}_i^*$ in (47) is *not* a refutation of the free model. If y is endogenous, it is reasonable to expect a significant $\hat{\theta}_i^*$ in the equation so that the appropriate test of the free model is not (47), but the comparisons at the first stage.

Before carrying out these tests in Section 5.6, I discuss data, econometric, and specification problems in the next section, while in Section 5.5 I discuss whether, under the hypothesis of free choice, the separability embodied in (41) and (42) is an acceptable specialization over the nonseparable model in (32) and (33).

5.4 THE DATA AND ECONOMETRIC PROBLEMS

This research is intended in part to complement that of Atkinson and Stern (1981a, b) and, for that reason, the data are identical. A full account is given in the first of their papers; I give only a brief description here.

The underlying sample is the Department of Employment's Family Expenditure Survey 1973, a cross-section stratified sample of 10 500 households with a response rate of 68 %. Information is collected on, among many other things, hours worked, income, and expenditures on various items. Following Atkinson and Stern, the sample is restricted to those households with male heads who are in employment, are aged between 18 and 64, and who have a normal wage between £0.85 and £3.00 per hour. This reduces the sample size to 1617 households. If, as is assumed here, the wage rate is exogenous to the labour supply decisions of male household heads, such sample selection does not bias the results and it has the effect of ruling out most individuals who do not have straightforward linear budget sets. With a normal wage between £0.85 and £3.00 few individuals attract either higher rates of tax or means-tested benefits. The expenditure categories used are those collected via a 14 day diary (although all magnitudes are re-expressed at weekly rates) and are: (1) food, (2) alcoholic drink, (3) tobacco, (4) clothing, (5) durable household goods, (6) other goods, (7) transport and vehicles, (8) services, and (9) composite. The data give figures for 'normal' hours worked and for 'normal' weekly earnings; the gross wage rate is then obtained by dividing the latter by the former. (It is worth noting that although it is true that many workers report 40 or 42 hours worked, there is still substantial variation in hours across individuals; mean hours reported over the 1617 observations is 42.8 with a standard deviation of 6.7.) Unearned income, μ above, is net income of the household excluding the earnings of the head. The composite is then defined by adding-up, once basic tax rates and National Insurance Contributions have been taken into account. These imply an average deduction of 32.5 % for most households, see Atkinson and Stern, so that the net wage is 0.675 of the gross wage and the composite is 0.675 times gross earnings *plus* unearned income *less* the sum of expenditures on the other commodities. This ignores the cash value of tax allowances; these are assumed to be constant for each household and absorbed into the constant term of the regressions. To the extent that they vary with the wage rate or other household characteristics (to be discussed below) the effects will be absorbed into the other parameters. Note that, given the definition of the other goods, the composite includes such important expenditures as housing, fuel, light, and power as well as saving.

Atkinson and Stern allow for three household characteristics: the number of children (NCH), the number of earners in the family (NEARN), and a binary variable reflecting whether or not the household owns its own home (OWN). These can be regarded as affecting household preferences and legitimately and unrestricted versions of the model.

$$\gamma_i = \gamma_{io} + \gamma_{i1}\mathrm{NCH} + \gamma_{i2}\mathrm{NEARN} + \gamma_{i3}\mathrm{OWN}. \tag{48}$$

It is easily shown that these variables will then appear linearly in both restricted and unrestricted versions of the model.

There is a large number of very severe problems in using the data as described in the way that I am about to use it. For the timc being, I can do very little more than list them. First, it is clear that obtaining wages by dividing imperfectly measured earnings by imperfectly measured hours induces spurious negative correlation between hours and the wage and spurious positive correlation between earnings and the wage. Treatment for this requires instrumenting the wage and the construction of a wage equation in terms of education, experience, age, and so on. Secondly, there is a similar problem of measurement with unearned income and, in addition, even if perfectly measured, it may well be positively correlated with omitted (and largely unobservable) effects. For example, households with a 'taste' for work are likely both to work long hours *and* to possess high income from assets representing the fruits of their earlier labours. Adequate resolution of these difficulties requires the use of panel data. Nevertheless, the literature contains much ingenious work designed to circumvent the typical 'untreated' results of a measured *positive* effect of unearned income on hours. Thirdly, the current treatment of family labour supply is extremely crude and the procedure of absorbing non-head of household income into unearned income is very hard to defend. Similarly, NEARN would not be an exogenous variable if family labour supply decisions were seriously modelled. Fourthly, several of the consumption categories distinguished take a zero value for some households, alcoholic drink and tobacco being the obvious examples. Tobin's (1958) procedure is now standard for such cases considered in isolation but it is far from so when there are several such in a system of equations, although see the attempt by Wales and Woodland (1979). Nor is it obvious that the Tobin model is a correct representation of why the zeros occur; some households may consume the good but simply not purchase it over the 14 day diary period. For the present work, all the data are used, including zeros.

The presence of these difficulties reduces much of the current work to an illustrative exercise although it can still be regarded as a starting point for more refined analysis. Even so, it is never possible to solve all such problems simultaneously and many of those listed above comprise major research projects in their own right. Perhaps inevitably then, I proceed as if the data are a perfect representation of the model discussed in Section 5.3.

5.5 TESTING FOR SEPARABILITY

The substitution of the household characteristics specification (48) into the unrationed nonseparable demand system (32) and (33) yields a system of 10 equations, 9 of which are independent, and each of which represents a linear relationship between expenditure (or income), the number of children NCH, the number of earners NEARN, whether or not the household owns its own home OWN, unearned income μ, and the wage rate ω. Since there are no cross-equation restrictions, FIML estimation is equivalent to OLS applied equation by equation, the results of which are given in Table 5.1

Several features of these regressions are worth noting. The first nine elements of each column add to the tenth; hence if, for example, children increase the demand for food (as here they do), this must be met by a decrease elsewhere (transport, services, composite) and/or by an increase in hours worked. Note that there is no evidence here of children increasing the demand for drink or tobacco as might be suggested, for example, by the Barten (1964) model of the effects of family composition on consumption. The number of earners exerts a significantly positive effect on several items of consumption; surprisingly, this is reflected in a negative effect on the composite rather than a positive effect on total income. Given the possible biases from the inappropriate treatment of family labour supply, these coefficients are difficult to interpret. Owner-occupiers smoke and drink a good deal less than non-owners; they also spend more on transport and vehicles. These are interesting effects. On smoking in particular, anti-smoking propaganda has had well-known differential effects across class lines so that expenditure on tobacco in 1973 (as now) tends to be strongly negatively related to

Table 5.1 Linear model without separability

	Constant	NCH	NEARN	OWN	μ	ω	R^2	Ratio
1. Food	4.58	1.56	1.37	0.07	0.10	2.86	0.278	30
	(8.8)	(16.9)	(5.0)	(0.3)	(8.4)	(6.6)		
2. Drink	0.32	0.03	0.88	−0.82	0.05	0.79	0.161	15
	(0.9)	(0.5)	(4.5)	(−4.8)	(6.6)	(2.6)		
3. Tobacco	1.76	0.05	0.45	−0.90	0.02	−0.55	0.164	−31
	(8.9)	(1.5)	(4.3)	(−9.8)	(4.2)	(−3.4)		
4. Clothing	0.14	0.54	0.72	0.15	0.09	1.97	0.099	21
	(0.2)	(4.4)	(2.0)	(0.5)	(6.3)	(3.4)		
5. Durable household goods	0.88	−0.15	0.16	1.11	0.04	2.64	0.011	70
	(0.6)	(−0.6)	(0.2)	(1.7)	(1.3)	(2.3)		
6. Other goods	0.90	0.19	0.11	0.26	0.05	1.94	0.076	36
	(2.0)	(2.4)	(0.5)	(1.2)	(5.6)	(5.3)		
7. Transport and vehicles	1.56	−0.45	0.20	1.24	0.13	5.02	0.099	40
	(1.6)	(−2.5)	(0.4)	(2.7)	(5.8)	(6.0)		
8. Services	−1.85	−0.39	0.03	0.06	0.09	7.72	0.070	87
	(−1.6)	(−1.9)	(0.0)	(0.1)	(3.5)	(8.1)		
9. Composite	−5.40	−0.85	−3.94	−1.27	0.43	15.9	0.100	37
	(−2.1)	(−1.9)	(−3.0)	(−1.1)	(7.8)	(7.6)		
10. Total income	2.89	0.53	−0.02	−0.11	1.00	38.3		38
	(4.4)	(4.6)	(−0.1)	(−0.14)	(70.5)	(70.9)		

$W = 28.6 \quad W_{3,8} = 8.1 \quad 2 \log L = -88647$

any variable which is positively linked with social class. Home ownership is almost certainly such a proxy. Unearned income and wages both have positive signs throughout, except for the effect of wages on tobacco expenditure. Once again, I suspect a proxy effect for omitted class variables; it is hard to believe that tobacco is as strongly complementary with leisure as the results would indicate. The income supply equation, category 10, is not atypical of the kind of results usually obtained by crude regression on wages and unearned income. The latter has essentially no effect on hours while the coefficient on the wage rate, being less than the sample mean, implies that, at least at the mean, the labour supply curve is backward sloping. The combination of these two results is theoretically impossible under the standard model of labour supply, although, until the problems discussed in Section 5.4 are dealt with, there is no way of knowing whether or not the phenomenon is real.

Separability can be tested in two different (but asymptotically equivalent) ways. The first is to use the unrestricted estimates in Table 5.1 to test whether or not the ratio β_i/α_i is indeed common to each equation. The ratios implied by the coefficients are given in the final column of Table 5.1 and show considerable variability, from −31 for tobacco (but see the remarks in the previous paragraph) to 87 for services. Under separability, these ratios would be identical and would give an estimate of the number of free hours available per week for work and leisure together. As it is, tobacco is more of a complement to leisure and transport more of a complement to work than would be permitted under separability. A formal test on the Wald principle can be based on testing, for $i = 1, \ldots, 8$

$$h_i(\hat{\alpha}, \hat{\beta}) = \hat{\beta}_i \hat{\alpha}_9 - \hat{\beta}_9 \hat{\alpha}_i = 0 \tag{49}$$

for OLS estimates $\hat{\beta}$ and $\hat{\alpha}$. The variances and covariances of the $\hat{\alpha}$'s and $\hat{\beta}$'s are easily determined, e.g.

$$\operatorname{cov}(\hat{\alpha}_i \hat{\beta}_j) = \hat{\omega}_{ij}(X'X)^{56} \tag{50}$$

where $\boldsymbol{X}$ is the matrix of independent variables in the order listed in Table 5.1, $(X'X)^{ij}$ is the i,jth element of $(\boldsymbol{X}'\boldsymbol{X})^{-1}$, and $\hat{\omega}_{ij}$ is the estimated variance–covariance matrix based on the OLS residuals. Hence, defining

$$\begin{aligned} v_{ij} = & \sum_r \sum_s (\delta_{ir}\hat{\alpha}_9 - \delta_{r9}\hat{\alpha}_i)(X'X)^{55}\hat{\omega}_{rs}(\delta_{jr}\hat{\alpha}_9 - \delta_{r9}\hat{\alpha}_j) \\ & + \sum_r \sum_s (\delta_{ir}\hat{\alpha}_9 - \delta_{r9}\hat{\alpha}_i)(X'X)^{56}\hat{\omega}_{rs}(\hat{\beta}_j\delta_{9s} - \hat{\beta}_9\delta_{js}) \\ & + \sum_r \sum_s (\hat{\beta}_i\delta_{9r} - \hat{\beta}_9\delta_{ir})(X'X)^{65}\hat{\omega}_{rs}(\delta_{jr}\hat{\alpha}_9 - \delta_{r9}\hat{\alpha}_i) \\ & + \sum_r \sum_s (\hat{\beta}_i\delta_{9r} - \hat{\beta}_9\delta_{ir})(X'X)^{66}\hat{\omega}_{rs}(\hat{\beta}_j\delta_{9s} - \hat{\beta}_9\delta_{js}) \end{aligned} \tag{51}$$

the statistic

$$W = \sum_i \sum_j h_i(\hat{\alpha}, \hat{\beta}) v^{ij} h_j(\hat{\alpha}, \hat{\beta}) \tag{52}$$

is the Wald test for separability and is asymptotically distributed as χ^2_8 under the null hypothesis.

As reported at the foot of Table 5.1, W has the value 28.6 which, using the asymptotic criterion, is significant at 1%. There are two reasons for treating the result with caution. First, the negative coefficient for ω in the tobacco equation is suspect for the reasons given above. Secondly, the majority of these equations suffer from considerable residual heteroskedasticity as gauged, for example, by the test proposed by Breusch and Pagan (1979). Experience elsewhere suggests that such heteroskedasticity implies an overstating of t-values by perhaps 10–15%. A similar effect may well operate on W.

The cause of the rejection (if indeed it is to be so interpreted) can be traced further by examining the likelihood function in the following way. A separable group, excluding for example food, can be tested for by testing (49) for $i = 2, \ldots, 8$, excluding 1. This was done for each of the goods in turn and in no case was W_i (i being the excluded good) small enough to change the results obtained for no exclusions. The test was then repeated for all possible permutations of *two* excluded goods. In this case, for one permutation, and for that one only, the W statistic dropped below conventional significance limits. This was the case where (not surprisingly) tobacco and transport and vehicles were excluded, so that the other 7 goods could be treated as separable from labour (leisure). Of course, this sort of likelihood mining does not constitute a proper test but it does indicate the direction of the difficulty.

Table 5.2 provides an alternative approach to testing separability through the estimation of the separable model itself, i.e. of (41) and (42) plus the household characteristics. This model is nonlinear but all the parameters except τ can be concentrated out of the first-order likelihood maximization conditions, so that iteration can be carried out in one dimension (it is still relatively expensive, however).[2] The parameter τ is estimated to be 38.9, which reconciles by force the

Table 5.2 Linear model with separability (LES)

	Constant	NCH	NEARN	OWN	$\mu + \hat{\tau}\omega$	R^2
1. Food	4.14	1.56	1.58	0.04	0.08	0.278
	(10.7)	(17.0)	(7.3)	(0.9)	(12.0)	
2. Drink	−0.34	0.03	1.20	−0.88	0.04	0.158
	(1.2)	(0.5)	(7.8)	(−5.1)	(7.2)	
3. Tobacco	1.11	0.05	0.76	−0.95	0.00	0.152
	(7.5)	(1.4)	(9.3)	(−10.4)	(0.7)	
4. Clothing	−0.76	0.54	1.16	0.08	0.07	0.097
	(1.5)	(4.4)	(4.1)	(0.2)	(8.0)	
5. Durable household goods	1.49	−0.15	−0.14	1.16	0.05	0.011
	(1.5)	(0.6)	(0.2)	(1.8)	(2.8)	
6. Other goods	0.81	0.19	0.16	0.25	0.05	0.076
	(2.5)	(2.4)	(0.8)	(1.2)	(8.7)	
7. Transport and vehicles	1.61	−0.45	0.18	1.24	0.13	0.099
	(2.2)	(2.5)	(0.4)	(2.7)	(9.1)	
8. Services	0.37	−0.39	−1.04	0.24	0.15	0.066
	(0.4)	(−1.9)	(−2.2)	(0.4)	(9.1)	
9. Composite	−5.87	−0.85	−3.71	−1.31	0.42	0.100
	(−3.1)	(−1.9)	(−3.5)	(−1.13)	(12.4)	
10. Total income	2.55	0.53	0.14	−0.13	0.99	

$\hat{\tau} = 38.9$ (45.8) $2 \log L = -88682$

different ratios in Table 5.1. In common with other investigators' results for the linear income supply model, this figure is absurdly low as an estimate of free hours. Twice the logarithm of the likelihood drops by 35, a number which yields a χ_8^2 figure asymptotically if separability is correct. Once again, the null is rejected, perhaps not surprisingly since this likelihood ratio test and the earlier Wald test are asymptotically equivalent and there are 1617 observations. (Even so, there are 45 parameters in the variance–covariance matrix and 45 in the model so that it may be over-optimistic to think of the sample as being 'large'.)

In spite of these rejections, I shall proceed entirely in terms of the separable model. This is partly because of the arguments on the rejection given above but largely because I wish to look at the empirical counterparts of the separable models discussed in Section 5.3. Testing for quantity restrictions in a nonseparable framework is a rather different problem and I hope to discuss it in another paper.

5.6 DOES THE LABOUR MARKET CLEAR?

The tests of rationing versus free choice are carried out starting with the constrained model. The first line for each good in Table 5.3 gives the regression of expenditure on the characteristics and money income. This is the correct model if all consumers have fixed hours and if separability is true. Qualitatively, these results are very similar to those in Tables 5.1 and 5.2. In the line below each set of results are those with $\omega\hat{\tau} + \mu$ included as a separate regressor, $\hat{\tau}$ being taken from Table 5.2. Under the truth of the rationed model, this is an irrelevant variable and although its presence can be expected to reduce the efficiency of estimation, it should not affect the other parameter estimates or be itself significant. This is fairly close to what happens. The standard errors of the parameters on y are reduced in roughly equal proportions ($\omega\hat{\tau} + \mu$ is clearly most highly correlated with y of all the variables) and, overall, the $\omega\hat{\tau} + \mu$ variable is not significant in the system, the $2 \log LR$ taking a value of 16. On a generous interpretation, the rationed model passes the test.

Even so, there are a number of disquieting features in the table. In particular, the coefficients on $\omega\hat{\tau} + \mu$ in both durable household goods and transport and vehicles equations are (marginally) significantly different from zero at 5% and in these two cases, as well as in a few others, there are marked changes in the coefficient on y on the introduction of the additional regressor. Such effects may well be due to chance, and it is important to bear in mind the relatively high correlation between y and $\omega\hat{\tau} + \mu$, but there must remain at least some doubt as to the consistency of the rationed model with these data.

Table 5.4 contains the results of testing the free model. The first part, labelled 'Conditional regression coefficients' contains the estimates of $(\gamma_i - \alpha_i\gamma_0/\alpha_0)$ and α_i/α_0 in equation (43) and are calculated from the ML estimates of the parameters of the free model from Table 5.2. If the free model were correct and had true

Table 5.3 Disequilibrium model and nested composite

	Constant	NCH	NEARN	OWN	y	$\omega\hat{\tau} + \mu$	R^2
1. Food	3.85	1.52	1.51	0.02	0.09		0.292
	(10.0)	(16.5)	(7.2)	(0.8)	(13.3)		
	3.84	1.50	1.57	0.05	0.12	−0.03	0.293
	(10.0)	(16.3)	(7.3)	(0.22)	(5.9)	(−1.5)	
2. Drink	−0.50	0.01	1.15	−0.89	0.04		0.166
	(−1.8)	(0.2)	(7.6)	(−5.2)	(8.3)		
	−0.50	−0.00	1.19	−0.87	0.06	−0.02	0.167
	(−1.8)	(−0.0)	(7.8)	(−5.1)	(4.3)	(−1.6)	
3. Tobacco	1.07	0.05	0.74	−0.97	0.00		0.153
	(7.2)	(1.4)	(9.1)	(−10.6)	(1.2)		
	1.07	0.04	0.76	−0.95	0.02	−0.13	0.154
	(7.2)	(1.2)	(9.3)	(−10.4)	(2.0)	(−1.6)	
4. Clothing	−0.93	0.50	1.16	0.09	0.07		0.101
	(−1.8)	(4.1)	(4.1)	(0.3)	(8.2)		
	−0.93	0.50	1.15	0.09	0.07	0.01	0.101
	(−1.8)	(4.1)	(4.0)	(0.3)	(2.5)	(0.2)	
5. Durable household goods	1.10	−0.18	−0.36	1.07	0.07		0.014
	(1.1)	(−0.7)	(−0.6)	(1.7)	(3.7)		
	1.08	−0.23	−0.16	1.18	0.16	−0.11	0.117
	(1.1)	(−0.9)	(−0.3)	(1.9)	(3.1)	(−1.97)	
6. Other goods	0.64	0.16	0.12	0.24	0.05		0.085
	(1.9)	(2.0)	(0.65)	(1.2)	(9.6)		
	0.64	0.15	0.15	0.26	0.07	−0.01	0.086
	(1.9)	(1.9)	(0.8)	(1.3)	(4.0)	(−0.8)	
7. Transport and vehicles	1.51	−0.52	0.35	1.35	0.12		0.096
	(2.0)	(−2.9)	(0.8)	(2.9)	(9.2)		
	1.53	−0.47	0.17	1.25	0.03	0.09	0.099
	(2.0)	(−2.6)	(0.4)	(2.7)	(0.9)	(2.3)	
8. Services	0.03	−0.46	−1.02	0.27	0.14		0.071
	(0.04)	(−2.2)	(−2.2)	(0.5)	(9.7)		
	0.04	−0.45	−1.06	0.26	0.13	0.02	0.071
	(0.04)	(−2.2)	(−2.2)	(0.5)	(2.9)	(0.37)	
9. Composite	−6.8	−1.08	−3.63	−1.19	0.41		0.107
	(−3.6)	(−2.4)	(−3.5)	(−1.0)	(12.8)		
	−6.8	−1.04	−3.77	−1.26	0.35	0.07	0.108
	(−3.6)	(−2.3)	(−3.6)	(−1.1)	(3.6)	(0.7)	

$2 \log LR = 16$

parameters as given in Table 5.2, these would be the parameters of (43). However, estimating (43) when the free model is true produces inconsistent parameter estimates because of the simultaneity bias. The maximum likelihood estimates of the probability limits of these inconsistent parameter estimates are given in the second half of the table and are labelled 'Predicted disequilibrium values under equilibrium'. The differences between these numbers and those given immediately above are simply the estimates of the simultaneity bias. According to (45), if $\mathbf{b}_i$ is the vector of coefficients for equation i ($i = 1,\ldots, 9$) comprising 5 elements (coefficients of constant, NCH, NEARN, OWN, and y)

$$(\text{plim}\,\tilde{\mathbf{b}}_i - \mathbf{b}_i) = A^{-1}\mathbf{f}_i \tag{53}$$

where

$$A = \text{plim}\left\{\frac{1}{n}Z'Z\right\} \tag{54}$$

estimated by $n^{-1}\,Z'Z$, and $\mathbf{f}_i$ is a vector of 5 elements all of which are zero save the last, i.e.

$$f_{ij} = \delta_{5j}\left\{\sum_k \omega_{ik} - \frac{\alpha_i}{\alpha_0}\sum_k\sum_l \omega_{kl}\right\} \tag{55}$$

for $i = 1,\ldots,9; j = 1,\ldots,5$. These quantities are estimated from the parameters in Table 5.2 and the corresponding estimated variance covariance matrix. As it turns out, the estimates of $\boldsymbol{\Omega}$ and α approximately satisfy (45) so that there is very little predicted bias except in the few cases printed in italic in Table 5.4. Apart from these, the first part of the table looks very much like the second. However, the second is even closer to the third which presents the *actual* disequilibrium values, replicated from Table 5.3. I have not so far been able to calculate the variance–covariance matrix of the estimated differences, but the figures are so close that there seems little need to do so. In particular, if attention is focused on the italicized cases, in every case that a simultaneity bias is predicted, it appears almost exactly. In fact of these extraordinarily accurate predictions of the free model, the (minor) failures of the rationed model in Table 5.3 seem comparatively very large.

Of course, the basic result is that both models do rather well in predicting the outcome of estimating the other, so that there are few grounds for favouring one over the other.

I conclude this section by referring back briefly to Table 5.3. It might at first be thought that the truth of the free model should not imply significant coefficients for y when $(\omega\hat{\tau} + \mu)$ is included. Hence the fact that y remains a significant variable in the extended regressions might be thought to contradict the results in Table 5.4. This is not in fact the case given the dependence of y on $(\omega\hat{\tau} + \mu)$ in the free model. Indeed, just as in Table 5.4, the free model can be used to predict the

Table 5.4 Predicted disequilibrium estimates

	Constant	NCH	NEARN	OWN	*y*
Conditional regression coefficients					
F	3.9238	1.5166	1.5718	*0.04842*	0.08472
D	−0.43741	0.01221	1.1966	−0.87261	0.03677
T	1.1011	0.04879	0.76307	−0.95365	*0.00165*
C	−0.94651	0.49949	1.1441	0.08825	0.07289
H	1.3553	−0.17347	*−0.14480*	1.1682	0.05358
O	0.67710	0.15936	0.14713	0.25572	0.05254
TV	1.2855	−0.52193	*0.15774*	1.2616	0.12879
S	*−0.00691*	−0.46278	−1.0576	0.25913	0.14590
R	−6.9519	−1.0782	−3.7780	−1.2550	0.42317
Predicted disequilibrium values under equilibzium					
F	3.8498	1.5176	1.5027	*0.01608*	0.08865
D	−0.49474	0.01305	1.1430	−0.89769	0.03982
T	1.0697	0.04925	0.73371	−0.96740	*0.00332*
C	−0.93165	0.49927	1.1580	0.09475	0.07210
H	1.1006	−0.16974	*−0.38270*	1.0568	0.06712
O	0.64154	0.15988	0.11392	0.24017	0.05443
TV	1.5103	−0.52523	*0.36774*	1.3599	0.11684
S	*0.03417*	−0.46338	−1.0192	0.27710	0.14371
R	−6.7797	−1.0807	−3.6172	−1.1797	0.41402
Actual disequilibrium values					
F	3.8487	1.5156	1.5096	*0.02000*	0.08826
D	−0.49561	0.01150	1.1483	−0.89464	0.03951
T	1.0692	0.04840	0.73663	−0.96573	*0.00315*
C	−0.93143	0.49967	1.1566	0.09396	0.07218
H	1.0967	−0.17664	*−0.35903*	1.0704	0.06576
O	0.64100	0.15892	0.11722	0.24206	0.05424
TV	1.5137	−0.51914	*0.34685*	1.3480	0.11804
S	*0.03480*	−0.46227	−1.0230	0.27491	0.14393
R	−6.7771	−1.0761	−3.6332	−1.1889	0.41494

results of estimating the extended regression reported in Table 5.3. As one would expect, the expected and actual parameter estimates are extraordinarily close and there is no contradiction, either in methodology or results, between the two tables.

5.7 CONCLUSIONS

In this paper, I have suggested a methodology for testing for quantity restrictions in the labour market and I have reported some results using the 1973 British Family Expenditure Survey. The results, although slightly favouring the market clearing hypothesis, are basically unable to distinguish between that and constrained hours. Given that my prior expectations were that the tests would be decisive in favour of the disequilibrium model, I find the results surprising. Others may not do so, and still others will emphasize the meaninglessness of the results in the face of all the data and econometric problems which I have discussed (and ignored). However, I believe that the framework is a useful one and that the general methodology will survive the improvements of data, of technique, and of modelling which are so clearly required. Obviously it would be better to allow some consumers to be on their supply curves and others to be off them; it would be better to allow for the errors of measurement in wages and in income; it would be better to use a wider variety of household characteristics; and it would be better if I knew better how to deal with zero recorded purchases. There is clearly much work to be done.

ACKNOWLEDGEMENTS

The work for this paper was done while the author was visiting the Industrial Relations Section in Princeton. I should like to thank the Section and Princeton University for their hospitality. I had helpful comments from and/or discussion with Joe Altonji, Orley Ashenfelter, William Brainard, Naorayex Dastoor, Robert Engle, John Ham, David Hendry, Dale Jorgenson, David Lillian, Michel Mouchart, Marc Nerlove, Peter Phillips, Jean-François Richard, Paul Schultz, and James Tobin. I am grateful for all this help but retain all responsibility for the contents.

NOTES

[1] Note that, if the models were nested, this variance would vanish since $\boldsymbol{Q}_{10}^{-1}\boldsymbol{G}_{10}\boldsymbol{Q}_{10}^{-1} = \boldsymbol{Q}_{10}^{-1}$, a submatrix of $\boldsymbol{Q}_0^{-1}$, while, apart from deletions, $\boldsymbol{J}$ is the identity matrix. Of course, in this case $\tilde{\beta}_{10} = \hat{\beta}_1$ identically as we would expect.

[2] Table 5.2 represents a model which is essentially equivalent, on these data, to the linear expenditure system (LES). However, given the parameter estimates in the table, the parameters of the LES itself are essentially unidentified. The problem is that the γ_i's estimated are equal to $(p_i d_i - \alpha_i \Sigma p_k d_k)$ where d_i is the ith 'subsistence' quantity of good i and $p_i d_i$ is subsistence expenditure; see equations (35) and (36) above. The $p_i d_i$ values can be obtained from the γ_i's if and only if $\Sigma\alpha_i \neq 1$. In both Tables 5.1 and 5.2, $\Sigma\alpha_i$ is very close to unity and the subsistence expenditures correspondingly close to unidentification.

REFERENCES

Abbot, M., and Ashenfelter, O. (1976). 'Labour supply, commodity demand, and the allocation of time.' *Review of Economic Studies*, **43,** 389–411.

Ashenfelter, O. (1980). 'Unemployment as disequilibrium in a model of aggregate labour supply.' *Econometrica*, **48,** 547–564.

Atkinson, A. B., and Stern, N. (1981a). 'Labour supply, commodity demands and the switch from direct to indirect taxation.' *Journal of Public Economics*, **14,** 195–224.

Atkinson, A. B., and Stern, N. (1981b). 'On labour supply and commodity demands.' In A. S. Deaton (Ed.), *Essays in the Theory and Measurement of Consumer Behaviour*, Cambridge University Press, New York, pp. 265–296.

Atkinson, A. C. (1970). 'A method for discriminating between models.' *Journal of the Royal Statistical Society*, B, **32**, 323–344.

Barten, A. P. (1964). 'Family composition, prices and expenditure patterns.' In P. E. Hart, G. Mills, and J. K. Whitaker (Eds.), *Econometric Analysis for National Economic Planning*, Butterworth, London.

Breusch, T. S., and Pagan, A. R. (1979). 'A simple test for heteroskedasticity and random coefficient variation.' *Econometrica*, **47**, 1287–1294.

Cox, D. R. (1961). 'Tests of separate families of hypotheses.' *Proceedings of the Fourth Berkeley Symposium on Mathematical Statistics and Probability, Volume 1*, University of California Press, Berkeley.

Cox, D. R. (1962). 'Further results on tests of separate families of hypotheses.' *Journal of the Royal Statistical Society*, B, **24**, 406–424.

Dastoor, N. K. (1981). 'Some aspects of testing non-nested hypotheses.' University of Liverpool, mimeo.

Davidson, R., and MacKinnon, J. (1981). 'Several tests for model specification in the presence of alternative hypotheses.' *Econometrica*, **49**, 781–793.

Deaton, A. S. (1975). *Models and Projections of Demand in Post-war Britain*, Chapman Hall, London.

Deaton, A. S. (1981). 'Theoretical and empirical approaches to consumer demand under rationing.' In A. S. Deaton (Ed.), *Essays in the Theory and Measurement of Consumer Behaviour*, Cambridge University Press, New York, pp. 55–72.

Deaton, A. S., and Muellbauer, J. (1980). *Economics and Consumer Behaviour*, Cambridge University Press, New York.

Deaton, A. S., and Muellbauer, J. (1981). 'Functional forms for labor supply and commodity demands with and without quantity constraints.' *Econometrica*, **49**, 1521–1532.

Engle, R. F. (1979). 'A general approach to the construction of model diagnostics based upon the Lagrange multiplier principle.' University of Warwick, Economic Research Papers, Research Paper No. 156.

Hausman, J. A. (1978). 'Specification tests in econometrics.' *Econometrica*, **46**, 1251–1271.

Holly, A. (1980). 'A remark on Hausman's specification test.' Harvard University, mimeo.

Huber, P. J. (1967). 'The behaviour of maximum likelihood estimates under nonstandard conditions.' In *Proceedings of the Fifth Berkeley Symposium on Mathematical Statistics and Probability*, University of California Press, Berkeley, pp. 221–233.

Muellbauer, J. (1981). 'Linear aggregation in neoclassical labour supply.' *Review of Economic Studies*, **48**, 21–36.

Neary, J. P., and Roberts K. W. S. (1980). 'The theory of household behaviour under rationing.' *European Economic Review*, **13**, 25–42.

Pesaran, M. H. (1974). 'On the general problem of model selection.' *Review of Economic Studies*, **41**, 153–171.

Pesaran, M. H. (1981) 'Comparison of local power of alternative tests of non-nested regression models. 'Trinity College, Cambridge, mimeo to appear in Econometrica.

Pesaran, M. H., and Deaton, A. S. (1978). 'Testing non-tested nonlinear regression models.' *Econometrica*, **46**, 677–694.

Phlips, L. (1978). 'The demand for leisure and money.' *Econometrica*, **46**, 1025–1043.

Quandt, R. E. (1974). 'A comparison of methods for testing nonnested hypotheses.' *Review of Economics and Statistics*, **56**, 92–99.

Theil, H. (1971). 'An economic theory of the second moments of disturbances of behavioural equations.' *American Economic Review*, **61**, 190–194.
Theil, H. (1975). *Theory and Measurement of Consumer Demand, Volume I*, North-Holland, Amsterdam.
Tobin, J. (1958). 'Estimation of relationships for limited dependent variables.' *Econometrica*, **26**, 24–36.
Wales, T. J., and Woodland, A. D. (1979). 'A random preference model for the estimation of consumer demand systems with binding non-negativity constraints.' University of British Columbia, Discussion Paper No. 79–32.
White, H. (1982). 'Maximum likelihood estimation of misspecified models', *Econometrica*, **50**, 1–25.
Wu, D.-M. (1973). 'Alternative tests of independence between stochastic regressors and disturbances.' *Econometrica*, **41**, 733–750.

Discussion

M. MOUCHART
Center for Operations Research & Econometrics, Louvain

1 INTRODUCTION

I shall not comment on the analytics of this paper but rather on the underlying approach to model building.

I found this paper something like an example of what I regard as a good, a very good example of econometric practice; this involves serious thoughts on the statistical methods, on the economic theory, and on the data, and the conclusions are careful. Superficially viewed, the results seem inconclusive although the primary question is crucial: is the labour market in equilibrium? More precisely: do people allocate to work the quantity of time they are willing to, given the price structure? I felt quite disturbed by an inconclusive answer to such a question. As I did not find any source of dissatisfaction on the analytical side, I concluded I should look to the underlying framework. I must confess I will not end up with an alternative proposal; rather I shall conclude with the idea that such inconclusive results should be expected from this kind of analysis.

I will organize these comments according to three topics: first, on the relationships between statistical model building and economic models; secondly, on the problem of testing separate families; and thirdly, on some of the statistical specifications in the model presented in the paper under discussion.

2 STATISTICAL MODEL AND ECONOMIC MODEL

By statistical model building, I mean the following. I take a statistical model as a family of sampling distributions; in other words, it is not simply a deterministic function plus some noise. There are two basic aspects when we want to model an economic phenomenon. In other words, I think that economic theory bears on two types of questions. First, there is some statistical independence which is asserted by the theory, and, roughly speaking, this is specified by the list of the involved variables. Secondly, there is asserted some structural invariance. By this we mean that, for some parametrization of a model, some parameters are going to be relatively invariant or relatively stable: they receive a 'structural' interpretation; in other words, they represent something 'structural' as opposed to something 'incidental' or 'accidental'.

Let me just give an example of the kind of thing I have in mind. Consider a very naive agricultural model. Suppose that I model the sector by saying that given past and given some exogenous variable, the quantity is fixed by the supply side: $q_t = f_1(p_0^{t-1}, q_0^{t-1}$, climatic hazard, etc). On the demand side, price is adjusted to quantity and to other exogenous variables: $p_t = f_2(q_t, z_t)$.

Now I consider three 'different' statistical models. Model 1 would be the following. For each observation, the marginal distribution of the quantity is a normal distribution and I summarize the influence of 'past' and of the exogenous variables by means of a variable expectation and then I say that the demand side is represented by the conditional distribution of the price given quantity and the other variables:

Model 1

$$(q_t| \ldots) \sim N(\mu_t, \sigma_1^2)$$
$$(p_t|q_t \ldots) \sim N(\beta_1 + \beta_2 q_t + \beta_3' z_t, \sigma_{2.1}^2).$$

For model 2, I consider that the pair (q_t, p_t) is jointly normal:

Model 2

$$\begin{pmatrix} q_t \\ p_t \end{pmatrix} \Bigg| \ldots \sim N\left[\begin{pmatrix} \mu_t \\ \beta_1 + \beta_2\mu_t + \beta_3' z_t \end{pmatrix}, \begin{pmatrix} \sigma_1^2 & \beta_2\sigma_1^2 \\ \beta_2\sigma_1^2 & \sigma_{2.1}^2 + \beta_2^2\sigma_1^2 \end{pmatrix}\right].$$

For model 3, I just reverse the decomposition in model 1:

Model 3

$$(p_t| \ldots) \sim N(\gamma_t, \sigma_{2.1}^2 + \beta_2^2\sigma_1^2)$$
$$(q_t|p_t \ldots) \sim N(\alpha_{1,t} + \alpha_2 p_t + \alpha_3' z_t, \sigma_{1.2}^2)$$

where, evidently,

$$\gamma_t = \beta_1 + \beta_2\mu_t + \beta_3' z_t$$
$$\alpha_2 = \frac{\beta_2\sigma_1^2}{\sigma_{2.1}^2 + \beta_2^2\sigma_1^2}$$
$$\alpha_{1,t} = \mu_t - \alpha_2(\beta_1 - \beta_2\mu_t)$$
$$\alpha_3 = -\alpha_2\beta_3$$

$$\sigma_{1.2}^2 = \sigma_1^2 - \frac{\beta_2^2\sigma_1^4}{\sigma_{2.1}^2 + \beta_2^2\sigma_1^2} = \sigma_1^2(1 - \beta_2\alpha_2).$$

What to choose about these models? These three models are basically one model. They are different parametrizations of a same model that says that given exogenous variables the pair (q_t, p_t) is distributed according to a bivariate normal law. If I prefer model 1, I actually prefer the parametrization in model 1 because I think that β_1, β_2 and β_3 do represent some economic behaviour; I hope that they will reveal some structural stability so that my model is really to say that β_1, β_2, and β_3 are structural parameters: in particular μ_t (or σ_1^2) can be time-dependent without affecting the second equation of model 1: that is precisely the basic model.

3 TESTING SEPARATE FAMILIES

When we say that a model is basically concerned with (conditional) independence among variables and with structural stability, we have in mind approximate statements. We do not mean we have exact independence nor absolute stability of some parameters. In this context, what is the meaning of testing a model? Clearly, testing a model means testing the stability of some parameters or testing the sufficiency of the involved variables, i.e. for instance is it really true that no other variables than q_t and z_t enter the demand equation? Even if we state the null hypothesis in the form of a sharp hypothesis, we really have in mind that the hypothesis being tested regards, for instance, a regression coefficient to be 'approximately zero' or to be 'approximately constant'. It is therefore important to give some meaning to a neighbourhood of parameter values.

In other words, I have no particular sympathy with the idea of testing separate families; this is so mainly for two reasons. First, it does not correspond, in my mind, to the natural way of building a model. Economic theory provides us with some general idea about the way economic variables are being generated. Surely there are several 'theories' involving different judgments about the actual importance of certain behaviours. But if some economists for instance think that the labour market is constrained on the supply side while other economists think that constraints come from rigidities on the demand side, this does not imply that we have to 'choose' one of two completely separated representations of the world. Every economist is aware of both types of constraints but they may disagree as to the degree of effectiveness of these constraints. If two economists with different opinions want to question the data in order to decide upon their theories, I think they should first agree on some 'super model' coherent not only with their two views but also with what I would call 'the rest of the profession' and then to consider in which neighbourhood of the parameter space the data suggest a good model should be. Secondly, I find it difficult to visualize a model being composed by two separate families because it is too difficult to imagine which values of the parameters of the model correspond to distributions 'close to' distributions associated with parameter values of the other model. I therefore tend to think that it is a question the data cannot answer in general. Consider, for instance, the following situation:

$$M_1: \mathbf{y} = X\boldsymbol{\beta}_1 + \boldsymbol{\varepsilon}_1$$
$$M_2: \mathbf{y} = Z\boldsymbol{\beta}_2 + \boldsymbol{\varepsilon}_2$$

along with the usual assumptions about the standard linear models. What can be the sense of 'choosing' between M_1 or M_2? As far as representation of the real world is concerned they are surely both 'false' but if, for instance, we accept a generalized normality assumption on $(\mathbf{y} \quad X \quad Z)$ both models are 'true' in the sense that in the normal case every regression function is linear and homoskedastic. In fact, the economically meaningful questions are the following. In self-explanatory notation, $\boldsymbol{\beta}_1$ and $\boldsymbol{\beta}_2$ are parameters of the joint distributions of $(\mathbf{y} \quad X \quad Z)$:

$$\boldsymbol{\beta}_1 = \Sigma_{XX}^{-1}\,\Sigma_{Xy}$$
$$\boldsymbol{\beta}_2 = \Sigma_{ZZ}^{-1}\,\Sigma_{Zy}$$

and one may consider the following:

1. Is $\boldsymbol{\beta}_1$ or $\boldsymbol{\beta}_2$ 'structural'? Then we test the structural stability of these parameters.

2. *If* the complete model:

$$M_3: \mathbf{y} = X\boldsymbol{\gamma}_1 + Z\boldsymbol{\gamma}_2 + \boldsymbol{\varepsilon}_3$$

is economically meaningful, one may ask whether X (or Z) is sufficient. Then we test $H_0: \boldsymbol{\gamma}_1 = \mathbf{0}$ (or $H_0: \boldsymbol{\gamma}_2 = \mathbf{0}$). Actually, M_1, M_2, and M_3 are part of three different decompositions of the process generating jointly $(\mathbf{y} \quad X \quad Z)$ and I would find it difficult to assert that *both* M_1 and M_2 would be economically meaningful *and* that the data would be helpful to decide that M_1 is more or less 'true' than M_2.

4 THE ECONOMIC PROBLEM AND ITS STATISTICAL SPECIFICATION

The economic problem analysed in this paper may be briefly sketched as follows. Consider a direct utility function defined over leisure q_0, and a vector of goods $\mathbf{q}: v(q_0, \mathbf{q})$ and to be maximized subject to a budget constraint. The problem is to analyse how far the quantity q_0 is freely chosen by the consumer or is constrained on the labour market. (Analytically the problem is simplified under a weak separability assumption.)

If q_0 is freely chosen by the consumer it is endogenous, while if q_0 is constrained then it becomes (partly or completely) exogenous. An assumption of weak separability of the utility function ensures that the demand function of the unconstrained goods have the same form whether q_0 is constrained or not. The problem is then asserted to be reduced to that of testing for the exogeneity of income, with a qualification on the nature of this exogeneity.

I want to argue that even if I were to accept that the above qualifications lead to separate families, such tests will crucially depend on the *stochastic* specification of the model. In other words, such sentences as 'The terms u_i and u_0, with $u_0 = \Sigma u_i$, are stochastic error terms which it is convenient to add at this point' are particularly unfortunate as far as they suggest that the core of the problem lies in the deterministic specification. More precisely, I would like to stress two points related to the residual terms:

1. The analysis of disequilibrium economics reveals the crucial importance of the adjustment processes: an individual who has met a rigidity at period t will not 'forget it' at period $t + 1$; it is therefore doubtful that the sequence of this behaviour will reveal independence and, more importantly, the nature of that time-dependence will precisely represent both the magnitude of the disequilibrium and the nature of the adjustment process. One may therefore doubt whether cross-section data are helpful to analyse a (rather subtle) form of disequilibrium unless the data provide some information about the status of the individual in the period before the sample period.

2. The stochastic treatment of the budget constraint may also be questioned. Traditionally, it is realized by specifying a singular covariance matrix of the residuals with an intraclass correlation structure. This implicitly assumes a 'neutral' role of the restriction; is it reasonable to believe that, especially in the case of endogenous leisure time, all the residuals will form a symmetric (or exchangeable) sequence? I am personally reluctant to accept such a specification and would rather prefer to specify for instance that, *conditionally* on the residual relative to q_0, the residuals relative to $q_1, \ldots, q_n$ form a symmetric sequence.

In conclusion, this paper has shown how important it is to think of economic models in terms of stochastic systems instead of deterministic systems plus some noise. This is far from being new but this paper has shown that this is a substantial problem.

Evaluating the Reliability of Macro-economic Models
Edited by G. C. Chow and P. Corsi

CHAPTER 6

Tests of Misspecification Using Locally Equivalent Alternative Models

L. G. GODFREY
University of York

M. R. WICKENS
University of Southampton

6.1 INTRODUCTION

Among the more important criteria for evaluating the reliability of a macro-economic model is the model's ability to pass a test of misspecification. In specifying an econometric model it is necessary to impose restrictions in order to bring evidence to bear on the model. Whether these restrictions are derived from economic theory or are introduced to simplify statistical analysis, the failure of the model to pass a test of their validity indicates the presence of some form of misspecification and implies that the model may be unlikely to be reliable for forecasting or policy use.

To help avoid misspecified models, it is now routine to test for various types of misspecification such as omitted variables, serially correlated errors, and structural change; other tests made less routinely are for the correctness of the functional form and for heteroskedasticity. These tests are usually carried out in an *ad hoc* way: one test at a time and in an arbitrary order. This paper is concerned with providing a unified framework for the construction of tests for misspecification, with showing that many existing tests can be re-interpreted within this framework, and with deriving a number of new tests, including joint tests suitable for detecting the presence of more than one kind of misspecification. It is hoped that the paper will be of use to model builders not only for the suggested new tests and for its pedagogic value, but also because all the tests proposed are fairly simple to compute.

There are two common approaches to the construction of tests of misspecification for econometric models. The first of these simply involves deriving some statistic which has a known (asymptotic) distribution when the assumed model is correct and interpreting significant values of the statistic as evidence that this model is misspecified in some undetermined way. Tests of this type are known as *pure significance tests* and do not require the specification of a particular alternative model against which to judge the assumed model. A well-known example of such a test is the Box–Pierce (1970) procedure for checking the adequacy of fitted time series relationships.

The second approach involves choosing a more general (or alternative) model than that which is assumed to be correct. The assumed model is then obtained from the alternative model by imposing certain restrictions on the alternative model and a test is made of the validity of these restrictions. Such *nested hypothesis tests* often reduce to investigating whether constraining certain coefficients of the alternative model to be zero is consistent with the sample data. An example of this second kind of test is the widely used h-statistic proposed by Durbin (1970) which tests the assumption that the errors of a dynamic regression are independent against the alternative of first-order autoregressive errors.

In practice the distinction between pure significance and nested hypothesis tests is often blurred, with rejection of the null hypothesis being interpreted as evidence that the model is misspecified but not necessarily due to having incorrectly imposed the restrictions whose validity is in question. Rejection of the null does not necessarily imply, therefore, that the alternative should be mechanically adopted. In such a situation the nested hypothesis test is being treated as though it was a pure significance test. In seeking to justify such a procedure, at a minimum one would require that the hypothesis test has the correct size and his reasonable power against the other types of misspecification envisaged. Carr (1972) has provided an example which indicates that a significant Durbin–Watson statistic can reflect structural change rather than autoregressive errors, while Blattberg (1973) has shown that the Durbin–Watson test can be powerful against autocorrelation models other than the first-order autoregressive scheme for which it was devised.

In this paper, using the nested hypothesis test approach, we show how it is possible to derive misspecification tests against a set of alternative hypotheses comprising, say, autoregressive or moving average errors, heteroskedasticity, variables omitted from the null, and a different functional form from the null. Such tests are obtained for single regression equations and simultaneous-equation models. The unifying principle which underlies these tests is based upon the use of the Lagrange multiplier test with locally equivalent alternative models. The Lagrange multiplier test has been used frequently in recent papers dealing with tests for misspecification (e.g. Breusch and Pagan, 1980; Engle, 1978, 1980; Godfrey, 1978a, b). With complex alternative models it is often easier to compute the Lagrange multiplier test than the other two well-known hypothesis testing procedures, the likelihood ratio test and the Wald test, and it is asymptotically equivalent to them. For many problems a further simplification is to use a locally equivalent alternative model rather than the original alternative model. These locally equivalent alternatives are constructed in such a way that they provide statistics which have the same asymptotic distribution as the Lagrange multiplier test based on the original alternative model; see Godfrey (1981). In fact, in many important cases the test statistic for the null model will be the same for all members of the set of locally equivalent alternatives. Using this approach it is possible to show that each type of misspecification can be incorporated in the locally equivalent alternative model as additional regressor variables, which is an enormous simplification.

The plan of this paper is as follows. In Section 6.2 we provide the theoretical underpinnings for tests against locally equivalent alternative models and we derive various test statistics. These tests are then applied to single-equation regressions in Sections 6.3 and to simultaneous-equation models in Section 6.4.

6.2 TESTS FOR MISSPECIFICATION AND LOCALLY EQUIVALENT ALTERNATIVES

6.2.1 Maximum likelihood estimation

We begin by describing the model for which our results are applicable and then establish the foundations of the tests for misspecification to be examined in this paper (see also Godfrey, 1981).

Consider the (possibly) nonlinear model

$$\mathbf{f}(\mathbf{y}_t, \mathbf{z}_t, \mathbf{d}_{t-1}; \boldsymbol{\theta}) = \mathbf{e}_t, \qquad t \Rightarrow 1, 2, \ldots, T, \tag{2.1}$$

where $\mathbf{y}_t$ is an M-dimensional vector of endogenous variables, $\mathbf{z}_t$ is an N-dimensional vector of exogenous variables, $\mathbf{d}_{t-1}$ is a vector of the past values of $\mathbf{y}_t$ and $\mathbf{z}_t$, $\boldsymbol{\theta}$ is a K-dimensional vector of parameters, and $\mathbf{e}_t$ is an M-dimensional vector of stochastic variables. It will be assumed that the $\mathbf{e}_t$ are NID $(0, \boldsymbol{\Sigma})$ where $\boldsymbol{\Sigma}$ is positive definite but otherwise unrestricted.

Suppose that the parameter vector is partitioned as $\boldsymbol{\theta}' = (\boldsymbol{\theta}_1', \boldsymbol{\theta}_2')$ where $\boldsymbol{\theta}_2$ is a $G\,(\leqslant K)$ dimensional vector, and that the model specified by the researcher is the special case of (2.1) obtained by setting $\boldsymbol{\theta}_2$ equal to a null vector. A test for misspecification can then be obtained by testing the null hypothesis $H_0{:}\boldsymbol{\theta}_2 = \mathbf{0}$. The cases examined in this paper do not involve restrictions on the variance–covariance matrix of the $\mathbf{e}_t$ and, in order to simplify the notation, $\boldsymbol{\theta}_1$ will be regarded as containing the distinct elements of $\boldsymbol{\Sigma}$ although these elements will not actually appear as coefficients in system (2.1).

Equation (2.1) is sufficiently general to encompass many of the models used in applied work; for example, dynamic simultaneous equation models with vector autoregressive moving average (VARMA) disturbances (Reinsel, 1979b), nonlinear simultaneous-equation systems (Amemiya, 1977), and models with heteroskedastic disturbances. (Since $\mathbf{d}_{t-1}$ is explicitly included in (2.1), invertible moving average error schemes can be handled by rewriting them as restricted autoregressive processes of infinite order. Also, although (2.1) does not itself have heteroskedastic disturbances, many such models can be rewritten in the form of (2.1).)

The tests to be derived below are based on the assumption that the unrestricted maximum likelihood estimator (MLE) $\tilde{\boldsymbol{\theta}}$ of $\boldsymbol{\theta}$ exists and possesses the usual asymptotic properties and, in particular, that

$$T^{1/2}(\tilde{\boldsymbol{\theta}} - \boldsymbol{\theta}) \underset{D}{\rightarrow} N(0,V)$$

where

$$V^{-1} = -\text{plim}\, T^{-1}\, \partial^2 L_T(\boldsymbol{\theta})/\partial\boldsymbol{\theta}\, \partial\boldsymbol{\theta}'$$

and $L_T(\boldsymbol{\theta})$ denotes the log likelihood function based upon a sample of T observations. It is also assumed that the standard large-sample tests, namely the Lagrange multiplier (LM), likelihood ratio (LR), and Wald (W) procedures, can be applied to test $H_0{:}\boldsymbol{\theta}_2 = \mathbf{0}$. Thus the asymptotic information matrix must be nonsingular when evaluated under the null hypothesis. The set of conditions necessary for these assumptions to hold will depend upon the particular model being considered. Amemiya (1977) and Reinsel (1979a, b) have considered the conditions required for nonlinear simultaneous-equation models which have no lagged endogenous variables and for a linear system with lagged endogenous variables and autoregressive moving average disturbances, respectively. At present there do not seem to be corresponding results for the more general case of a dynamic nonlinear system with autoregressive moving average error terms. Consequently, the large-sample properties of the tests derived below are not yet known in this general case.

The LM test of $H_0{:}\boldsymbol{\theta}_2 = \mathbf{0}$ is based upon testing for the joint significance from zero of the Lagrange multipliers associated with maximizing $L_T(\boldsymbol{\theta})$ subject to the restriction $\boldsymbol{\theta}_2 = \mathbf{0}$. This is equivalent to testing the joint significance from zero of the elements of the 'score vector' $\partial L_T(\hat{\boldsymbol{\theta}})/\partial\boldsymbol{\theta}$ where $\hat{\boldsymbol{\theta}}' = (\hat{\boldsymbol{\theta}}_1', \mathbf{0}')$ maximizes $L_T(\boldsymbol{\theta})$ subject to $\boldsymbol{\theta}_2 = \mathbf{0}$. The LM test statistic is derived from the limiting null distribution of

$$T^{-1/2}\, \partial L_T(\hat{\boldsymbol{\theta}})/\partial\boldsymbol{\theta}$$

and can be written as

$$\phi = T^{-1}(\partial L_T(\hat{\boldsymbol{\theta}})/\partial\boldsymbol{\theta})' V (\partial L_T(\hat{\boldsymbol{\theta}})/\partial\boldsymbol{\theta})$$

where $\phi \underset{D}{\rightarrow} \chi^2(G)$ on H_0. In general, V will be unknown and hence ϕ cannot be used. However, by replacing V with a consistent estimator, it is possible to generate a class of asymptotically equivalent test statistics each with a limiting $\chi^2(G)$ distribution on H_0.

Among this class there is a subset of test statistics that are constructed from estimators of V which are consistent only on H_0. The standard LM statistic due to Silvey (1959) belongs to this subset and is given by

$$s = -(\partial L_T(\hat{\boldsymbol{\theta}})/\partial \boldsymbol{\theta})'(\partial^2 L_T(\hat{\boldsymbol{\theta}})/\partial \boldsymbol{\theta}\, \partial \boldsymbol{\theta}')^{-1}(\partial L_T(\hat{\boldsymbol{\theta}})/\partial \boldsymbol{\theta}). \tag{2.2}$$

Another member of this subset enables the resulting statistic to be written as the product of the sample size and a coefficient of determination which is measured about the origin. In order to derive this test statistic, it is necessary to re-write the log likelihood function $L_T(\boldsymbol{\theta})$ as

$$L_T(\boldsymbol{\theta}) = \sum_t l_t(\boldsymbol{\theta}). \tag{2.3}$$

where $l_t(\boldsymbol{\theta})$ is the log likelihood for the tth observation. Also, the results of Berndt *et al.* (1974) imply that, under H_0,

$$\operatorname{plim} T^{-1}(\partial^2 L_T(\hat{\boldsymbol{\theta}})/\partial \boldsymbol{\theta}\, \partial \boldsymbol{\theta}') = -\operatorname{plim} T^{-1} \sum_{t=1}^{T} (\partial l_t(\hat{\boldsymbol{\theta}})/\partial \boldsymbol{\theta})(\partial l_t(\hat{\boldsymbol{\theta}})/\partial \boldsymbol{\theta})'. \tag{2.4}$$

Thus, s of (2.2) is asymptotically equivalent to

$$s^* = \left(\sum_{t=1}^{T} \partial l_t(\hat{\boldsymbol{\theta}})/\partial \boldsymbol{\theta}\right)'\left[\sum_{t=1}^{T} (\partial l_t(\hat{\boldsymbol{\theta}})/\partial \boldsymbol{\theta})(\partial l_t(\hat{\boldsymbol{\theta}})/\partial \boldsymbol{\theta})'\right]^{-1}\left(\sum_{t=1}^{T} \partial l_t(\hat{\boldsymbol{\theta}})/\partial \boldsymbol{\theta}\right). \tag{2.5}$$

If $\boldsymbol{W}(\boldsymbol{\theta})$ is the T by K matrix with typical element $w_{ts} = \partial l_t(\boldsymbol{\theta})/\partial \theta_s$ $(t = 1, \ldots, T;$ $s = 1, \ldots, K)$ and $\mathbf{i}$ is a T-dimensional vector with each element equal to unity, then (2.5) can be rewritten as

$$\begin{aligned} s^* &= \mathbf{i}'\boldsymbol{W}(\hat{\boldsymbol{\theta}})\,[\boldsymbol{W}(\hat{\boldsymbol{\theta}})'\boldsymbol{W}(\hat{\boldsymbol{\theta}})]^{-1}\boldsymbol{W}(\hat{\boldsymbol{\theta}})'\mathbf{i} \\ &= T\,[\mathbf{i}'\boldsymbol{W}(\hat{\boldsymbol{\theta}})\,[\boldsymbol{W}(\hat{\boldsymbol{\theta}})'\boldsymbol{W}(\hat{\boldsymbol{\theta}})]^{-1}\boldsymbol{W}(\hat{\boldsymbol{\theta}})'\mathbf{i}/\mathbf{i}'\mathbf{i}] \\ &= T \times R^2_{\mathbf{i}.\hat{W}}, \end{aligned} \tag{2.6}$$

where $R^2_{\mathbf{i}.\hat{W}}$ is the coefficient of determination of the regression of $\mathbf{i}$ on $\boldsymbol{W}(\hat{\boldsymbol{\theta}})$.[1]

Note that since $\partial L_T(\hat{\boldsymbol{\theta}})/\partial \boldsymbol{\theta}_1 = 0$, s and s^* are asymptotic tests of the joint significance of the elements of

$$\partial L_T(\hat{\boldsymbol{\theta}})/\partial \boldsymbol{\theta}_2 = \sum_{t=1}^{T} \partial l_t(\hat{\boldsymbol{\theta}})/\partial \boldsymbol{\theta}_2. \tag{2.7}$$

If $H_0{:}\boldsymbol{\theta}_2 = \mathbf{0}$ is true then s and s^* both have a limiting $\chi^2(G)$ distribution. Under the Pitman sequence of local alternatives $H_T{:}\boldsymbol{\theta}_2 = T^{-1/2}\boldsymbol{\eta}$, $\boldsymbol{\eta}'\boldsymbol{\eta} < \infty$, s and s^* are both asymptotically distributed as noncentral $\chi^2(G, \mu^2)$ with noncentrality parameter μ^2 given by

$$\mu^2 = \boldsymbol{\eta}'\boldsymbol{V}_{22}^{-1}\boldsymbol{\eta}, \tag{2.8}$$

$\boldsymbol{V}_{22}$ being the variance–covariance matrix of the limiting distribution of $T^{1/2}(\tilde{\boldsymbol{\theta}}_2 - \boldsymbol{\theta}_2)$.

Having set out the results which constitute the foundations of the tests for misspecification to be discussed below, we shall now show that although s and s^* are derived on the assumption that (2.1) is the alternative model, they are not specific to this alternative model but, in fact, are appropriate for certain other alternatives. If the analysis above is repeated for one of these other alternatives, then the new s and s^* statistics so derived will be asymptotically equivalent (and sometimes numerically equal) to those of (2.2) and (2.6). These other alternatives are obtained from local approximations to (2.1) and will be called locally equivalent alternative (LEA) models.

Suppose that

$$\mathbf{f}_t^*(\mathbf{y}_t, \mathbf{z}_t, \mathbf{d}_{t-1}; \boldsymbol{\theta}) = \mathbf{e}_t, \qquad \mathbf{e}_t \text{ NID}(0, \boldsymbol{\Sigma}), \qquad t = 1, \ldots, T, \tag{2.9}$$

is a model which is different from (2.1) except when $\boldsymbol{\theta}_2 = \mathbf{0}$ and that its log likelihood function is written as

$$L_T^*(\boldsymbol{\theta}) = \sum_{t=1}^{T} l_t^*(\boldsymbol{\theta}). \tag{2.10}$$

If this new alternative model is specified so that:

(i) $\hat{\boldsymbol{\theta}}$ maximizes $L_T^*(\boldsymbol{\theta})$ subject to $H_0: \boldsymbol{\theta}_2 = \mathbf{0}$;

and

(ii) $\partial l_t^*(\hat{\boldsymbol{\theta}})/\partial \boldsymbol{\theta}_2 = \partial l_t(\hat{\boldsymbol{\theta}})/\partial \boldsymbol{\theta}_2$,

then s and s^* would obviously be appropriate LM tests of $H_0: \boldsymbol{\theta}_2 = \mathbf{0}$ against either (2.1) or (2.9), i.e. (2.1) and (2.9) would be LEA models.

In order to derive a specification for (2.9) which satisfies conditions (i) and (ii), consider

$$l_t(\boldsymbol{\theta}) = \text{const} - \tfrac{1}{2} \ln |\boldsymbol{\Sigma}| - \tfrac{1}{2} [\mathbf{f}_t(\boldsymbol{\theta})' \boldsymbol{\Sigma}^{-1} \mathbf{f}_t(\boldsymbol{\theta})] + \ln \|\partial \mathbf{f}_t(\boldsymbol{\theta})/\partial \mathbf{y}_t\|, \tag{2.11}$$

where $\mathbf{f}_t(\boldsymbol{\theta})$ denotes $\mathbf{f}(\mathbf{y}_t, \mathbf{z}_t, \mathbf{d}_{t-1}; \boldsymbol{\theta})$.

A Taylor series expansion of $l_t(\boldsymbol{\theta})$ about $\boldsymbol{\theta}_2 = \mathbf{0}$ yields

$$l_t(\boldsymbol{\theta}) = \text{const} - \tfrac{1}{2} \ln |\boldsymbol{\Sigma}| - \tfrac{1}{2} [\mathbf{f}_t^*(\boldsymbol{\theta})' \boldsymbol{\Sigma}^{-1} \mathbf{f}_t^*(\boldsymbol{\theta}) + R_1] + \ln \|\partial \mathbf{f}_t^*(\boldsymbol{\theta})/\partial \mathbf{y}_t + R_2\|, \tag{2.12}$$

where[2]

$$\mathbf{f}_t^*(\boldsymbol{\theta}) = \mathbf{f}_t(\boldsymbol{\theta}_1, \mathbf{0}) + [\partial \mathbf{f}_t(\boldsymbol{\theta}_1, \mathbf{0})/\partial \boldsymbol{\theta}_2] \boldsymbol{\theta}_2. \tag{2.13}$$

The remainder terms R_1 and R_2 of (2.12) represent the effects of second and higher order terms in the elements of $\boldsymbol{\theta}_2$ and, therefore, make no contribution to $\partial l_t(\boldsymbol{\theta}_1, \mathbf{0})/\partial \boldsymbol{\theta}_2$. (In particular, ignoring R_1 and R_2 will not affect the value of $\partial l_t(\hat{\boldsymbol{\theta}}_1, \mathbf{0})/\partial \boldsymbol{\theta}_2 = \partial l_t(\hat{\boldsymbol{\theta}})/\partial \boldsymbol{\theta}_2$.) If R_1 and R_2 are omitted, then we obtain

$$l_t^*(\boldsymbol{\theta}) = \text{const} - \tfrac{1}{2} \ln |\boldsymbol{\Sigma}| - \tfrac{1}{2} [\mathbf{f}_t^*(\boldsymbol{\theta})' \boldsymbol{\Sigma}^{-1} \mathbf{f}_t^*(\boldsymbol{\theta})] + \ln \|\partial \mathbf{f}_t^*(\boldsymbol{\theta})/\partial \mathbf{y}_t\| \tag{2.14}$$

which is the log likelihood for a single observation when $\mathbf{f}_t^*(\boldsymbol{\theta})$ is defined by (2.13) with $\partial l_t^*(\boldsymbol{\theta}_1,\mathbf{0})/\partial\boldsymbol{\theta}_2 = \partial l_t(\boldsymbol{\theta}_1,\mathbf{0})/\partial\boldsymbol{\theta}_2$. The log likelihood function $L_T^*(\boldsymbol{\theta})$, which is equal to the sum of the T terms given by (2.14), is clearly maximized by $\hat{\boldsymbol{\theta}}$ when the restrictions of $H_0:\boldsymbol{\theta}_2 = \mathbf{0}$ are imposed. Moreover, since $\partial l_t(\boldsymbol{\theta}_1,\mathbf{0})/\partial\boldsymbol{\theta}_2 = \partial l_t^*(\boldsymbol{\theta}_1,\mathbf{0})/\partial\boldsymbol{\theta}_2$, it follows that $\partial L_T(\hat{\boldsymbol{\theta}})/\partial\boldsymbol{\theta}_2 = \partial L_T^*(\hat{\boldsymbol{\theta}})/\partial\boldsymbol{\theta}_2$. Thus $\mathbf{f}_t^*(\boldsymbol{\theta})$ of (2.13) is an LEA model to $\mathbf{f}_t(\boldsymbol{\theta})$ of (2.1).

It was remarked earlier that the s and s^* statistics based on an LEA model will sometimes be numerically equal to the corresponding statistics based on $\mathbf{f}_t(\boldsymbol{\theta})$. If the LEA model used is $\mathbf{f}_t^*(\boldsymbol{\theta})$ above, it is possible to be more precise since, in this case, the s^* statistics will always be numerically equal to each other whereas, in general, the s statistics will not; they will, of course, be asymptotically equivalent. Similar results will be obtained if $\mathbf{f}_t(\boldsymbol{\theta})$ is only linearized with respect to a subset of the elements of $\boldsymbol{\theta}_2$. In addition to LEA's of the $\mathbf{f}_t^*(\boldsymbol{\theta})$ variety defined by (2.13) it is often helpful to consider other approximations. If (2.13) implies that

$$\begin{aligned}\mathbf{f}_t(\boldsymbol{\theta}_1,\boldsymbol{\theta}_2) &= \mathbf{f}_t^*(\boldsymbol{\theta}) + \mathbf{R}_3\\ &= \mathbf{f}_t(\boldsymbol{\theta}_1,\mathbf{0}) + [\partial\mathbf{f}_t(\boldsymbol{\theta}_1,\mathbf{0})/\partial\boldsymbol{\theta}_2]\boldsymbol{\theta}_2 + \mathbf{R}_3\end{aligned}$$

then an alternative approximation is given by

$$\begin{aligned}\mathbf{f}_t(\boldsymbol{\theta}_1,\boldsymbol{\theta}_2) &= \mathbf{f}_t(\boldsymbol{\theta}_1,\mathbf{0}) + [\partial\mathbf{f}_t(\hat{\boldsymbol{\theta}}_1,\mathbf{0})/\partial\boldsymbol{\theta}_2]\boldsymbol{\theta}_2 + \mathbf{R}_4\\ &= \mathbf{f}_t^+(\boldsymbol{\theta}) + \mathbf{R}_4\end{aligned} \tag{2.15}$$

where

$$\mathbf{f}_t^+(\boldsymbol{\theta}) = \mathbf{f}_t(\boldsymbol{\theta}_1,\mathbf{0}) + [\partial\mathbf{f}_t(\hat{\boldsymbol{\theta}}_1,\mathbf{0})/\partial\boldsymbol{\theta}_2]\boldsymbol{\theta}_2 \tag{2.16}$$

and $\mathbf{R}_3$ and $\mathbf{R}_4$ are remainder terms. As $(\hat{\boldsymbol{\theta}}_1 - \boldsymbol{\theta}_1)$ is $O_p(T^{-1/2})$ under H_T, it is possible to show that $\mathbf{f}_t^+(\boldsymbol{\theta})$ represents an LEA model to $\mathbf{f}_t(\boldsymbol{\theta})$. This can be done in much the same way as for $\mathbf{f}_t^*(\boldsymbol{\theta})$. The only new complication arises from the presence in (2.16) of $\hat{\boldsymbol{\theta}}_1$, a function of the total sample, which makes the Jacobian term $\partial\mathbf{f}_t^+(\boldsymbol{\theta})/\partial\bar{\mathbf{y}}_s$ slightly awkward. But furtunately this difficulty with the Jacobian can be ignored when establishing the asymptotic equivalence of test procedures as we need only consider what happens on H_0 and H_T.

A simple example may help to clarify this point. Consider testing $H_0:\theta_2 = 0$ for the single-equation model

$$f_t(\theta) = y_t - \theta_1 z_{t1} - \theta_1\theta_2 z_{t2} = e_t, \tag{2.17}$$

where e_t is distributed as $N(0,1)$ and the $z_{ti}\ (i = 1,2)$ are uniformly bounded nonstochastic variables whose sample cross-product moment matrix tends to a positive definite matrix as $T\to\infty$. From (2.16) and (2.17),

$$f_t^+(\theta) = y_t - \theta_1 z_{t1} - (\hat{\theta}_1 z_{t2})\theta_2, \tag{2.18}$$

where

$$\hat{\theta}_1 = \sum_{t=1}^{T} y_t z_{t1} \Big/ \sum_{t=1}^{T} z_{t1}^2,$$

and so

$$\partial f_t^{+}(\theta)/\partial y_s = \delta_{ts} - \left[\left(z_{s1}\Big/\sum_{r=1}^{T} z_{r1}^2\right) z_{t2}\right]\theta_2 \tag{2.19}$$

with δ_{ts} being the Kronecker delta. As $\left(z_{s1}z_{t2}\Big/\sum_{r=1}^{T} z_{r1}^2\right)$ is $O(T^{-1})$ and θ_2 is at most $O(T^{-1/2})$ under H_0 and H_T, it is valid to omit the second term on the right-hand side of (2.19) in the neighbourhood of $\theta_2 = 0$.[3]

Using $\mathbf{f}_t^{+}(\boldsymbol{\theta})$ as the model on the alternative hypothesis, and noting that the resulting difficulty with the Jacobian is asymptotically irrelevant, leads to an important simplification which provides a unifying principle for tests of misspecification. The problem of testing H_0 can now be formulated as one of testing the joint significance of a subset of regressors which are constructed from $\partial\mathbf{f}_t(\hat{\boldsymbol{\theta}})/\partial\boldsymbol{\theta}_2$ and which enter $\mathbf{f}_t^{+}(\boldsymbol{\theta})$ linearly. Moreover, as will be seen below, it is possible to use this approach to test against combinations of specification errors; the more types of misspecification are entertained, the larger the number of additional variables generated by $\partial\mathbf{f}_t(\hat{\boldsymbol{\theta}})/\partial\boldsymbol{\theta}_2$. Although the discussion above has been concerned with the use of LM tests, testing the validity of omitting $\partial\mathbf{f}_t(\hat{\boldsymbol{\theta}})/\partial\boldsymbol{\theta}_2$ from $\mathbf{f}_t^{+}(\boldsymbol{\theta})$ can also be carried out using LR or W tests if it is more convenient. Finally, it should perhaps be noted that, in contrast to $\mathbf{f}_t^{*}(\boldsymbol{\theta})$, using $\mathbf{f}_t^{+}(\boldsymbol{\theta})$ as the LEA model will not, in general, lead to s and s^* statistics which are numerically equal to the corresponding statistics based on $\mathbf{f}_t(\boldsymbol{\theta})$. Further discussion of testing models for functional form can be found in Godfrey and Wickens (1981).

6.2.2 Instrumental variable estimation

The results above concern the use of LEA models for tests based upon maximum likelihood estimation. It is possible, however, to extend the use of LEA models for tests based upon instrumental variable (IV) estimation, e.g. by two-stage least squares (2SLS) or three-stage least squares (3SLS). Hypothesis tests which depend on the principle of overfitting (corresponding to the LR and W tests) for systems of simultaneous nonlinear implicit equations have been considered by Gallant and Jorgenson (1979) who describe the necessary regularity conditions.[4] The extension of the results of the previous subsection, however, involves the use of LM type tests.

The following additional notation is required: $f_{ti}(\boldsymbol{\theta})$ $(i = 1,\ldots, M)$ is the ith element of $\mathbf{f}_t(\boldsymbol{\theta})$ $(t = 1,\ldots, T)$; $\mathbf{f}(\boldsymbol{\theta})$ is a TM-dimensional vector defined by

$$\mathbf{f}(\boldsymbol{\theta}) = (f_{11}(\boldsymbol{\theta}),\ldots,f_{T1}(\boldsymbol{\theta}),\ldots,f_{TM}(\boldsymbol{\theta}))'; \tag{2.20}$$

X is a $T \times L$ matrix of instrumental variables; and $\dot{\boldsymbol{\Sigma}}$ is an estimator of $\boldsymbol{\Sigma}$ with $(\dot{\boldsymbol{\Sigma}} - \boldsymbol{\Sigma})$ being $O_p(T^{-1/2})$ under H_T. Also the distinct elements of $\boldsymbol{\Sigma}$ will now be omitted from the parameter vector $\boldsymbol{\theta}$.

The Jorgenson–Laffont (1974) nonlinear 3SLS estimator is the value of $\boldsymbol{\theta}$ which minimizes

$$S_T(\boldsymbol{\theta}) = \mathbf{f}(\boldsymbol{\theta})'(\dot{\Sigma}^{-1} \otimes X(X'X)^{-1}X')\mathbf{f}(\boldsymbol{\theta}). \quad (2.21)$$

The Gallant and Jorgenson (1979) test of $H_0:\boldsymbol{\theta}_2 = \mathbf{0}$ corresponding to the LR test is given by

$$T^0 = S_T(\hat{\boldsymbol{\theta}}) - S_T(\tilde{\boldsymbol{\theta}}), \quad (2.22)$$

where $\hat{\boldsymbol{\theta}}' = (\hat{\boldsymbol{\theta}}'_1, \mathbf{0}')$ minimizes $S_T(\boldsymbol{\theta})$ subject to $\boldsymbol{\theta}_2 = \mathbf{0}$ and $\tilde{\boldsymbol{\theta}}$ is the unrestricted 3SLS estimator. The limiting distribution of T^0 under the null hypothesis is $\chi^2(G)$.

In order to obtain the IV analogue of the LM test, expand $S_T(\tilde{\boldsymbol{\theta}})$ and $\partial S_T(\tilde{\boldsymbol{\theta}})/\partial\boldsymbol{\theta}$ about $\boldsymbol{\theta} = \hat{\boldsymbol{\theta}}$ to obtain the approximations

$$S_T(\tilde{\boldsymbol{\theta}}) \simeq S_T(\hat{\boldsymbol{\theta}}) + (\partial S_T(\hat{\boldsymbol{\theta}})/\partial\boldsymbol{\theta})'(\tilde{\boldsymbol{\theta}} - \hat{\boldsymbol{\theta}}) + \tfrac{1}{2}(\tilde{\boldsymbol{\theta}} - \hat{\boldsymbol{\theta}})'(\partial^2 S_T(\hat{\boldsymbol{\theta}})/\partial\boldsymbol{\theta}\,\partial\boldsymbol{\theta}')(\tilde{\boldsymbol{\theta}} - \hat{\boldsymbol{\theta}}) \quad (2.23)$$

and

$$\partial S_T(\tilde{\boldsymbol{\theta}})/\partial\boldsymbol{\theta} \simeq \partial S_T(\hat{\boldsymbol{\theta}})/\partial\boldsymbol{\theta} + (\partial^2 S_T(\hat{\boldsymbol{\theta}})/\partial\boldsymbol{\theta}\,\partial\boldsymbol{\theta}')(\tilde{\boldsymbol{\theta}} - \hat{\boldsymbol{\theta}}). \quad (2.24)$$

The approximation errors associated with (2.23) and (2.24) are asymptotically negligible under H_T. Thus, substituting (2.23) and (2.24) into (2.22) yields

$$s = \tfrac{1}{2}(\partial S_T(\hat{\boldsymbol{\theta}})/\partial\boldsymbol{\theta})'(\partial^2 S_T(\hat{\boldsymbol{\theta}})/\partial\boldsymbol{\theta}\,\partial\boldsymbol{\theta}')^{-1}(\partial S_T(\hat{\boldsymbol{\theta}})/\partial\boldsymbol{\theta}) \quad (2.25)$$

which is asymptotically equivalent to T^0. As s uses only the constrained estimates $\hat{\boldsymbol{\theta}}$, it can, therefore, be interpreted as the IV analogue of the LM test. Moreover, using the LEA's $\mathbf{f}^*(\boldsymbol{\theta})$ and $\mathbf{f}^+(\boldsymbol{\theta})$ in (2.21) instead of $\mathbf{f}(\boldsymbol{\theta})$ provides further asymptotically equivalent tests. The specialization of these results to the case of an individual equation estimated by IV/2SLS is straightforward.

In the case of a single structural equation, $\mathbf{f}_t(\boldsymbol{\theta})$ is a scalar function of the vectors $(\mathbf{y}_t, \mathbf{z}_t, \boldsymbol{\theta})$, the $\mathbf{e}_t$ are independent $N(0, \sigma^2)$ variates, $\mathbf{f}(\boldsymbol{\theta})$ is a $T \times 1$ vector, and the criterion function of (2.21) specializes to

$$S_T(\boldsymbol{\theta}) = \mathbf{f}(\boldsymbol{\theta})'X(X'X)^{-1}X'\mathbf{f}(\boldsymbol{\theta})/\dot{\sigma}^2, \quad (2.26)$$

where $\dot{\sigma}^2$ is an estimator of σ^2, the equation error variance, which is consistent under H_0. The generation of LEA's proceeds as before with $\boldsymbol{\theta}$ now being interpreted as the parameter vector for the equation of interest under the alternative hypothesis. For future reference, Gallant and Jorgenson refer to the single-equation specialization of the T^0 test as the T_α^0 test.

6.3 MISSPECIFICATION TESTS FOR A SINGLE EQUATION USING LEA MODELS

6.3.1 Serial correlation

Consider the following model

$$g(y_t, \mathbf{z}_t, \mathbf{d}_{t-1}; \boldsymbol{\theta}_1) = u_t \quad (3.1)$$

for which the assumption that the u_t are serially independent is to be tested against the Gth order moving average [MA(G)] process

$$u_t = [1 + \alpha(B)]e_t, \qquad e_t \, \mathrm{NID}(0, \sigma^2), \tag{3.2}$$

where $\alpha(B) = \alpha_1 B + \cdots + \alpha_G B^G$ and B is the backward shift operator, $B^j w_t = w_{t-j}$. The hypothesis to be tested is $H_0\colon \alpha_1 = \cdots = \alpha_G = 0$ so that u_t is e_t on H_0. On the alternative hypothesis, equations (3.1) and (3.2) can be written in a form corresponding to (2.1) to give

$$f_t(\boldsymbol{\theta}) = [1 + \alpha(B)]^{-1} g_t(\boldsymbol{\theta}_1) \tag{3.3}$$

with $g_t(\boldsymbol{\theta}_1)$ denoting $g(y_t, \mathbf{z}_t, \mathbf{d}_{t-1}; \boldsymbol{\theta}_1)$ and $\boldsymbol{\theta}_2' = (\alpha_1, \ldots, \alpha_G) = \boldsymbol{\alpha}'$. Equation (3.1) is a sufficiently general model to represent a stochastic linear difference equation with autoregressive moving average (ARMA) errors (Reinsel, 1979a) and the nonlinear regression model with autoregressive errors recently studied by Frydman (1980). It also provides a framework suitable for testing univariate ARMA (p, q) time series models against the alternative of an ARMA $(p, q + G)$ scheme. In each of these cases, the error serial correlation model is expressed in autoregressive form and (3.1) represents the corresponding restricted transformed equation. For example, the univariate ARMA model can be written as

$$g(y_t, \mathbf{d}_{t-1}; \boldsymbol{\theta}_1) = \mu(B)^{-1} \rho(B) y_t = u_t, \tag{3.4}$$

where

$$\begin{aligned} \mu(B) &= 1 + \mu_1 B + \cdots + \mu_q B^q, \\ \rho(B) &= 1 + \rho_1 B + \cdots + \rho_p B^p, \\ \mathbf{d}_{t-1} &= (y_{t-1}, y_{t-2}, \ldots) \end{aligned}$$

and

$$\boldsymbol{\theta}_1' = (\mu_1, \ldots, \mu_q, \rho_1, \ldots, \rho_p, \sigma^2).$$

Consider the problem of testing $H_0\colon \boldsymbol{\theta}_2 = \mathbf{0}$ for the model of (3.3) using the LEA models $f_t^*(\boldsymbol{\theta})$ and $f_t^+(\boldsymbol{\theta})$ instead of $f_t(\boldsymbol{\theta})$ itself. In order to construct the LEA's it is necessary to form $\partial f_t(\boldsymbol{\theta}_1, \mathbf{0})/\partial \boldsymbol{\theta}_2$. As

$$\partial f_t(\boldsymbol{\theta})/\partial \alpha_i = -[1 + \alpha(B)]^{-2} B^i g_t(\boldsymbol{\theta}_1),$$

it follows that

$$\partial f_t(\boldsymbol{\theta}_1, \mathbf{0})/\partial \alpha_i = -B^i g_t(\boldsymbol{\theta}_1) = -g_{t-i}(\boldsymbol{\theta}_1).$$

Noting that $f_t(\boldsymbol{\theta}_1, \mathbf{0}) = g_t(\boldsymbol{\theta}_1)$ we find that

$$\begin{aligned} f_t^*(\boldsymbol{\theta}) &= g_t(\boldsymbol{\theta}_1) - \alpha_1 g_{t-1}(\boldsymbol{\theta}_1) - \cdots - \alpha_G g_{t-G}(\boldsymbol{\theta}_1) \\ &= [1 - \alpha(B)] g_t(\boldsymbol{\theta}_1) = e_t. \end{aligned} \tag{3.5}$$

The LEA $f_t^*(\boldsymbol{\theta})$ is therefore an autoregressive transform of $g_t(\boldsymbol{\theta}_1)$ since it can be obtained by treating the u_t of (3.1) as if they were generated by the Gth order autoregressive [AR(G)] process.

$$[1 - \alpha(B)]u_t = e_t, \qquad e_t \text{ NID}(0, \sigma^2). \tag{3.6}$$

Thus the AR(G) scheme is an LEA for an MA(G) and *vice versa*. This implies that the LM statistic s^* for testing the serial independence of the u_t will be numerically the same whether the alternative is the MA(G) model or the AR(G) model. If the s form of the LM statistic is used, then the choice of alternative model will affect the estimate of the information matrix and hence the sample value of s. The two statistics s and s^* will, however, be asymptotically equivalent to each other and to the corresponding LR and W tests.

Given the generality of $g_t(\boldsymbol{\theta}_1)$ this result has a number of important special cases. For example, if $g_t(\boldsymbol{\theta}_1)$ is an econometric model with ARMA (p, q) errors (or simply a univariate ARMA (p, q) time series model), then this result implies that s^* can be used to test against both the ARMA ($p + G, q$) and ARMA ($p, q + G$) alternatives. It is only necessary to decide upon G, the number of additional coefficients in the alternative model, and not upon whether to extend the AR or the MA component. It is not possible, however, to extend both components. To see this consider the ARMA (1, 1) alternative

$$(1 - \alpha_1 B)u_t = (1 + \alpha_2 B)e_t. \tag{3.7}$$

The LEA's corresponding to (3.7) are the AR(1) model

$$[1 - (\alpha_1 + \alpha_2)B]u_t = e_t \tag{3.8}$$

and the MA(1) model

$$u_t = [1 + (\alpha_1 + \alpha_2)B]e_t. \tag{3.9}$$

Thus the coefficients α_1 and α_2 are locally under-identified. This under-identification is reflected in the information matrix for the alternative comprising (3.1) and (3.7), which is singular under the null hypothesis $\alpha_1 = \alpha_2 = 0$. This singularity implies that the standard results on LM, LR, and W tests are not applicable.[5]

The results above are derived from the LEA $f_t^*(\boldsymbol{\theta})$. Similar results with the added advantage of computational simplicity can be obtained by using $f_t^+(\boldsymbol{\theta})$ as the LEA. From (3.5)

$$f_t^+(\boldsymbol{\theta}) = g_t(\boldsymbol{\theta}_1) - \alpha(B)g_t(\hat{\boldsymbol{\theta}}_1) = e_t. \tag{3.10}$$

The test statistic for the null hypothesis that the u_t are serially independent against either the AR(G) or MA(G) alternative can now be obtained by testing $H_0\colon \alpha_1 = \cdots = \alpha_G = 0$ in the augmented model

$$g_t(\boldsymbol{\theta}_1) - \alpha_1 \hat{u}_{t-1} - \cdots - \alpha_G \hat{u}_{t-G} = e_t, \tag{3.11}$$

where $\hat{u}_{t-1} = g_{t-1}(\hat{\boldsymbol{\theta}}_1)$ are the lagged residuals from the MLE of (3.1).

An example

In order to illustrate the use of LEA's and to relate our results to earlier work in this area, we shall examine the important special case where (3.1) is a linear dynamic model with unrestricted coefficients:

$$g_t(\boldsymbol{\theta}_1) = y_t - \mathbf{x}_t'\boldsymbol{\beta} = u_t \tag{3.12}$$

in which $\mathbf{x}_t$ is an H-dimensional vector of exogenous and lagged dependent variables. The alternative hypothesis is that u_t is generated by the AR(G) process (3.6) and on $H_0:\alpha_1 = \cdots = \alpha_G = 0$ we have $u_t = e_t$.

Consider first testing the null hypothesis by means of the s^* test statistic defined in (2.5). The construction of s^* requires the evaluation of $\boldsymbol{W}(\hat{\boldsymbol{\theta}})$, $\boldsymbol{\theta}' = (\boldsymbol{\beta}', \sigma^2, \boldsymbol{\alpha}')$, which has typical element $w_{ts}(\hat{\boldsymbol{\theta}}) = \partial l_t(\hat{\boldsymbol{\theta}})/\partial \boldsymbol{\theta}_s$. It can be shown that

$$\left.\begin{array}{lr} \text{(a)}\ \partial l_t(\hat{\boldsymbol{\theta}})/\partial \beta_i = x_{ti}\hat{u}_t/\hat{\sigma}^2 & (i = 1, \ldots, H) \\ \text{(b)}\ \partial l_t(\hat{\boldsymbol{\theta}})/\partial \sigma^2 = (2\hat{\sigma}^4)^{-1}(\hat{u}_t^2 - \hat{\sigma}^2) & \\ \text{(c)}\ \partial l_t(\hat{\boldsymbol{\theta}})/\partial \alpha_i = \hat{u}_t\hat{u}_{t-i}/\hat{\sigma}^2 & (i = 1, \ldots, G) \end{array}\right\} \tag{3.13}$$

where x_{ti} is the ith element of $\mathbf{x}_t$, $\hat{u}_t$ is the OLS residual of (3.12), and $\hat{\sigma}^2 = T^{-1}\sum_{t=1}^{T}\hat{u}_t^2$. Thus s^* can be constructed as T times the R^2 of the regression of the unit vector on the regressors of (3.13) or, equivalently, on

$$\{x_{t1}\hat{u}_t, \ldots, x_{tH}\hat{u}_t, \hat{u}_t^2 - \hat{\sigma}^2, \hat{u}_t\hat{u}_{t-1}, \ldots, \hat{u}_t\hat{u}_{t-G}\}.$$

The s statistic is equal to the LM criterion proposed by Godfrey (1978a) and differs from the s^* statistic constructed from (3.13) by asymptotically negligible terms. The difference between s and s^* arises from the fact that

$$\sum_t (\partial l_t(\hat{\boldsymbol{\theta}})/\partial \boldsymbol{\theta})(\partial l_t(\hat{\boldsymbol{\theta}})/\partial \boldsymbol{\theta})' + \partial^2 L_T(\hat{\boldsymbol{\theta}})/\partial \boldsymbol{\theta}\,\partial \boldsymbol{\theta}' \tag{3.14}$$

is not equal to zero in finite samples. For example, consider T^{-1} times the (1, 1) element of the matrix of (3.14):

$$T^{-1}\left(\sum_t x_{t1}^2\hat{u}_t^2/\hat{\sigma}^4 - \sum_t x_{t1}^2/\hat{\sigma}^2\right). \tag{3.15}$$

It is straightforward to verify that the quantity given in (3.15), while being nonzero for finite sets of data, does have a probability limit of zero.

Turning to the different forms of LEA models, it has already been shown that the use of the $f_t^*(\boldsymbol{\theta})$ variant yields the result that the AR(G) and MA(G) models are locally equivalent. This finding is implied by the work of Breusch (1978a) and Godfrey (1978a) who both established that the vector of estimated multipliers for testing the serial independence assumption depended only upon the order of the alternative autocorrelation model (i.e. the value of G) and not upon its form (AR or MA).

If the LEA $f_t^+(\boldsymbol{\theta})$ is used then the test statistic for H_0 can be obtained very simply. For the linear model (3.12), equation (3.11) can be rewritten as

$$y_t = \mathbf{x}_t'\boldsymbol{\beta} + \alpha_1\hat{u}_{t-1} + \cdots + \alpha_G\hat{u}_{t-G} + e_t. \tag{3.16}$$

Instead of using s or s^*, the test statistic for H_0 can now be constructed as G times the usual F statistic for the subset of regression coefficients $(\alpha_1, \ldots, \alpha_G)$ and this product is asymptotically distributed as $\chi^2(G)$ on H_0.

Relating this W-type procedure to the literature, it can be noted firstly that, for the alternative hypothesis of an AR(G), Durbin (1970) used (3.16) but with y_t replaced by $\hat{u}_t$. Due to the orthogonality properties of least squares, the test statistic is unaffected by this substitution. Secondly, Godfrey (1978b) proposed that the test statistic be calculated as T times the R^2 associated with OLS estimation of (3.16) again with y_t replaced by $\hat{u}_t$. This proposal yields the LM-type test of H_0 against the alternative represented by (3.16).

Finally, if $g_t(\boldsymbol{\theta}_1)$ is a nonlinear function, then the LM test may be more attractive than the LR and W procedures as a means of testing H_0 against the unrestricted LEA (3.11). For example, if $g_t(\boldsymbol{\theta}_1)$ is the nonlinear regression function

$$g_t(\boldsymbol{\theta}_1) = y_t - h_t(\boldsymbol{\theta}_1) = u_t$$

then the results of Breusch and Pagan (1980) imply that the LM statistic can be calculated as T times the R^2 from the regression of $\hat{u}_t$ on $\{\hat{H}_t, \hat{u}_{t-1}, \ldots, \hat{u}_{t-G}\}$ where $\hat{H}_t = \partial h_t(\hat{\boldsymbol{\theta}}_1)/\partial\boldsymbol{\theta}_1$. This result can be related to (3.11) by noting that a linear approximation to $g_t(\boldsymbol{\theta}_1)$ about $\boldsymbol{\theta}_1 = \hat{\boldsymbol{\theta}}_1$ is

$$\begin{aligned} g_t(\boldsymbol{\theta}_1) &\approx y_t - h_t(\hat{\boldsymbol{\theta}}_1) - \hat{H}_t(\boldsymbol{\theta}_1 - \hat{\boldsymbol{\theta}}_1) \\ &= \hat{u}_t - \hat{H}_t(\boldsymbol{\theta}_1 - \hat{\boldsymbol{\theta}}_1) \end{aligned}$$

which combined with (3.11) yields

$$\hat{u}_t = \hat{H}_t(\boldsymbol{\theta}_1 - \hat{\boldsymbol{\theta}}_1) + \alpha_1\hat{u}_{t-1} + \cdots + \alpha_G\hat{u}_{t-G} + e_t^*. \tag{3.17}$$

Thus, testing for the significance of the regressors of (3.17) provides the test given by Breusch and Pagan (1980).

6.3.2 Heteroskedasticity

On the null hypothesis the model will be defined as before and will consist of equation (3.1) with $u_t = e_t$ where e_t is NID$(0, \sigma^2)$. On the alternative hypothesis it is assumed that u_t is NID$(0, \sigma_t^2)$ where

$$\begin{aligned} \sigma_t^2 &= \sigma^2 v(\mathbf{Q}_t'\boldsymbol{\alpha}) \\ &= \sigma^2 v_t(\boldsymbol{\theta}_2) \end{aligned} \tag{3.18}$$

where $\mathbf{Q}_t$ is a G-dimensional vector of nonstochastic variables, $\boldsymbol{\theta}_2' = \boldsymbol{\alpha}' = (\alpha_1, \ldots, \alpha_G)$, $v(0) = 1$ and $\partial v(0)/\partial(\mathbf{Q}_t'\boldsymbol{\alpha}) \neq 0$.[6] Thus on $H_0: \boldsymbol{\theta}_2 = \boldsymbol{\alpha} = \mathbf{0}$, u_t is homoskedastic and on the alternative $H_1: \boldsymbol{\theta}_2 \neq \mathbf{0}$, u_t is heteroskedastic.

As Breusch and Pagan (1980) point out, the alternative defined by (3.18) can represent most of the error variance schemes studied in the literature, and in particular the additive model

$$\sigma_t^2 = \sigma^2(1 + \mathbf{Q}_t'\boldsymbol{\alpha}) \tag{3.19}$$

and the multiplicative model

$$\sigma_t^2 = \sigma^2 \exp(\mathbf{Q}_t'\boldsymbol{\alpha}). \tag{3.20}$$

Estimation under the additive scheme has been studied by Amemiya (1977, 1978) and under multiplicative schemes by Harvey (1976, 1977).

In order to use the inferential framework developed above it is necessary first to rewrite equations (3.1) and (3.18) in the form of (2.1). Thus the required alternative model which has homoskedastic errors is

$$f_t(\boldsymbol{\theta}) = g_t(\boldsymbol{\theta}_1) v_t(\boldsymbol{\theta}_2)^{-1/2} = e_t. \tag{3.21}$$

Next we consider the corresponding LEA's which are derived using

$$\partial f_t(\boldsymbol{\theta})/\partial\alpha_i = -\tfrac{1}{2} g_t(\boldsymbol{\theta}_1) v_t(\boldsymbol{\theta}_2)^{-3/2} [\partial v(\mathbf{Q}_t'\boldsymbol{\alpha})/\partial(\mathbf{Q}_t'\boldsymbol{\alpha})] Q_{ti} \tag{3.22}$$

where Q_{ti} is the ith element of $\mathbf{Q}_t$. Evaluating (3.22) at $(\boldsymbol{\theta}_1', \mathbf{0})$ gives

$$\partial f_t(\boldsymbol{\theta}_1, \mathbf{0})/\partial\alpha_i = h g_t(\boldsymbol{\theta}_1) Q_{ti} \tag{3.23}$$

where

$$h = -\tfrac{1}{2} \partial v_t(0)/\partial(\mathbf{Q}_t'\boldsymbol{\alpha}) \tag{3.24}$$

is a constant. It follows that the LEA model $f_t^*(\boldsymbol{\theta})$ can now be written as

$$f_t^*(\boldsymbol{\theta}) = g_t(\boldsymbol{\theta}_1) + h \sum_{i=1}^{G} \alpha_i g_t(\boldsymbol{\theta}_1) Q_{ti} = e_t. \tag{3.25}$$

The test of H_0 based upon (3.25) is clearly independent of the value of h. Furthermore, the form chosen for $\mathbf{v}(.)$ will only affect h in (3.25); in particular the test will be the same whichever of the alternatives (3.19) or (3.20) is selected. The choice of the Q_{ti} will of course affect the test and, as Godfrey (1978c) remarks, this choice is not entirely independent of the form of $\mathbf{v}(.)$. For example, if the additive model is being entertained the Q_{ti} might include the *levels* of some of the regressor variables of the original model (3.1), whereas if the multiplicative model is chosen as the alternative the Q_{ti} might include the *logarithms* of some of the regressors.

The LEA model $f_t^+(\boldsymbol{\theta})$ can be written as

$$f_t^+(\boldsymbol{\theta}) = g_t(\boldsymbol{\theta}_1) - \sum_{i=1}^{G} \alpha_i g_t(\hat{\boldsymbol{\theta}}_1) Q_{ti}$$
$$= g_t(\boldsymbol{\theta}_1) - \sum_{i=1}^{G} \alpha_i(\hat{u}_t Q_{ti})$$
$$= e_t \tag{3.26}$$

where $\hat{u}_t = g_t(\hat{\boldsymbol{\theta}}_1)$ is the residual obtained from the MLE of (3.1) on H_0 and h has been set equal to -1 for analytical convenience (this is equivalent to redefining the original $-h\alpha_i$ as α_i).

The derivation of test statistics for the LEA's $f_t^*(\boldsymbol{\theta})$ and $f_t^+(\boldsymbol{\theta})$ is complicated by the presence of a nonconstant Jacobian. Even without this, however, it can be seen from (3.25) that using $f_t^*(\boldsymbol{\theta})$ will in general lead to more nonlinearities than will $f_t^+(\boldsymbol{\theta})$. We shall, therefore, concentrate below on the use of $f_t^+(\boldsymbol{\theta})$.

To illustrate the derivation of the test statistic in general, we shall consider once more the important special case where $g_t(\boldsymbol{\theta}_1)$ is the linear model (3.12), when (3.26) becomes

$$f_t^+(\boldsymbol{\theta}) = y_t - \mathbf{x}_t'\boldsymbol{\beta} - \sum_{i=1}^{G} \alpha_i(\hat{u}_t Q_{ti}) = e_t \tag{3.27}$$

where $\hat{u}_t$ is the OLS residual of (3.12). Neglecting terms which are unimportant asymptotically, the Jacobian term for (3.27) is derived from

$$\partial f_t^+(\boldsymbol{\theta})/\partial y_t = 1 - \sum_{i=1}^{G} \alpha_i Q_{ti} \tag{3.28}$$

as

$$\sum_{t=1}^{T} \ln \|\partial f_t^+(\boldsymbol{\theta})/\partial y_t\| = \sum_{t=1}^{T} \ln \left(1 - \sum_{i=1}^{G} \alpha_i Q_{ti}\right)$$
$$\simeq -\sum_{i=1}^{G} \alpha_i \left(\sum_{t=1}^{T} Q_{ti}\right) \tag{3.29}$$

where the approximation is taken on the sequence of local alternatives H_T. If the Q_{ti} are measured as deviations about their sample means then $\sum_{t=1}^{T} Q_{ti} = 0$ for $i = 1, \ldots, G$ and (3.29) vanishes. With this simplifying assumption there is no need to consider the Jacobian further. The problem has now been reduced to that of testing for the joint significance of the regressors $\hat{u}_t Q_{ti}$ in (3.27).

Two approaches to constructing test statistics for H_0 will be considered; the first involves using s^*, defined by (2.6), together with $f_t^+(\boldsymbol{\theta})$ and the second uses (3.27) directly. In constructing s^* it is necessary to evaluate $w_{ts}(\hat{\boldsymbol{\theta}}) = \partial l_t^+(\hat{\boldsymbol{\theta}})/\partial \theta_s$.

Noting that the jacobian does not vanish for $l_t^+(\boldsymbol{\theta})$ as it does for $\sum_{t=1}^{T} l_t^+(\boldsymbol{\theta})$, we obtain

$$\left.\begin{aligned} &\text{(a)}\ \partial l_t^+(\hat{\boldsymbol{\theta}})/\partial \beta_i = x_{ti}\hat{u}_t/\hat{\sigma}^2 && (i = 1,\ldots,H) \\ &\text{(b)}\ \partial l_t^+(\hat{\boldsymbol{\theta}})/\partial \sigma^2 = (2\hat{\sigma}^4)^{-1}(\hat{u}_t^2 - \hat{\sigma}^2) && \\ &\text{(c)}\ \partial l_t^+(\hat{\boldsymbol{\theta}})/\partial \alpha_i = (\hat{u}_t Q_{ti})\hat{u}_t/\hat{\sigma}^2 - Q_{ti} && (i = 1,\ldots,G). \end{aligned}\right\} \tag{3.30}$$

Thus s^* is constructed as T times the R^2 of the regression of the unit vector on the regressors

$$\{x_{t1}\hat{u}_t,\ldots,x_{tH}\hat{u}_t,(\hat{u}_t^2 - \hat{\sigma}^2),(\hat{u}_t^2 - \hat{\sigma}^2)Q_{t1},\ldots,(\hat{u}_t^2 - \hat{\sigma}^2)Q_{tG}\}.$$

The direct approach involves testing for the joint significance of the regressors $\hat{u}_t Q_{ti}$ in (3.27). However, the standard inference results of regression theory cannot be used because the $\hat{u}_t Q_{ti}$ do not satisfy the normal assumption that for the linear model '$\mathbf{y} = \boldsymbol{X\beta} + \mathbf{u}$', the limiting distribution of '$T^{-1/2}\boldsymbol{X}'\mathbf{u}$' is '$N(0, \sigma^2 \operatorname{plim} T^{-1}\boldsymbol{X}'\boldsymbol{X})$'.[7] A typical element of the subvector of '$T^{-1/2}\boldsymbol{X}'\mathbf{u}$' corresponding to the added regressors $\hat{u}_t Q_{ti}$ is $T^{-1/2}\sum_{t=1}^{T} u_t(\hat{u}_t Q_{ti})$ which has the same limiting distribution on H_0 as

$$T^{-1/2}\sum_{t=1}^{T} u_t^2 Q_{ti} = T^{-1/2}\sum_{t=1}^{T}(u_t^2 - \sigma^2)Q_{ti}.$$

But on H_0 the variates $(u_t^2 - \sigma^2)$ are i.i.d. with mean zero and finite variance $2\sigma^4$ and hence, given the usual assumptions about Q_{ti}, the limiting distribution of $T^{-1/2}\sum_{t=1}^{T} u_t(\hat{u}_t Q_{ti})$ is $N(0, \Delta_i)$ where

$$\begin{aligned} \Delta_i &= 2\sigma^4 \operatorname{plim} T^{-1}\sum_{t=1}^{T} Q_{ti}^2 \\ &= 2\sigma^2 \operatorname{plim} T^{-1}\sum_{t=1}^{T}(\hat{u}_t Q_{ti})^2. \end{aligned} \tag{3.31}$$

The standard regression formulae would omit the factor 2 in (3.31) and are, therefore, invalid. The necessary correction is, however, trivial.

Assuming that the x_{ti} and Q_{ti} of (3.27) are nonstochastic and uniformly bounded with moment matrices satisfying the usual conditions, we have

$$\operatorname{plim} T^{-1}\sum_{t=1}^{T} x_{tj}(\hat{u}_t Q_{ti}) = 0$$

implying that the x_{tj} and $u_t Q_{ti}$ are asymptotically uncorrelated. It follows that a valid large-sample test of H_0 is obtained by calculating F, the usual F-test statistic for $H_0\colon \alpha_1 = \cdots = \alpha_G = 0$, in (3.27) and then multiplying it by $G/2$ (not by G). The resulting statistic $GF/2$ has a limiting $\chi^2(G)$ distribution when the u_t are homoskedastic.

At first sight this test is quite unlike those proposed by Breusch and Pagan (1980) and Godfrey (1978d) whose suggestions amount to using

$$\mathbf{r}'\boldsymbol{Q}(\boldsymbol{Q}'\boldsymbol{Q})^{-1}\boldsymbol{Q}'\mathbf{r}/2\hat{\sigma}^4 \tag{3.32}$$

where $\mathbf{r}$ is a T-dimensional vector with typical element $\hat{\mathbf{u}}_t^2$ and $\boldsymbol{Q}$ is a $T \times G$ matrix with typical element Q_{ti}.[8] A slightly different test was given by Godfrey (1978c) who pointed out that (3.32) was asymptotically equivalent to T times the R^2 of the regression of $\hat{u}_t^2$ on the Q_{ti} and an intercept term.[9] These earlier tests are, in fact, closely related to an LM test of H_0 against the LEA model of (3.27). Since the x_{tj} and $\hat{u}_t Q_{ti}$ are asymptotically uncorrelated, a valid LM-type test of H_0 against (3.27) is

$$\left[\sum_{t=1}^{T} \hat{u}_t(\hat{u}_t Q_{ti})\right]' \left[2\hat{\sigma}^2 \sum_{t=1}^{T} \hat{u}_t^2 Q_{ti} Q_{tj}\right]^{-1} \left[\sum_{t=1}^{T} \hat{u}_t(\hat{u}_t Q_{ti})\right]$$

which, as required, has the same limiting distribution on H_0 as

$$\left[\sum_{t=1}^{T} \hat{u}_t^2 Q_{ti}\right]' \left[2\hat{\sigma}^4 \sum_{t=1}^{T} Q_{ti} Q_{tj}\right]^{-1} \left[\sum_{t=1}^{T} \hat{u}_t^2 Q_{ti}\right] = \mathbf{r}'\boldsymbol{Q}(\boldsymbol{Q}'\boldsymbol{Q})^{-1}\boldsymbol{Q}'\mathbf{r}/2\hat{\sigma}^4.$$

The results above have been based on the assumption that on the alternative hypothesis σ_t^2 can be represented by (3.18) which may not always be appropriate. Suppose instead that a more general nonlinear function is preferred involving the nonstochastic variables $\mathbf{q}_t$:

$$\sigma_t^2 = \sigma^2 h(\mathbf{q}_t, \boldsymbol{\theta}_2)$$

where $h(\mathbf{q}_t, \mathbf{0}) = 1$ but that there is uncertainty about the precise form of $h(.)$. In these circumstances, it may be useful to adopt the variant of Ramsey's (1969) RESET test suggested by the results of Thursby and Schmidt (1977). This involves deriving the vector $\mathbf{Q}_t$ using powers of the $\mathbf{q}_t$ variables. For example, using up to the third powers of $\mathbf{q}_t$ gives

$$\mathbf{Q}_t' \underset{a}{=} \{\mathbf{q}_t', (\mathbf{q}_t^2)', (\mathbf{q}_t^3)'\}^{\mathrm{d}}$$

where $\mathbf{q}_t^2$ and $\mathbf{q}_t^3$ consist of terms like $q_{ti}q_{tj}$ and $q_{ti}q_{tj}q_{tk}$ respectively, $\{.\}^{\mathrm{d}}$ denotes that redundant variables of the vector are deleted and $\underset{a}{=}$ is an equality which holds after the right-hand side variables have been measured as deviations about their sample means. It is now possible to use the test procedure described above (see also White, 1980).

6.3.3 Combination of specification errors

Although in the previous subsections we have considered testing the null model for only one type of misspecification, it is often useful to test against several (typically) non-nested alternatives, e.g. omitted variables, serially correlated errors, heteroskedasticity, structural instability, and wrong functional form. Rather than carry out a number of separate tests of the null model against each alternative in turn, it is attractive to examine the construction of joint tests in order to avoid the problems associated with induced tests and to obtain an overall test of misspecification.[10]

It would be possible to form a general alternative which included all the individual alternatives of interest as special cases. The log likelihood function for this general alternative could then be written down and the appropriate expression for the LM statistic could be obtained by differentiation in the usual way. However, when it is reasonable to assume that the parameters which distinguish the various alternatives from the null are functionally independent, a simpler approach is available. Suppose that there are J different types of misspecification and that $\hat{\boldsymbol{W}}_j$ is the regressor matrix required to calculate the s^* test of the null model against the jth alternative ($j = 1, \ldots, J$), then the regressor matrix for the s^* test against the combination of all J alternatives is simply

$$\hat{\boldsymbol{W}} = \{\hat{\boldsymbol{W}}_1, \ldots, \hat{\boldsymbol{W}}J\}^{\mathrm{d}},$$

where $\{.\}^{\mathrm{d}}$ denotes that redundant columns corresponding to nuisance parameters are deleted.

In order to illustrate this result we shall consider the problem of testing jointly for serially correlated and heteroskedastic errors; let serial correlation be the first type of specification error and heteroskedasticity the second. The maintained model on the null hypothesis will again be defined as equation (3.1) with $u_t = e_t$ where e_t is NID$(0, \sigma^2)$. On the alternative hypothesis it is now assumed that

$$u_t = [1 + \alpha(B)]\varepsilon_t \tag{3.33}$$

where ε_t is NID$(0, \sigma_t^2)$ and

$$\sigma_t^2 = \sigma^2 v(\mathbf{Q}_t'\boldsymbol{\lambda}) \tag{3.34}$$

where $\alpha(B)$ and $\mathbf{Q}_t$ are defined as above except that here $\alpha(B)$ is a G_1-dimensional polynomial and $\mathbf{Q}_t$ is a G_2-dimensional vector with $G_1 + G_2 = G$. Also $\boldsymbol{\lambda}' = (\lambda_1, \ldots, \lambda_{G_2})$, $v(0) = 1$, and $\partial v(0)/\partial(\mathbf{Q}_t'\boldsymbol{\lambda}) \neq 0$. Thus, if $\boldsymbol{\theta}_2' = (\alpha_1, \ldots, \alpha_{G_1}, \lambda_1, \ldots, \lambda_{G_2})$, then we have once more that $H_0: \boldsymbol{\theta}_2 = \mathbf{0}$ and $H_1: \boldsymbol{\theta}_2 \neq \mathbf{0}$.

The model on the alternative hypothesis of MA(G_1) and heteroskedastic errors can now be written as

$$f_t(\boldsymbol{\theta}) = [1 + \alpha(B)]^{-1} g_t(\boldsymbol{\theta}_1) v_t(\mathbf{Q}_t'\boldsymbol{\lambda})^{-1/2} = e_t. \tag{3.35}$$

The LEA model $f_t^*(\boldsymbol{\theta})$ can be obtained with only minor modifications to the earlier results. Thus

$$\partial f_t(\boldsymbol{\theta}_1, \mathbf{0})/\partial \alpha_i = -B^i g_t(\boldsymbol{\theta}_1)$$

and

$$\partial f_t(\boldsymbol{\theta}_1, \mathbf{0})/\partial \lambda_i = h g_t(\boldsymbol{\theta}_1) Q_{ti}$$

where $h = \frac{1}{2}\partial v_t(\mathbf{0})/\partial(\mathbf{Q}_t'\boldsymbol{\lambda})$ and hence

$$f_t^*(\boldsymbol{\theta}) = [1 - \alpha(B)]g_t(\boldsymbol{\theta}_1) + h \sum_{i=1}^{G_2} \lambda_i g_t(\boldsymbol{\theta}_1) Q_{ti} = e_t. \tag{3.36}$$

The LEA model $f_t^+(\boldsymbol{\theta})$ can, therefore, be written as

$$f_t^+(\boldsymbol{\theta}) = g_t(\boldsymbol{\theta}_1) - \sum_{i=1}^{G_1} \alpha_i \hat{u}_{t-i} - \sum_{i=1}^{G_2} \lambda_i(\hat{u}_t Q_{ti}) = e_t \tag{3.37}$$

where $\hat{u}_{t-i}$ is the lag i residual from the MLE of (3.1) on H_0 and h has been set equal to -1 as before. Despite the fact that the misspecifications affect $g_t(\boldsymbol{\theta}_1)$ multiplicatively in $f_t(\boldsymbol{\theta})$, in $f_t^+(\boldsymbol{\theta})$ they enter as separate additive effects. The test statistics will again be derived for the case where $g_t(\boldsymbol{\theta}_1)$ is the linear model (3.12), when $f_t^+(\boldsymbol{\theta})$ becomes

$$f_t^+(\boldsymbol{\theta}) = y_t - \mathbf{x}_t'\boldsymbol{\beta} - \sum_{i=1}^{G_1} \alpha_i \hat{u}_{t-i} - \sum_{i=1}^{G_2} \lambda_i(\hat{u}_t Q_{ti}) = e_t. \tag{3.38}$$

Consider first the use of the s^* statistic for $H_0: (\boldsymbol{\alpha} = \mathbf{0}, \boldsymbol{\lambda} = \mathbf{0})$ against $H_{A1}: (\boldsymbol{\alpha} \neq \mathbf{0}, \boldsymbol{\lambda} = \mathbf{0})$. Using (3.13) the $\hat{\boldsymbol{W}}_1$ matrix, which is associated with the first specification error, is the $T \times (H + G_1 + 1)$ matrix with tth row

$$\{x_{t1}\hat{u}_t, \ldots, x_{tH}\hat{u}_t, \hat{u}_t^2 - \hat{\sigma}^2, \hat{u}_t\hat{u}_{t-1}, \ldots, \hat{u}_t\hat{u}_{t-G_1}\}.$$

From (3.30) the corresponding $\hat{\boldsymbol{W}}_2$ matrix for H_0 against $H_{A2}: (\boldsymbol{\alpha} = \mathbf{0}, \boldsymbol{\lambda} \neq \mathbf{0})$ is a $T \times (H + G_2 + 1)$ matrix with tth row

$$\{x_{t1}\hat{u}_t, \ldots, x_{tH}\hat{u}_t, \hat{u}_t^2 - \hat{\sigma}^2, (\hat{u}_t^2 - \hat{\sigma}^2)Q_{t1}, \ldots, (\hat{u}_t^2 - \hat{\sigma}^2)Q_{tG_2}\}.$$

Thus, in order to test H_0 against $H_1: (\boldsymbol{\alpha} \neq \mathbf{0}, \boldsymbol{\lambda} \neq \mathbf{0})$ by the s^* approach, the test statistic should be calculated as $T \times R^2_{i\hat{W}}$ where $\hat{\boldsymbol{W}}$ is a $T \times (H + G + 1)$ matrix with tth row

$$\{x_{t1}\hat{u}_t, \ldots, x_{tH}\hat{u}_t, \hat{u}_t^2 - \hat{\sigma}^2, \hat{u}_t\hat{u}_{t-1}, \ldots, \hat{u}_t\hat{u}_{t-G_1}, (\hat{u}_t^2 - \hat{\sigma}^2)Q_{t1}, \ldots, (\hat{u}_t^2 - \hat{\sigma}^2)Q_{tG_2}\}.$$

It is straightforward to show that the last G_2 columns of $\boldsymbol{W}$ (corresponding to $\boldsymbol{\lambda}$) are asymptotically uncorrelated with the other $(H + G_1 + 1)$ columns. In this case it would, therefore, be valid to compute a joint test of H_0 against H_1 as the sum of the two separate tests for serial correlation and heteroskedasticity.

The direct test of H_0 against H_1 involves evaluating the joint significance of $\boldsymbol{\alpha}$ and $\boldsymbol{\lambda}$ in (3.38) but, as with the case of pure heteroskedasticity derived above, a correction to the standard F-test formulae is required. Once again x_{tj} and $\hat{u}_t Q_{ti}$ will be asymptotically uncorrelated. Moreover, on the null hypothesis of serial independence and homoskedasticity $\hat{u}_{t-j}$ and $\hat{u}_t Q_{ti}$ will also be asymptotically uncorrelated for $j \geqslant 1$. It follows that on H_0 the statistic $G_2F/2$ has a limiting $\chi^2(G_2)$ distribution where F is the usual F-statistic for testing $\lambda_1 = \cdots = \lambda_{G_2} = 0$ when the residual variance under H_1 is calculated with the x_{ti}, the $\hat{u}_t\hat{u}_{t-i}$, and the $\hat{u}_t Q_{ti}$ all included as explanatory variables. Similarly on H_0 the statistic G_1F^* has a limiting $\chi^2(G_1)$ distribution on H_0 where F^* is the usual F-statistic for testing the subset of coefficients $(\alpha_1, \ldots, \alpha_{G_1})$. Since these two statistics are independent asymptotically, a joint test statistic for H_0 is given by $(G_1F^* + G_2F/2)$, which has a limiting $\chi^2(G)$ distribution on H_0.

6.4 MISSPECIFICATION TESTS FOR SIMULTANEOUS-EQUATION MODELS

In this section we shall be concerned with the construction of tests suitable for detecting misspecification due to serially correlated or heteroskedastic disturbances.[11] Like the previous misspecification tests, these will be asymptotically equivalent to overfitting tests involving estimation of the alternative model. Although there has been much work on the estimation of simultaneous-equation models with serially correlated errors (see for example Hendry (1976) and Reinsel (1979b)), far less attention has been paid to the estimation of systems with heteroskedastic disturbances. In fact, as will be seen below, certain problems arise in modifying conventional estimators such as IV for use with heteroskedastic errors and these problems affect the derivation of diagnostic statistics. In contrast, the construction of tests for serial correlation is straightforward and the results of Subsection 6.3.1 can be readily extended.

6.4.1 Testing for serially correlated errors

In order to make use of the earlier results on testing for serially correlated errors it is necessary to re-define the terms entering (3.1) and (3.2). The quantities $\mathbf{g}(.)$, $\mathbf{y}_t$, $\mathbf{u}_t$, and $\mathbf{e}_t$ in (3.1) should now be regarded as $M \times 1$ vectors and σ^2 should be replaced by the $M \times M$ positive-definite symmetric matrix $\boldsymbol{\Sigma}$. The vector moving average (VMA) scheme corresponding to (3.2) is

$$(I_M + \boldsymbol{\alpha}_1 B + \cdots + \boldsymbol{\alpha}_G B^G)^{-1}\mathbf{u}_t = \mathbf{e}_t \tag{4.1}$$

where the $\boldsymbol{\alpha}_i$ are now $M \times M$ matrices. The vector of coefficients constrained on H_0 is defined by the $GM^2 \times 1$ vector

$$\boldsymbol{\theta}_2' = (\text{vec}\,(\boldsymbol{\alpha}_1)', \ldots, \text{vec}\,(\boldsymbol{\alpha}_G)'). \tag{4.2}$$

With these re-definitions the model on the alternative hypothesis can again be written as $\mathbf{f}_t(\boldsymbol{\theta})$ of equation (3.3). The LEA model $\mathbf{f}_t^*(\boldsymbol{\theta})$ corresponding to (3.5) can be shown to be the Gth order vector autoregressive (VAR(G)) scheme.

$$(I_M - \boldsymbol{\alpha}_1 B - \cdots - \boldsymbol{\alpha}_G B^G)\mathbf{u}_t = \mathbf{e}_t \tag{4.3}$$

which can be compared with (3.6). More generally, the alternatives VARMA $(p + G, q)$ and VARMA $(p, q + G)$ are LEA models when the null model is a VARMA (p, q) specification. Thus, if the s^* form of the LM criterion is used to test the null hypothesis of VARMA (p, q) disturbances, then its value is the same for each LEA.

Similarly, once the variables are re-defined, the LEA $\mathbf{f}_t^+(\boldsymbol{\theta})$ is given by (3.10) or (3.11). The residuals $\hat{\mathbf{u}}_{t-i} = \mathbf{g}_{t-i}(\hat{\boldsymbol{\theta}}_1)$ entering (3.11) can be obtained either as before from the maximum likelihood estimation of the null model, or from any asymptotically equivalent estimator on H_0. The null hypothesis can now be tested by evaluating the joint significance of the estimated $\boldsymbol{\alpha}_i$ coefficient matrices in the model corresponding to (3.11).

(*a*) *A linear simultaneous-equation system*

In order to illustrate these general results we consider first the important special case in which the null model consists of a linear system with serially independent errors and the alternative model is linear with either VAR(1) or VMA(1) errors. The null model can be written as

$$\boldsymbol{B}\mathbf{y}_t + \boldsymbol{C}\mathbf{x}_t = \mathbf{u}_t \qquad \text{with} \quad \mathbf{u}_t \ \mathrm{NID}(0, \boldsymbol{\Sigma}), \tag{4.4}$$

where $\mathbf{x}_t$ contains lagged endogenous and current and lagged exogenous variables. The LEA model $\mathbf{f}_t^+(\boldsymbol{\theta})$ is given by

$$\mathbf{f}_t^+(\boldsymbol{\theta}) = \boldsymbol{B}\mathbf{y}_t + \boldsymbol{C}\mathbf{x}_t + \boldsymbol{R}\hat{\mathbf{u}}_{t-1} = \mathbf{e}_t, \qquad \mathbf{e}_t \ \mathrm{NID}(0, \boldsymbol{\Sigma}), \tag{4.5}$$

where $\hat{\mathbf{u}}_{t-1}$ is the lagged value of the residual vector associated with the FIML estimator (or an estimator asymptotically equivalent to FIML on H_0, e.g. 3SLS) and $\boldsymbol{R} = -\boldsymbol{\alpha}_1$ is the $M \times M$ coefficient matrix of the alternative serial correlation model. Thus we have $H_0\!:\boldsymbol{\theta}_2 = \mathrm{vec}(\boldsymbol{R}) = \mathbf{0}$.[12]

The null hypothesis can now be tested using the LM, LR, or W procedures directly on (4.5). Although the LM test does not require estimation on the alternative hypothesis, it does require some modification to the standard FIML programs to compute it; see Breusch and Godfrey (1981, Appendix A) for the derivation of the direct LM test.[13] Due to these (short run) computational problems it may be easier to use either the LR or the W approach. If the LR or W test is applied to (4.5), then it would seem sensible to concentrate the log likelihood function for this model with respect to $\boldsymbol{R}$ since $\boldsymbol{R}$ is an unrestricted $M \times M$ matrix; see Breusch and Godfrey (1981) for further discussion.

(*b*) *A single structural equation*

Suppose that a single structural equation of a (possibly incomplete) model is written as

$$\mathbf{y} = \boldsymbol{Y}\boldsymbol{\beta} + \boldsymbol{Z}\boldsymbol{\gamma} + \mathbf{u}, \tag{4.6}$$

where $\mathbf{y}$ and $\mathbf{u}$ are $T \times 1$ stochastic vectors, Y is the matrix of current endogenous regressors, and Z is the matrix of regressors which can be treated as predetermined when the errors of (4.6) are serially independent. It is simple to show that, as in Subsection 6.3.1, the AR (G) and MA (G) schemes are LEA's when testing the null hypothesis that $\mathbf{u}$ is serially uncorrelated and so only the former will be considered. The alternative hypothesis is then that $\mathbf{u}$ is generated by the AR (G) scheme

$$\mathbf{u} = \alpha_1 \mathbf{u}_{-1} + \cdots + \alpha_G \mathbf{u}_{-G} + \mathbf{e}, \tag{4.7}$$

where $\mathbf{e}$ is $N(0, \sigma^2 I_T)$ and $\mathbf{u}_{-i}$ is the vector $\mathbf{u}$ lagged i periods. The null hypothesis to be tested is $H_0 : \boldsymbol{\theta}_2 = \mathbf{0}$ with $\boldsymbol{\theta}_2' = (\alpha_1, \ldots, \alpha_G)$.

The alternative model $\mathbf{f}(\boldsymbol{\theta})$ can be obtained by combining (4.6) and (4.7), and the LEA model corresponding to $\mathbf{f}^+(\boldsymbol{\theta})$ can be shown to be

$$\mathbf{y} = Y\boldsymbol{\beta} + Z\boldsymbol{\gamma} + \alpha_1 \hat{\mathbf{u}}_{-1} + \cdots + \alpha_G \hat{\mathbf{u}}_{-G} + \mathbf{e}, \tag{4.8}$$

where $\hat{\mathbf{u}}_{-i}$ is the residual vector $\hat{\mathbf{u}}$ lagged i periods. The residuals of $\hat{\mathbf{u}}$ are derived from (4.6) on H_0 using the single-equation estimates of $\boldsymbol{\beta}$ and $\boldsymbol{\gamma}$ obtained by LIML, 2SLS, or IV.

If both (4.6) and (4.8) are estimated using the same set of instruments, then H_0 can be tested by means of the T_α^0 statistic defined in Section 6.2. It will be recalled that the T_α^0 statistic is obtained from the T^0 statistic of (2.21) with $S_T(\boldsymbol{\theta})$ defined by (2.26) and with $\mathbf{f}(\boldsymbol{\theta})$ given by (4.8); $\tilde{\boldsymbol{\theta}}$ is now the 2SLS/IV estimate of (4.8) and $\hat{\boldsymbol{\theta}}' = (\hat{\boldsymbol{\theta}}_1', \mathbf{0}_G')$ where $\boldsymbol{\theta}_1'$ is the 2SLS/IV estimate of $(\boldsymbol{\beta}', \boldsymbol{\gamma}')$ and $\mathbf{0}_G$ is a G-dimensional null vector. The asymptotic properties of the T_α^0 test will, however, not be affected if we use $\hat{\sigma}^2$ for $\dot{\sigma}^2$ when evaluating $S_T(\hat{\boldsymbol{\theta}})$ and $\tilde{\sigma}^2$ for $\dot{\sigma}^2$ when calculating $S_T(\tilde{\boldsymbol{\theta}})$. Breusch and Godfrey (1981) point out that this modified T_α^0 test can be implemented in the following way:

(i) Estimate the null model (4.6) by 2SLS/IV using the instrument matrix X. Regress the associated residual vector $\hat{\mathbf{u}}$ on X and obtain R_1^2, the coefficient of determination for this OLS regression.

(ii) Estimate the alternative model (4.8) using the same set of instruments X, obtain the associated residual vector $\tilde{\mathbf{u}}$ and calculate R_2^2, the coefficient of determination from the OLS regression of $\tilde{\mathbf{u}}$ on X.

(iii) Evaluate the test statistic as

$$\phi(G) = T(R_1^2 - R_2^2). \tag{4.9}$$

If only the null model (4.6) is estimated, then H_0 can be tested using the LM-type procedure provided by s of (2.25), with $\mathbf{f}(\boldsymbol{\theta})$, $\hat{\boldsymbol{\theta}}$, and $S_T(\boldsymbol{\theta})$ specified as in the discussion of the T^0 test.

Whichever of these three tests is employed, the test statistic will be asymptotically distributed as $\chi^2(G)$ under $H_0 : \alpha_1 = \cdots = \alpha_G = 0$ with significantly large values leading to the rejection of H_0. It should be noted that the instruments of $\boldsymbol{X}$ must be sufficient in number to permit the estimation of the alternative model (4.8) and cannot consist entirely of exogenous variables since otherwise $\boldsymbol{X}$ would be asymptotically uncorrelated with the $\hat{\mathbf{u}}_{-i}$ regressors of (4.8). These restrictions apply to all three tests discussed above.

6.4.2 Testing for heteroskedasticity

Comparatively little attention has been paid to the problems of estimating simultaneous-equation models when the error variance–covariance matrix is time varying, or to tests for the presence of such variation. Szroeter (1978) has considered the problem of testing for the constancy of the variance of the error of an individual structural equation, but assumes that there is a known ordering such that the T variances are nondecreasing (with at least one increase in the sequence) under the alternative. If it is believed that magnitudes of variances (and covariances) depend upon several variables (as in the single-equation analyses of Amemiya (1977) and Harvey (1976)) then, in general, such a known ordering will not exist. We shall, therefore, generalize the results of Subsection 6.3.2 and consider first tests for heteroskedasticity based upon results obtained by applying a full information estimator.

In Subsection 6.3.2, the disturbances u_t of a single equation were assumed to be heteroskedastic on the alternative hypothesis, with $u_t\,\mathrm{NID}(0, \sigma_t^2)$ and $\sigma_t^2 = \sigma^2 v(\mathbf{Q}_t'\boldsymbol{\alpha})$. It was noted that this formulation was sufficiently general to encompass the additive model $\sigma_t^2 = \sigma^2(1 + \mathbf{Q}_t'\boldsymbol{\alpha})$. A natural generalization of single-equation heteroskedasticity to the case of the linear simultaneous-equation model

$$\boldsymbol{B}\mathbf{y}_t + \boldsymbol{C}\mathbf{x}_t = \mathbf{u}_t = (u_{t1}, \ldots, u_{tm})', \qquad t = 1, \ldots, T \tag{4.4}$$

is to assume that on the alternative hypothesis

$$u_{ti} = (1 + \mathbf{Q}_t(i)'\boldsymbol{\alpha}_i)e_{ti}, \qquad i = 1, \ldots, M \tag{4.10}$$

where the $\mathbf{Q}_t(i)$ are finite-dimensional nonstochastic vectors with uniformly bounded elements and the $\mathbf{e}_t = (e_{t1}, \ldots, e_{tm})'$ are NID $(0, \boldsymbol{\Sigma})$. If the set of variables determining the heteroskedasticity is the same for each equation, then $\mathbf{Q}_t(i)$ can be replaced in (4.10) by $\mathbf{Q}_t$ which might, for example, be equal to $\mathbf{x}_t$. Equation (4.10) can be expressed in matrix–vector form as

$$\mathbf{u}_t = \boldsymbol{D}_t\mathbf{e}_t \tag{4.11}$$

where $\boldsymbol{D}_t = \mathrm{diag}\,\{1 + \mathbf{Q}_t(1)'\boldsymbol{\alpha}_1, \ldots, 1 + \mathbf{Q}_t(M)'\boldsymbol{\alpha}_m\}$.

The log likelihood corresponding to a single observation on the alternative model consisting of (4.4) and (4.11) is

$$l_t(\boldsymbol{\theta}) = \mathrm{const} + \tfrac{1}{2}\ln|\boldsymbol{\Sigma}^{-1}| + \ln|\boldsymbol{B}| - \ln|\boldsymbol{D}_t| - \tfrac{1}{2}\mathbf{e}_t(\boldsymbol{\theta})'\boldsymbol{\Sigma}^{-1}\mathbf{e}_t(\boldsymbol{\theta}) \tag{4.12}$$

with

$$\mathbf{e}_t(\boldsymbol{\theta}) = \boldsymbol{D}_t^{-1}(\boldsymbol{B}\mathbf{y}_t + \boldsymbol{C}\mathbf{x}_t), \tag{4.13}$$

where $\boldsymbol{\theta}' = (\boldsymbol{\theta}_1', \boldsymbol{\theta}_2')$, $\boldsymbol{\theta}_1$ contains the unrestricted elements of $\boldsymbol{B}$ and $\boldsymbol{C}$ and also the distinct elements of $\boldsymbol{\Sigma}^{-1}$, and $\boldsymbol{\theta}_2 = (\boldsymbol{\alpha}_1', \ldots, \boldsymbol{\alpha}_m')'$. The null hypothesis is then $H_0 : \boldsymbol{\theta}_2 = \mathbf{0}$.

The null hypothesis can now be tested using the LM statistic s^* defined by (2.4). In order to calculate s^* it is necessary to obtain $\partial l_t(\hat{\boldsymbol{\theta}})/\partial\boldsymbol{\theta}$ where $\hat{\boldsymbol{\theta}}' = (\hat{\boldsymbol{\theta}}_1', \mathbf{0}')$ and $\hat{\boldsymbol{\theta}}_1$ is the FIML (or an asymptotically equivalent) estimator of $\boldsymbol{\theta}_1$ on H_0. Since s^* is T times the (uncentred) R^2 statistic from an OLS regression with regressor matrix $\boldsymbol{W}(\hat{\boldsymbol{\theta}})$ whose tth row equals $(\partial l_t(\hat{\boldsymbol{\theta}})/\partial\boldsymbol{\theta})'$, any constants like -1 or $-\frac{1}{2}$ appearing in every element of a column of $\boldsymbol{W}(\hat{\boldsymbol{\theta}})$ can be ignored. Thus $\boldsymbol{W}(\hat{\boldsymbol{\theta}})$ can be constructed as follows.

(i) For columns of $\boldsymbol{W}(\hat{\boldsymbol{\theta}})$ corresponding to partial differentiation with respect to one of the distinct elements of $\boldsymbol{\Sigma}^{-1}$, use the appropriate elements of the matrix

$$\{\hat{u}_{ti}\hat{u}_{tj} - \hat{\sigma}_{ij}\} \tag{4.14}$$

where $\hat{u}_{ti}$ is a typical FIML residual, $\hat{\boldsymbol{\Sigma}} = \{\hat{\sigma}_{ij}\}$, and $\hat{\sigma}_{ij} = \{T^{-1}\Sigma_t \hat{u}_{ti}\hat{u}_{tj}\}$.

(ii) For columns of $\boldsymbol{W}(\hat{\boldsymbol{\theta}})$ corresponding to partial differentiation with respect to one of the unrestricted elements of $\boldsymbol{B}$, set $w_{tm}(\hat{\boldsymbol{\theta}})$ equal to the appropriate element of the matrix

$$\left\{\sum_{j=1}^{M} \hat{\sigma}^{ij}\hat{u}_{tj}\bar{y}_{tk}\right\} \tag{4.15}$$

where $\hat{\sigma}^{ij}$ is the (i,j)th element of $\hat{\boldsymbol{\Sigma}}^{-1}$ and $\bar{y}_{tk}$ is the kth element of $\bar{\mathbf{y}}_t = -\hat{\boldsymbol{B}}^{-1}\hat{\boldsymbol{C}}\mathbf{x}_t$, the solved reduced form after restricted FIML estimation.

(iii) For columns of $\boldsymbol{W}(\hat{\boldsymbol{\theta}})$ corresponding to partial differentiation, with respect to one of the unrestricted elements of $\boldsymbol{C}$, set $w_{tn}(\hat{\boldsymbol{\theta}})$ equal to the appropriate element of the matrix

$$\left\{\sum_{j=1}^{M} \hat{\sigma}^{ij}\hat{u}_{tj}x_{tk}\right\}. \tag{4.16}$$

(iv) Finally, the part of $\boldsymbol{W}(\hat{\boldsymbol{\theta}})$ corresponding to partial differentiation with respect to the elements of $\boldsymbol{\theta}_2$ can be calculated using

$$\partial l_t(\hat{\boldsymbol{\theta}})/\partial\boldsymbol{\alpha}_k = \mathbf{Q}_t(k)\sum_{j=1}^{M}(\hat{u}_{tk}\hat{\sigma}^{kj}\hat{u}_{tj} - 1). \tag{4.17}$$

The test statistic s^* can now be calculated from substituting the expressions (4.14)–(4.17) into (2.4). Under H_0, s^* is asymptotically distributed as a central χ^2 with degrees of freedom equal to the total number of elements in $\boldsymbol{\theta}_2$.

The above test is based on the exact alternative model $\mathbf{f}_t(\boldsymbol{\theta})$ defined by (4.4) and (4.10). The LEA model of type $\mathbf{f}_t^+(\boldsymbol{\theta})$ can be written as:

$$\boldsymbol{B}\mathbf{y}_t + \boldsymbol{C}\mathbf{x}_t + \boldsymbol{\Lambda}\mathbf{Q}_t^+ = \mathbf{e}_t \qquad \mathbf{e}_t \ \text{NID}(0, \boldsymbol{\Sigma}) \tag{4.18}$$

where $\mathbf{Q}_t^+$ is the $G \times 1$ vector

$$\mathbf{Q}_t^+ = \{\hat{u}_{t1}\mathbf{Q}_t(1)', \ldots, \hat{u}_{tM}\mathbf{Q}_t(M)'\}' \tag{4.19}$$

and $\boldsymbol{\Lambda}$ is the $M \times G$ matrix

$$\boldsymbol{\Lambda} = \begin{bmatrix} \boldsymbol{\alpha}_1' & \mathbf{0}_2' & \mathbf{0}_3' & \cdots & \mathbf{0}_M' \\ \mathbf{0}_1' & \boldsymbol{\alpha}_2' & \mathbf{0}_3' & \cdots & \mathbf{0}_M' \\ \vdots & \vdots & \vdots & & \vdots \\ \mathbf{0}_1' & \mathbf{0}_2' & \mathbf{0}_3' & & \boldsymbol{\alpha}_M' \end{bmatrix} \tag{4.20}$$

where $\mathbf{0}_i$ is a null vector with the same dimension as $\boldsymbol{\alpha}_i$ $(i = 1, 2, \ldots, M)$.

Although it is now possible to test for the presence of system heteroskedasticity directly from (4.18) by testing for the joint significance of the unrestricted elements of $\boldsymbol{\Lambda}$ using for example one of the IV analogues of the LM, LR, and W procedures, there are a number of complications which must be overcome first. One problem is the choice of IV's. A natural choice of IV's is to select only from the $\mathbf{x}_t$ and the $\mathbf{Q}_t(i)$, but the sample covariances between $\mathbf{Q}_t^+$ of (4.18) and such variables vanish as $T \to \infty$.[14] One way of overcoming this problem is to use the $\hat{u}_{ti}\mathbf{Q}_t(i)$ of $\mathbf{Q}_t^+$ as IV's. Provided the $\mathbf{Q}_t(i)$ variables are measured as deviations from sample averages, the $\hat{u}_{ti}\mathbf{Q}_t(i)$ would be valid instruments. Similar comments apply to the choice of the IV set when constructing heteroskedasticity tests for individual structural equations.

In the case of single structural equations there is a further problem arising from the assumptions which need to be made about the properties of the disturbances of the remaining $(M - 1)$ equations. In order to make use of standard large-sample theory, as for example in Szroeter (1978, Section 6), it is necessary to assume that the variance–covariance matrix of the reduced form errors is almost always constant or has changes generated by some underlying Pitman sequence which can therefore be neglected as $T \to \infty$.[15] Given the relationship between the disturbances of the structural form (4.4) and those of its reduced form, this assumption implies that the null hypothesis that the errors of the structural equation of interest are homoskedastic is being tested conditional upon the other structural equations having homoskedastic errors.[16] The reasonableness of this conditioning is open to question and presumably this approach would have to be abandoned as soon as the first significant test result was obtained. Having made the assumption that the $\boldsymbol{\alpha}_j$ are at most $O(T^{-1/2})$ for $j = 1, \ldots, M$ and $j \neq i$, however, asymptotic tests of $H_0^i\!:\boldsymbol{\alpha}_i = \mathbf{0}$ can be derived.

In fact valid large-sample tests of H_0^i can be obtained which are very similar to the expression given for the case of the single regression equation (3.27). These tests are of the significance of $\mathbf{p}_i = T^{-1/2}\boldsymbol{Q}_i'\mathbf{r}_i$ where the tth row of $\boldsymbol{Q}_i$ is $\mathbf{Q}_t(i)$ and $\mathbf{r}_i$ is a $T \times 1$ vector with typical element $\hat{u}_{ti}^2$.[17] The limiting distribution of $\mathbf{p}_i$ on H_0^i can be derived from Szroeter's (1978) results and is $N(0, 2\sigma_i^4 \lim T^{-1}(\boldsymbol{Q}_i'\boldsymbol{Q}_i))$ where $\sigma_i^2 = E(u_{ti}^2)$. The obvious test statistic is therefore

$$\xi_i = \mathbf{r}_i'\boldsymbol{Q}_i(\boldsymbol{Q}_i'\boldsymbol{Q}_i)^{-1}\boldsymbol{Q}_i'\mathbf{r}_i/2\hat{\sigma}_i^4 \tag{4.21}$$

where $\hat{\sigma}_i^2 = T^{-1}\Sigma_t\hat{u}_{ti}^2$. Under H_0^i, ξ_i is asymptotically distributed as a central χ^2 with degrees of freedom equal to the number of elements of $\boldsymbol{\alpha}_i$.

If the assumption that all other structural equations have homoskedastic errors is thought inappropriate, then an alternative test is to use a test procedure based on Neyman's (1959) $C(\boldsymbol{\alpha})$ principle; see Breusch and Pagan (1980) and Breusch and Godfrey (1981, Appendix A) for a discussion of $C(\boldsymbol{\alpha})$ tests. This test is based on the use of a single-equation estimator which is consistent on $H_0:\boldsymbol{\alpha}_1 = \mathbf{0}_1, \ldots, \boldsymbol{\alpha}_M = \mathbf{0}_M$ such as 2SLS, and is asymptotically equivalent to the LM test of H_0.

For the general problem examined in Section 6.2, the $C(\boldsymbol{\alpha})$ test of $H_0:\boldsymbol{\theta}_2 = \mathbf{0}$ can be written as

$$\begin{aligned} c = {} & (\partial L_T(\hat{\boldsymbol{\theta}})/\partial\boldsymbol{\theta}_1)'(\partial^2 L_T(\hat{\boldsymbol{\theta}})/\partial\boldsymbol{\theta}_1\,\partial\boldsymbol{\theta}_1')^{-1}(\partial L_T(\hat{\boldsymbol{\theta}})/\partial\boldsymbol{\theta}_1) \\ & - (\partial L_T(\hat{\boldsymbol{\theta}})/\partial\boldsymbol{\theta})'(\partial^2 L_T(\hat{\boldsymbol{\theta}})/\partial\boldsymbol{\theta}\,\partial\boldsymbol{\theta}')^{-1}(\partial L_T(\hat{\boldsymbol{\theta}})/\partial\boldsymbol{\theta}) \end{aligned} \tag{4.22}$$

where $\hat{\boldsymbol{\theta}}$ now denotes an estimator of $\boldsymbol{\theta}$ which is consistent but not necessarily asymptotically efficient on H_0. If $\hat{\boldsymbol{\theta}}$ maximizes $L_T(\boldsymbol{\theta})$ subject to $\boldsymbol{\theta}_2 = \mathbf{0}$ then (4.22) reduces to the LM expression (2.2). An asymptotically equivalent test statistic can be obtained using (2.3) and can be expressed as

$$c^* = T(R^2 - R_1^2) \tag{4.23}$$

where R^2 is the (uncentred) coefficient of determination for the OLS regression of $\mathbf{i}$ on $\boldsymbol{W}(\hat{\boldsymbol{\theta}})$ and R_1^2 is the corresponding statistic for the regression of $\mathbf{i}$ on $\boldsymbol{W}_1(\hat{\boldsymbol{\theta}})$, a $T \times (K - G)$ matrix with tth row $\partial l_t(\hat{\boldsymbol{\theta}})/\partial\boldsymbol{\theta}_1'$. In calculating (4.23), the expressions (4.14)–(4.17) are used but with $\hat{\boldsymbol{\theta}}$ now defined as above; the vector $\boldsymbol{\theta}_2 = (\boldsymbol{\alpha}_1', \ldots, \boldsymbol{\alpha}_M')'$ can be estimated once more by the null vector.

NOTES

[1] Gallant and Holly (1980) have considered the asymptotic properties of s and s^* in the context of hypothesis testing for systems of implicit nonlinear equations.

[2] The notation of (2.13) is slightly inaccurate but is less cumbersome than the correct expression which uses $\mathbf{f}_t((\boldsymbol{\theta}_1', \mathbf{0}'('))$.

[3] This example is provided to illustrate the nature of the problem associated with the Jacobian when using the model $\mathbf{f}_t^+(\boldsymbol{\theta})$. We are not arguing that this approach is the best way to test $\theta_2 = 0$ in (2.17).

[4] See also Sargan (1976) for an important unpublished paper dealing with testing for misspecification after IV estimation.

[5] See Breusch (1978a) and Godfrey (1978a) for detailed discussion of this result for the special case of a linear dynamic regression model with $p = q = 0$.
[6] The condition $\partial v(0)/\partial(\mathbf{Q}_i'\boldsymbol{\alpha}) \neq 0$ is required in order to avoid a problem of under-identification under the null hypothesis of homoskedasticity which would affect the LM, LR, and W tests.
[7] We use quote marks to indicate that the notation is that used in conventional text-book discussion of the classical regression model, rather than that specified in this paper.
[8] In relating (3.32) to the corresponding formulae of Breusch and Pagan (1980) and Godfrey (1978d), it should be recalled that the Q_{ti} of (3.32) are measured as deviations from sample means.
[9] White (1980) has shown that this '$T \times R^2$' form of the LM test for heteroskedasticity is applicable to quite general stochastic models.
[10] See Darroch and Silvey (1963) for a discussion of induced tests.
[11] Barten and Bronsard (1970) have discussed tests for structural stability in simultaneous-equation models.
[12] Breusch (1978b) derives this version of the test of the serial independence of the $\mathbf{u}_t$ using Hatanaka's (1976) results on two-step estimators.
[13] This direct LM test is very similar to the correct generalization of Durbin's (1970) *h*-test. Guilkey's (1975) derivation is, unfortunately, marred by errors and Maritz (1978) does not provide a complete correction.
[14] See Gallant (1977) for a discussion of such problems.
[15] See Szroeter (1978, assumption 6.1).
[16] Or, more strictly, that any heteroskedasticity in the errors of these other equations is negligible in large samples.
[17] As usual the variables of $\boldsymbol{Q}_i$ are measured as deviations from sample means implying that $\Sigma_t \mathbf{Q}_t(i) = \mathbf{0}$. Also '˜' denotes an IV/2SLS estimate.

REFERENCES

Amemiya, T. (1977). 'A note on a heteroskedastic model.' *Journal of Econometrics*, **6**, 365–370.

Amemiya, T. (1978). 'Corrigenda.' *Journal of Econometrics*, **8**, 265.

Barten, A. P., and Bronsard, L. S. (1970). 'Two-stage least squares estimators with shifts in the structural form.' *Econometrica*, **38**, 938–941.

Berndt, E. K., Hall, B. H., Hall, R. E., and Hausman, J. A. (1974). 'Estimation and inference in nonlinear structural models.' *Annals of Economic and Social Measurement*, **3**, 653–666.

Blattberg, R. C. (1973). 'Evaluation of the power of the Durbin–Watson statistic for non-first order serial correlation alternatives.' *Review of Economics and Statistics*, **55**, 508–515.

Box, G. E. P., and Pierce, D. A. (1970). 'Distribution of residual autocorrelations in autoregressive integrated moving average time series models.' *Journal of the American Statistical Association*, **65**, 1509–1526.

Breusch, T. S. (1978a). 'Testing for autocorrelation in dynamic linear models.' *Australian Economic Papers*, **17**, 334–355.

Breusch, T. S. (1978b). *Some aspects of statistical inference for econometrics.* Unpublished Ph.D. Thesis, ANU, Canberra.

Breusch, T. S., and Godfrey, L. G. (1981). 'A review of recent work on testing for autocorrelation in dynamic economic models.' In D. Currie, R. Nobay and D. Peel (Eds.), *Macroeconomic Analysis*, Croom Helm, London.

Breusch, T. S., and Pagan, A. R. (1980). 'The Lagrange multiplier test and its application to model specification in econometrics.' *Review of Economic Studies*, **47**, 239–254.

Carr, J. (1972). 'A suggestion for the treatment of serial correlation: A case in point.' *Canadian Journal of Economics*, **5**, 301–306.

Darroch, J. N., and Silvey, S. D. (1963). 'On testing more than one hypothesis.' *Annals of Mathematical Statistics*, **34**, 555–567.

Durbin, J. (1970). 'Testing for serial correlation in least squares regression when some of the regressors are lagged dependent variables.' *Econometrica*, **38**, 410–421.

Engle, R. F. (1978). 'The Lagrange multiplier test as a regression diagnostic.' University of California, San Diego, Discussion Paper No. 78–6.

Engle, R. F. (1980). 'A general approach to the construction of model diagnostics based upon the Lagrange multiplier principle.' University of California, San Diego, Discussion Paper No. 80.

Frydman, R. (1980). 'A proof of the consistency of maximum likelihood estimators of nonlinear regression models with autocorrelated errors.' *Econometrica*, **48**, 853–860.

Gallant, A. R. (1977). 'Three-stage least-squares estimation for a system of simultaneous, nonlinear, implicit equations.' *Journal of Econometrics*, **5**, 71–88.

Gallant, A. R., and Jorgenson, D. W. (1979). 'Statistical inference for a system of simultaneous non-linear implicit equations in the context of instrumental variable estimation.' *Journal of Econometrics*, **11**, 275–302.

Gallant, A. R., and Holly, A. (1980). 'Statistical inference in an implicit, nonlinear, simultaneous equation model in the context of maximum likelihood estimation.' *Econometrica*, **48**, 697–720.

Godfrey, L. G. (1978a). 'Testing against general autoregressive and moving average error models when the regressors include lagged dependent variables.' *Econometrica*, **46**, 1293–1302.

Godfrey, L. G. (1978b). 'Testing for higher order serial correlation in regression equations when the regressors include lagged dependent variables.' *Econometrica*, **46**, 1303–1310.

Godfrey, L. G. (1978c). 'Some tests for specification error.' University of York, unpublished paper.

Godfrey, L. G. (1978d). 'Testing for multiplicative heteroskedasticity.' *Journal of Econometrics*, **8**, 227–236.

Godfrey, L. G. (1981). 'On the invariance of the Lagrange multiplier test with respect to certain changes in the alternative hypothesis.' *Econometrica*, **49**, 1443–1455.

Godfrey, L. G., and Wickens, M. R. (1981). 'Testing linear and log-linear regression models for functional form.' *Review of Economic Studies*, **XLVIII**, 487–496.

Guilkey, D. K. (1975). 'A test for the presence of first-order vector autoregressive errors when lagged endogenous variables are present.' *Econometrica*, **43**, 711–718.

Harvey, A. C. (1976). 'Estimating regression models with multiplicative heteroskedasticity.' *Econometrica*, **44**, 461–466.

Harvey, A. C. (1977). 'Erratum.' *Econometrica*, **45**, 1302.

Hatanaka, M. (1976). 'Several efficient two-step estimators for the dynamic simultaneous equations model with autoregressive disturbances.' *Journal of Econometrics*, **4**, 189–204.

Hendry, D. F. (1976). 'The structure of simultaneous equations estimators.' *Journal of Econometrics*, **4**, 51–88.

Jorgenson, D. W., and Laffont, J.-J. (1974). 'Efficient estimation of non-linear simultaneous equations with additive disturbances.' *Annals of Economic and Social Measurement*, **3**, 615–640.

Maritz, A. (1978). 'A note of correction to Guilkey's test for serial independence in simultaneous equations models.' *Econometrica*, **46**, 471.

Neyman, J. (1959). 'Optimal asymptotic tests of composite statistical hypotheses.' In U.

Grenander (Ed.), *Probability and Statistics, The Harald Cramer Volume*, Wiley, New York.
Ramsey, J. B. (1969). 'Tests for specification errors in classical least-squares regression analysis.' *Journal of the Royal Statistical Society, Series B*, **31**, 350–371.
Reinsel, G. (1979a). 'Maximum likelihood estimation of stochastic linear difference equations with autoregressive moving average errors.' *Econometrica*, **47**, 129–152.
Reinsel, G. (1979b). 'FIML estimation of the dynamic simultaneous equations model with ARMA disturbances.' *Journal of Econometrics*, **9**, 263–281.
Sargan, J. D. (1976). 'Testing for misspecification after estimating using instrumental variables.' London School of Economics, unpublished paper.
Silvey, S. D. (1959). 'The Lagrange multiplier test.' *Annals of Mathematical Statistics*, **30**, 389–407.
Szroeter, J. (1978). 'A class of parametric tests for heteroskedasticity in linear econometric models.' *Econometrica*, **46**, 1311–1328.
Thursby, J. G., and Schmidt, P. (1977). 'Some properties of tests for specification error in a linear regression model.' *Journal of the American Statistical Association*, **72**, 635–641.
White, H. (1980). 'A heteroskedasticity-consistent covariance-matrix estimator and a direct test for heteroskedasticity.' *Econometrica*, **48**, 817–838.

Discussion

P. K. SCHOENFELD
University of Bonn

Professors Godfrey and Wickens are to be congratulated on their fine contribution to the theory of large-sample tests in econometrics. The main idea they dwell upon is the concept of locally equivalent alternative models (LEA's). This concept has many interesting aspects and calls for future research.

Let me briefly restate the idea of the LEA approach for ease of reference. Suppose we are given a (possibly nonlinear) model

$$\mathbf{f}(\mathbf{x};\bar{\boldsymbol{\theta}}_1,\boldsymbol{\theta}_2) = \boldsymbol{\varepsilon},$$

$\mathbf{x}$ = the data, $\boldsymbol{\varepsilon} = \text{IID}\,N(0,\boldsymbol{\Sigma})$ error, $\boldsymbol{\theta}_1 = (\bar{\boldsymbol{\theta}}_1, \text{vec}\,\boldsymbol{\Sigma})$, leading to a logarithmic likelihood $L_T(\boldsymbol{\theta}) = \sum_{t=1}^{T} l_t(\boldsymbol{\theta})$, $\boldsymbol{\theta} = (\boldsymbol{\theta}_1, \boldsymbol{\theta}_2)$. The misspecification is assumed to consist in erroneously adopting the null hypothesis $H_2\colon\boldsymbol{\theta}_2 = \mathbf{0}$. Now $\mathbf{f}$ can be expanded with respect to $\boldsymbol{\theta}_2$ around the point $(\boldsymbol{\theta}_1, \mathbf{0})$ according to Taylor's formula. Neglecting nonlinear remainders this yields another model $\mathbf{f}^* = \boldsymbol{\varepsilon}$. Moreover, if $\boldsymbol{\theta}_1$ in $\mathbf{f}^*$ is replaced by its ML estimate $\hat{\boldsymbol{\theta}}_1$ under H_0 still another model $\mathbf{f}^+ = \boldsymbol{\varepsilon}$ results. Let s, s^*, and s^+, respectively, denote the Lagrange multiplier statistics corresponding to $\mathbf{f}$, $\mathbf{f}^*$, and $\mathbf{f}^+$, respectively. Under regularity assumptions the statistics s^* and s^+ are valid approximations to s in the sense that under the null all three statistics have the same limiting χ^2 distribution and under a Pitman sequence of local alternatives $H_T\colon\boldsymbol{\theta}_2 = T^{-1/2}\boldsymbol{\delta}_T$, $\lim \boldsymbol{\delta}_T = \boldsymbol{\delta} \neq \mathbf{0}$, $\boldsymbol{\delta}$

fixed, they have the same limiting noncentral χ^2 distribution with noncentrality parameter $\boldsymbol{\delta}'V^{-1}\boldsymbol{\delta}$ where V is the limiting variance–covariance of the unrestricted ML estimator $\tilde{\boldsymbol{\theta}}_2$.

There are obvious merits to the LEA approach. Firstly, the LEA approach is a substantial step towards achieving a classification of econometric large-sample tests by showing that they are approximations to the LM test. The LEA approach is thus in the spirit of the major stream of econometric research that has been devoted to demonstrating that most econometric estimators are just approximations to the ML estimator.[1] The paper has many results of this kind, in particular on tests for serial correlation and for heteroskedasticity. As, under the null, s^* can be given an appealing interpretation as a (noncentral) coefficient of determination all these tests amount to checking the significance of a group of regressors in a suitable regression model which is linear with respect to $\boldsymbol{\theta}_2$. This yields a unified framework for specification tests in terms of a formal F test.

Secondly, the approximate LM test based on a LEA has the attractive feature that different sources of specification error can be tested jointly. This avoids the problem of finding the appropriate critical points in a sequence of induced tests for the different kinds of misspecification. Different types of misspecification can often be lumped together by jointly extending the original model to a super-model. For example, serial correlation, heteroskedasticity, and omitted variables can be jointly allowed for. Whatever the degree of nonlinearity and of interaction between different kinds of misspecification incorporated into the super-model might be the LEA approach is likely to end up with a regression that is linear in the additional regressors, reflecting the various sources of misspecification (provided the components of $\boldsymbol{\theta}$ are not functionally dependent on each other). It is quite an achievement that virtually any mix of various kinds of misspecification can be tested in a single step. In practice, of course, the joint test might not mean too much because it amounts to a mere significance test. If, upon rejection of the null, one is eager to trace out the particular kind of misspecification causing the trouble one is back with induced tests.

Thirdly, a very useful result, in my opinion, is that the Gallant and Jorgenson (1979) analogue to the LR test based on the Jorgenson and Laffont (1974)[2] nonlinear 3SLS estimator can formally be put into either the s, s^*, or s^+ versions of the LM test analogue. Although some care has to be taken in deriving the asymptotic distributions of these statistics and in proving their asymptotic equivalence within the framework of Quasi-ML estimation it is clear intuitively that, in view of the structural similarity between the GLS objective function and the kernel of the likelihood L_T on the one hand and the similarity in the construction of the ML and the NL-3SLS estimators on the other hand, results analogous to the LEA ML case will obtain for the LEA Quasi-ML case as well. Thus the normality assumption for $\boldsymbol{\varepsilon}$ can be weakened substantially.

Nevertheless, I envisage a basic conceptual drawback in the LEA approach. I am presently not concerned with the problem of non-nested hypotheses which cannot be dealt with adequately in the present set-up although I believe—contrary to an earlier statement—that non-nested conflicting models are an important issue to the econometrician. My present subject is the power of the LEA LM tests which on theoretical prior grounds I suspect to be fairly low in general. It has been mentioned earlier that the alternatives H_T are chosen to form a Pitman sequence of local alternatives. Technically, local alternatives can be admitted only in order to keep the remainders in Taylor's formula down to negligibility. From the point of view of constructing a reasonable test the choice of a Pitman sequence is justifiable. Hopefully a good test would be able to discriminate between hypotheses that become arbitrarily close together provided that the sample size increases indefinitely. If the Pitman choice leads to different distributions under the null and under the alternatives, we know that the distance between H_0 and H_T may decrease as fast as $\sqrt{T}$. This is a desirable local property of the test.

It is a different matter, however, to use local alternatives on $\boldsymbol{\theta}_2$ in the approximation of the underlying model $\mathbf{f} = \boldsymbol{\varepsilon}$. Thus the models $\mathbf{f}^*$ and $\mathbf{f}^+$ are valid approximations to the original model $\mathbf{f}$ only in a small neighbourhood of $\boldsymbol{\theta}_2 = \mathbf{0}$ in the parameter space. Only for an indefinitely shrinking sequence of neighbourhoods of $\boldsymbol{\theta}_2 = \mathbf{0}$ do the tests based on s, s^* and s^+ become equivalent. Their equivalence basically stems from the fact that locally all models are linear. The LEA approach therefore is fully valid only in the situation that the specification error decreases and eventually vanishes as the sample size increases indefinitely. The authors do not provide a justification why we would be entitled to concentrate on local alternatives in the parameter space. In my opinion, a specification error typically would lead to an alternative model which remains at some 'finite distance' from the original model even asymptotically. But then the performance of the LM test s and the asymptotic equivalences established in the paper do not necessarily imply much for the actual power performance of the LEA tests s^* and s^+. Thus a low power of LEA tests is to be suspected, in general. This conclusion is backed by the results of the paper that various different models have the same LEA. For example, an LEA would not discriminate between an MA and an AR process and between certain additive and multiplicative schemes of heteroskedasticity. The LEA of a sum and a product is the same.

To illustrate the problem consider a special case of the heteroskedastic scheme in formula (3.19). Let $g_t(\overline{\boldsymbol{\theta}}_1) = y_t - \boldsymbol{\beta}'\mathbf{x}_t = u_t$ with $\text{var}(u_t) = \sigma^2(1 + \alpha t)$, $\sigma^2 = \text{var}(\varepsilon_t)$. Then the correct model is

$$(1 + \alpha t)^{-1/2} y_t = (1 + \alpha t)^{-1/2} \boldsymbol{\beta}'\mathbf{x}_t + \varepsilon_t$$

and the LEA model $f^* = \varepsilon$ is

$$y_t = \boldsymbol{\beta}'\mathbf{x}_t + \tfrac{1}{2}\alpha(t \,.\, u_t) + \varepsilon_t.$$

Although the LEA is a valid approximation to the correct model for small $|\alpha|$ both models look quite different for $|\alpha|$ not small. Clearly the LEA does provide a test for the hypothesis $H_0: \alpha = 0$ since heteroskedasticity as specified here should be reflected by the regressor $t \,.\, u_t$. However, one would be inclined to believe that the power of a test built up explicitly on the precise nonlinear form of the correct model would be much better than the power of the LEA test.

The conjectured low power of the LEA tests is just the other side of what appears as the strength of the LEA approach. Often we are confident about the general nature of the misspecification (its heteroskedasticity, say). But we rarely know the particular scheme for the specification error. It then is an advantage that, for example, the s^+ statistic is invariant under a vast class of alternative schemes. The trade-off between a test that reacts on a 'broad' alternative and a test that takes into account the specific form of the alternative presumably is in terms of the power function.

A general lesson to be learnt from this is that apparently innocent substitutions in asymptotic expressions could make up sizable effects in the performance of the test statistics (of course *not* in their local asymptotic behaviour). For instance, under the null we have

$$\frac{1}{T}\left(\sum_t \frac{\partial l_t(\hat{\boldsymbol{\theta}})}{\partial \boldsymbol{\theta}}\right)\left(\sum_t \frac{\partial l_t(\hat{\boldsymbol{\theta}})}{\partial \boldsymbol{\theta}}\right)' \underset{\substack{P \\ \text{or a.s.}}}{\approx} -\left(\frac{1}{T}\sum_t \frac{\partial^2 l_t(\hat{\boldsymbol{\theta}})}{\partial \boldsymbol{\theta}\,\partial \boldsymbol{\theta}'}\right)$$

in large samples where $\hat{\boldsymbol{\theta}}$ is the restricted ML estimator. Thus one would not hesitate to replace the right-hand side expression which appears in the LM statistic s by the much simpler left-hand side expression. The left-hand side expression, however, is precisely the variance–covariance used in s^*, i.e. it results from approximating the correct model locally. If this approximation is bad the performance of the test might become sizably worse under this substitution.

In the final part of his presentation Professor Wickens reported on some Monte Carlo experiments on the power performance of the test statistics involved. Professor Godfrey has some more results in another paper.[3] These results indicate that the generally conjectured low power of the LEA LM tests does not always occur. At least the LM test does not seem to be inferior to the LR test which incorporates an ML estimate under the alternative hypothesis. This might be due to the fact that the properties of the LR test that can be ascertained are also local asymptotic only. The authors' results are not yet fully conclusive. Thus the analysis of the power of LEA tests would seem to be an important field of future research. Hopefully occasional reports in the literature on the low power of certain test variants will become explainable if those tests are identified as LEA approximations and the nature of the approximation involved is understood. The possible improvement over the LEA if the approximation is performed up to quadratic terms would thus be an interesting subject of study.

Let me add a brief remark on the specification of σ_t^2 in (3.18). As is stated in the paper the variables $\mathbf{Q}_t$ should be chosen such that their sum over the sample is $\mathbf{0}$. But then the heteroskedastic pattern depends on T. Thus we have u_{tT} rather than

$\mathbf{u}_t$ which unpleasantly complicates the asymptotics of maximum likelihood. The authors might wish to reconsider the choice of the $\mathbf{Q}_t$'s.

The paper is focused on the local asymptotics whereas my criticism has mostly been in terms of what happens in finite, say medium-size, samples and what happens under nonlocal alternatives. Thus for finite samples there is a difference between s^* and s^+ due to the Jacobian in L_t^+. This correction term could have some influence on the power of the test in finite samples. I suggest that this issue be studied in more detail. In the same spirit one could consider $\boldsymbol{\theta}_1$ as a nuisance parameter and concentrate L_T with respect to $\boldsymbol{\theta}_1$. If $\boldsymbol{\theta}_1$ is replaced in $\mathbf{f}$ by its conditional ML estimate $\tilde{\boldsymbol{\theta}}_1(\mathbf{x}, \boldsymbol{\theta}_2)$ the derivative $\partial \mathbf{f}/\partial \boldsymbol{\theta}_2$ required in passing to $\mathbf{f}^*$ would be modified. Possibly this modification also could improve the performance of the LEA LM test.

NOTES

[1] See, for example, David Hendry's paper in the *Journal of Econometrics*, 1976, cited among the references of the paper by Godfrey and Wickens.
[2] Also for these papers see the list of references in the papers by Godfrey and Wickens.
[3] See Godfrey, L. G. (1980). 'On the invariance of the Lagrange multiplier test with respect to certain changes in the alternative hypothesis.' University of York, discussion paper.

Evaluating the Reliability of Macro-economic Models
Edited by G. C. Chow and P. Corsi

CHAPTER 7

Exogeneity, Causality, and Structural Invariance in Econometric Modelling

J.-F. RICHARD[1]
Center for Operations Research & Econometrics, Louvain

7.1 INTRODUCTION

In spite of the importance of the concept of exogeneity in econometric modelling, most definitions which are found in the literature (and especially in econometric textbooks) are elusive. They are often formulated either for limited classes of models (typically linear and Gaussian models) or in terms of unobservable disturbances from relationships which contain unknown parameters. Also it is generally unclear what is entailed for inference on modelling by the discovery that a variable is exogenous on any given definition.

The object of our current research is not only to provide clarification on these critical issues but, more importantly, to develop accordingly concepts which are useful for inference and modelling. Definitions are proposed for *weak* and *strong* exogeneity in terms of the distribution of the *observable* variables: essentially, a variable z_t in a model is defined to be weakly exogenous for a set of parameters ψ if inference on ψ conditional on z_t involves no loss of sample information. This definition builds on the important paper by Koopmans (1950) using concepts of statistical inference which are developed, for example, in Barndorff-Nielsen (1978), Florens and Mouchart (1980), and Richard (1980). If in addition to being weakly exogenous, z_t is not caused—in the sense of Granger (1969)—by the endogenous variables in the system, then z_t is defined to be strongly exogenous.

It is argued below that the concepts of weak and strong exogeneity are useful in that they put the emphasis on some of the key aspects of econometric modelling: distribution of the *observable* variables, parameters of interest, structurality, conditionalization, forecasting, ...

7.2 NOTATION AND DEFINITIONS

Let $\mathbf{x}_t \in \mathbb{R}^n$ be a vector of observable random variables generated at time t on which T observations are available. Let X_t^1 denote the $t \times n$ matrix

$$X_t^1 = (\mathbf{x}_1 \quad \dots \quad \mathbf{x}_t)'. \tag{1}$$

The analysis is conducted conditionally on X_0, the matrix of initial conditions. Let X_{t-1} represent the matrix

$$X_{t-1} = \begin{pmatrix} X_0 \\ X_{t-1}^1 \end{pmatrix}. \tag{2}$$

The process generating the T observations is represented by the joint data density $D(X_T^1 | X_0, \boldsymbol{\theta})$ where $\boldsymbol{\theta} \in \Theta$ is a vector of unknown parameters. The likelihood function of $\boldsymbol{\theta}$, given X_0, is denoted by $L^0(\boldsymbol{\theta}; X_T^1)$. Since most econometric models describe how the observations are generated at time t, conditionally on the past, the joint data density is factorized as

$$D(X_T^1 | X_0, \boldsymbol{\theta}) = \prod_{t=1}^{T} D(\mathbf{x}_t | X_{t-1}, \boldsymbol{\theta}). \tag{3}$$

Often the model user is interested only in some functions of $\boldsymbol{\theta}$, say

$$f: \boldsymbol{\theta} \to \psi; \qquad \boldsymbol{\theta} \rightharpoondown \psi = f(\boldsymbol{\theta}). \tag{4}$$

These functions are denoted *parameters of interest*. Parameters may be of interest, for example, because they are related to economic theories. More generally parameters which remain constant in changing environments, i.e. which are *structurally invariant*, are obviously of interest in particular for forecasting or control.

Since data sets often consist of a relatively small number of observations on a large number of variables, the analysis must focus on a subset of the variables to be manageable. Let us, therefore, partition $\mathbf{x}_t$ into

$$\mathbf{x}_t = \begin{pmatrix} \mathbf{y}_t \\ \mathbf{z}_t \end{pmatrix} \qquad \mathbf{x}_t \in \mathbb{R}^p,\ \mathbf{z}_t \in \mathbb{R}^q, \quad p + q = n, \tag{5}$$

where $\mathbf{y}_t$ is the vector of variables to be modelled and $\mathbf{z}_t$ the vector of variables to be treated as 'exogenous' for the purpose of the analysis. The matrices X_0, X_t^1, and X_{t-1} are partitioned conformably with $\mathbf{x}_t$

$$X_0 = (Y_0 \quad Z_0) \qquad X_t^1 = (Y_t^1 \quad Z_t^1) \qquad X_{t-1} = (Y_{t-1} \quad Z_{t-1}). \tag{6}$$

The joint density $D(\mathbf{x}_t | X_{t-1}, .)$ is then factorized into a conditional density $D(\mathbf{y}_t | \mathbf{z}_t, X_{t-1}, .)$ supposedly describing the economy under consideration and a marginal density $D(\mathbf{z}_t | X_{t-1}, .)$ characterizing the exogenous process. The object of exogeneity assumptions is precisely to provide conditions under which the marginal density of $\mathbf{z}_t$ does not need to be specified. Such factorizations of the model usually entail reparametrizations. Let, therefore, $\boldsymbol{\lambda}_1$ denote the parameters of the conditional model, $\boldsymbol{\lambda}_2$ those of the marginal model, and Λ_i the set of admissible values of $\boldsymbol{\lambda}_i$. The factorization under consideration may then be written as

$$D(\mathbf{x}_t|X_{t-1}, \boldsymbol{\lambda}) = D(\mathbf{y}_t|\mathbf{z}_t, X_{t-1}, \boldsymbol{\lambda}_1) \,.\, D(\mathbf{z}_t|X_{t-1}, \boldsymbol{\lambda}_2), \qquad t{:}1 \rightarrow T. \tag{7}$$

Let us first restate in this framework the definition of noncausality by Granger (1969).

Definition 2.1 Y_{t-1}^1 *does not Granger cause* $\mathbf{z}_t$ with respect to X_{t-1} if and only if

$$\mathrm{D}(\mathbf{z}_t|X_{t-1}, \boldsymbol{\lambda}_2) \equiv D(\mathbf{z}_t|Z_{t-1}, Y_0, \boldsymbol{\lambda}_2) \qquad t{:}1 \rightarrow T. \tag{8}$$

This definition often takes the weaker form of an assumption of *linear* independence between $\mathbf{z}_t$ and Y_{t-1}^1, conditionally on (Y_0, Z_{t-1}). Also, in contrast with Granger's population definition, Definition 2.1 applies only to the *finite* sample X_T^1 and is *conditional* on X_0. So are the other definitions given below. Our analysis could also be conducted marginally with respect to X_0 (whether X_0 is treated as an unobservable random variable generated by the process itself or as an unknown parameter under a suitable prior density). Conditions such as (8) might then no longer apply to the first r observations, where r denotes the order of the process under study. On the other hand these r first observations would be lost anyway for inference if they were used as initial conditions under which the analysis of the remaining observations would then be conducted. How to handle initial conditions is, therefore, a practical matter to be solved for each individual case taking into account such conflicting aims as numerical tractability, efficiency, and also, obviously, robustness. For the purpose of exposition, we have found it convenient to treat X_0 as given, as most practitioners do anyway.

Also, as discussed by Zellner (1979), it is unfortunate that the wording 'noncausality' is used in connection with Definition 2.1 (it is, however, current practice and we follow it here for ease of reference). More appropriately one might refer to the *self-predictability* of the $\mathbf{z}$'s (conditionally on X_0), since, when (8) holds over the sample period, the joint data density $D(X_T^1|X_0, \boldsymbol{\lambda})$ factorizes as in

$$D(X_T^1|X_0, \boldsymbol{\lambda}) = D(Y_T^1|Z_T^1, X_0, \boldsymbol{\lambda}_1) \,.\, D(Z_T^1|X_0, \boldsymbol{\lambda}_2). \tag{9}$$

The concept of self-predictability offers the advantage that, conceptually at least, exogeneity and causality can be discussed without reference to each other. In practice, however, exogeneity is often one of the essential components of causality in the sense of Zellner's 'predictability according to a law'.

It is important to realize that the concept of Granger noncausality is not oriented *per se* towards inference on specific parameters of interest mainly for two reasons:

(a) Definition 2.1 does not entail that the parameters of interest $\boldsymbol{\psi}$ are functions of $\boldsymbol{\lambda}_1$ (or $\boldsymbol{\lambda}_2$) only.

(b) If we except the special case of linear, Gaussian, and just identified simultaneous-equation models, $\boldsymbol{\lambda}_1$ and $\boldsymbol{\lambda}_2$ are generally subject to cross-restrictions so that independent estimation of $\boldsymbol{\lambda}_1$ and $\boldsymbol{\lambda}_2$ typically entails a loss of efficiency.

These two conditions are precisely those which are covered by the concept of weak exogeneity whose objective, in contrast with the concept of Granger noncausality, is to validate conducting inference on $\boldsymbol{\psi}$ conditionally on $\mathbf{z}_t$.

Definition 2.2 $\mathbf{z}_t$ is *weakly exogenous* over the sample period for $\boldsymbol{\psi}$ if and only if there exists a reparametrization $\boldsymbol{\lambda} = (\boldsymbol{\lambda}_1, \boldsymbol{\lambda}_2)$ such that under (7)

(i) $\boldsymbol{\psi}$ is a function of $\boldsymbol{\lambda}_1$ only[2]

(ii) $\boldsymbol{\lambda}_1$ and $\boldsymbol{\lambda}_2$ are variation free, i.e. $(\boldsymbol{\lambda}_1, \boldsymbol{\lambda}_2) \in \Lambda_1 \times \Lambda_2$.

If $\mathbf{z}_t$ is weakly exogenous (over the sample period) for $\boldsymbol{\psi}$, then $L^0(\boldsymbol{\lambda}; \boldsymbol{X}_T^1)$ factorizes as in

$$L^0(\boldsymbol{\lambda}; \boldsymbol{X}_T^1) = L_1^0(\boldsymbol{\lambda}_1 . \boldsymbol{X}_T^1) . L_2^0(\boldsymbol{\lambda}_2; \boldsymbol{X}_T^1) \tag{10}$$

where

$$L_1^0(\boldsymbol{\lambda}_1; \boldsymbol{X}_T^1) = \prod_{t=1}^{T} D(\mathbf{y}_t | \mathbf{z}_t, \boldsymbol{X}_{t-1}, \boldsymbol{\lambda}_1) \tag{11}$$

$$L_2^0(\boldsymbol{\lambda}_2; \boldsymbol{X}_T^1) = \prod_{t=1}^{T} D(\mathbf{z}_t | \boldsymbol{X}_{t-1}, \boldsymbol{\lambda}_2) \tag{12}$$

and the two factors in (10) can be analysed independently of each other. Therefore, if it is known that $\mathbf{z}_t$ is weakly exogenous for $\boldsymbol{\psi}$, then the marginal process $D(\mathbf{z}_t | \boldsymbol{X}_{t-1}, \boldsymbol{\lambda}_2)$ does not need to be specified. Tests of the weak exogeneity of $\mathbf{z}_t$ are discussed below.

Definition 2.3 $\mathbf{z}_t$ is *strongly exogenous* over the sample period for $\boldsymbol{\psi}$ if and only if it is weakly exogenous for $\boldsymbol{\psi}$ and in addition $\boldsymbol{Y}_{t-1}^1$ does not Granger cause $\mathbf{z}_t$ over the sample period.

7.3 COMMENTS

(a) In a non-Bayesian framework, the concept of weak exogeneity provides a sufficient condition for conducting inference on $\boldsymbol{\psi}$ conditionally on $\mathbf{z}_t$ without loss of relevant sample information. In a Bayesian framework, the issue is whether or not the posterior density of $\boldsymbol{\psi}$, based on the joint model $D(\mathbf{x}_t | \boldsymbol{X}_{t-1}, .)$ coincides with the posterior density of $\boldsymbol{\psi}$ based solely on the conditional model $D(\mathbf{y}_t | \mathbf{z}_t, \boldsymbol{X}_{t-1}, .)$. This is obviously the case if $\mathbf{z}_t$ is weakly exogenous for $\boldsymbol{\psi}$ and if, in addition, $\boldsymbol{\lambda}_1$ and $\boldsymbol{\lambda}_2$—and, therefore, $\boldsymbol{\psi}$ and $\boldsymbol{\lambda}_2$—are *a priori* independent. However, as discussed in Florens and Mouchart (1980), these conditions are not necessary since, even when $\mathbf{z}_t$ is not weakly exogenous for $\boldsymbol{\psi}$, the prior density on $\boldsymbol{\lambda}$

may be such that inference on $\boldsymbol{\psi}$ may still be conducted conditionally on $\mathbf{z}_t$ without loss of information.

(b) The definitions of weak and strong exogeneity are formulated in terms of the distribution of the observable variables. This does not preclude formulating theories in terms of unobservables (expectations, disturbances, ...) but these should be integrated out first in order to apply the definitions in Section 7.2. There are two reasons for doing so:

— Most definitions which are found in the literature (and especially in textbooks) are formulated for limited classes of models, typically linear and Gaussian simultaneous-equation models. In contrast the concept of weak exogeneity is applicable to a wide range of statistical models.

— Definitions which are formulated in terms of unobservables are often ambiguous. Consider, for example, the traditional single-equation model

$$\mathbf{y} = X\boldsymbol{\beta} + \mathbf{u} \tag{13}$$

where the notation is that found in most textbooks. The condition that the covariances between X and $\mathbf{u}$ are zero may either be viewed as a *definition* of $\boldsymbol{\beta}$, in which case it is obviously not testable, or as an over-identifying *constraint* on $\boldsymbol{\beta}$, provided $\boldsymbol{\beta}$ is unambiguously defined elsewhere. Much of the ambiguity in the literature arises from the fact that these two fundamentally different situations are not always distinguished from each other. In contrast, a reasoning which focuses on the distribution of the observables calls for defining $\boldsymbol{\beta}$ in terms of this distribution and automatically removes such ambiguities. (See the discussion in Geweke (1978) and Richard (1980).)

(c) As already discussed in Section 7.2, the condition that Y_{t-1}^{1} does not cause $\mathbf{z}_t$ is neither sufficient nor necessary for the weak exogeneity of $\mathbf{z}_t$ for $\boldsymbol{\psi}$ and the two concepts serve essentially different purposes. In fact, if $\mathbf{z}_t$ is weakly exogenous for $\boldsymbol{\psi}$, then the condition that Y_{t-1}^{1} does not cause $\mathbf{z}_t$ is irrelevant (for inference on $\boldsymbol{\psi}$) since it then affects only the parameters of the marginal model $D(\mathbf{z}_t|Z_{t-1}, X_0, .)$. Evidently, if one wishes to construct parametric tests of the weak exogeneity of $\mathbf{z}_t$, as discussed in Section 7.5, then noncausality restrictions which are typically overidentifying restrictions may usefully be taken into account to increase the efficiency of the test procedure.

(d) The concept of weak exogeneity is not directly related to validating specific estimation method and later selection of an inappropriate estimator may produce inefficiency even though weak exogeneity conditions are fulfilled.

(e) Econometric models are often used for predictions or simulations of control policies rather than for inference on a well-defined set of parameters of interest. The question of whether or not predictions which are run conditionally on *preassigned* values of the exogenous variables make sense then becomes essential. In order to validate such conditional predictions, one has to assume *jointly* that:

(i) $\mathbf{z}_t$ is weakly exogenous for a parameter vector $\boldsymbol{\psi}$ which implicitly consists of the parameters of the conditional model $D(\mathbf{y}_t|\mathbf{z}_t, X_{t-1}, \cdot)$ and (ii) that $\mathbf{z}_t$ is self-predictable over the forecast horizon, i.e. that $\mathbf{z}_t$ is *strongly* exogenous for the parameters of the conditional model. Evidently, even under such conditions, one may still have to generate forecasts for the exogenous variables, but, at least, these forecasts may be generated independently of those of the endogenous variables under consideration. The simulation of control policies raises an additional problem of parameter constancy which is discussed below.

Further comments together with examples may be found in Engle *et al.* (1980).

7.4 STRUCTURAL INVARIANCE AND EXOGENEITY

In worlds where parameters may shift, it becomes essential to identify parameters which are *structurally invariant* with respect to a class of parameter changes, denoted below *interventions*, in the sense that they remain constant under these interventions. Such parameters are obviously of interest to model users. In econometric modelling the question often arises of whether or not $\boldsymbol{\lambda}_1$, the parameter of the conditional model $D(\mathbf{y}_t|\mathbf{z}_t, X_{t-1}, \boldsymbol{\lambda}_1)$ under consideration, is structurally invariant with respect to interventions affecting $\boldsymbol{\lambda}_2$, the parameter of the marginal model $D(\mathbf{z}_t|X_{t-1}, \boldsymbol{\lambda}_2)$, where $\mathbf{z}_t$ typically regroups policy variables. Obviously, the concept of weak exogeneity, whereby $\boldsymbol{\lambda}_1$ and $\boldsymbol{\lambda}_2$ are variation free, offers a natural framework for analysing the potential invariance of $\boldsymbol{\lambda}_1$ with respect to interventions affecting $\boldsymbol{\lambda}_2$ even though weak exogeneity is not sufficient for structural invariance (one cannot rule out the possibility that economic agents modify their behaviour in reaction to interventions). However, weak exogeneity and structural invariance are related in two essential ways:

— Estimation under invalid exogeneity assumptions, e.g. estimation of structural relationship by Ordinary Least Squares, typically loses structural invariance in the estimated model and may, therefore, lead to the erroneous conclusion of a structural break. Conversely, correctly interpreting parameter shifts or predictive failure requires an understanding of the weak exogeneity structure of a model in particular to ensure that the observed shifts do not simply result from invalid exogeneity assumptions.

— The fact that the parameters of a conditional submodel are found to be structurally invariant with respect to interventions affecting the process generating the supposedly exogenous variables provides strong support to the validity of these exogeneity assumptions.

7.5 EXOGENEITY TESTS

For limited classes of models, e.g. simultaneous-equation models, it is often possible to find parametric conditions under which some variables are weakly exogenous for specific parameters of interest. For example, the zero covariance restrictions analysed by Wu (1973) are sufficient for weak exogeneity, provided the simultaneous-equation model under consideration is just identified (except for the equation of interest, which may be over-identified). Such over-identifying conditions are testable in a straightforward way and in fact exogeneity tests already exist for special cases (see, for example, Wu, 1973; Revankar and Hartley, 1973; Revankar, 1978; Hausman, 1978; Engle, 1979; Richard, 1979; *inter alia*).

However, the construction of such parametric tests requires the specification of the marginal model $D(\mathbf{z}_t|\boldsymbol{X}_{t-1}, \boldsymbol{\lambda}_2)$ which is undesirable at least for two reasons:

— It is paradoxical that, in order to test whether or not the marginal model is required for inference on the parameters of interest, this marginal model should first be specified.
— The process generating the exogenous variables is often difficult to specify and may vary over the sample period. Consequently, specification errors are likely to occur in the formulation of the exogenous process and may completely distort the evidence concerning weak exogeneity assumptions.

More generally, as soon as we consider nonlinear or non-Gaussian models (disequilibrium models, ...) it is often difficult to test the null hypothesis of exogeneity within a more general model generating all the variables under consideration in such a way that exogeneity can be tested parametrically.

In the light of our discussion of structural invariance, an indirect test of weak exogeneity based on constancy tests for the parameters of interest yields an operational alternative to direct parametric tests of exogeneity, unless evidently there has been a genuine structural shift in the conditional model. It is, therefore, suggested that the predictive performance of models estimated under specific exogeneity assumptions should insofar as possible always be tested in changing environments.

NOTES

[1] The present note summarizes a communication presented at the Symposium on 'Criteria for Evaluating the Reliability of Macro-economic Models' organized by I.B.M. and held in Pisa on December 16–18, 1980. The note draws heavily on the paper 'Exogeneity, Causality and Structural Invariance in Econometric Modelling' written jointly with R. F. Engle and D. F. Hendry and presently available as CORE Discussion Paper No. 8038 (CORE, Louvain-la-Neuve, Belgium).

A. Zellner's thoughtful discussion of our communication is based on this joint discussion paper. I have tried to incorporate in the present note the information required for the understanding of the discussion. The interested reader is referred to the Discussion Paper for a more complete analysis, for an extensive list of references on the topic, and for illustrative examples.

[2] $\boldsymbol{\lambda}_2$ is then a 'nuisance parameter'. As rightly pointed out by A. Zellner, the wording 'incidental parameter' which has been used instead in our discussion paper is inappropriate.

REFERENCES

Barndorff-Nielsen, O. (1978). *Information and Exponential Families in Statistical Theory*, Wiley, New York.

Engle, R. F. (1979). 'The Lagrange multiplier test as a regression diagnostic.' London School of Economics, unpublished paper.

Engle, R. F., Hendry, D. F., and Richard, J.-F. (1980). 'Exogeneity, causality and structural invariance in econometric modelling.' Université Catholique de Louvain, CORE Discussion Paper 808, to appear in Econometrica.

Florens, J.-P. and Mouchart, M. (1980). 'Initial and sequential reduction of Bayesian experiments.' Université Catholique de Louvain, CORE Discussion Paper 8015.

Geweke, J. (1978). 'Testing the exogeneity specification in the complete dynamic simultaneous equations model.' *Journal of Econometrics*, **7**, 163–185.

Granger, C. W. J. (1969). 'Investigating causal relations by econometric models and cross-spectral methods.' *Econometrica*, **37**, 424–438.

Hausman, J. A. (1978). 'Specification tests in econometrics.' *Econometrica*, **46**, 1251–1271.

Koopmans, T. C. (1950). 'When is an equation system complete for statistical purposes?' In T. C. Koopmans (Ed.), *Statistical Inference in Dynamic Economic Models*, Wiley, New York, pp. 393–409.

Revankar, N. S. (1978). 'Asymptotic relative efficiency analysis of certain tests of independence in structural systems.' *International Economic Review*, **19**, 165–179.

Revankar, N. S., and Hartley, M. J. (1973). 'An independence test and conditional unbiased predictions in the context of simultaneous equations systems.' *International Economic Review*, **14**, 625–631.

Richard, J.-F. (1979). 'Exogeneity, inference and prediction in so-called incomplete dynamic simultaneous equation models.' Université Catholique de Louvain, CORE Discussion Paper 7922.

Richard, J.-F. (1980). 'Models with several regimes and changes in exogeneity.' *Review of Economic Studies*, **47**, 1–20.

Wu, D. M. (1973). 'Alternative tests of independence between stochastic regressors and disturbances.' *Econometrica*, **41**, 733–750.

Zellner, A. (1970). 'Causality and econometrics.' In K. Brunner and A. H. Meltzer (Eds), *Three Aspects of Policy and Policymaking*, North-Holland, Amsterdam.

Discussion

A. ZELLNER

University of Chicago[1]

The authors' stated objective is to provide a discussion of exogeneity, causality, and structural invariance that will facilitate econometric modelling. In this very long paper, the authors provide a useful discussion of these basic concepts. One important concept that they do not discuss and which is very relevant is the concept of probability that is employed in their paper and in econometrics generally. Without a clear-cut definition of probability, it is difficult to impute precise meaning to likelihood functions and other basic concepts in the paper, particularly in circumstances in which there is just a single realization of a process as with data relating to a particular national economy.

With respect to facilitating econometric modelling, it is relevant to consider some objectives of econometric modelling. One level of objectives involves obtaining good predictions and forecasts. Obtaining good predictions and forecasts from econometric models is very important. This is in part the objective of time series analysts using Box–Jenkins and other time series models. I believe that this objective fits in well with the emphasis on empirical analysis that Pasinetti stressed earlier in discussion. We want to have models that fit the data reasonably well, describe the major movements in series, and forecast well. If such models are empirical time series models, then economic theorists can attempt to rationalize their good performance. Thus, instead of always starting with a full-blown economic theory before analysing data, it may be fruitful to determine what works well from the data and then rationalize the results. Further empirical analyses using new data can be conducted to test these rationalizations. I put forward to you the idea that many important results are obtained in this way. At the extremes, Koopman's 'measurement without theory' is a sin, but 'theory without measurement' is also a sin. We have to get a more fruitful interaction between empirical work and economic theory established. Thus an important objective of econometric modelling is to describe the variation in series, most of which have important seasonal variation with which many empirical workers are not familiar since X-11 or some other seasonal adjustment method has been employed to take it out in one way or another. With a good understanding of the data, it is possible that relatively simple time series models can be constructed which forecast reasonably well. Time series analysts are pursuing this approach quite vigorously. A recent example of this approach in the economic literature is provided in the work of Litterman (1980) who has implemented vector autoregressions with informative prior distributions and obtained forecasts that compare very favourably with those made by other methods. In his work, no distinction between exogenous and endogenous variables is employed, a case not analysed by the authors. Clearly, incorrect exogeneity assumptions can lead to poor estimates and forecasts.

The second level of objectives involves control as well as prediction and forecasting. That is, some variables may be subject to policy-makers' control and the problem is how to control them in order to obtain good system behaviour. It may be possible to accomplish this objective using just reduced form or transfer function equations. The third level of objectives, much more ambitious than the preceding two, involves obtaining good forecasts, predictions, control policies, and structural analyses. Among other things, structural analyses involve behavioural models and permit analysts to predict the effects of structural changes. Also, this range of considerations extends to include Lucas' effects associated with changes in policy-makers' policies. Finally, the objectives of econometric modelling include the testing of alternative economic theories, an area of activity that can lead to profound results. As regards these objectives of econometric modelling, I believe that the present paper would have benefited from a clearer explanation of the objectives of econometric modelling and more precise indications of how the results in the paper relate to specific objectives.

With respect to structural econometric modelling, with which the authors are mainly concerned, it is relevant, and perhaps shocking, to ask, 'How do we know that any variables are exogenous?' It is my impression that the separation of variables into the endogenous–exogenous categories is often done in an informal way. Note that, in some cases, variables may shift their status within a given historical period. For example, at times one variable, say a monetary aggregate, may be exogenously controlled while at other times an interest rate may be exogenously controlled. Further, the nature of control policies relating to a single variable can change from time to time. These difficulties have not been analysed too well in the past in my opinion. Close study of how these problems are treated in connection with currently operating models would be of great interest. Such study could indicate a number of important hypotheses to be tested.

On exogenous variables, the paper did not put enough emphasis on determining stochastic processes for them. The future values of the exogenous variables are needed to generate forecasts of the endogenous variables and thus determining processes for the exogenous variables from which they can be forecast well is important. For example, in consulting with a private utility company on forecasting electricity sales from a structural model, forecasting the weather is a central problem. That is, if summers are unusually cool, electricity demand for air-conditioning falls while if winters are unusually mild, electricity demand for heating falls. Thus various measures of weather conditions, that you will agree are exogenous, must be forecast well in order to obtain good forecasts of electricity sales. This aspect of the forecasting problem is not considered in the authors' discussion of exogeneity.

The paper is somewhat difficult to read because some incorrect definitions appear. For example, the terms 'incidental parameters' and 'nuisance parameters' are sometimes used as being equivalent, which is incorrect. In other places, one term is used when the other is appropriate. As is well known, incidental parameters are parameters that grow in number as the sample size increases, a concept that Neyman and Scott introduced in about 1948. For example, if

$$x_i = \xi_i + v_i, \qquad \text{with} \quad Ex_i = \xi_i, \qquad i = 1, 2, \ldots, n,$$

the ξ_i's grow in number with the sample size n and are thus incidental parameters. On the other hand, if the parameters θ and ϕ appear in a model and interest centres on θ while ϕ is of no interest, then ϕ is a nuisance parameter. For example, in fitting a regression model, an autocorrelation parameter is a nuisance parameter, and a nuisance, when interest is centred on the regression coefficients. Incidental parameters can be nuisance parameters, though they need not be in general. In models with incidental parameters, difficult inference problems often arise and delicate issues arise in asymptotic properties of estimation procedures.

Another definition that does not seem to be entirely correct is the authors' definition of Granger 'causality'. The authors state that $\boldsymbol{Y}_{t-1}$ does not cause $\mathbf{z}_t$ with respect to $\boldsymbol{X}_{t-1}$ if, and only if,

$$D(\mathbf{z}_t|\boldsymbol{X}_{t-1},\boldsymbol{\theta}) \equiv D(\mathbf{z}_t|\boldsymbol{Z}_{t-1},\boldsymbol{Y}_0,\boldsymbol{\theta}),$$

where $\mathbf{z}_t = (\mathbf{y}_t, \mathbf{x}_t)$. The appearance of $\boldsymbol{Y}_0$ on the right-side of the identity is not in accord with Granger's 1969 population definition that relates to the entire past history of the $\boldsymbol{Y}$ process. The initial value, $\boldsymbol{Y}_0$, could be helpful in predicting $\mathbf{z}_t$ and therefore Granger's population definition is not satisfied. Also, if $\boldsymbol{Y}_0$ is random and generated by the process, its distribution will usually involve some of the elements of $\boldsymbol{\phi}$ and this has to be taken into account in defining the status of $\boldsymbol{Y}_{t-1}$.

Further, I believe that exogeneity can be discussed, as it usually is in the literature, without any reference to causality. All that one has to say is that variables enter models in particular ways, that is certain coefficients and/or covariances are zero or nonzero. There is no basic need to get enmeshed in the quagmire of causality. Since the authors do get into this quagmire quite deeply in terms of their definition of strong exogeneity, I believe that it is important to point out that Granger's definition of causality is very inadequate and his recent thoughts on this issue are quite different from those expressed in his 1969 *Econometrica* paper.[2] Briefly, in that paper he equated causality with statistical prediction. Thus on this definition, if changes in sunspot activity are helpful in predicting changes in business activity, then changes in sunspot activity cause changes in business activity. This is absurd since we know from elementary statistics texts that correlation does not necessarily imply causation. Thus just cross-correlating variables does not establish causality. Generally, causality is defined to be 'predictability according to a law or set of laws,' that is according to a model which provides understanding of the underlying economic behaviour. Also, the predictability in this definition is *actual* predictability, not *potential* predictability. For example, if a model which has a strong subject matter basis and provides understanding of economic behaviour is used on many occasions and found to make very good predictions of certain variables given others' values, then causality may be cautiously asserted. Some such discussion of these and other concepts of causality in the paper are needed to provide readers with guidance.

In my opinion, the concept of exogeneity should be linked to the concept of ancillary statistics in the statistical literature—see, for example, Cox and Hinkley (1974). In terms of the normal multiple regression model, $\mathbf{y} = \boldsymbol{X}\boldsymbol{\beta} + \mathbf{u}$ with $\boldsymbol{X}$ random and $\mathbf{u}$ normal with zero mean vector and covariance matrix $\sigma^2\boldsymbol{I}$, the joint pdf for $\mathbf{y}$ and $\boldsymbol{X}$ is $p(\mathbf{y}|\boldsymbol{X},\boldsymbol{\beta},\sigma)g(\boldsymbol{X}|\boldsymbol{\phi})$, where the first factor is the conditional likelihood function and $g(\boldsymbol{X}|\boldsymbol{\phi})$ is the marginal pdf for $\boldsymbol{X}$ given $\boldsymbol{\phi}$, the parameters of this pdf. For fixed parameters, if $\boldsymbol{\phi}$ does not include $\boldsymbol{\beta}$ and σ, then $\boldsymbol{X}$ is an ancillary statistic.[3] The implications of this state of affairs is that the conditional likelihood function $p(\mathbf{y}|\boldsymbol{X},\boldsymbol{\beta},\sigma)$ can be used for estimation. Also, in testing usual t

and F statistics are valid whether $\boldsymbol{X}$ is fixed or random. That is, the joint pdf for a t statistic and $\boldsymbol{X}$ is

$$f(t, \boldsymbol{X}) = h(t|\boldsymbol{X})\mathbf{g}(\boldsymbol{X}|\boldsymbol{\phi}) = h(t)g(\boldsymbol{X}|\boldsymbol{\phi})$$

since $h(t|\boldsymbol{X}) = h(t)$ from properties of the univariate Student-t pdf. Similarly for an F statistic, $f(F|\boldsymbol{X}) = f(F)$ and F has the same pdf whether $\boldsymbol{X}$ is random or fixed. While the authors mention estimation results similar to these, they do not analyse results relating to test statistics for structural models. Also, they do not mention how unconditional prediction intervals will differ from those conditional on given values of stochastic exogenous variables.

The examples in the paper are well worth studying and helpful in understanding features of models. On the issue of which parametrization to employ, I believe that there are some results in the statistical and engineering literature on optimal parametrization. With respect to structural econometric models, Basmann (1965) has shown how any linear interdependent or simultaneous model can be transformed into an observationally equivalent fully recursive model. Also, linear multivariate time series models have a number of observationally equivalent representations. Further work to understand the relative advantages and disadvantages of alternative representations would be valuable.

On testing for exogeneity, it is well known that a variety of test statistics including the likelihood ratio, Wald, and Lagrange multiplier statistics are available. In choosing among them, one should, of course, take account of their associated finite sample power functions which, unfortunately, have not as yet been tabulated. To use power functions, it is necessary to have some prior information about probable values of parameters under alternative hypotheses. If such prior information is available, it seems to me that it would be useful to represent it by a prior distribution and to compute posterior odds ratios for exogeneity and endogeneity hypotheses. Indeed, Reynolds (1977, 1980, 1981) has derived Bayesian posterior odds ratios that are the Bayesian analogues of Wu–Hausman sampling theory test statistics and applied them in analysing data on health, income, and other variables. This analysis yields posterior probabilities associated with hypotheses of exogeneity and endogeneity. It is important to be able to quantify uncertainty about the exogeneity status of a variable or variables. In addition, in testing for autocorrelation in a simple regression model, work of Fomby and Guilkey (1978) and Griffiths and Dao (1980) indicates that Bayesian procedures produce better results than standard non-Bayesian procedures.

The above tests of exogeneity and autocorrelation are usually not the main objectives of an analysis. Rather they are steps along the way to obtaining coefficient estimates and/or forecasts. Technically they are called 'pre-tests' and the effects of pre-tests on subsequent estimation and forecasting results must be carefully considered.[4] In this connection, Fomby and Guilkey (1978) considered the problem of choosing a significance level for the Durbin–Watson test in order to get a good regression coefficient estimate. They found that using a significance level of about 50 % led to best estimation results when a test result of no autocorrelation was followed by least squares estimation and of autocorrelation followed by generalized least squares estimation. That a 50 % level of significance produces better estimation results than a 5 % level can be understood by noting that an error of the first kind is much less important than an error of the second kind in terms of getting good estimation results using the procedure described above. The general range of pre-testing problems is extremely important in econometric model construction.

In connection with pre-testing problems, Bayesians can compute posterior probabilities associated with hypotheses and use them to average estimates and forecasts—see for example, Geisel (1973), Zellner and Vandaele (1975), and Griffiths and Dao (1980). However, more work is needed to take proper account of the many kinds of pre-tests including tests of autocorrelation, overidentifying restrictions, homoskedasticity, exogeneity, etc., that are employed in constructing econometric models and using them for forecasting and policy-making.

In closing, as my discussion indicates, I found this paper very stimulating and an interesting contribution to the literature.

NOTES

[1] This discussion was prepared while the author was on leave at the National Bureau of Economic Research and the Hoover Institution, Stanford, California. As already mentioned in Chapter 7, A. Zellner's discussion is based on the paper 'Exogeneity, Causality and Structural Invariance in Econometric Modelling', by R. F. Engle, D. F. Hendry, J. F. Richard, CORE Discussion Paper No. 8038 (CORE, Louvain-la-Neuve, Belgium).

[2] See my paper, 'Causality and Econometrics', which the authors cite for information about Granger's more recent views.

[3] In a Bayesian setting, prior independence of $(\boldsymbol{\beta}, \sigma)$ and $\boldsymbol{\phi}$ results in the posterior pdf for $(\boldsymbol{\beta}, \sigma)$ being proportional to $\pi(\boldsymbol{\beta}, \sigma)p(\mathbf{y}|X, \boldsymbol{\beta}, \sigma)$. Similar considerations relate to random parameter models.

[4] See Zellner (1979) for further discussion.

REFERENCES

Basmann, R. L. (1965). 'A Note on the statistical testability of "Explicit Causal Chains" against the class of "Interdependent models.' *Journal of the American Statistical Association*, **60,** 1080–1093.

Cox, D. R., and Hinkley, D. V. (1974). *Theoretical Statistics*, Chapman and Hall, London.

Fomby, T. B., and Guilkey, D. K. (1978). 'On choosing the optimal level of significance for the Durbin–Watson test and the Bayesian alternative.' *Journal of Econometrics*, **8,** 203–213.

Geisel, M. S. (1973). 'Bayesian comparisons of simple macroeconomic models.' *Journal of Money and Credit*. Reprinted in S. E. Fienberg and A. Zellner (Eds), *Studies in Bayesian*

Econometrics and Statistics in Honor of Leonard J. Savage, North-Holland, Amsterdam. pp. 227–256.

Griffiths, W., and Dao, D. (1980). 'A note on a Bayesian estimator in an autocorrelated error model.' *Journal of Econometrics*, **12,** 389–392.

Litterman, R. B. (1981). 'A Bayesian procedure for forecasting with vector autoregressions.' To appear in *Journal of Econometrics*.

Reynolds, R. A. (1980). 'A study of the relationship between health and income.' Unpublished doctoral dissertation, Department of Economics, University of Chicago.

Reynolds, R. A. (1981). 'Posterior odds for the hypothesis of independence between stochastic regressors and disturbances.' To appear in *International Economic Review*.

Reynolds, R. A. (1981). 'The joint determination of health and income.' Department of Economic Research, American Medical Association, Chicageo, Illinois.

Zellner, A. (1979). 'Statistical analysis of econometric models.' Invited paper with discussion. *Journal of American Statistical Association*, **74,** 628–651.

Zellner, A., and Vandaele, W. (1975). 'Bayes–Stein estimators for *k*-means, regression and simultaneous equation models.' In S. E. Fienberg and A. Zellner (Eds). *Studies in Bayesian Econometrics and Statistics in Honor of Leonard J. Savage*, North-Holland, Amsterdam. pp. 627–653.

Evaluating the Reliability of Macro-economic Models
Edited by G. C. Chow and P. Corsi

CHAPTER 8

Econometric Model Diagnostics

E. KUH
Massachusetts Institute of Technology

J. NEESE
Massachusetts Institute of Technology

8.1 INTRODUCTION

The topic of this conference is important. We also believe that the papers to be presented here attest to progress already made and an awareness that many substantive issues of model reliability need to be resolved.

Since econometric models as we now know them began to emerge about 30 years ago, it is fair to say that they have at least reached adolescence; some would say they are in a state of delayed adolescence.

Some problems of immaturity are endemic. We will comment on these summarily under four headings: complexity, inadequacy of theory, data problems, and lack of experimental control. First, there is the inherent complexity of social and economic phenomena. We can never expect to understand reality more than partially. It remains an open question whether that fraction we can expect to understand is miniscule, or just small.

Secondly, and not unrelated to the first point, are large gaps that pervade economic theory. Our understanding of how to incorporate institutions into theory is limited. We imperfectly understand imperfect competition. Other areas on which hard work is being done and the results are not yet satisfactory include expectations and dynamics.

Thirdly, there are troublesome questions about data. One is that theory often does not have data which corresponds to it. As we all know, most theory is at the micro level, yet much of our data is aggregated. There is also a fact we would like to forget, that data often are of dubious quality. Finally, there are innate limits to data when there is technical or other change.

Fourthly, we normally lack experimental control. This lacuna, with only a few exceptions, greatly weakens our ability to identify causal structures, although there is emerging statistical theory that provides some solace in the pursuit of understanding causality. A correlative point is that, typically, we have only weak power to discriminate among (even quite different) competing hypotheses, given the nature of most economic data.

In a more positive vein, the substance of this paper is devoted to three different procedures for improving model reliability and our understanding of models.[1] It provides a survey of some ongoing work at the MIT Center for Computational Research in Economics and Management Science and is based on our own work and that of our colleagues; this research is in turn part of an inter-university project on model reliability.[2] While we believe these three topics are important, we must exclude others of interest because of time limitations.

The first of the three topics to be addressed is concerned with methods that lead to coefficient estimates which more nearly reflect typical behaviour uncontaminated by uncharacteristic data. In turn, this will allow judgment and other nonstatistical elements (e.g. 'add factors') to enter into forecasts and policy analysis, separately and cleanly. A paramount criterion of estimation, 'goodness of fit' over an historical period (perhaps supplemented by ex-post simulations), can be misleading. Even for intelligently chosen theories or hypotheses elements of data can be atypical, yet pass unnoticed by conventional goodness of fit tests. Regression diagnostics to detect influential data and bounded influence estimation to mitigate their impact are intended to promote this initial objective.

A second objective of modelling which we wish to discuss is the detection of those parameters to which model response is especially sensitive. Economic models are sometimes inaccurate because their outputs are highly sensitive to certain estimated parameters of the model, which are not precisely known. The methodology for examining this sensitivity is well developed and we will present some results regarding it. A related goal is to design model structures that are relatively insensitive to small subsets of parameters. Since in practice we have many different possible ways to model a particular process, we can include among our criteria the choice of structures which are not excessively sensitive in this specific sense. We do not believe this notion has been discussed much in existing literature, where models are assumed (perhaps misleadingly) to be handed down from on high.

The third worthwhile objective of modelling concerns better ways to understand strategic aspects of models and to allow more scope for intuitive understanding of important elements of model structure. Models have become extremely large and often quite complicated 'black boxes' customarily studied by observing output responses to variations in model inputs. The standard procedure, of course, is multiplier analysis through exogenous variable changes. In the absence, however, of compelling theory it is extraordinarily difficult to understand models at intuitive levels because of size, nonlinearity, and adhocery. Thus the basic mechanisms of the model are obscure, except perhaps to the model proprietor. The main tool will be linear systems analysis of linearized models.

8.2 REGRESSION DIAGNOSTICS AND INFLUENTIAL DATA

The purpose of the regression diagnostics that have been developed in Chapter 2 of Belsley *et al.* (1980) is the detection of influential observations in regression analysis. We define an influential observation as one with unusually large impact on regression outputs such as predictions or coefficients. Thus influential data yield estimated quantities that are outside the patterns set by the majority of data, in the context of a given model, estimator (here, least squares), and sample. We present some scatter diagrams to illustrate how influential data can affect regression estimates to motivate methods that apply to multiple regression.

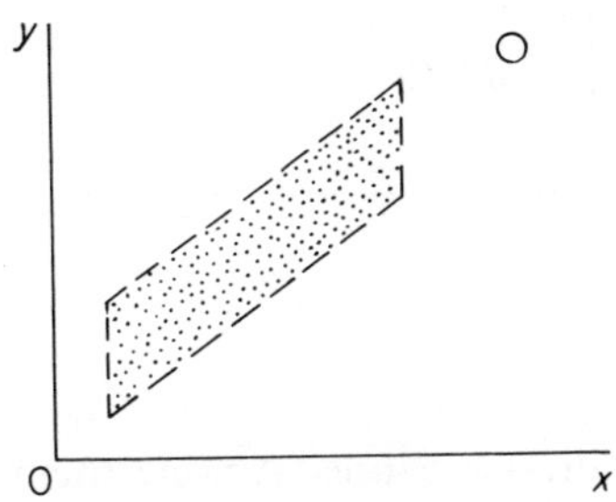

Figure 8.1

Figure 8.1 shows that outlying points can help as well as hurt. Even when helpful in the sense of improving precision, it is useful to locate such observations and to determine the extent of their influence.

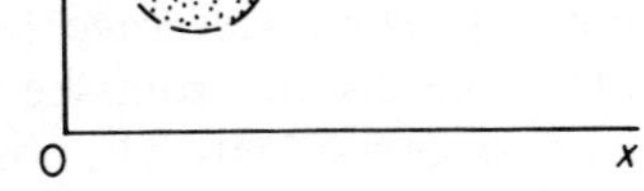

Figure 8.2

Figure 8.2 illustrates a situation where influential points can be the source of apparently highly precise estimation when there may not be any valid relationship whatsoever. In the diagram shown we might even think that, for a straight line, there were no degrees of freedom despite the clear possibility that there are actually a large number of observations. While this illustration may appear extreme, configurations like this occur in practice and ought to be ferreted out for further analysis.

Finally, in Figure 8.3 we indicate a circumstance where a small subset of influential points can cause ordinary least squares coefficients to diverge from those which are consistent with the majority of the data. Useful methods for determining the existence and influence of such subsets are described below.

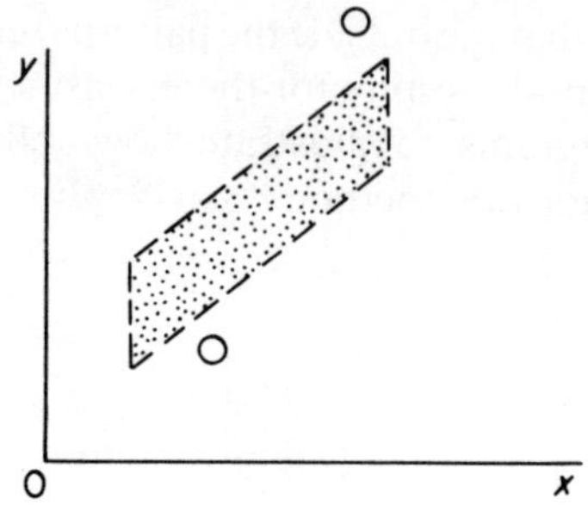

Figure 8.3

Influential points have diverse causes. Among them are strong experimental evidence (see Figure 8.1), recording or data entry errors, innate errors (sampling errors or errors of observation), and sporadic model failure. This type of model failure happens when occasional unusual circumstances occur that are poorly represented by a model that otherwise performs well enough.

The remedies for influential data are also varied. One obvious thing to do is nothing: it is often inadvisable to modify the sample after having discovered some influential points. Secondly, newly discovered errors should obviously be fixed. Thirdly, one might re-specify the model in ways that bring the influential observations more appropriately within the scope of the systematic part of the model. A final new possibility that holds great promise is the use of bounded-influence estimation.

In a more formal treatment of regression diagnostics, we characterize influential data by two attributes. The first is leverage: leverage points are data in explanatory variable space that are distant from the majority of the X data. Secondly, and more familiar, are large residuals. The notation we use is in Figure 8.4. We note that $\mathbf{b} = (X'X)^{-1}X'\mathbf{y}$ for OLS and further by way of definition let

$$H = X(X'X)^{-1}X' \text{ be the } \textit{hat matrix} \text{ and } h_{ik} = \mathbf{x}_i(X'X)^{-1}\mathbf{x}_k'.$$

Then $\hat{\mathbf{y}} = X\mathbf{b} = H\mathbf{y}$, which is how the hat matrix got its name. We can describe the predicted value as

$$\hat{y}_i = \sum_{k=1}^{n} h_{ik} y_k.$$

Figure 8.4 Notation

Population regression $\mathbf{y} = X\boldsymbol{\beta} + \boldsymbol{\varepsilon}$	Estimated regression $\mathbf{y} = X\mathbf{b} + \mathbf{e}$ and $\hat{\mathbf{y}} = X\mathbf{b}$
$\mathbf{y}$: $n \times 1$ column vector for response variable	same
X: $n \times p$ matrix of explanatory variables	same
$\boldsymbol{\beta}$: $p \times 1$ column vector of regression parameters	$\mathbf{b}$: estimate of $\boldsymbol{\beta}$
$\boldsymbol{\varepsilon}$: $n \times 1$ column vector of errors	$\mathbf{e}$: residual vector: $\mathbf{y} - \hat{\mathbf{y}}$
σ^2: error variance	s^2: estimated error variance
Additional notation	
$\mathbf{x}_i$: ith row of X matrix	$\mathbf{b}(i)$: estimate of $\boldsymbol{\beta}$ when ith row of X and $\mathbf{y}$ have been deleted.
$\mathbf{X}_j$: jth column of X matrix	$s^2(i)$: estimated error variance when ith row of X and $\mathbf{y}$ have been deleted

Using the above results the last expression can be rewritten as

$$\hat{y}_i = \sum_{k \neq i} h_{ik} y_k + h_{ii} y_i.$$

We see that the impact of y_i on $\hat{y}_i$ is dominated by the corresponding diagonal element h_i, since from the Cauchy–Schwarz inequality, $h_{ik} \leq h_{ii}^{1/2} h_{kk}^{1/2}$. [3]

If we let $\hat{y}_i(i) = \mathbf{x}_i \mathbf{b}(i)$, then $\hat{y}_i$ for the full data set is the following weighted average of $\hat{y}_i(i)$ and y_i:

$$\hat{y}_i = (1 - h_i)\,\hat{y}_i(i) + h_i y_i. \tag{2.1}$$

Strong leverage points (those with large h_i) increasingly dominate predicted or fitted values.

There is also a direct distance interpretation of h_i. Let $\tilde{X}$ be the X matrix centred by column means $\bar{\mathbf{x}}$, so that $\tilde{h}_i = (\mathbf{x}_i - \bar{\mathbf{x}})(\tilde{X}'\tilde{X})^{-1}(\mathbf{x}_i - \bar{\mathbf{x}})'$. It is apparent that large $\tilde{h}_i$ are relatively far removed from the centre of the data measured in the $(\tilde{X}'\tilde{X})$ coordinate system since H is a quadratic form.[4] For simple bivariate regression

$$\tilde{h}_i = \frac{(x_i - \bar{x})^2}{\sum_{i=1}^{n} (x_i - \bar{x})^2},$$

so that (for given $(y_i - \bar{y}) \neq 0$) a large hat matrix diagonal corresponds in the most transparent fashion to a point with strong leverage or influence or impact on the estimated slope regression coefficient as

$$b = \frac{\sum(x_i - \bar{x})(y_i - \bar{y})}{\sum(x_i - \bar{x})^2}.$$

Since $\boldsymbol{H}$ is a projection matrix, it has the following properties:

$$\text{(i) } 0 \leq h_i \leq 1$$
$$\text{(ii) } \sum h_i = p. \tag{2.2}$$

Thus a perfectly balanced $\boldsymbol{X}$ matrix—with equal leverage for all observations—is one for which $h_i = p/n$. As further elaborated in Belsley *et al.* (1980), when h_i exceeds $2p/n$ and certainly when it exceeds $3p/n$, we are inclined to consider that row of data as potentially influential.

Relatively large residuals have long been viewed as indicators of regression problems. Since for spherically distributed errors $\boldsymbol{\varepsilon} \sim (0, \sigma^2 \boldsymbol{I})$ the error variance for the ith observation is $\sigma^2(1 - h_i)$ in least squares, we prefer in practice to scale residuals by $\hat{\sigma}^2(1 - h_i)$. Instead of using s (the sample standard deviation) estimated from all the data to estimate σ, we prefer to use $s(i)$ (an estimate excluding the ith row) so that the denominator is stochastically independent of the numerator. We thus obtain the *studentized residual* e_i^*, which is the t-distribution when $\boldsymbol{\varepsilon}$ is normally distributed:

$$e_i^* = \frac{e_i}{s(i)\sqrt{1 - h_i}}. \tag{2.3}$$

One can observe the influence of an individual data row by comparing OLS regression quantities based on the full data set with estimates obtained when one row of data at a time has been deleted. We will restrict ourselves here to two such measures: coefficients and the predicted dependent variable or fitted values. Thus for the latter:

$$\mathbf{x}_i\mathbf{b} - \mathbf{x}_i\mathbf{b}(i) = \mathbf{x}_i(\mathbf{b} - \mathbf{b}(i)) = \frac{h_i e_i}{1 - h_i},$$

with variance $(\mathbf{x}_i\mathbf{b}) = \sigma^2 h_i$. Replacing σ by $s(i)$ gives a measure we have designated

$$\text{DFFITS}_i = \frac{h_i e_i/(1 - h_i)}{s(i)\sqrt{h_i}} = \left[\frac{h_i}{1 - h_i}\right]^{1/2} e_i^*. \tag{2.4}$$

It is evident that the ith data point will:

(i) have little influence even if e_i^* is large provided h_i is small, reinforcing our belief that residuals alone are an inadequate diagnostic, and

(ii) that substantial leverage points can be a major source of influence on predicted fit even when e_i^* is small.

A second direct measure of influence is the vector of estimated regression coefficients when the *i*th row has been deleted:

$$\text{DFBETA}_i \equiv \mathbf{b} - \mathbf{b}(i) = \frac{(X'X)^{-1}\mathbf{x}_i' e_i}{1 - h_i}. \tag{2.5}$$

This can be scaled by $s(i)$ diag $\sqrt{(X'X)^{-1}}$, yielding an expression called DFBETAS.[5]

We have also found *partial regression leverage plots* (scatter diagram of residuals from $\mathbf{y}$ regressed on all but the jth column of X plotted against the residuals of column $\mathbf{X}_j$ regressed on the remaining columns of X; its OLS slope is just b_j) contain much valuable qualitative information about influential data, especially the 'masking' problem alluded to earlier in Note 5. However, when we turn to bounded influence regression, in its weighted least squares context, we find that the weights provide an alternative and valid source of information about subset influences, an additionally appealing aspect of bounded influence estimation.

We turn next to a brief illustration of row deletion diagnostics. Useful qualitative diagnostic information about influential data appears in Figure 8.5, a

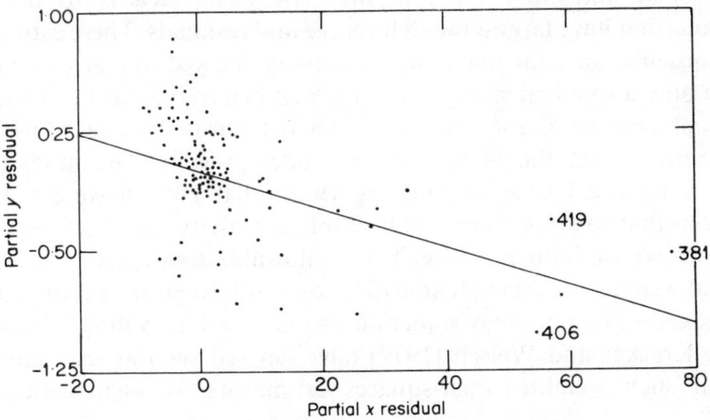

Figure 8.5 Partial regression leverage plot for B_2 (CRIM), S.E. = 0.00124; housing-price equation

Diagnostic magnitudes

Observation	h_i	RSTUDENT	DFFITS
381	0.2949	2.559	1.6551
406	0.1533	2.141	−0.9112
419	0.1843	2.316	1.1009
Cut off	$2p/n$ [7]	[8]	$2\sqrt{p/n}$ [9]
	0.0550	2.0	0.3333

partial regression leverage plot from a housing price equation of Harrison and Rubinfeld (1978) based on a 1970 sample of 506 census tracts in the Boston Standard Metropolitan Statistical Area.[6] Three points (census tracts 381, 419, and 406) effectively determine the slope for one of the fourteen explanatory variables that appear in this cross-section relation. The diagnostic measures for the hat matrix diagonals, studentized residuals, and DFFITS for these three unusual census tracts are also reported. Hat matrix diagonals exceed the $2p/n$ cutoff, the studentized residuals are well in excess of 2, the conventional level where we begin to look for large residuals, and DFFITS substantially exceeds its usual cutoff. It is interesting to note that by deleting only one observation, the predicted value for each of these observations changes anywhere from 1 to $1\frac{2}{3}$ standard deviations.

Exactly which remedies (if any) should be invoked in these circumstances is not clear, although we might think hard about excluding the three most influential observations and then re-estimate, since there is some reason to believe that they are vastly different from the remainder of the sample.

A less arbitrary remedy, bounded-influence estimation, offers both diagnostic information and alternative estimates which first locate and then counteract the effects of such influential observations. The basic idea is to downweight observations that have large enough leverage and residuals. These estimators are initially chosen so that the maximum sensitivity allowed to a given observation will cause only a small efficiency loss with well-behaved data. For instance, the bounded influence estimator can be chosen with a sensitivity level consistent with 95% efficiency when the normal error model prevails. The next step is to construct a weighted least squares algorithm that gives a weight of one to observations that have less than the allowable sensitivity but which downweights observations whose influence exceeds the allowable sensitivity.

The final weights contain valuable diagnostic information and the alternative set of regression estimates may sometimes be preferred to ordinary least squares estimates. Krasker and Welsch (1979) have devised such an estimator which, among all such weighted-least-squares estimators, is asymptotically most efficient.[10]

8.3 DETERMINISTIC PARAMETER SENSITIVITY[11]

We now turn to parameter sensitivity, which is studied by comparing model simulations generated with perturbed and unperturbed parameters. This analysis can become a valuable complement to more familiar multipliers in several ways. It identifies parameters to which model outputs are most sensitive. Thus, the analysis helps direct research efforts toward reducing uncertainty about influential coefficients. It goes beyond multiplier analysis in illuminating model structure; the influence of an individual parameter in a given equation is uncovered through structural coefficient variations. In these ways parameter sensitivity analysis can help to confront current scepticism about model robustness and reliability and further our quest for methods which improve our understanding and ability to communicate model strengths and weaknesses.

We illustrate with a single linear equation

$$y_t = \beta_0 + \beta_1 y_{t-1} + \beta_2 x_t \tag{3.1}$$

$$\eta(y, \beta_2)_t \equiv \frac{\beta_2}{y_t}\frac{\mathrm{d}y_t}{\mathrm{d}\beta_2} = \left[\left(\frac{\beta_2}{y_t}\right)\left(\frac{\beta_1\,\mathrm{d}y_{t-1}}{\mathrm{d}\beta_2} + x_t\right)\right] \tag{3.2}$$

$$= \left[\beta_1\left(\frac{\beta_2}{y_t}\frac{\mathrm{d}y_{t-1}}{\mathrm{d}\beta_2}\right) + \frac{\beta_2 x_t}{y_t}\right]. \tag{3.3}$$

(3.3) is the total differential of (3.1) converted to elasticity form. The transformation in (3.4) enables (3.3) to be rewritten in the straightforward way it appears in (3.5).

$$\frac{\beta_2}{y_t}\frac{\mathrm{d}y_{t-1}}{\mathrm{d}\beta_2} \equiv \left(\frac{\mathrm{d}y_{t-1}}{\mathrm{d}\beta_2}\frac{\beta_2}{y_{t-1}}\right)\left(\frac{y_{t-1}}{y_t}\right) \equiv \eta(y, \beta_2)_{t-1}\left(\frac{y_{t-1}}{y_t}\right), \tag{3.4}$$

$$\eta(y, \beta_2)_t = \left(\frac{\beta_1 y_{t-1}}{y_t}\right)\eta(y, \beta_2)_{t-1} + \frac{\beta_2 x_t}{y_t}. \tag{3.5}$$

The other elasticities can be written equivalently as:

$$\eta(y, \beta_0)_t = \left(\frac{\beta_1 y_{t-1}}{y_t}\right)\eta(y, \beta_0)_{t-1} + \frac{\beta_0}{y_t} \tag{3.6}$$

$$\eta(y, \beta_1)_t = \left(\frac{\beta_1 y_{t-1}}{y_t}\right)\eta(y, \beta_1)_{t-1} + \frac{\beta_1 y_{t-1}}{y_t}. \tag{3.7}$$

We note the following general features. The forcing function turns out to be the parameter's share in determining the dependent variable: for instance, $\beta_2 x_t/y_t$ in (3.5). Since, by definition, the impact elasticity is the parameter share, the sum of the impact elasticities is one in the linear case. Homogeneous elasticity dynamics depend on previous period endogenous variable shares in ways that closely resemble linear dynamics. We wish to draw your attention to the fact that impact elasticities are greatly magnified in later periods when the lagged dependent variable coefficient β_1 is large.

Although we have described the parameter sensitivity analysis for elasticities using a linear equation, the results generalize readily to linear time invariant simultaneous systems. While nonlinear systems do not yield to analysis in the same way, for many mildly nonlinear systems that typify econometric models linear analysis can be expected to provide valid insights. Even for more strongly nonlinear models, linear analysis holds for small perturbations.

We shall describe some parameter sensitivity experiments using the Michigan Quarterly Economic Model (MQEM), a 98-equation model of the U.S. economy.[12] Our focus is on the sensitivity of two major real magnitudes—constant dollar Gross National Product and constant dollar investment in residential construction—to one-at-a-time perturbations of several coefficients in the money demand equation.[13] For these two endogenous variables we compute the difference (DELTA) between a benchmark (or 'base case') simulation, and a perturbed simulation, where one money demand coefficient alone has been changed by 1%. We then calculate the ratio of the finite differences $\Delta y/\Delta\beta$ and convert to elasticities (ELAST) in the conventional manner.

The equation for real money demand has been singled out because of its pivotal role in the 12-equation MQEM monetary sector. Some information about the equation and our perturbation experiments is shown in Figure 8.6. The money demand specification derives from a partial adjustment process governing asset demand. The main arguments are permanent and transitory income, short and long interest rates, and inflation. A first-order or Koyck lag governs the dynamics; since the associated coefficient is nearly 1, we anticipate large magnification of impact elasticities in subsequent periods.

We briefly examine in Figure 8.7 responses of GNP and residential construction to perturbations in three parameters in the money demand equation 4, 8, and 35 quarters after the parameter change. Turning first to the column associated with GNP elasticities in Experiment 3 (where the Koyck lag coefficient, MON8, has been perturbed), we note a factor of 10 growth in sensitivity from quarter 4 to quarter 35 (ELAST $= -0.317$ at 4 quarters, -3.144 at 35 quarters). The corresponding 35 quarter DELTA indicates that a surprisingly large $41.996 billion drop in GNP has been produced by the 1% increase in MON8. A similar perusal of Experiments 1 and 2 shows a quite large sensitivity to the permanent income coefficient, MON2, while the major real magnitudes are largely insensitive to the treasury bill rate coefficient, MON4.

The graph in Figure 8.8 shows, for elasticities with respect to MON8 scaled to have a maximum of ± 1, that the timepath of GNP elasticities and the timepath of residential construction elasticities are quite similar.[14] The maximum elasticity of GNP is -5.34; that for IRC, investment in residential construction, is -76.0, indicating extreme sensitivity of residential construction to this one money demand coefficient. Given similarity of timepaths (and dissimilarity to most other perturbation timepaths we have examined) residential construction appears to be a primary link between the monetary sector and aggregate output.

These results are informative about model structure and parameter sensitivity. In the first instance, it is of course widely believed that monetary magnitudes influence GNP through residential construction, although perhaps the intensity

Figure 8.6 Basic information about parameter perturbation for M2 equation

Perturbed parameter and experiment	Associated variable	Unperturbed parameter value	Parameter perturbation	Perturbation % of standard error
MON 1	Intercept	−0.37259	−0.003726	—
MON 2	Permanent income	0.15289	0.001529	4.3
MON 3	Transitory income	0.11815	0.001181	2.2
MON 4	RTB: Bill rate	−0.020627	−0.000206	5.8
MON 5	RAAA	−0.035635	−0.000356	2.4
MON 6	Inflation rate	−0.45674	−0.004567	5.0
MON 7	Public debt	−0.028	−0.00028	—
MON 8	M2 lagged	0.93125	0.009312	29.1

The M2 equation is linear in logarithms and the dependent variable M2 is measured in constant dollars.

Figure 8.7 Response of GNP and residential construction to perturbations of three parameters in the money demand equation

Periods after parameter change	Experiment 1 Treasury Bill Rate MON 4				Experiment 2 Permanent Income MON 2				Experiment 3 Lagged M2 MON 8			
	GNP		IRC		GNP		IRC		GNP		IRC	
	DELTA	ELAST	DELTA	ELAST	DELTA	ELAST	DELTA	ELAST	DELTA	ELAST	DELTA	ELAST
4 Quarter	0.022	0.002	0.010	0.028	−0.617	−0.057	−0.302	−0.808	−3.428	−0.317	−1.678	−4.569
8 Quarter	0.081	0.007	0.035	0.068	−2.574	−0.224	−1.085	−2.093	−15.087	−1.320	−6.386	−12.982
35 Quarter	0.187	0.013	0.099	0.090	−6.121	−0.452	−3.127	−2.869	−41.996	−3.144	−20.028	−19.911

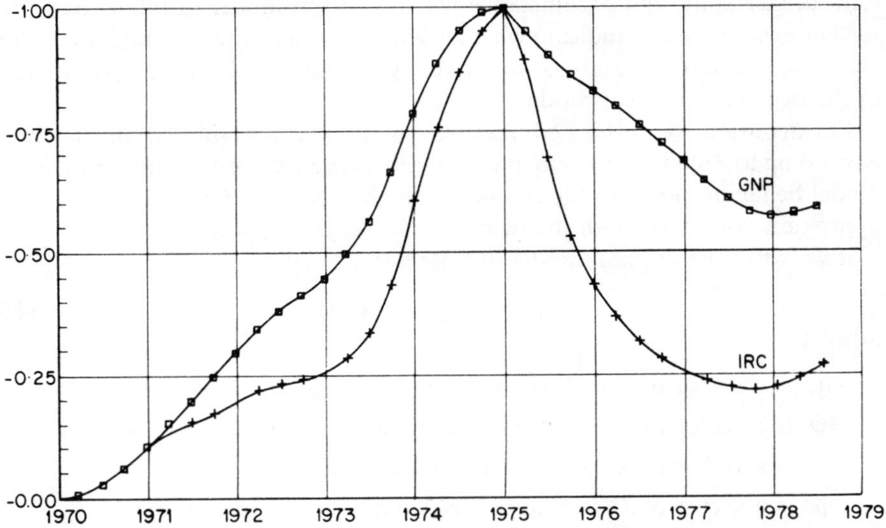

Figure 8.8 Scaled elasticities: MON8 perturbations for GNP and IRC. Each series is scaled so that its largest magnitude will be $= +^{1}$. The GNP scale factor is 5.34. The IRC (Residential Construction) scale factor is 76.0

with which this effect occurs and its dependence on particular parameters are new insights. Secondly, we observe quite exceptional sensitivity of residential construction itself to just one parameter in the money demand equation.

8.4 DETERMINISTIC LINEAR ANALYSIS[15]

Our motivation for pursuing linear analysis rests on a basic presumption: despite the size and complexity of econometric models, only a few model elements determine important aspects of model behaviour. Current large macro models may have in excess of 1000 (often nonlinear) equations with a potential for highly complex interactions. However, we believe that for many purposes, there are few critical model elements and important interactions. It thus becomes possible to arrive at model representations that are much smaller than the original model and thereby greatly improve intuitive understanding.

We propose to identify essential model features by studying properties of the linearized model, rather than the original nonlinear model, thereby taking advantage of the considerable analytic understanding of linear structures. Our goal in this analysis is to identify one or a few small models that capture essential model features.

The obvious difficulty with this approach is the possibility of distorting critical model nonlinearities in the linearization stage. It is our belief and experience that models are often only mildly nonlinear—hence nonlinearities are seldom critical. Certainly this circumstance will vary from model to model and only further experience can indicate whether linearization is often a fatal flaw. In any event, we intend to keep tabs on ourselves by verifying our linear results with tests of the original nonlinear model.

Linearization is performed relative to a reference simulation timepath. According to Taylor's theorem, then, we generate a first-order approximation to model behaviour local to the simulation path, and the range of validity for the approximation varies with the degree of model nonlinearity.

If we write the original model in state space form as:

$$\mathbf{y}_t = \boldsymbol{\psi}(\mathbf{y}_t, \mathbf{y}_{t-1}, \mathbf{x}_t, \boldsymbol{\beta}) \tag{4.1}$$

where:

- $\mathbf{y}_t$ is a vector of G endogenous variables,
- $\boldsymbol{\psi}$ is a vector of G (nonlinear) functions,
- $\mathbf{x}_t$ is a vector of K exogenous variables, and
- $\boldsymbol{\beta}$ is a vector of J (constant) coefficients,

we can then express the linearization of (4.1), the *linearized structural form deviations model*, as:

$$\boldsymbol{D}.\Delta\mathbf{y}_t = \boldsymbol{E}.\Delta\mathbf{y}_{t-1} + \boldsymbol{F}.\Delta\mathbf{x}_t + \boldsymbol{G}.\Delta\boldsymbol{\beta} \tag{4.2}$$

where $\Delta\mathbf{y}_t$, $\Delta\mathbf{x}_t$, $\Delta\boldsymbol{\beta}$ are deviations about the simulation timepaths, and $\boldsymbol{D}, \boldsymbol{E}, \boldsymbol{F}, \boldsymbol{G}$ are partial derivative matrices (which are held constant for this presentation despite their time-varying nature).

Assuming that the $\boldsymbol{D}$ matrix is invertible, as will normally be the case, we can derive the familiar *reduced form deviations model*:

$$\begin{aligned}\Delta\mathbf{y}_t &= \boldsymbol{D}^{-1}\boldsymbol{E}.\Delta\mathbf{y}_{t-1} + \boldsymbol{D}^{-1}\boldsymbol{F}.\Delta\mathbf{x}_t + \boldsymbol{D}^{-1}\boldsymbol{G}.\Delta\boldsymbol{\beta} \\ &= \boldsymbol{A}.\Delta\mathbf{y}_{t-1} + \boldsymbol{B}.\Delta\mathbf{x}_t + \boldsymbol{C}.\Delta\boldsymbol{\beta}.\end{aligned} \tag{4.3}$$

As expressed diagrammatically beneath equation (4.3), the reduced form is composed of three basic components. The system's homogeneous dynamics are governed by the $\boldsymbol{A}$ matrix. Multipliers are generated by exogenous variable changes ($\Delta\mathbf{x}_t$) and their coefficients $\boldsymbol{B}$, together with the homogeneous dynamics. Similarly, parameter perturbations ($\Delta\boldsymbol{\beta}$) drive the endogenous variables through the $\boldsymbol{C}$ and $\boldsymbol{A}$ matrices.

There are many things one might want to do with the linearized structural form and reduced form deviations models to identify essential model features. Rather than attempt to catalogue the possibilities here we prefer to concentrate on our most recent and ongoing research.[16] We address three questions about multipliers:

1. What exogenous variables are most important in determining the endogenous variables?
2. What elements of the homogeneous dynamics contribute most to influential multipliers?
3. Where in the model's structure do the important elements of the dynamics originate?

The answer to the first question can be found through conventional reduced-form multiplier analysis. It is easily verified that:

$$\Delta \mathbf{y}_{t_0+n} = \sum_{s=0}^{n-1} \boldsymbol{A}^s \boldsymbol{B} . \Delta \mathbf{x}_{t_0+n-s} \tag{4.4}$$

where t_0 is the period preceding the initial exogenous variable perturbation (the initial condition period), $t_0 + n$ is the current time period, and s is the running time index for the perturbed values of $\Delta\mathbf{x}$ between $t_0 + 1$ and $t_0 + n$.

Since important exogenous variables create large endogenous variable response, we seek to identify these after normalizing the response as an elasticity to remove effects of units of measurement.

Answering the second question requires defining 'elements of the homogeneous dynamics.' It is customary to define dynamic elements in terms of the characteristic roots and vectors of the A matrix:[17]

$$\boldsymbol{A}\mathbf{r}_h = \mathbf{r}_h \lambda_h \qquad (h = 1, \ldots, H) \tag{4.5}$$

$$\mathbf{l}_h' \boldsymbol{A} = \lambda_h \mathbf{l}_h' \qquad (h = 1, \ldots, H) \tag{4.6}$$

where

λ_h is a characteristic root of $\boldsymbol{A}$,
$\mathbf{r}_h$ is the right characteristic vector associated with λ_h, and
$\mathbf{l}_h$ is the left characteristic vector associated with λ_h.

If we normalize the characteristic vectors so that:

$$\boldsymbol{L}'\boldsymbol{R} = \boldsymbol{I} \tag{4.7}$$

where

$\boldsymbol{R}$ is the $H \times H$ matrix of right characteristic vectors,
$\boldsymbol{L}$ is the $H \times H$ matrix of left vectors, and
$\boldsymbol{I}$ is the $H \times H$ identity matrix,

$\boldsymbol{A}$ can then be written as the sum of elements associated with individual characteristic roots:

$$\boldsymbol{A} = \sum_{h=1}^{H} \mathbf{r}_h \cdot \lambda_h \cdot \mathbf{l}'_h. \tag{4.8}$$

Moreover, powers of $\boldsymbol{A}$ may be similarly expressed:

$$\boldsymbol{A}^s = \sum_{h=1}^{H} \mathbf{r}_h \cdot \lambda_h^s \cdot \mathbf{l}'_h. \tag{4.9}$$

The conventional multiplier equation (4.4) can be broken up into dynamic elements by substituting equation (4.9) into equation (4.4). This yields a characteristic root decomposition for multipliers:

$$\Delta \mathbf{y}_{t_0+n} = \sum_{s=0}^{n-1} \left(\sum_{h=1}^{H} \mathbf{r}_h \cdot \lambda_h^s \cdot \mathbf{l}'_h \right) \boldsymbol{B} \cdot \Delta \mathbf{x}_{t_0+n-s}. \tag{4.10}$$

For any single root, λ_h, we can express that portion of endogenous variable response associated with λ_h as:

$$(\Delta y_{t_0+n}|\lambda_h) = \sum_{s=0}^{n-1} \mathbf{r}_h \cdot \lambda_h^s \cdot \mathbf{l}'_h \cdot \boldsymbol{B} \cdot \Delta \mathbf{x}_{t_0+n-s}. \tag{4.11}$$

Hence, the elements of homogeneous dynamics that contribute most to multipliers are those for which $(\Delta \mathbf{y}_{t_0+n}|\lambda_h)$ is large. To aid interpretation, components of $(\Delta \mathbf{y}_{t_0+n}|\lambda_h)$ are normalized to elasticities.[18]

We relate the characteristic roots to elements of the coefficient matrices in the linearized structural form model to determine where in the model's structure important elements of the dynamics arise. Remembering that the roots are functions of the reduced form $\boldsymbol{A}$ matrix, and that the $\boldsymbol{A}$ matrix is determined by the structural form $\boldsymbol{D}$ and $\boldsymbol{E}$ matrices, we see that the roots are functions of the $\boldsymbol{D}$ and $\boldsymbol{E}$ matrices. Elements of $\boldsymbol{D}$ and $\boldsymbol{E}$ which importantly influence a given λ_h are those for which partial derivatives $\partial\lambda_h/\partial d_{ij}$ and $\partial\lambda_h/\partial e_{ij}$ are large.[19] These derivatives are also normalized into elasticities.

Since real GNP behaviour has been one classical focus of macro-economic modelling, we shall look at its behaviour in MQEM to illustrate how the processes described above work out in practice.[20]

We would normally expect to find that only a few of the 51 exogenous variables and 239 roots in the MQEM are important to GNP multipliers since the MQEM coefficient matrices are $2\frac{2}{3}\%$ sparse or less, a percent that typifies macro models more generally. We should thus be able to isolate a small number of significant model elements.

Descriptive information about the most meaningful exogenous variables and characteristic roots is available in Figure 8.9. The initial focus is on conventional reduced form multiplier elasticities for the period 1 or impact, period 4, and

Figure 8.9 Descriptive information for GNP72 particular response

A: Exogenous Variable Definitions

DQMH	– Dummy for change in productivity growth rate (0 to 1966-1, 1 thereafter)
GFD	– Government purchases of goods and services: defence
GSL	– Government purchases of goods and services: state and local
GTROF	– Government transfers minus unemployment benefits: federal
MBASE	– Monetary base including borrowed reserves
PAUTO	– Consumer price index component for new autos, 1967 = 100
PCRUDE	– Wholesale price index for crude materials less raw food and food stocks, 1967 = 100
PGAS	– Consumer price index component for gasoline and motor oil
PM	– Deflator for imports, 1972 = 100
PX	– Deflator for exports, 1972 = 100
RDIS	– Discount rate, Federal Reserve Bank of NY
TIME	– Time: equals 1.0 in 1954.I, increasing by 1 per quarter
X	– Exports, current $
YGWS	– Government wage and salary disbursements: all
YPINT	– Personal interest income

B: Characteristic root properties

Root index	*Real part*	*Imag. part*	*Magnitude*	*Period*
4	0.436	0.461	0.635	7.72
5	0.277	0.551	0.617	5.69
9	−0.294	0.498	0.578	2.99
11	−0.004	0.547	0.547	3.98
12	−0.425	0.337	0.542	2.54
13	−0.443	0.264	0.516	2.41
51	0.936	0.069	0.939	85.30
52	0.925	0.061	0.927	96.10
56	0.779	0.145	0.793	34.20
59	0.730	0.081	0.734	57.00
61	0.698	0.045	0.699	98.00
71	0.589	0.026	0.589	145.00
72	0.578	—	0.578	—
75	0.495	0.005	0.495	569.00
76	0.307	0.363	0.475	7.23
79	0.119	0.394	0.411	4.92
82	0.045	0.363	0.366	4.34
89	−0.221	0.165	0.276	2.51

period 8, shown in Figure 8.10. The dominant impression from the period 1 elasticities is that GSL matters a lot at impact; GFD, YGWS, PAUTO, PX, and X count for something, while the two primary monetary variables do not matter. Thus fiscal variables (and to a lesser extent some sectoral prices) have short term clout.

Figure 8.10 Total GNP72 particular elasticity to exogenous variable changes. Elasticities less than 0.05 in magnitude are set to 0

Period	Monetary		Fiscal				Prices					Other			
	MBASE	RDIS	GFD	GSL	GTROF	YGWS	PAUTO	PCRUDE	PGAS	PM	PX	DQMH	TIME	X	YPINT
1	0	0	0.050	0.159	0.019	0.041	−0.046	0	−0.034	−0.026	−0.063	0	0	0.064	0.024
4	0.032	−0.024	0.074	0.237	0.048	0.085	−0.037	−0.035	−0.038	−0.081	−0.094	0.010	0	0.095	0.050
8	0.086	−0.064	0.081	0.256	0.076	0.107	−0.039	−0.053	−0.047	−0.115	−0.103	0.021	0	0.103	0.063

At four quarters some changes in relative importance emerge. PM and YPINT take on significance, while the fiscal variables, GFD, GSL, and YGWS, have nearly doubled their impact elasticities. Monetary elasticities for RDIS and MBASE are small but no longer zero.

Further interesting changes emerge at eight quarters. GTROF appears for the first time as another sizable fiscal variable. Although fiscal variables still have the largest elasticities, their influence has ceased to grow much over the previous 4 quarters, while the two monetary variables, RDIS and MBASE, have twice the influence that they had 4 quarters earlier.

One original goal, obtaining a better understanding of structure through simplification, has at least been partly achieved. We have found for short–intermediate run behaviour that a small handful of the model's 51 exogenous variables really make a difference to real GNP. We also have a rough notion about some aspects of dynamic behaviour. To refine our understanding of the dynamics further, we look at how the characteristic roots interact with exogenous variables. For this purpose we will initially limit attention to the 8 quarter elasticities in Figure 8.11, Part C.

Root 56 seems to dominate real GNP's response as it appears with sizable elasticities across most of the important exogenous variables while other roots have much more restricted, and typically smaller, exogenous variable associations. This complex root (see Figure 8.9, Part B) has a magnitude of 0.79 and a periodicity of $8\frac{1}{2}$ years; we will soon investigate it more thoroughly. All the roots shown except Root 72 are complex. About half have periodicities less than two years, which for quarterly data seem largely devoid of meaning. A number of roots have a periodicity greater than 20 years; while perhaps not biased, these are only of independent interest for those with faith in the Kondratief cycle.

According to Figure 8.11, nine of the 18 roots (4, 5, 9, 11, 12, 13, 71, 79, and 82) are only associated with the exogenous price terms PGAS, PCRUDE, and PAUTO as well as PM (which is linked to many other roots as well). Three roots (61, 72, 75) are only connected to policy monetary variables RDIS and MBASE, while two other 'monetary roots' (51 and 52) have one or two other related exogenous variables. Two roots (59, 76) have fiscal variable associations, GSL and YGWS, and one or two price variables, also.

Thus we see clear patterns emerging. One root is strongly connected to most exogenous variables; a majority of roots, of short periodicity, are tied only to exogenous prices and a set of five roots is exclusively or primarily linked to the monetary policy variables.

The next stage in the process establishes which linearized model coefficients are most responsible for determining each of the above roots. We confine our attention in this paper to the dominating Root 56. Figure 8.12 lists by sector definitions of the variables whose coefficients are involved with this root. Elasticities of the root with respect to linearized model coefficients ($\boldsymbol{D}$ and $\boldsymbol{E}$ matrix entries) are presented in Figure 8.13.

Figure 8.11 Partial GNP72 particular elasticity response to exogenous variable changes associated with characteristic roots. Elasticities less than 0.05 in magnitude are set to 0.

A: One period or impact response

Root index	Monetary		Fiscal				Prices					Other			
	MBASE	RDIS	GFD	GSL	GTROF	YGWS	PAUTO	PCRUDE	PGAS	PM	PX	DQMH	TIME	X	YPINT
4	0	0	0	0	0	0	−0.053	0	0	−0.104	0	0	0	0	0
8	0	0	0	0	0	0	0	0.067	0	0.086	0	0	0	0	0
9	0	0	0	0	0	0	−0.071	0	−0.059	−0.068	0	0	0	0	0
10	0	0	0	0	0	0	0	0.102	0	0.063	0	0	0	0	0
11	0	0	0	0	0	0	0.063	−0.124	0.052	−0.065	0	0	0	0	0
12	0	0	0	0	0	0	0	−0.104	0	−0.122	0	0	0	0	0
13	0	0	0	0	0	0	0	0.100	0	0.151	0	0	0	0	0
56	0	0	0	0.070	0	0	0	0	0	0	0	0	0	0	0
61	−0.072	0.052	0	0	0	0	0	0	0	0	0	0	0	0	0
75	0.054	0	0	0	0	0	0	0	0	0	0	0	0	0	0
76	0	0	0	0	0	0	0	0.056	0	0.101	0	0	0	0	0
79	0	0	0	0	0	0	−0.080	0	−0.060	−0.121	0	0	0	0	0
82	0	0	0	0	0	0	0.067	0	0.055	0.074	0	0	0	0	0
89	0	0	0	0	0	−0.064	0	0	0	0	0	0	0	0	0
Summation*	0	0	0.050	0.159	0.019	0.041	−0.046	0	−0.034	−0.026	−0.063	0	0	0.064	0.024

*Summation over all roots, not just for the ones greater than 0.05 which appear above.

B: Four period response

Root index	Monetary		Fiscal				Prices					Other				
	MBASE	RDIS	GFD	GSL	GTROF	YGWS	PAUTO	PCRUDE	PGAS	PM	PX	DQMH	TIME	X	YPINT
4	0	0	0	0	0	0	−0.095	0	−0.095	−0.151	0	0	0	0	0
5	0	0	0	0	0	0	0	0.075	0	0.088	0	0	0	0	0
9	0	0	0	0	0	0	−0.055	0	0	−0.063	0	0	0	0	0
11	0	0	0	0	0	0	0.051	−0.064	0	0	0	0	0	0	0
12	0	0	0	0	0	0	0	−0.077	0	−0.072	0	0	0	0	0
13	0	0	0	0	0	0	0	0.074	0	0.097	0	0	0	0	0
51	−0.105	0.065	0	0	0	0	0	0	0	−0.063	0	0	−0.061	0	0
52	0.100	−0.063	0	0	0	0	0	0	0	0	0	0	0	0	0
56	0.125	−0.081	0.069	0.191	0	0.062	0	0.052	−0.067	−0.103	−0.076	0	0	0.076	0
59	0	0	0	−0.068	0	0	0	−0.106	0	0	0	0	0	0	0
61	−0.185	0.133	0	0	0	0	0	0	0	0	0	0	0	0	0
72	−0.063	0	0	0	0	0	0	0	0	0	0	0	0	0	0
75	0.102	−0.077	0	0	0	0	0	0	0	0	0	0	0	0	0
76	0	0	0	0	0	−0.066	0	0	0.051	0.122	0	0	0	0	0
79	0	0	0	0	0	0	−0.107	0	−0.092	−0.138	0	0	0	0	0
82	0	0	0	0	0	0	0.070	0	0.063	0.086	0	0	0	0	0
89	0	0	0	0	0	−0.054	0	0	0	0	0	0	0	0	0
Summation	0.032	−0.024	0.074	0.237	0.048	0.085	−0.037	−0.035	−0.038	−0.081	−0.094	0.010	0	0.095	0.050

C: Eight period response

Root index	Monetary		Fiscal				Prices					Other				
	MBASE	RDIS	GFD	GSL	GTROF	YGWS	PAUTO	PCRUDE	PGAS	PM	PX	DQMH	TIME	X	YPINT
4	0	0	0	0	0	0	−0.080	0	−0.080	−0.128	0	0	0	0	0
5	0	0	0	0	0	0	0	0.072	0	0.082	0	0	0	0	0
9	0	0	0	0	0	0	−0.051	0	0	−0.062	0	0	0	0	0
11	0	0	0	0	0	0	0.056	−0.070	0.051	0	0	0	0	0	0
12	0	0	0	0	0	0	0	−0.071	0	−0.070	0	0	0	0	0
13	0	0	0	0	0	0	0	0.071	0	0.096	0	0	0	0	0
51	−0.218	0.139	0	0	0	0	0	−0.069	0	−0.107	0	0.061	−0.107	0	0
52	0.191	−0.124	0	0	0	0	0	0	0	0	0	0	0.066	0	0
56	0.298	−0.202	0.084	0.229	0.077	0.079	0	0.100	0.068	−0.088	−0.091	0	0.062	0.091	0
59	0	0	0	−0.082	0	0	0	−0.144	0	−0.060	0	0	0	0	0
61	−0.231	0.166	0	0	0	0	0	0	0	0	0	0	0	0	0
71	0	0	0	0	0	0	0	0	0	0.055	0	0	0	0	0
72	−0.070	0.052	0	0	0	0	0	0	0	0	0	0	0	0	0
75	0.109	−0.082	0	0	0	0	0	0	0	0	0	0	0	0	0
76	0	0	0	0	0	−0.062	0	0	0	0.107	0	0	0	0	0
79	0	0	0	0	0	0	−0.107	0	−0.092	−0.140	0	0	0	0	0
82	0	0	0	0	0	0	0.071	0	0.064	0.087	0	0	0	0	0
89	0	0	0	0	0	−0.054	0	0	0	0	0	0	0	0	0
Summation	0.086	−0.064	0.081	0.256	0.076	0.107	−0.039	−0.053	−0.047	−0.115	−0.103	0.021	0	0.103	0.063

Figure 8.12 Background information on elasticities of characteristic Root 56 with respect to linearized model coefficient matrices ***D***, ***E***

Final Demand (consumption and investment) variables

C72	– Real personal consumption
GNP72	– Real gross national product
FS72	– Real final sales
GNPAVEQ	– 6-quarter moving average of GNP: Production
GNPAVEA	– 6-quarter moving average of GNP: Agriculture
AUTOS	– Unit retail sales of new autos
IBFNC72	– Real nonresidential investment: Structures
IINV72	– Real inventory investment
IRC72	– Real residential fixed investment
IPDAG72	– Real nonresidential investment: Producer durables, Agriculture
IPDO72	– Real nonresidential investment: Producer durables, Other
IPDQ72	– Real nonresidential investment: Producer durables, Production

Income flow variables

YPWS	– Private wages and salaries

Productivity and employment variables

QMH67	– Real output per hour of all persons (Business nonfarm)
RUM	– Rate of unemployment (Males 20+ years)

Monetary variables

M2	– Currency in circulation and demand deposits
RTB	– Treasury bill rate
RAAA	– Corporate AAA bond rate
RCD	– 90-day Certificate deposit rate, Market yield

Wage and price variables

JCMH	– Real compensation per man hour
PPNF	– Deflator for business nonfarm GNP
PCN	– Deflator for nondurable consumption
PCS	– Deflator for consumption of services
PC	– Deflator for personal consumption

Part A of Figure 8.13 focuses on important coefficients in the final demand (consumption and investment) sector of the MQEM. Three identities and seven behavioural equations are involved. The identities determine real GNP, its major component, real consumption (C72), and real final sales (FS72). The 'own' current coefficient is the only one in C72's equation which exceeds the 0.1 elasticity cutoff.[21] Likewise, the coefficients on GNP72 and IINV72 are most influential in the GNP identity, and that for GNP72 naturally has a strong effect in the FS72 identity. As these identities are static, they cannot be the source for a nonzero root like Root 56; rather they serve to link dynamic behavioural equations.

Figure 8.13 Elasticity of the modulus of Root 56 with respect to linearized model coefficients (***D*** and ***E*** matrix entries)

A: Final demand (consumption and investment) equations

Equation number	Left-hand side endogenous variable	Final demand variables																		
		C72	GNP72	GNPAVEQ			GNPAVEA		AUTOS		IINV72		IRC72		IPDAG72		IPDO72		IPDQ72	
		(0)	(0)	(−1)	(−3)	(−2)	(−3)	(−4)	(−5)	(0)	(−1)	(0)	(−1)	(0)	(−1)	(0)	(−1)	(0)	(−1)	(−1)
14	C72	−0.117	0	0	0	0	0	0	0	0	0	0	0	0	0	0	0	0	0	0
27	GNP72	0	−0.237	0	0	0	0	0	0	0	0	0.105	0	0	0	0	0	0	0	0
31	FS72	0	0.100	0	0	0	0	0	0	0	0	0	0	0	0	0	0	0	0	0
57	AUTOS	0	0	0	0	0	0	0	0	−0.115	0.104	0	0	0	0	0	0	0	0	0
65	IBFNC72	0	0	0	0.124	0	0	0	0	0	0	0	0	0	0	0	0	0	0	0
66	IINV72	0	0	0	0	0	0	0	0	0	0	−0.206	0.113	0	0	0	0	0	0	0
67	IRC72	0	0	0	0	0	0	0	0	0	0	0	0	−0.241	0.290	0	0	0	0	0
73	IPDAG72	0	0	0	0	0	0	−0.127	0.154	0	0	0	0	0	0	0.136	−0.150	0	0	0
77	IPDO72	0	0	0	0	0	0	0	0	0	0	0	0	0	0	0	0	−0.278	0.244	0
81	IPDQ72	0	0	0	0	−0.159	0.241	0	0	0	0	0	0	0	0	0	0	0	0	−0.121

The horizontal dashed line separates static identities from dynamic stochastic equations and the vertical dashed line distinguishes variables defined by identities from variables determined by dynamic stochastic equations. Elasticities less than 0.1 are set to zero

B: Income flow equations

Equation number	Left-hand side endogenous variable	Income flow Variable YPWS (−1)	Final demand interaction GNP72 (0)	(−1)
82	YPWS	−0.144	−0.122	0.171

C: Productivity and unemployment equations

Equation number	Left-hand side endogenous variable	Unemployment variable RUM (0)	(−1)	Final demand interaction GNP72 (0)	(−1)
53	QMH67	0	0	0	−0.125
54	RUM	−0.334	0.324	0.157	0

D: Monetary equations

Equation number	Left-hand side endogenous variable	Monetary variables M2 (0)	(−1)	RTB (0)	(−1)	Price interaction PPNF (−2)	(−3)	(−4)
97	M2	0.175	−0.209	0	0	0	0	0
98	RTB	0	0	−0.356	0.212	0.286	0.721	−0.406
107	RAAA	0	0	0.103	−0.129	0	0	0
111	RCD	0	0	0.182	0	0	0	−0.156

E: Wage and price equations

Equation number	Left-hand side endogenous variable	Wage and price variables												
		JCMH				PPNF		PCN		PCS		PC		
		(0)	(−1)	(−3)	(−5)	(0)	(−1)	(0)	(−1)	(0)	(−1)	(−1)	(−3)	(−4)
38	JCMH	0.478	−0.741	0.163	0	0	0	0	0	0	0	−0.178	0.264	−0.125
39	PPNF	0	0	0	0.102	0	0	0	0	0	0	0	0	0
43	PCN	0	0	0	0	−0.120	0.146	0.133	−0.173	0	0	0	0	0
44	PCS	0	0	0	0	0	0.114	0	0	0.234	−0.327	0	0	0

The seven behavioural equations with coefficients which strongly influence Root 56 are all investment equations. A notable pattern is evident: own current and/or own lag coefficients are important in each investment equation (with the exception of the IBFNC72 equation), which shows up in the lower right partition of Figure 8.13, Part A. Three of the investment equations exhibit influential dependence on GNP or variables derived from GNP (GNPAVEQ, GNPAVEA). While a high degree of sectoral simultaneity is evident in light of the number of behavioural equations implicated, it is striking that coefficients governing interactions between the equations are not the most influential. Rather, it is first-order or Koyck lags that control behaviour, which appear as column (0) for the current value and (−1) for the associated first-order lag.

The same pattern appears in Parts B and C of Figure 8.13, which display important elasticities of Root 56 with respect to coefficients in the income flow and productivity and unemployment sectors. In both cases Koyck lags dominate within the sector and real GNP provides linkage to final demand.

Part D of Figure 8.13 shows a different pattern for the monetary sector. In addition to Koyck lags in the money demand (97) and money supply (98) equations, the dependences of RAAA and RCD on RTB in their respective structural equations turn up here as important influences on Root 56 sensitivity. Moreover, large weight falls on price interaction, primarily through the money supply equation.

Finally, within-sector simultaneity is more important in the wage and price sector (Part E of Figure 8.13). Compensation per man hour (JCMH) depends importantly on the deflator for personal consumption (PC), the components of which (PCN, PCS) derive from the business nonfarm GNP deflator (PPNF), which in turn has an influential dependence on JCMH. First and/or higher order own lags have coefficients with large elasticities in the JCMH, PCN, and PCS equations.

We started out this part of the paper with a description of linear analysis that we thought would help to winnow out some of the more important elements of model behaviour. We found at the outset that a small subset of the 51 exogenous variables in MQEM is important in determining real GNP response. This response is associated with a handful of the 239 MQEM roots but dominated by the contribution of Root 56. This root has been traced to a small group of coefficients in the linearized model. Root 56 is most sensitive to Koyck lag coefficients that appear in the linearized structural equations. Apart from identities that definitionally link equations, there is little simultaneous sensitivity determination. There are exceptions to this generalization: prices and wages interact, as does price with monetary equations. Thus we have identified those elements of the MQEM which are most influential in determining the characteristic response of real GNP to exogenous variables. These are some early results of ongoing research that, with time, should help point the way toward one or a few small models that capture the most salient features of this econometric model.

NOTES

[1] We are grateful to the National Science Foundation for Grant No. NSF/77-2690MCS, to IBM, and to the Energy Information Administration, Department of Energy, for their support.

[2] Participants from other universities include: Professors Gregory C. Chow, James Durbin, Jean-Marie Dufour, Robert F. Engle, Clive Granger, E. Philip Howrey, Saul H. Hymans, Edward E. Leamer, and G. S. Maddala.

[3] We use the notations h_{ii} and h_i interchangeably.

[4] See page 16 of Belsley *et al.* (1980).

[5] When several data points in X space form a relatively tight cluster that is distant from the bulk of the remaining data, the single row deletion methods described here might not work well, since influential subsets could have their effects masked by the presence of nearby points. Various multiple subset deletion procedures (which can, however, become uncomfortably expensive for large data sets) described in Belsley *et al.* (1980) can be used instead.

[6] Belsley *et al.* (1980), Chapter 4, has the full data set and a more detailed discussion of both the equation and regression diagnostics.

[7] Belsley *et al.* (1980), p. 17.

[8] Conventional magnitude for approximate '95% significance'.

[9] Belsley *et al.* (1980), p. 28.

[10] Mallows (1973), Schweppe (see Handschin *et al.*, 1975) and Huber (1981) have proposed other bounded influence estimators. These, along with the Krasker–Welsch algorithm, are presently available in the TROLL Program BIFMOD, CCREMS Technical Report No. 16.

[11] For a more complete development, see Kuh and Neese (1982).

[12] The 1979 version of the MQEM to which these results pertain was recently updated. The two versions are basically similar. We greatly appreciate the cooperation of Professors Hymans and Howrey in making the MQEM available. For a description of the model's structure, see Hymans and Shapiro (1974).

[13] In Kuh and Neese (1982) we discuss the pros and cons of alternative perturbation procedures.

[14] The purpose in scaling is to facilitate graphical comparisons of timepaths.

[15] This section is current research of Peter Hollinger and ourselves. Recent work by Deleau and Malgrange (1978) is in much the same spirit.

[16] Two books which describe applications of linear analysis in depth are Aoki (1976) and Chow (1975).

[17] We assume for this presentation that A possesses a full set of H roots and vectors (where $H = G$) as the exposition would be unfruitfully complicated by considering the defective case.

[18] A valuable text by Baumol (1979) provides background on how characteristic roots illuminate understanding of dynamic economic model behaviour.

[19] Formulas for computing these derivatives are available in Faddeev and Faddeeva (1963), pp. 228–229.

[20] The model has been initialized in 1973–2 after all exogenous variables were given 'stylized trend' values (historical geometric growth or typical constant value) beginning in 1969–2 in order to get rid of historical behavioural transients. Further work is needed to show how sensitive the results reported in this paper are to initialization procedures.

[21] All nonzero coefficients in these identities are of course unity. Obviously coefficients, and elasticities that embed these coefficients, will generally differ.

REFERENCES

Aoki, M. (1976). *Optimal Control and System Theory in Dynamic Economic Analysis*, Elsevier, New York.

Baumol, W. (1979). *Economic Dynamics: An Introduction*, 3rd Ed. MacMillan, New York.

Belsley, D. A., Kuh, E., and Welsch, R. E. (1980) *Regression Diagnostics: Identifying Influential Data and Sources of Collinearity*, Wiley, New York.

Chow, G. C. (1975). *Analysis and Control of Dynamic Economic Systems*, Wiley, New York.

Deleau, M., and Malgrange, P. (1978). *'L'analyse des modèles macroéconomiques quantitatifs.'* Economica, Paris.

Faddeev, D. K., and Faddeeva, V. N. (1963). *Computational Methods of Linear Algebra*, Freeman, San Francisco.

Handschin, E., Kohlas, J., Fiechter, A., and Schweppe, F. (1975). 'Bad data analysis for power system state estimation.' *IEEE Transactions on Power Apparatus and Systems*, **PAS-94,** 329–337.

Harrison, D., and Rubinfeld, D. L. (1978). 'Hedonic prices and the demand for clean air.' *Journal of Environmental Economics and Management*, **5,** 81–102.

Huber, P. J. (1981). *Robust Statistics*, Wiley, New York.

Hymans, S. H., and Shapiro, H. T. (1974). 'The structure and properties of the Michigan Quarterly Econometric Model of the U.S. Economy.' *International Economic Review*, **15,** 632–653.

Krasker, W. S., and Welsch, R. E. (1979). 'Efficient bounded-influence regression estimation using alternative definitions of sensitivity.' Massachusetts Institute of Technology, CCREMS Technical Report No. 3.

Kuh, E., and Neese, J. (1982). 'Parameter sensitivity, dynamic behaviour and model reliability: An initial exploration with the MQEM monetary sector.' Chapter in *Proceedings of the Econometric Society European Meeting 1979, Selected Econometric Papers–in Memory of Stefan Valavanis*, North-Holland, Amsterdam.

Mallows, C. L. (1973). 'Influence functions.' Talk at the National Bureau of Economic Research Conference on Robust Regression in Cambridge, Mass.

Discussion

J. WAELBROECK
Free University, Bruxelles

It is useful to distinguish three stages in building up a model. The first is gathering and checking data; the second is estimation; the third is simulation to assess the model's properties. All three stages are important, though for various reasons a large fraction of methodological studies is devoted to stage 2. This is true for the present meeting also, as illustrated earlier by the subtle discussion of exogeneity, nested versus non-nested hypotheses, locally equivalent specifications, Lagrange multiplier tests, and other topics. The present paper focuses on better methods for stages 1 and 3; in fact the authors have been kind and have provided us with two papers, which are only loosely related.

The first stage is the most tedious, but not the least important. Because it is unglamorous there is something of a tendency for econometricians to pick up any data which happen to be lying around and put them uncritically into the computer. Anyone who has taught econometrics has probably felt the need to exhort students to criticize sources, to plot the data to see what they seem to imply, to have a close look at seemingly aberrant observations; not infrequently these turn out to be wrong, the result of a punching error for example. Data plots become very difficult to analyse when the sample exceeds, say, 100 observations. The Kuh–Neese method provides a heuristic way of singling out the critical observations which may deserve a close look.

Perhaps I can illustrate what is at stake by an anecdote. Many years ago—econometrics were young in Belgium then—I was on the thesis committee of a Ph.D. on projections of the OECD economy. The relation highlighted in the thesis was a production function relating growth with the investment share; I think the R^2 was around 0.9 and everything seemed lovely. Plotting data made it immediately clear however that this consisted in a tight cluster, with one outlier for Iceland: 2000 fishing boats were responsible for policy implications for the whole of the developed world.

For this simple case there was no need for the Kuh–Neese approach; this would not be true for a larger sample. The programs developed can thus greatly help in the stage 1 process of checking important data, pointing out observations which might be erroneous or atypical. For small samples I would prefer the traditional look at data plots. For very large samples, say over 1000 observations, I suspect that the method may not work very well. The choice of influential observation is, as analysis of the formula shows, a combinatorial problem, as each observation which is removed changes the 'influentiality' of the others; results will not, I suspect, be clearcut if there are many outliers, though only experience can say how important the problem is. My impression therefore is that the Kuh–Neese technique will be most useful for samples numbering in the hundreds.

I do feel it necessary to break a lance for orthodoxy. There is a real danger of being led by the method into what a colleague at CORE has called 'John Wayne econometrics', in which the valiant hero strides through the sample, his trusted Kuh–Neese gun at the cock, shooting down in the best Western tradition villainous observations from rooftops and balconies, to finally marry the beautiful regression. The sample should be tampered with only for strong reasons; as my Iceland example shows this may worsen the R^2 and t ratios.

The other contribution of the paper is the methodology for the study of dynamic properties of models. Much of this is well known, such as the multiplier analysis. What I found new and interesting is the work on eigenvectors and eigenvalues. I believe that the first calculations of eigenvectors for large models are those of Mori at the Wharton School. Soon after he developed his program we tried this approach on our models in Bruxelles, and I must say that after great hopes we gradually became disappointed. It turned out that there were acute problems of accuracy; scale changes or use of different programs to calculate eigenvectors and eigenvalues made a large impact on the results; the same model would be stable with one program and unstable with another. Here the Kuh group has made a contribution not reported in the paper, in developing much needed highly accurate software, thanks to which it will be possible to get results which at least are numerically correct.

The other reason for our disappointment was that the results seemed so hard to understand. In particular cases, we did trace unstable eigenvalues to small sets of unstable equations which were not strongly connected with the rest of the model; but there were often quite a few fairly large eigenvalues, which did not depend in any obvious way on the structure of the model. Here the Kuh group, using the Faddeev–Faddeeva formulae, has been able to relate eigenvectors and eigenvalues to individual coefficients. And quite surprisingly to me, it seems that most of the eigenvalues depend largely on a small set of coefficients. In fact eigenvector values seem to be related to individual equations. This result suggests a kind of dynamic decomposability of models which we should understand better; I suggest that the authors should try to relate it to an analysis of the quasi recursiveness or quasi diagonality of the models which they study.

Evaluating the Reliability of Macro-economic Models
Edited by G. C. Chow and P. Corsi

CHAPTER 9

Analysing Econometric Models by Control Methods

G. C. CHOW
Princeton University

In building an econometric model, one can find no guarantee that it will produce good forecasts in the future. There are a number of statistical tests that one can apply, but these only measure how well the model fits the sample data by various criteria, and not how well the model will predict. As is well-known, a finite amount of data can be well fitted by many different models, depending on the ingenuity and resourcefulness of the model builder. Therefore, economists have relied on the theoretical reasonableness of each equation in judging a model, besides its statistical goodness of fit. However, theoretical weaknesses of a model may escape one's attention when the equations are examined individually but may become apparent when the properties of the model as a whole are investigated. It is thus useful to study the dynamic properties of the entire model by simulations or analytical methods, such as the cyclical properties of the individual endogenous variables, the lead–lag relations among them, the various short-run and long-run multipliers, and the stability properties of the system. Some of these methods for analysing the dynamic properties of an econometric model are discussed in Part 1 of my *Analysis and Control of Dynamic Economic Systems*, Wiley, 1975. The main purpose of this paper is to present a set of new tools for studying the properties of an econometric model by the use of optimal control methods. These tools are discussed in detail in my book, *Econometric Analysis by Control Methods*, Wiley, 1981.

9.1 METHOD OF OPTIMAL CONTROL

Before presenting the tools for model analysis, let us review briefly the method of feedback control as applied to systems of nonlinear simultaneous econometric equations, using a quadratic objective function. Let a system of structural equations be written as

$$\mathbf{y}_t = \boldsymbol{\Phi}(\mathbf{y}_t, \mathbf{y}_{t-1}, \mathbf{x}_t, \mathbf{w}_t) + \boldsymbol{\varepsilon}_t \tag{1.1}$$

where $\mathbf{y}_t$ is a vector of endogenous variables at time t, $\mathbf{x}_t$ is a vector of control variables, $\mathbf{w}_t$ is a vector of exogenous variables not subject to control, and $\boldsymbol{\varepsilon}_t$ is a random vector of residuals with zero mean and independently distributed through time. $\boldsymbol{\Phi}$ is a vector of functions Φ_i. Lagged variables $\mathbf{y}_{t-2}, \mathbf{y}_{t-3}, \ldots, \mathbf{x}_{t-1}, \mathbf{x}_{t-2}$, etc. have been eliminated by the introduction of identities. The vector $\mathbf{x}_t$ is incorporated as a subvector in $\mathbf{y}_t$ by definition, so that the quadratic loss function can be written as

$$W = \sum_{t=1}^{T} (\mathbf{y}_t - \mathbf{a}_t)' \boldsymbol{K}_t (\mathbf{y}_t - \mathbf{a}_t) = \sum_{t=1}^{T} (\mathbf{y}_t' \boldsymbol{K}_t \mathbf{y}_t - 2\mathbf{y}_t' \boldsymbol{K}_t \mathbf{a}_t + \mathbf{a}_t' \boldsymbol{K}_t \mathbf{a}_t). \tag{1.2}$$

The problem is to minimize EW subject to (1.1). Its solution consists of the following steps.

1. Starting with a tentative policy path $\mathbf{x}_1^0, \mathbf{x}_2^0, \ldots, \mathbf{x}_T^0$, and given $\mathbf{w}_1, \mathbf{w}_2, \ldots, \mathbf{w}_T$, we apply the Gauss–Seidel method to the model (1.1) with $\boldsymbol{\varepsilon}_t = \mathbf{0}$ for T periods to obtain a solution path $\mathbf{y}_1^0, \mathbf{y}_2^0, \ldots, \mathbf{y}_T^0$ of the endogenous variables. Thus, for each period t, the following system of equations holds:

$$\mathbf{y}_t^0 = \boldsymbol{\Phi}(\mathbf{y}_t^0, \mathbf{y}_{t-1}^0, \mathbf{x}_t^0, \mathbf{w}_t) \qquad (t = 1, \ldots, T). \tag{1.3}$$

2. Equations (1.1) are linearized about the point $\mathbf{y}_t^0$, $\mathbf{y}_{t-1}^0$, and $\mathbf{x}_t^0$ to yield

$$\mathbf{y}_t = \mathbf{y}_t^0 + \boldsymbol{B}_{1t}(\mathbf{y}_t - \mathbf{y}_t^0) + \boldsymbol{B}_{2t}(\mathbf{y}_{t-1} - \mathbf{y}_{t-1}^0) + \boldsymbol{B}_{3t}(\mathbf{x}_t - \mathbf{x}_t^0) + \boldsymbol{\varepsilon}_t. \tag{1.4}$$

The ij elements of $\boldsymbol{B}_{1t}$, $\boldsymbol{B}_{2t}$, and $\boldsymbol{B}_{3t}$ are, respectively, the derivatives of Φ_i in (1.1) with respect to the jth elements of $\mathbf{y}_t$, $\mathbf{y}_{t-1}$, and $\mathbf{x}_t$. They are easily computed numerically by changing the jth element of $\mathbf{y}_t$, $\mathbf{y}_{t-1}$, or $\mathbf{x}_t$ by a small amount and evaluating the resulting changes in Φ_i.

3. The linear simultaneous equations (1.4) are solved to obtain the linearized reduced-form equations

$$\mathbf{y}_t = \boldsymbol{A}_t \mathbf{y}_{t-1} + \boldsymbol{C}_t \mathbf{x}_t + \mathbf{b}_t + \mathbf{u}_t \tag{1.5}$$

where

$$\begin{aligned} (\boldsymbol{A}_t; \boldsymbol{C}_t; \mathbf{u}_t) &= (\boldsymbol{I} - \boldsymbol{B}_{1t})^{-1} (\boldsymbol{B}_{2t}; \boldsymbol{B}_{3t}; \boldsymbol{\varepsilon}_t) \\ \mathbf{b}_t &= \mathbf{y}_t^0 - \boldsymbol{A}_t \mathbf{y}_{t-1}^0 - \boldsymbol{C}_t \mathbf{x}_t^0. \end{aligned} \tag{1.6}$$

4. Using the linear model (1.5) with additive random disturbances $\mathbf{u}_t$ and the quadratic loss function (1.2), we compute the optimal linear feedback control equations

$$\hat{\mathbf{x}}_t = \boldsymbol{G}_t \mathbf{y}_{t-1} + \mathbf{g}_t \tag{1.7}$$

by the algorithm of Chow (1975, pp. 178–179).

5. A new tentative policy path $\mathbf{x}_1^0, \ldots, \mathbf{x}_T^0$ and solution path $\mathbf{y}_1^0, \ldots, \mathbf{y}_T^0$ are obtained by solving (1.7) and (1.1) with $\boldsymbol{\varepsilon}_t = \mathbf{0}$ consecutively for $\mathbf{x}_t$ and $\mathbf{y}_t$ ($t = 1, \ldots, T$).

6. We go back to step 2 to linearize the model about the new solution path and then compute the optimal feedback solution for the linear–quadratic problem until the process converges.

7. The stochastic system under control is approximately described by (1.5) and (1.7), i.e.

$$\mathbf{y}_t = (A_t + C_t G_t)\mathbf{y}_{t-1} + (\mathbf{b}_t + C_t \mathbf{g}_t) + \mathbf{u}_t = R_t \mathbf{y}_{t-1} + \mathbf{r}_t + \mathbf{u}_t. \tag{1.8}$$

The mean path of this system is given by $\bar{\mathbf{y}}_t = R_t \bar{\mathbf{y}}_{t-1} + \mathbf{r}_t$, or equivalently by the solution vector $\mathbf{y}_t^0$ in the last iteration which also satisfies (1.7) and (1.5) with $\mathbf{u}_t = \mathbf{0}$. The covariance matrix of the system is computed by, for $\mathbf{y}_t^* = \mathbf{y}_t - \bar{\mathbf{y}}_t$,

$$E\mathbf{y}_t^* \mathbf{y}_t^{*\prime} = R_t (E\mathbf{y}_{t-1}^* \mathbf{y}_{t-1}^{*\prime}) R_t^* + E\mathbf{u}_t \mathbf{u}_t' \tag{1.9}$$

where $E\mathbf{u}_t\mathbf{u}_t' = (\boldsymbol{I} - \boldsymbol{B}_{1t})^{-1}(E\boldsymbol{\varepsilon}_t\boldsymbol{\varepsilon}_t')(\boldsymbol{I} - \boldsymbol{B}_{1t})^{-1\prime}$ because of (1.6). The covariance matrix of the random residuals in (1.1) is assumed to have been estimated together with the other unknown parameters in the econometric model. The expected total loss in T periods when the system is under feedback control can be calculated by a formula given in Chow (1975, p. 179).

A computer program is available to perform the above calculations. A user's guide to this program is contained in Chapter 5 of Chow (1981). The program is being distributed by the Econometric Research Program, 207 Dickinson Hall, Princeton University.

9.2 DERIVING THE TRADE-OFF POSSIBILITIES BETWEEN VARIABLES

An important characteristic of an econometric model is the trade-off relations between pairs of variables, such as between inflation and unemployment in the Phillips curve or between consumption goods and investment goods in a planning model. These relations can be ascertained only by optimal control techniques. For example, to derive the inflation–unemployment trade-off relation implicit in an econometric model, economists have tried to vary the timepaths of certain exogenous variables in an econometric model and observe the resulting paths of inflation and unemployment generated by simulations of the model. High inflation and low unemployment have often been found to associate with expansionary fiscal and monetary policies according to the model used. It is hoped that, by simulations, the trade-off relationship between inflation and unemployment can be ascertained. However, it is quite likely that the policies used in the simulation experiment can be dominated, in the sense that an outcome corresponding to both lower inflation and lower unemployment rates could be obtained. By the use of stochastic control techniques, one can trace out the lowest inflation rate compatible with a given unemployment rate according to the specification of an econometric model and given a set of initial conditions, thus yielding an econometric definition of the inflation–unemployment trade-off. The procedure is as follows.

Let y_{1t} and y_{2t} denote the inflation and the unemployment rates respectively. By setting the target a_{2t} for y_{2t} at 5 % and the weight k_{22} in the matrix $\boldsymbol{K}_t$ of the loss function very large in an optimal control experiment, one insures that the unemployment rate generated by the model under optimal control will be close to 5 %. In this experiment, the target a_{1t} for the inflation rate may be set equal to 0 % and the weight k_{11} to a small number. Thus the inflation rate will be minimized subject to the condition that unemployment is at 5 %. By varying the target unemployment rate in a set of optimal control experiments, one can trace out the trade-off relationship between the two variables of interest. The same method can be applied to trace out the production possibilities among different outputs in an econometric model for planning purposes which includes a number of production functions sharing a common set of inputs limited in supply. The optimal control problem is to allocate these inputs in different uses through time efficiently so that given the targeted output of any one commodity, the output of a second commodity is maximized.

The usefulness of performing these trade-off calculations using optimal control methods cannot be overemphasized. It was discovered, as reported in Chapter 2 of Chow (1981), that the Klein–Goldberger model did not impose a trade-off between inflation and real output. That is, by manipulating the control variable of that model, one can achieve any combination of the price level and real GNP in the 1950's that one desires. It was also discovered, as reported in Chapter 13 of Chow (1981), that an experimental econometric model of the Soviet Union constructed by Donald Green along the lines of the SOVMOD of Green and Higgins (1977) did not impose a trade-off between consumption and investment. The discovery that the production constraints were not tight enough led to re-specification of the model. On the positive side, the trade-off relations between inflation and employment were derived for the Michigan Quarterly Econometric Model and the St. Louis Model. They serve to characterize these models, as reported in Chapter 7 of Chow (1981).

9.3 THE VALUE FUNCTION $V(x)$ FOR CHARACTERIZING ECONOMETRIC MODELS

As a by-product of the optimal control calculations described in Section 9.1, one obtains a linearized reduced form (1.5) from which a set of multipliers can be derived. We now define a different type of multipliers which measure the effects of the control variables on the expected loss, rather than on any individual endogenous variables. The expected loss can be viewed as a composite dependent variable. It can be calculated once the loss function (1.2) is specified. The logic of the calculation is as follows.

Given a loss function (1.2) and a linearized reduced form (1.5), we apply the method of dynamic programming to find the optimal feedback control equations for all periods t, beginning with the last period T. Specifically, we first find the optimal strategy for the last period by minimizing the expected loss $E(\mathbf{y}_T - \mathbf{a}_T)' \boldsymbol{K}_T(\mathbf{y}_T - \mathbf{a}_T)$ for only the last period T with respect to $\mathbf{x}_T$. Substituting (1.5) for $\mathbf{y}_T$ in this expectation and differentiating the result with respect to $\mathbf{x}_T$ we obtain a linear feedback control equation $\mathbf{x}_T = \boldsymbol{G}_T\mathbf{y}_{T-1} + \mathbf{g}_T$. We then minimize the sum of the expected losses for the last two periods with respect to $\mathbf{x}_{T-1}$, assuming that the last-period policy $\mathbf{x}_T$ shall be optimal, i.e. substituting the minimum expected loss for period T into the minimand. Continuing the process backward in time, we finally minimize the sum of the expected losses for all T periods with respect to $\mathbf{x}_1$ of the first period, assuming that $\mathbf{x}_2, \ldots, \mathbf{x}_T$ shall be optimal. This sum, after all the future minimum expected losses from period 2 onward have been duly inserted, is the expectation of a quadratic function of the economic variables $\mathbf{y}_1$ for the first period only:

$$V_1 = E(\mathbf{y}_1' \boldsymbol{H}_1 \mathbf{y}_1 - 2\mathbf{y}_1'\mathbf{h}_1 + c_1) \tag{3.1}$$

where the coefficients $\mathbf{H}_1$, $\mathbf{h}_1$, and c_1 can be calculated by the formulas of Chow (1975, p. 179). Using (1.5) to substitute for $\mathbf{y}_1$ in (3.1) and taking expectations, we have

$$\begin{aligned} V_1 &= \mathbf{x}_1' \boldsymbol{C}_1' \boldsymbol{H}_1 \boldsymbol{C}_1 \mathbf{x}_1 + 2\mathbf{x}_1' \boldsymbol{C}_1'(\boldsymbol{H}_1 \boldsymbol{A}_1 \mathbf{y}_0 + \boldsymbol{H}_1 \mathbf{b}_1 - \mathbf{h}_1) \\ &\quad + (\boldsymbol{A}_1 \mathbf{y}_0 + \mathbf{b}_1)' \boldsymbol{H}_1 (\boldsymbol{A}_1 \mathbf{y}_0 + \mathbf{b}_1) + E\mathbf{u}_1' \boldsymbol{H}_1 \mathbf{u}_1 - 2(\boldsymbol{A}_1 \mathbf{y}_0 + \mathbf{b}_1)' \mathbf{h}_1 + c_1 \\ &= \mathbf{x}_1' \boldsymbol{Q} \mathbf{x}_1 + 2\mathbf{x}_1' \mathbf{q} + d. \end{aligned} \tag{3.2}$$

Thus, assuming that the policies from period 2 onward shall be optimal, the expected multiperiod loss is a quadratic function of $\mathbf{x}_1$, as given by (3.2). The optimal first-period policy $\hat{\mathbf{x}}_1$ is obtained by minimizing (3.2) with respect to $\mathbf{x}_1$, yielding the associated minimum expected multiperiod loss $\hat{V}_1 = V_1(\hat{\mathbf{x}}_1)$. Note that the subscript of V denotes the fact that this cumulated expected loss is computed from period 1 onward.

We propose to use the quadratic function $V_1(\mathbf{x}_1)$ as given by (3.2) to characterize and compare econometric models. This function gives the total expected loss from period 1 to period T in terms of the control variables $\mathbf{x}_1$ in the first period, assuming that future policies from period 2 to period T shall be optimally chosen. It appears to capture the essential information contained in an econometric model concerning the effects of the current policy variables on economic welfare as measured by the loss function. It is applicable to deterministic models as a special case where the vectors $\mathbf{u}_t$ of random disturbances for all periods are set equal to zero.

Several uses of the function $V_1(\mathbf{x}_1)$ can be mentioned. First, the derivatives of V_1, or $2Q\mathbf{x}_1 + 2\mathbf{q}$, measure the effects of the current control variables on total expected loss (under the assumption that all future policies be optimal) and can be viewed as a set of multipliers for a composite dependent variable. Secondly, when the function $V_1(\mathbf{x}_1)$ is evaluated at the optimal current period policy $\hat{\mathbf{x}}_1$, the vector of first derivatives $2Q\hat{\mathbf{x}}_1 + 2\mathbf{q}$ is of course zero, but the difference between $V_1(\hat{\mathbf{x}}_1 + \Delta\mathbf{x})$ and $V_1(\hat{\mathbf{x}}_1)$, where the vector $\Delta\mathbf{x}$ has only one finite, nonzero element, will measure the sensitivity of the minimum expected loss with respect to the corresponding control variable. If this difference is small, the specified variation in that control variable will not materially affect the expected loss. Thirdly, once an econometric model and a loss function are agreed upon, the historical policy $\mathbf{x}_1$ for any period (considered as the first period in the optimal control calculations) can be evaluated by the difference $V_1(\mathbf{x}_1) - V_1(\hat{\mathbf{x}}_1)$, as explained in Chapter 8 of Chow (1981).

9.4 EFFECT OF POLICY RULE ON MODEL STABILITY

As is by now fairly generally recognized, one way to check the proper working of an econometric model is to subject it to a set of optimal control experiments, and observe whether it will behave in a strange fashion when the control variables depart from their historical pattern. This can be done through a set of deterministic control experiments where the random disturbances in the model are set equal to zero. The optimal feedback control equation $\mathbf{x}_t = G_t\mathbf{y}_{t-1} + \mathbf{g}_t$ will in this case generate deterministic timepaths for the optimal control variables as well as the endogenous variables in the model. If the paths of the control variables are not far from their historical values and yet the dependent variables could reach their desired targets which are deemed historically impossible (such as achieving a stable price level in 1980), one would question the validity of the model. On the other hand, if the control experiments show that the control variables are required to change drastically in order to change slightly certain endogenous variables which are considered easy to influence, one will also question the validity of the model.

The above analysis is confined to deterministic models. In the case of stochastic models, the optimal policy takes the form of feedback control equations. The historical policies of the government are also depicted by a set of feedback control equations, on a set of reaction functions. Different policy regimes are therefore represented by different reaction functions. To test the sensitivity of the model to changes in policy, one can insert different reaction functions or policy rules for the control variables and observe the stability properties of the resulting systems. One would be concerned if a given change in policy rule leads to unreasonably large or small changes in the stability of the system.

In Chapter 9 of Chow (1981), three different regimes are used to describe the policy instruments. The first is a set of historical reaction functions estimated from sample data. The second is a set of passive reaction functions which set the policy instruments according to smooth trends, irrespective of current economic conditions. The third is a set of optimal control rules derived by minimizing a weighted average of the variances of certain important variables and of the deviations of their means from specified target variables, i.e. the expectation of a quadratic loss function. The purpose of that study is to compare the stability properties of the three regimes, using the Michigan Quarterly Econometric Model, in order to find out to what extent government policy as depicted by the historical reaction functions actually contributed to economic stability. However, for the purpose of analysing the properties of an econometric model, the same method can be used to discover to what extent the stability properties of the model would be affected by different policy regimes. This is a comparative dynamic analysis. The different conditions are the different feedback control equations or reaction functions while the outcome is the stability properties of the system in terms of its first two moments. The analysis will reveal the properties of the model used for the purpose of its validation; it will reveal the properties of the economy if the model is regarded as a good description of the economy.

9.5 EFFECT OF POLICY RULE ON OTHER BEHAVIOURAL EQUATIONS

The analysis of Section 9.4 assumes that when the rule or equation for the government control variables changes, the remaining behavioural equations of the private sector remain constant. This might not be the case since government policies could affect the behaviour of the private sector, as pointed out by Lucas (1976). To study the effect of government policy on the properties of the econometric system, allowing for possible changes in other equations, the method of optimal control can be applied, as pointed out in Chapters 16 and 17 of Chow (1981). Assume that other equations in the econometric model describing the behaviour of the private sector are obtained by the maximization of the latter's objective function subject to the constraints of a stochastic environment. Since government policy is a part of this environment, the behavioural equations or optimal rules of the private sector will change when the government policy rule changes. If an econometrician has estimated the parameters of the objective function of the private sector, he or she can derive the optimal behavioural equations for that sector once the government policy rule and the remainder of the environment facing the private sector are known.

Specifically, let

$$\mathbf{y}_t = A\mathbf{y}_{t-1} + C_1\mathbf{x}_{1t} + C_2\mathbf{x}_{2t} + \mathbf{b} + \mathbf{u}_t \tag{5.1}$$

represent the environment facing the private sector which has the control variables $\mathbf{x}_{1t}$, while the government adopts the decision rule

$$\mathbf{x}_{2t} = G_2\mathbf{y}_{t-1} + \mathbf{g}_2 \tag{5.2}$$

for its policy variables x_{2t}. The environment facing the private economic agents then becomes

$$\begin{aligned} \mathbf{y}_t &= (A + C_2G_2)\mathbf{y}_{t-1} + C_1\mathbf{x}_{1t} + (\mathbf{b} + C_2\mathbf{g}_2) + \mathbf{u}_t \\ &= A_1\mathbf{y}_{t-1} + C_1\mathbf{x}_{1t} + \mathbf{b}_1 + \mathbf{u}_t. \end{aligned} \tag{5.3}$$

Given the objective function of the private sector to be

$$W_1 = \sum_{t=1}^{T} (\mathbf{y}_t - \mathbf{a}_1)' K_{1t} (\mathbf{y}_t - \mathbf{a}_1) \qquad K_{1t} = \beta^t K_1 \tag{5.4}$$

one can derive a set of time-invariant optimal behaviour equations

$$\mathbf{x}_{1t} = G_1\mathbf{y}_{t-1} + \mathbf{g}_1 \tag{5.5}$$

for the private sector using the method of optimal control, provided that the time horizon T is reasonably long and the matrices A_1 and C_1 satisfy certain stability conditions. Equation (5.5) may represent consumption functions, investment functions, and demand equations for inputs. If the parameters of both (5.1) and (5.4) are known, the econometrician can solve the behavioural equations (5.5) for the private sector by optimal control methods, once the government policy rule (5.2) is specified. It is therefore important to estimate the parameters of (5.1) and (5.4) in order to study the effects of government policy on the econometric model.

The estimation of (5.1) and (5.4) is also an important problem in the optimal control literature; it is the problem of estimating the parameters of the preference function. If we regard the parameters of (5.1) and (5.4) as the 'structural' parameters of the model, and the parameters of the behavioural equations (5.5) as the 'reduced-form' parameters derived from them, we can apply the method of maximum likelihood and the method of two-stage least squares to estimate them. These methods are described in Chapter 16 of Chow (1981).

Maximum likelihood estimates of the parameters of (5.5) can be obtained as follows. (The subscript 1 for the private sector will be dropped.) By the dynamic programming algorithm of Chow (1975, pp. 178–179), the coefficients G_t and $\mathbf{g}_t$ of the optimal feedback control equations are solutions of the following four equations:

$$(C_t'H_tC_t)G_t + C_t'H_tA_t = O \tag{5.6}$$

$$H_{t-1} - K_{t-1} - (A_t + C_tG_t)'H_t(A_t + C_tG_t) = O \tag{5.7}$$

$$(C_t'H_tC_t)\mathbf{g}_t + C_t'(H_t\mathbf{b} - \mathbf{h}_t) = O \tag{5.8}$$

$$\mathbf{h}_{t-1} - \mathbf{k}_{t-1} - (A_t + C_tG_t)'(\mathbf{h}_t - H_t\mathbf{b}_t) = O. \tag{5.9}$$

G_t and H_t are found by solving the first two equations backward in time, with the initial conditions $H_T = K_T$, $\mathbf{g}_t$ and $\mathbf{h}_t$ are found by solving the last two equations backward in time, with the initial condition $\mathbf{h}_T = K_T\mathbf{a}_T$.

Confining ourselves here to a special but important case, let $\boldsymbol{K}_t = \beta^t \boldsymbol{K}$, β being the discount rate, and $\mathbf{a}_t = \mathbf{a}$. Let the model be linear and time-invariant, thus omitting the time subscript t in $\boldsymbol{A}_t$, $\boldsymbol{C}_t$, and $\mathbf{b}_t$. Assume that the solution to the above difference equations converge, so that $\boldsymbol{G}$, $\boldsymbol{H}$, $\mathbf{g}$, and $\mathbf{h}$ will satisfy

$$(\boldsymbol{C}'\boldsymbol{H}\boldsymbol{C})\boldsymbol{G} + \boldsymbol{C}'\boldsymbol{H}\boldsymbol{A} = \boldsymbol{O} \tag{5.10}$$

$$\boldsymbol{H} - \boldsymbol{K} - \beta(\boldsymbol{A} + \boldsymbol{C}\boldsymbol{G})'\boldsymbol{H}(\boldsymbol{A} + \boldsymbol{C}\boldsymbol{G}) = \boldsymbol{O} \tag{5.11}$$

$$(\boldsymbol{C}'\boldsymbol{H}\boldsymbol{C})\mathbf{g} + \boldsymbol{C}'(\boldsymbol{H}\mathbf{b} - \mathbf{h}) = \boldsymbol{O} \tag{5.12}$$

$$\mathbf{h} - \mathbf{k} - \beta(\boldsymbol{A} + \boldsymbol{C}\boldsymbol{G})'(\mathbf{h} - \boldsymbol{H}\mathbf{b}) = \boldsymbol{O}. \tag{5.13}$$

Assume that the residuals of (5.3) and (5.5) are normal and independent, with covariance matrices $\boldsymbol{\Sigma}$ and $\boldsymbol{V}$ respectively. The constrained maximum likelihood estimates of the parameters $\boldsymbol{\Sigma}$, $\boldsymbol{V}$, $\boldsymbol{A}$, $\boldsymbol{C}$, $\mathbf{b}$, $\boldsymbol{K}$, β, $\mathbf{a}$, $\boldsymbol{G}$, $\boldsymbol{H}$, $\mathbf{g}$, and $\mathbf{h}$ can be obtained by maximizing the Lagrangian expression

$$\begin{aligned} L = \text{constant} &- \frac{n}{2}\log|\boldsymbol{\Sigma}| - \frac{n}{2}\log|\boldsymbol{V}| \\ &- \tfrac{1}{2}\operatorname{tr}[\boldsymbol{\Sigma}^{-1}(\boldsymbol{Y}' - \boldsymbol{A}\boldsymbol{Y}'_{-1} - \boldsymbol{C}\boldsymbol{X}' - \mathbf{b}\mathbf{z}')(\boldsymbol{Y} - \boldsymbol{Y}_{-1}\boldsymbol{A}' - \boldsymbol{X}\boldsymbol{C}' - \mathbf{z}\mathbf{b}')] \\ &- \tfrac{1}{2}\operatorname{tr}[\boldsymbol{V}^{-1}(\boldsymbol{X}' - \boldsymbol{G}\boldsymbol{Y}'_{-1} - \mathbf{g}\mathbf{z}')(\boldsymbol{X} - \boldsymbol{Y}_{-1}\boldsymbol{G}' - \mathbf{z}\mathbf{g}')] - \operatorname{tr}[\boldsymbol{\Omega}(10)] \\ &- \tfrac{1}{2}\operatorname{tr}[\boldsymbol{\Phi}(11)] - \boldsymbol{\omega}'[(12)] - \boldsymbol{\varphi}'[(13)] \end{aligned}$$

where $\boldsymbol{Y}$ is an $n \times p$ matrix of observations on the endogenous variables; $\boldsymbol{Y}_{-1}$ is an $n \times p$ matrix of observations on the lagged endogenous variables; $\boldsymbol{X}$ is an $n \times q$ matrix of observations on the control variables; z represents a dummy variable being a vector consisting of n ones; $\boldsymbol{\Omega}$ $(p \times q)$ and $\boldsymbol{\Phi} = \boldsymbol{\Phi}'(p \times p)$ are matrices of Lagrangian multipliers; $\boldsymbol{\omega}$ $(q \times 1)$ and $\boldsymbol{\varphi}$ $(p \times 1)$ are vectors of Lagrangian multipliers, and the numbers 10 to 13 in parentheses denote respectively the constraints (5.10) to (5.13). By setting the partial derivatives of L with respect to all parameters equal to zero, we obtain a set of first order conditions for maximum. In Chapter 16 of Chow (1981), we discuss the numerical solution to this maximization problem and to the problems of maximum likelihood and two-stage least squares estimation in more general cases.

For the purpose of studying the properties of an econometric model, ordinarily consisting of equation (5.1) and (5.5) rather than (5.1) and (5.4), the following experiments may be useful. First, for certain behavioural equations (5.5) whose properties we would like to examine critically, we may wish to go back to basics and postulate an objective function (5.4) from which the equation (5.5) can be derived through optimal control. This assumption will be used to estimate the parameters of (5.1) and (5.4), and hence also the parameters of (5.5) which are functions of the former parameters according to the optimal control algorithm. In other words, the parameters of (5.5) are now estimated subject to a set of restrictions resulting from the solution of the optimal control problem of (5.1) and (5.4). These restricted estimates can be compared with the unrestricted estimates to check the reasonableness of the optimization model.

Secondly, after the parameters of (5.1) and (5.4) are estimated, one can study the effect of a new government policy rule $\mathbf{x}_{2t} = \boldsymbol{G}_2 \boldsymbol{y}_{t-1} + \mathbf{g}_2$ on the behaviour of the private sector, and thus of the stability and other dynamic properties of the system. One may be able to exercise judgment as to whether the effects of a given change in government policy rule on the dynamic properties of the econometric system is reasonable, as was suggested in the last section. There is a difference in methodology, however. While in the last section we regarded all other equations in the model as fixed when the government policy was assumed to change, in this section we are able to incorporate the possible changes in the other equations in the model which are themselves induced by the assumed government policy change.

9.6 CONCLUDING COMMENT

In this paper, we have presented several applications of stochastic control methods in analysing the dynamic properties of an econometric model. Hopefully, through such analyses the weaknesses of the model can be revealed and its deficiencies corrected. Needless to say, the methods of stochastic control have other applications than the validation of econometric models. These include the analysis and evaluation of historical policies, the formulation of desirable policies, the comparison of econometric models, the prediction of future behaviour of the government and of private economic agents, and the study of many interesting macro-economic problems in finance and in the optimal exploration and use of natural resources, among others. However, these topics are beyond the scope of the present paper and of this Symposium.

REFERENCES

Chow, G. C. (1975). *Analysis and Control of Dynamic Economic Systems*, Wiley, New York.
Chow, G. C. (1981). *Econometric Analysis by Control Methods*, Wiley, New York.
Green, D. W., and Higgins, C. I. (1977). *SOVMOD I: A Macroeconomic Model of the Soviet Union*, Academic Press, New York.
Lucas, R., Jr. (1976). 'Econometric policy evaluation: A critique.' *Journal of Monetary Economics: Supplement*, **1**, 19–46.

Discussion

B. SITZIA
Università di Perugia

Econometric Analysis by Control Methods is the second book devoted by Professor Chow to such problems in economics and I think it will have, just as the previous one, a large impact on the appreciation and teaching of control methods in the twin fields of policy-making and model building. Concern for the evolution of the theory of policy-making and model building has in fact been a distinctive feature of Professor Chow's work.

The two books together span a period of research that covers the last ten years. Thus they present a large section of what has been the advancement of knowledge in this field during the 1970's.

Since the nature of this comment is that of the review of two books that are so closely linked I think I can take this opportunity to examine their content from the point of view of the perspective they offer on the developments of their subject matter.

A word may be said first on the scientific climate that has accompanied their elaboration. The book of 1975, *Analysis and Control of Dynamic Economic Systems*, which mainly reflected research done in the early 1970's, came out from an effort that was shared by many at that time to make the methods of optimal control operational in econometrics. In the early 1970's there was in fact a shift from the honoured tradition of Tinbergen and Theil to modern control theory. To remember just two names and two dates one might say that Ben Friedman's book (1975, but based on work done much earlier) was the last book in the Theil tradition while Bob Pindyck's book (1973, but also based on work done a couple of years before) was the first of the new wave. One might also remember that the *Annals of Economic and Social Measurement*, a journal that rapidly became prominent in this field, started its publication in October 1972.

Also, in the next year began the meetings of the Seminar on Comparison of Econometric Models, in which most of the model builders were involved and in which the attempt to assess the state of existing models from the point of view of their amenability to operational optimal control was more evident.

This objective presented two aspects, the first conceptual and the second technical. At the conceptual level there was the exigency to bring into econometrics the methods of established linear systems theory and the related state space approach, a methodology that dominates the work that Professor Chow has presented to us. This same exigency explains the content of the first part of the 1975 book, which is devoted to the characterization of econometric models from the point of view of systems theory both in the time and frequency domains. The second part of the 1975 book was instead more concerned with the second, technical, aspect. Under this name we indicate two problems. One is to show the nature of optimal control solutions and the feasibility of optimal control computation in the field of medium to large econometric models. The second is to show the applicability of optimal programs in realistic settings and to meaningful economic problems. The second part of Chow's 1975 book deals with the first of the two problems and culminates with the optimization procedures of which a summary view has been given in the present paper (Section 9.1) as an introduction to the second book.

The only debatable point in the procedure exposed by Chow is that of linearization. Carl Palash (1979) and others have criticized it on the grounds that the expectation of the reduced form of a nonlinear model is not equivalent to the deterministic solution (Howrey and Kelejian, 1971). As a result, 'if high order moments are significant, then the linear feedback rule obtained through Chow's procedure may be substantially suboptimal.'

This point carries a certain theoretical weight since we are not able in general to provide exact optimization rules for nonlinear models; however, I think it must not be over-emphasized. Chow's procedure is the obvious and natural one and may be iterated. Besides, we have evidence coming from a variety of sources (see, for instance, the stochastic simulation experiments performed by the IBM group in Pisa: Bianchi *et al.*, 1976) that tend to demonstrate that the point raised by Howrey and Kelejian is of no great practical importance. In any event now that Chow's procedure is readily available as a computer package it would be interesting to know whether some preliminary calculations are available to assess the extent of nonlinearity present in the model and hence the goodness of the approximation before running optimal control experiments.

As to the second problem, that of practical implementation, Chow's books are mainly theoretical and do not contain examples of realization of optimal control programs for stabilization purposes. One may notice, however, that the task of assessing the state of the art in this field has been performed elsewhere, namely in the NBER–NSF Seminar to which I have referred before.

My own reading of the results of the Seminar and of other similar studies is that the time is not yet ripe to profit from the direct advantages of optimal control in the field of policy-making, but a number of indirect advantages[1] can be gained in the fields of model analysis as well as model comparison or selection. My interpretation is that the second book by Chow, *Econometric Analysis by Control Methods*, is also in this vein of thought.

However, other things have happened in the economics profession since 1975. Briefly, we may recall the widespread consideration of Lucas' (1976) criticism of the methods of economic policy, the later development of the new macroeconomics, and the related issue of rational expectations models.

There has been in fact a cleavage among quantitative economists between the followers of the new fashion and the adherents of what Professor Klein has called mainstream econometrics. It is a cleavage that will not probably heal soon, but there are signs that the debate has reached a point in which participants begin to understand each other. Professor Chow has given important contributions to this area of understanding. The book we are discussing, while firmly in the tradition of mainstream econometrics, gives adequate recognition also to the point of view of the critics.

To illustrate this point I will comment briefly on two examples taken by Chow's presentation. One will be an example of mainstream econometrics, the other an example of how the arguments of the critics can be taken into account.

Both examples show what appears to me the main contribution of Professor

Chow's work, namely how our bag of simulation tools can be enriched by optimal control methods.

The first example is that of deriving trade-off curves implicit in the structure of existing econometric models. In considering the procedure suggested by Chow some points may be raised. First, as in every simulation exercise, the method is local in character: computed trade-offs will necessarily depend on initial conditions. Secondly, more important in my view, control variables are not restricted to belong to any particular feasible set. As a result, control variables may move outside the feasible region and in erratic fashion. Third, and at a different level, there might exist other characterizations of the same problem that may avoid some of the above difficulties and are worth investigating. If I may mention something that is related to my own work (Sitzia, 1976) I have tried to move in reverse fashion with respect to Chow's procedure, namely instead of starting from the concept of isoloss curves in the space of outputs one could start with isocost curves in the space of controls and then examine the shape of the reachability region in order to ascertain whether it contains any dominant trade-off.

The second example I wish to comment upon deals with the possibility of assessing the effects of policy rules on other behavioural equations. It is an interesting case because it provides a framework for appreciating some of the arguments of the critics of traditional policy evaluation. The structure of the problem can be brought forth, as Professor Chow does, considering at least two independent agents that face the same environment. Two possible agents worth considering are the government and the private sector, but other interpretations are obviously possible. This is clearly a game situation which has the potentiality of creating instability if the objective functions of the two agents are not consistent. Professor Chow shows how to use the methods of optimal control in this setting to estimate jointly the parameters of the systems and of the objective function, and how to relate changes in the reaction function of one agent to changes in the reaction function of the other. This seems to me a very useful simulation device but it raises a problem of general interpretation if we go beyond the present setting as a method for analysing the consistency properties of existing models and we then interpret this scheme as a realistic representation. In this event my feeling is that the procedure concedes too much to the position of the critics. Analysis of existing large-scale econometric models has shown in fact that their structure tends to be block-recursive. If we do not want to discard completely the research effort that has brought the construction of existing models and admit that they have captured some part of reality we also have to think of the decision process in the economy as a highly structured and hierarchical process, in which not every agent has access to the same information or possibilities. Along this line of thought one would expect that econometric policy evaluation could be enriched by some contribution coming from large-scale systems theory and decentralized control.

Professor Chow, of course, is not unaware of such developments. In fact, in a recent paper (Chow, 1980) whose results are not contained in the present paper, he has extended the basic model presented here considering a situation of dynamic game in which the government is allowed to anticipate the behaviour of the other agent and is thus assuming the role of a dominant player.

As a conclusion, if I had to guess the content of the next book by Professor Chow I would dare to say that it will contain more topics and applications that are akin to the literature of large-scale systems and I may also add that it will be a book which, like the present one we would all be eager to read.

NOTE

[1] I am borrowing here the terminology of Dr Livesey, who was on the board of the Royal Commission on Policy Optimization and in examining these issues reached the same conclusions (Livesey, 1979). It may be remembered that Professor Chow was among the referees of the Commission.

REFERENCES

Bianchu, C., Calzolari, G., and Corsi, P. (1976). 'Divergences in the results of stochastic and deterministic simulation of an Italian non linear economimetric model.' In L. Dekker (Ed.), *Simulation of Systems*, North-Holland, Amsterdam, p. 653–661.

Chow, G. C. (1975), *Analysis and Control of Dynamic Economic Systems*, Wiley, New York.

Chow, G. C. (1980). 'Estimation and Optimal Control of Models of Dynamic Games.' Presented at C.N.R.S., Paris, Dec. 1980.

Friedman, B. M. (1975). *Economic Stabilization Policy — Methods in Optimization*, North-Holland, Amsterdam.

Howrey, E. P., and Kelejian, H. (1971). 'Simulation verses Analytical Solutions: The Case of Econometric Models.' In T. Naylor (Ed.), *Computer Simulation Experiments with Models of Economic Systems*, Wiley, New York, pp. 299–319.

Livesey, D. A. (1979). 'Methodological Aspects of the Indirect Benefits of Optimal Control Theory.' In P. Ormerod (Ed.), *Economic Modelling*, Heineman, London.

Lucas, R. Jr. (1976). 'Econometric Policy Evaluation: A Critique.' *Journal of Monetary Economics: Supplement*, **1**, 19–46.

Palash, C. J. (1979). 'The Applications of Optimal control Techniques to Macroeconomics: A Survey.' *Research Paper No. 7903*, Fed. Res. Bank of New York, Feb. 1979.

Pindyck, R. (1973). *Optimal Planning for Economic Stabilization*, North-Holland, Amsterdam.

Sitzia, B. (1976). 'Controllability Considerations for Econometric Models.' Presented at 5th NBER Control and Economics Conference Palo Alto, May 1976.

Evaluating the Reliability of Macro-economic Models
Edited by G. C. Chow and P. Corsi

CHAPTER 10

The Chow Test in the Presence of Serially Correlated Errors

P. CORSI
Centro Scientifico IBM, Pisa

R. E. POLLOCK
IBM Corporation

J. L. PRAKKEN
IBM Corporation

10.1 INTRODUCTION

Users of large-scale econometric systems frequently must address the issue of whether the structural parameters underlying the model in question remain unchanged over time. To be useful as a device either for forecasting or for the evaluation of alternative policy measures, a model should be built from structural relationships that prove statistically 'robust' over various periods of both the past and the future. Consequently, econometricians have spent considerable effort developing techniques to test the sturdiness of regression coefficients across different time periods. Of such techniques, the Chow test is perhaps the most familiar and certainly the most frequently used.[1]

The Chow test compares estimates of a linear specification made over different sample periods and evaluates, by means of an F ratio, whether the null hypothesis of stability in the set of regression coefficients is rejected or not. The test proceeds on the usual assumptions that the residuals associated with the specification are normally and independently distributed with zero mean and a constant variance. In much time series work, however, disturbances are either heteroskedastic or serially dependent (or both). In such cases it is interesting to ask whether inferences drawn from the Chow test are seriously affected.

A partial analytical solution to the case of heteroskedastic disturbances has evolved in an exchange between Toyoda (1974), Jayatissa (1977), and Schmidt and Sickles (1977).[2] To our knowledge, however, problems introduced by serially correlated residuals have received little attention, in part because of the apparent intractability of a general analytical solution. In this paper we derive an expression for the extent to which the expectation of the test statistic is displaced when the Chow test is inappropriately applied to models characterized by first-order, serially correlated residuals. This derivation, however, is valid only asymptotically; futhermore, it does not consider higher-order moments of the distribution of the test statistic. Therefore, we also use Monte Carlo techniques to investigate the reliability of the Chow test in the case of a simple one-variable model with autocorrelated errors for a sample size of fifty.

Our results suggest that in instances typical of time series models, the Chow test is biased toward rejecting the hypothesis of stability in the regression coefficients. Frequently this bias is sufficient to render the test highly misleading unless corrective measures are applied to the data beforehand. Although these findings may not seem surprising, they do serve as a useful warning to the empirical practitioner.

The remainder of the paper is organized as follows: in Section 10.2 is derived an expression for the asymptotic displacement of the expectation of the test statistic when the Chow test is applied to models characterized by first-order, serially dependent disturbances; Section 10.3 discusses the methodology underlying the Monte Carlo experiments and presents results from a set of plausible cases; in Section 10.4 we present some examples of equations from the IBM quarterly model of the U.S. economy in which failure to correct for autocorrelation makes important differences in inferences drawn from the Chow test; Section 10.5 concludes the paper with a summary of the findings and some comments on judging the stability of regression models.

10.2 THE CHOW TEST WITH AUTOCORRELATED ERRORS

Consider the following time series model:

$$\begin{aligned} \mathbf{y} &= \boldsymbol{X\beta} + \mathbf{u} \\ E[\mathbf{u}] &= 0 \\ E[\mathbf{uu}'] &= \sigma^2 \boldsymbol{I}_n \end{aligned} \tag{1}$$

where $\mathbf{y}$ is an $n \times 1$ vector of chronologically ordered observations on the dependent variable, y_t, $t = 1, 2, \ldots, n$, $\boldsymbol{X}$ is an $n \times k$ matrix (of rank k) of corresponding observations on k independent variables, $\boldsymbol{\beta}$ is a $k \times 1$ vector of associated coefficients, $\mathbf{u}$ is an $n \times 1$ vector of normally, independently distributed disturbances with zero mean and common variance, σ^2, and $\boldsymbol{I}_n$ is an $n \times n$ identity matrix.

Suppose that the data are split after the first j observations, and separate regressions run over the two mutually exclusive subperiods thus created. These separate regressions are summarized in the following equivalent model:

$$\mathbf{y} = \begin{bmatrix} X_1 & 0 \\ 0 & X_2 \end{bmatrix} \begin{bmatrix} \boldsymbol{\beta}_1 \\ \boldsymbol{\beta}_2 \end{bmatrix} + \mathbf{u} \tag{2}$$

where, in obvious notation, X_1 is $j \times k$, X_2 is $(n-j) \times k$, and both $\boldsymbol{\beta}_1$ and $\boldsymbol{\beta}_2$ are $k \times 1$. For expositional simplicity, denote:

$$X^* = \begin{bmatrix} X_1 & 0 \\ 0 & X_2 \end{bmatrix}. \tag{3}$$

The null hypothesis of the Chow test is that $\boldsymbol{\beta}_1 = \boldsymbol{\beta}_2$, i.e. that the vector of coefficients associated with the first j observations of the model is identical to that associated with the last $n - j$ observations. The test is performed as follows.[3] First, estimate the 'restricted' model as in (1). Denote the resulting vector of residuals $\hat{\mathbf{u}}$. The sum of their squares is the quadratic form:

$$\hat{\mathbf{u}}'\hat{\mathbf{u}} = \mathbf{y}'(I_n - X(X'X)^{-1}X')\mathbf{y} = \mathbf{y}'M\mathbf{y} = \mathbf{u}'M\mathbf{u} \tag{4}$$

where $M = I_n - X(X'X)^{-1}X'$. M is symmetric idempotent and $\operatorname{tr}(M) = n - k$. Next, estimate the 'unrestricted' model as in (2). Call the resulting vector of residuals $\hat{\mathbf{u}}^*$. The sum of their squares is:

$$\hat{\mathbf{u}}^{*\prime}\hat{\mathbf{u}}^* = \mathbf{y}'(I_n - X^*(X^{*\prime}X^*)^{-1}X^{*\prime})\mathbf{y} = \mathbf{y}'M^*\mathbf{y} = \mathbf{u}'M^*\mathbf{u} \tag{5}$$

where $M^* = I_n - X^*(X^{*\prime}X^*)^{-1}X^{*\prime}$; again, M^* is idempotent and $\operatorname{tr}(M^*) = n - 2k$. Under the null hypothesis of stability, the test statistic

$$S = \frac{\left(\dfrac{\mathbf{y}'(M - M^*)\mathbf{y}}{k\sigma^2}\right)}{\left(\dfrac{\mathbf{y}'M^*\mathbf{y}}{(n-2k)\sigma^2}\right)} \tag{6}$$

is distributed as a central F with $(k, n-2k)$ degrees of freedom. The calculated test statistic is then compared to a tabled F distribution at the desired level of significance.

The proof that S obeys an F distribution proceeds by demonstrating that the quadratic forms appearing in both the numerator and denominator of (6) are distributed as Chi-squares (of k and $n - 2k$ degrees of freedom respectively) and that they are independent of each other. Consider, for example, the form:

$$\frac{\mathbf{y}'(M - M^*)\mathbf{y}}{\sigma^2} = \mathbf{u}'\left[\frac{1}{\sigma^2}(M - M^*)\right]\mathbf{u} \tag{7}$$

which appears in the numerator of S. Given our assumptions regarding the error structure of the model, it is clear that (7) is distributed as $\chi^2(k)$, since $(\boldsymbol{M} - \boldsymbol{M}^*)$ is idempotent of rank equal to tr $(\boldsymbol{M} - \boldsymbol{M}^*) = k$. Similar logic applies to the form:

$$\frac{\mathbf{y}'\boldsymbol{M}^*\mathbf{y}}{\sigma^2} = \mathbf{u}'\left[\frac{1}{\sigma^2}\boldsymbol{M}^*\right]\mathbf{u} \tag{8}$$

which appears in the denominator of S. The independence of (7) and (8) follows immediately from the fact that $(\boldsymbol{M} - \boldsymbol{M}^*)\boldsymbol{M} = \mathbf{0}$.[4] We also note in passing that the expectation of S is

$$E[S] = \frac{n - 2k}{n - 2k - 2}, \tag{9}$$

the expected value of an F distribution of $(k, n - 2k)$ degrees of freedom. The asymptotic expectation of S is thus:

$$\bar{E}[S] = \underset{n \to \infty}{E}\left[\frac{n - 2k}{n - 2k - 2}\right] = 1 \tag{10}$$

The situation becomes more complicated when the error process underlying the model deviates from that typically assumed in classical regression analysis. For example, suppose that the residuals display first-order serial correlation:

$$\begin{aligned} \mathbf{u} &= \rho\mathbf{u}_{-1} + \varepsilon \qquad -1 < \rho < 1 \\ E[\boldsymbol{\varepsilon}] &= \mathbf{0} \\ E[\boldsymbol{\varepsilon}\boldsymbol{\varepsilon}'] &= \boldsymbol{I}_n\sigma_\varepsilon^2. \end{aligned} \tag{11}$$

Then the variance–covariance matrix of $\mathbf{u}$ is:

$$E[\mathbf{u}\mathbf{u}'] = \frac{\sigma_\varepsilon^2}{1 - \rho^2}\boldsymbol{V} \tag{12}$$

where

$$\boldsymbol{V} = \begin{bmatrix} 1 & \rho & \rho^2 & \cdots & \rho^{n-1} \\ \rho & 1 & \rho & \cdots & \rho^{n-2} \\ \rho^2 & \rho & 1 & \cdots & \rho^{n-3} \\ \cdot & \cdot & \cdot & & \cdot \\ \cdot & \cdot & \cdot & & \cdot \\ \cdot & \cdot & \cdot & & \cdot \\ \rho^{n-1} & \rho^{n-2} & \rho^{n-3} & \cdots & 1 \end{bmatrix} \tag{13}$$

Under these circumstances it is not true in general that the quadratic forms (7) and (8) are distributed as Chi-squares because neither $(\boldsymbol{M} - \boldsymbol{M}^*)\boldsymbol{V}$ nor $\boldsymbol{M}^*\boldsymbol{V}$ are necessarily idempotent. Nor are (7) and (8) generally independent since it is not necessarily true that $(\boldsymbol{M} - \boldsymbol{M}^*)\boldsymbol{V}\boldsymbol{M}^* = \mathbf{0}$. Consequently, S is not guaranteed distributed as an F ratio, and proceeding with the Chow test on the assumption that S follows an F distribution may be misleading.

Once the assumptions of classical regression analysis are discarded, it is no longer possible to make precise statements about the distribution of (6). In general, the behaviour of S will depend on the properties of the regressors, the parameters underlying the model, and the nature of the error structure. Some insight into the performance of the Chow test in the presence of serially correlated errors can be gained, however, by considering the extent to which autocorrelation displaces the first moment of S away from the expectation of the F distribution falsely assumed to underlie the test.

Suppose that, for a given sample size n, we wish to test the hypothesis of stability in the regression coefficients before and after the midpoint of the sample. Thus, $j = n/2$, n even. Note that $\mathbf{u}$ can be partitioned as:

$$\mathbf{u} = \begin{bmatrix} \mathbf{u}_1 \\ \mathbf{u}_2 \end{bmatrix} \tag{14}$$

and that:

$$E[\mathbf{u}_1\mathbf{u}_1'] = E[\mathbf{u}_2\mathbf{u}_2'] = \frac{\sigma_\varepsilon^2}{1-\rho^2}\boldsymbol{V}_1 = \frac{\sigma_\varepsilon^2}{1-\rho^2}\boldsymbol{V}_2 \tag{15}$$

where:

$$\boldsymbol{V}_1 = \boldsymbol{V}_2 = \begin{bmatrix} 1 & \rho & \rho^2 & \cdots & \rho^{j-1} \\ \rho & 1 & \rho & \cdots & \rho^{j-2} \\ \rho^2 & \rho & 1 & \cdots & \rho^{j-3} \\ \cdot & \cdot & \cdot & & \cdot \\ \cdot & \cdot & \cdot & & \cdot \\ \cdot & \cdot & \cdot & & \cdot \\ \rho^{j-1} & \rho^{j-2} & \rho^{j-3} & \cdots & 1 \end{bmatrix} \tag{16}$$

Next, for large enough samples, let the product-moment matrix of the regressors converge to a fixed, $k \times k$, positive definite matrix:

$$\lim_{n\to\infty} \frac{1}{n}\boldsymbol{X}'\boldsymbol{X} = \lim_{n\to\infty} \frac{1}{j}\boldsymbol{X}_1'\boldsymbol{X}_1 = \lim_{n\to\infty} \frac{1}{j}\boldsymbol{X}_2'\boldsymbol{X}_2 = \boldsymbol{\Sigma}_{xx}. \tag{17}$$

In addition, assume that:

$$\lim_{n\to\infty} \frac{1}{n}\boldsymbol{X}'\boldsymbol{V}\boldsymbol{X} = \lim_{n\to\infty} \frac{1}{j}\boldsymbol{X}_1'\boldsymbol{V}_1\boldsymbol{X}_1 = \lim_{n\to\infty} \frac{1}{j}\boldsymbol{X}_2'\boldsymbol{V}_2\boldsymbol{X}_2 = \tilde{\boldsymbol{\Sigma}}_{xx}, \tag{18}$$

where $\tilde{\boldsymbol{\Sigma}}_{xx}$ is again a fixed, $k \times k$, positive definite matrix.[5]

Now the test statistic (6) can be expressed as:

$$S = S_n = \frac{[\mathbf{y}'(\boldsymbol{M} - \boldsymbol{M}^*)\mathbf{y}]((n-2k)/n)}{[\mathbf{y}'\boldsymbol{M}^*\mathbf{y}](k/n)}. \tag{19}$$

Using (3) and (14), the numerator of S_n is then easily rewritten as:

$$\begin{aligned} A_n &= [\mathbf{y}'(\boldsymbol{M} - \boldsymbol{M}^*)\mathbf{y}]\left(\frac{n-2k}{n}\right) \\ &= \left(\frac{n-2k}{n}\right)[\mathbf{u}_1'\boldsymbol{X}_1(\boldsymbol{X}_1'\boldsymbol{X}_1)^{-1}\boldsymbol{X}_1'\mathbf{u}_1 \\ &\quad + \mathbf{u}_2'\boldsymbol{X}_2(\boldsymbol{X}_2'\boldsymbol{X}_2)^{-1}\boldsymbol{X}_2'\mathbf{u}_2 - \mathbf{u}'\boldsymbol{X}(\boldsymbol{X}'\boldsymbol{X})^{-1}\boldsymbol{X}'\mathbf{u}]. \end{aligned} \tag{20}$$

The expectation of A_n is thus:

$$\begin{aligned} E[A_n] = \left(\frac{n-2k}{n}\right)\left(\frac{\sigma_\varepsilon^2}{1-\rho^2}\right)&[\operatorname{tr}\{(\boldsymbol{X}_1'\boldsymbol{X}_1)^{-1}\boldsymbol{X}_1'\boldsymbol{V}_1\boldsymbol{X}_1\} \\ &+ \operatorname{tr}\{(\boldsymbol{X}_2'\boldsymbol{X}_2)^{-1}\boldsymbol{X}_2'\boldsymbol{V}_2\boldsymbol{X}_2\} - \operatorname{tr}\{(\boldsymbol{X}'\boldsymbol{X})^{-1}\boldsymbol{X}'\boldsymbol{V}\boldsymbol{X}\}] \end{aligned} \tag{21}$$

or

$$\begin{aligned} E[A_n] = \left(\frac{n-2k}{n}\right)\left(\frac{\sigma_\varepsilon^2}{1-\rho^2}\right)&\left(\operatorname{tr}\left\{\left(\frac{1}{j}\boldsymbol{X}_1'\boldsymbol{X}_1\right)^{-1}\left(\frac{1}{j}\boldsymbol{X}_1'\boldsymbol{V}_1\boldsymbol{X}_1\right)\right\}\right. \\ &\left. + \operatorname{tr}\left\{\left(\frac{1}{j}\boldsymbol{X}_2'\boldsymbol{X}_2\right)^{-1}\left(\frac{1}{j}\boldsymbol{X}_2'\boldsymbol{V}_2\boldsymbol{X}_2\right)\right\} - \operatorname{tr}\left\{\left(\frac{1}{n}\boldsymbol{X}'\boldsymbol{X}\right)^{-1}\left(\frac{1}{n}\boldsymbol{X}'\boldsymbol{V}\boldsymbol{X}\right)\right\}\right) \end{aligned} \tag{22}$$

Given our assumptions in (17) and (18), and since $j = n/2$, the asymptotic expectation of A_n is simply:

$$\bar{E}[A_n] = \frac{\sigma_\varepsilon^2}{1-\rho^2}\operatorname{tr}\left(\boldsymbol{\Sigma}_{xx}^{-1}\tilde{\boldsymbol{\Sigma}}_{xx}\right) = \bar{A}. \tag{23}$$

The denominator of (19) can be handled in an analogous fashion. Hence:

$$\begin{aligned} B_n = \left(\frac{k}{n}\right)&[\mathbf{u}'\mathbf{u} - \mathbf{u}_1'\boldsymbol{X}_1'(\boldsymbol{X}_1'\boldsymbol{X}_1)^{-1}\boldsymbol{X}_1'\mathbf{u}_1 \\ &- \mathbf{u}_2'\boldsymbol{X}_2(\boldsymbol{X}_2'\boldsymbol{X}_2)^{-1}\boldsymbol{X}_2\mathbf{u}_2] \end{aligned} \tag{24}$$

the expectation of which is:

$$\begin{aligned} E[B_n] = \left(\frac{k}{n}\right)\left(\frac{\sigma_\varepsilon^2}{1-\rho^2}\right)&\left(n - \operatorname{tr}\left\{\left(\frac{1}{j}\boldsymbol{X}_1'\boldsymbol{X}_1\right)^{-1}\left(\frac{1}{j}\boldsymbol{X}_1'\boldsymbol{V}_1\boldsymbol{X}_1\right)\right\}\right. \\ &\left. - \operatorname{tr}\left\{\left(\frac{1}{j}\boldsymbol{X}_2'\boldsymbol{X}_2\right)^{-1}\left(\frac{1}{j}\boldsymbol{X}_2'\boldsymbol{V}_2\boldsymbol{X}_2\right)\right\}\right. \end{aligned} \tag{25}$$

Therefore, for large n (and thus j), (25) converges to:

$$\bar{E}[B_n] = k\frac{\sigma_\varepsilon^2}{1-\rho^2} = \bar{B}. \tag{26}$$

Consider next a truncated Taylor series approximation for the expectation of S_n:[6]

$$\begin{aligned} E[S_n] &= E\left[\frac{A_n}{B_n}\right] \\ &\doteq \frac{E[A_n]}{E[B_n]} - \frac{\operatorname{cov}[A_n, B_n]}{(E[B_n])^2} + \frac{E[A_n]\operatorname{var}[B_n]}{(E[B_n])^3} \end{aligned} \tag{27}$$

or, as n increases without bound:

$$\bar{E}[S_n] = \frac{\bar{A}}{\bar{B}} - \lim_{n\to\infty} \frac{\operatorname{cov}[A_n, B_n]}{\bar{B}^2} + \lim_{n\to\infty} \frac{\bar{A}(\operatorname{var}[B_n])}{\bar{B}^3}. \tag{28}$$

The variance of B_n is just k^2 times the variance of the least squares estimator of $\sigma_{\mathbf{u}}^2$ calculated from the residuals of the 'unrestricted' regression. This variance collapses to zero if the residuals are autocorrelated provided that $|\rho| < 1$ (see Goldberger (1964, pp. 149–152)). Thus, $\lim_{n\to\infty} \operatorname{var}[B_n] = 0$. To evaluate the covariance term recall that by Cauchy-Schwarz inequality:

$$|\operatorname{cov}[A_n, B_n]|^2 \leqslant \operatorname{var}[A_n]\operatorname{var}[B_n]. \tag{29}$$

Therefore, if $\lim_{n\to\infty} \operatorname{var}[A_n]$ exists and is finite, then $\lim_{n\to\infty} \operatorname{cov}[A_n, B_n] = 0$.[7] Hence, by (23) and (26):

$$\bar{E}[S_n] = \bar{S} \doteq \frac{\bar{A}}{\bar{B}} = \frac{\operatorname{tr}(\boldsymbol{\Sigma}_{xx}^{-1}\tilde{\boldsymbol{\Sigma}}_{xx})}{k}. \tag{30}$$

If $\rho = 0$, then $\boldsymbol{V} = \boldsymbol{I}_n$, $\boldsymbol{V}_1 = \boldsymbol{V}_2 = \boldsymbol{I}_j$, and $\tilde{\boldsymbol{\Sigma}}_{xx} = \boldsymbol{\Sigma}_{xx}$. Thus, $\operatorname{tr}(\boldsymbol{\Sigma}_{xx}^{-1}\boldsymbol{\Sigma}_{xx}) = \operatorname{tr}(\boldsymbol{\Sigma}_{xx}^{-1}\boldsymbol{\Sigma}_{xx}) = \operatorname{tr}(\boldsymbol{I}_k) = k$, and $S = 1$—the classical case. When the residuals are serially correlated, however, $\bar{S} \neq 1$ in general. The expectation of S will be displaced by an amount given by:

$$\bar{E}[S_n - 1] = \frac{\operatorname{tr}(\boldsymbol{\Sigma}_{xx}^{-1}\tilde{\boldsymbol{\Sigma}}_{xx}) - k}{k}. \tag{31}$$

This is true even though, as can be inferred from expression (26), the least squares estimator of $\sigma_{\mathbf{u}}^2$ is not biased asymptotically. Similar results obtain if the sample is split at different percentiles.

A simple example can serve to illustrate the type of problem involved. Consider the case of a single regressor ($k = 1$). Thus:

$$y_t = \beta x_t + u_t \qquad t = 1, 2, \ldots, n$$
$$u_t = \rho u_{t-1} + \varepsilon_t \tag{32}$$

where u_t is autocorrelated according to (11). It is readily demonstrated that:[8]

$$\begin{aligned} \operatorname{tr}(\boldsymbol{\Sigma}_{xx}^{-1}\tilde{\boldsymbol{\Sigma}}_{xx}) = 1 &+ 2\rho\left(\frac{\sum_{t=1}^{n-1} x_{t+1}x_t}{\sum_{t=1}^{n-1} x_t^2}\right)\left(\frac{\sum_{t=1}^{n-1} \frac{1}{n-1}x_t^2}{\sum_{t=1}^{n} \frac{1}{n}x_t^2}\right)\left(\frac{n-1}{n}\right) \\ &+ 2\rho^2\left(\frac{\sum_{t=1}^{n-2} x_{t+2}x_t}{\sum_{t=1}^{n-2} x_t^2}\right)\left(\frac{\sum_{t=1}^{n-2} \frac{1}{n-2}x_t^2}{\sum_{t=1}^{n} \frac{1}{n}x_t^2}\right)\left(\frac{n-2}{n}\right) \\ &+ \cdots + 2\rho^{n-1}\left(\frac{x_n x_1}{x_1}\right)\left(\frac{x_1^2}{\sum_{t=1}^{n} \frac{1}{n}x_t^2}\right)\left(\frac{1}{n}\right). \end{aligned} \tag{33}$$

For large n it follows from (17) that (33) is approximately equal to:

$$\operatorname{tr}(\boldsymbol{\Sigma}_{xx}^{-1}\tilde{\boldsymbol{\Sigma}}_{xx}) = 1 + 2\rho\hat{\phi}_1 + 2\rho^2\hat{\phi}_2 + \cdots + 2\rho^{n-1}\hat{\phi}_{n-1} \tag{34}$$

where $\hat{\phi}_1, \hat{\phi}_2, \ldots, \hat{\phi}_{n-1}$ is the sequence of least squares estimates of x_t regressed on $x_{t-1}, x_{t-2}, \ldots, x_{t-n-1}$. Furthermore, suppose for expositional purposes that this sequence is roughly geometric, as would be the case if the sample of x was itself generated by a first-order autoregressive process. Then we can approximate (34) by:

$$\operatorname{tr}(\boldsymbol{\Sigma}_{xx}^{-1}\tilde{\boldsymbol{\Sigma}}_{xx}) \doteq 1 + 2\rho\hat{\phi} + 2\rho^2\hat{\phi}^2 + \cdots = \frac{1 + \rho\hat{\phi}}{1 - \rho\hat{\phi}}. \tag{35}$$

where $\hat{\phi}$ is the sample analogue of the first-order autocorrelation coefficient of the regressor. Combining this expression with (31) shows that autocorrelated disturbances displace the asymptotic expectation of S by:

$$\bar{E}[S_n - 1] = \frac{2\rho\hat{\phi}}{1 - \rho\hat{\phi}}. \tag{36}$$

Several interesting implications for the Chow test arise from (36). First, autocorrelation in the residuals should not cause serious problems in large samples unless the x data display sample autocorrelation as well. If, however, $\rho, \hat{\phi} > 0$ or $\rho, \hat{\phi} < 0$, the expectation of the calculated test statistic will be larger than assumed. The contrary is true when ρ and $\hat{\phi}$ are opposite in sign. The extent of the displacement depends on the nonlinear interaction of ρ and $\hat{\phi}$, and can be quite large. This is seen in Table 10.1, which presents values of (36) for $|\rho, \hat{\phi}| < 1$. (We limit ourselves to these values of ρ and $\hat{\phi}$ to ensure the validity of assumptions made in the above derivations.) In time series work one typically encounters positive values of ρ and $\hat{\phi}$. In these instances, our analysis suggests the Chow test is biased towards rejecting the hypothesis of stability in the regression.

10.3 SMALL-SAMPLE EXPERIMENTS

It would be interesting to know something about the properties of S in small samples when residuals in the model are serially correlated. Monte Carlo techniques prove useful for this purpose. As seen above, the behaviour of S in these instances depends on the product-moment matrix of the regressors as well as the error process of the model. Quite obviously, an exhaustive search over all possibilities would be impracticably costly. Therefore we have limited ourselves to a closer examination of the one-variable model discussed at the end of the preceding section.

While the program used to generate the Monte Carlo experiments reported below is quite general, we consider only the following simple case of data creation:[9]

$$\psi_t \, \text{NID}(0, \sigma_\psi^2) \qquad t = 1, 2, \ldots, n \tag{37a}$$

$$x_t = \phi x_{t-1} + \psi_t \qquad |\phi| < 1 \tag{37b}$$

$$\varepsilon_t \, \text{NID}(0, \sigma_\varepsilon^2) \tag{37c}$$

$$u_t = \rho u_{t-1} + \varepsilon_t \qquad |\rho| < 1 \tag{37d}$$

$$y_t = \beta x_t + u_t. \tag{37e}$$

Parameters that can be varied include $n, \sigma_\psi^2, \phi, \sigma_\varepsilon^2, \rho$, and β. For a given set of parameters, then, a fixed sample of x_t is constructed by first drawing n values of ψ_t from a normal distribution with zero mean and variance σ_ψ^2. These values are next used to generate the autoregressive process x_t, which displays first-order serial correlation of ϕ.[10] Therefore, in each experiment the sample for x is drawn from a stationary ARMA process with zero mean and variance $\sigma_\psi^2/(1 - \phi^2)$. For values of $|\phi| < 1$, the assumptions of convergence postulated in (17) and (18) hold. Next, n values of ε_t are drawn from a distribution that is normal $(0, \sigma_\varepsilon^2)$, and these values are used to generate the autoregressive process u_t. Finally, x_t and u_t are combined in equation (37e) to produce data on y_t. The distributions of ψ and ε are independent, thereby guaranteeing that x_t is uncorrelated and hence independent of u_t. Once the data is manufactured, the sample can be split at any point desired, and equation (37e) subjected to the Chow test with the assurance that the null hypothesis of stability is in fact true. This is done by calculating the test statistic in (6) and comparing it to a tabled F distribution with the appropriate degrees of

Table 10.1 Displacement of $\bar{E}(S_n)$ as a function of ρ and ϕ in the one-variable model, calculated from equation (31). The matrix is symmetric

ϕ \ ρ	−0.9	−0.8	−0.7	−0.6	−0.5	−0.4	−0.3	−0.2	−0.1	0	0.1	0.2	0.3	0.4	0.5	0.6	0.7	0.8	0.9
−0.9	8.52	5.14	3.40	2.25	1.62	1.13	0.74	0.44	0.20	0	−0.17	−0.31	−0.43	−0.53	−0.62	−0.70	−0.77	−0.84	−0.90
−0.8		3.56	2.55	1.85	1.33	0.94	0.63	0.39	0.17	0	−0.15	−0.28	−0.39	−0.49	−0.57	−0.65	−0.72	−0.78	−0.84
−0.7			1.92	1.45	1.08	0.78	0.53	0.33	0.15	0	−0.13	−0.25	−0.35	−0.44	−0.52	−0.59	−0.66	−0.72	−0.77
−0.6				1.13	0.86	0.63	0.44	0.27	0.13	0	−0.11	−0.21	−0.31	−0.39	−0.46	−0.53	−0.59	−0.65	−0.70
−0.5					0.67	0.50	0.35	0.22	0.11	0	−0.10	−0.18	−0.26	−0.33	−0.40	−0.46	−0.52	−0.57	−0.62
−0.4						0.38	0.27	0.17	0.08	0	−0.08	−0.15	−0.21	−0.28	−0.33	−0.39	−0.44	−0.49	−0.53
−0.3							0.20	0.13	0.06	0	−0.06	−0.11	−0.17	−0.21	−0.26	−0.31	−0.35	−0.39	−0.43
−0.2								0.08	0.04	0	−0.04	−0.08	−0.11	−0.15	−0.18	−0.21	−0.25	−0.28	−0.31
−0.1									0.02	0	−0.02	−0.04	−0.06	−0.08	−0.10	−0.11	−0.13	−0.15	−0.17
0										0	0	0	0	0	0	0	0	0	0
0.1											0.02	0.04	0.06	0.08	0.11	0.13	0.15	0.17	0.20
0.2												0.08	0.13	0.17	0.22	0.27	0.33	0.39	0.44
0.3													0.20	0.27	0.35	0.44	0.53	0.63	0.74
0.4														0.38	0.50	0.63	0.78	0.94	1.13
0.5															0.67	0.86	1.08	1.33	1.62
0.6																1.13	1.45	1.85	2.25
0.7																	1.92	2.55	3.40
0.8																		3.56	5.14
0.9																			8.52

freedom. The experiment can be repeated any number of times by redrawing ε_t and then reformulating new data for y_t according to (37e).

In compiling results we have adopted the following procedure. A particular experiment (corresponding to a fixed set of parameters) was subjected to one thousand trials, each of which produces a calculated value of S. The empirical distribution of S, $d_s(S)$, was then compared to $d_f(F)$, the counterpart for the F distribution assumed to underlie the test statistic when the null hypothesis of stability in the regression coefficients is true. A hypothetical case appears in Figure 10.1(a).[11] Consider the shaded area

$$A(\alpha) = 1 - \int_0^{F_\alpha} d_s(S)\,dS,$$

where F_α is the critical value of the assumed F distribution at the α percent level of significance. If $A(\alpha)$ exceeds the hatched area

$$B(\alpha) = 1 - \int_0^{F_\alpha} d_f(F)\,dF = \alpha,$$

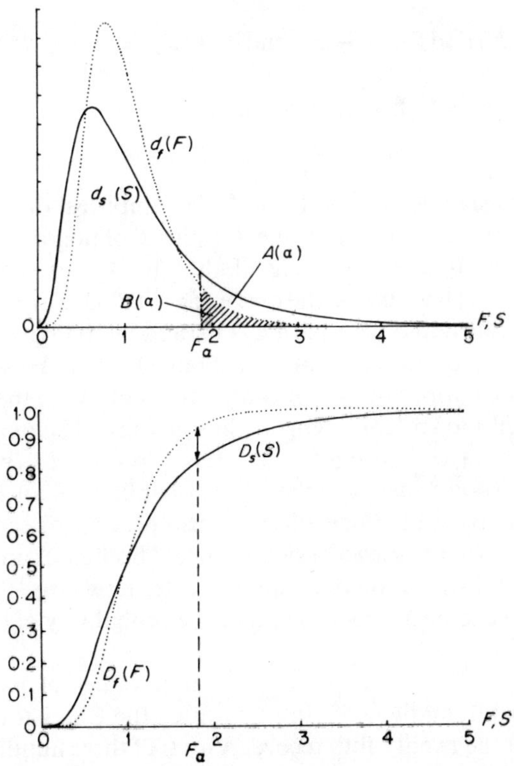

Figure 10.1 (a) Hypothetical densities of S and F. (b) Hypothetical cumulative distributions of S and F

there is a greater probability of type I error than presumed. That is, one tends to reject the null hypothesis of stability more often than is warranted. For each experiment, values of $A(\alpha)$ are presented for $\alpha = 0.05$ and $\alpha = 0.01$.

When $A(\alpha) \neq \alpha$, we say that the Chow test is 'biased'. Moreover, it is interesting to ask whether such bias is significant in some statistical sense. A direct test on $A(\alpha)$ is, of course, not possible because its distribution generally remains unknown. It is, however, possible to test whether $d_s(S)$ differs from $d_f(F)$ by means of the Kolmogorov–Smirnov test.[12] This test compares the largest vertical distance between the presumed and empirical *cumulative* distribution functions of F and S ($D_f(F)$ and $D_s(S)$ in Figure 10.1(b)) to a tabled critical value, K_δ, calculated at a prescribed significance level, δ.[13] If at any point $|D_f(F) - D_s(S)| > K_\delta$, one can reject the null hypothesis that S obeys the presumed F distribution. For current purposes, however, it is particularly interesting to know whether $D_s(S)$ differs significantly from $D_f(F)$ in the range typically considered when conducting the Chow test. Therefore, if $|D_f(F_\alpha) - D_s(F_\alpha)| > K_\delta$, we say that the bias in the Chow test is statistically significant at the δ percent level of significance. Since

$$D_f(F_\alpha) = \int_0^{F_\alpha} d_f(F)\,\mathrm{d}F = 1 - \alpha \quad \text{and} \quad D_s(F_\alpha) = \int_0^{F_\alpha} d_s(S)\,\mathrm{d}S = 1 - A(\alpha),$$

an equivalent statement of significance is that

$$A(\alpha) > \alpha + K_\delta \quad \text{or} \quad A(\alpha) < \alpha - K_\delta.$$

At the five percent significance level, and for an empirical distribution based on one thousand trials, the critical value for the Kolmogorov–Smirnov test is $K_\delta = 0.043$. Hence, as a general rule of thumb, $A(\alpha)$ is judged significantly different from α if $A(\alpha)$ lies outside the range of $\alpha \pm 0.043$. For $\alpha = 0.05$, this range is 0.007 to 0.093. Note that by comparing $D_s(S)$ and $D_f(F)$ at just one point, we do not adhere strictly to the Kolmogorov–Smirnov test. However, if, by our definition, the distributions are significantly different at F_α, they necessarily are different by the full-blown Kolmogorov–Smirnov test. The opposite is not true. Therefore, we have adopted a less powerful procedure than Kolmogorov–Smirnov to test whether S is distributed as an F ratio.

As an additional piece of information, we also present for each experiment S_α, the critical value of S at the α level of significance. This figure can be taken directly from the empirical distribution of S, and indicates how large the calculated test statistic would have to be in order to reduce the probability of type I error to the assumed value of α.

All experiments share the following common values of parameters: $\beta = 1$, $\sigma_\varepsilon^2 = 0.01$, $\sigma_\psi^2 = 0.001$, and $n = 50$. In performing the Chow test, each sample of fifty was split after the twenty-fifth record. A total of three hundred and sixty-one experiments were performed by considering all possible combinations of ρ and ϕ for $|\rho, \phi| < 0.9$ by intervals of 0.1.

As an example, consider Table 10.2 which, for any combination of ρ and ϕ, shows what percentage of the empirically generated distribution of S is to the right of $F_{0.05}(1, 48) = 4.04$. A single element in the grid corresponds to a fixed sample of x (of size fifty) and one thousand independent trials of y. The uppermost left element reveals that, for $\rho = \phi = -0.9$, if the researcher uses 4.04 as the critical value for testing the hypothesis of stability at the five percent level, the probability of falsely rejecting the null hypothesis is actually 0.512—ten times larger than assumed. The remainder of the table shows a pattern consistent with the theoretical considerations developed in Section 10.2. When ρ and ϕ are of the same sign, the actual probability of type I error is generally larger than presumed. The opposite is true when ρ and ϕ are different in sign. The extent of the bias is nonlinear in ρ and ϕ. Thus, if the x data show a low degree of serial correlation, the test is not much biased, even if the residuals are highly autocorrelated. The same is true for cases in which x displays considerable inertia but the residuals are nearly uncorrelated.[14]

Elements in excess of 0.093 or less than 0.007 correspond to instances when, as judged by our weak version of the Kolmogorov–Smirnov test, the cumulative distribution of S was significantly different from $F(1, 48)$ at the five percent level of significance, when evaluated at the point $F_{0.05} = 4.04$. As might be expected, these values are concentrated in the regions where there is at least moderate serial correlation of the same sign in both the regressor and the residuals of the equation. At least in time series work, it is fairly uncommon to find both ρ and ϕ to be negative. However, it is not unusual to find positive values for these parameters in the ranges suggested here to be problematic. Indeed, most econometric models are built from equations estimated on the level of trended time series data ($\phi > 1$) and in which the extent of serial correlation in regression residuals is also quite high.[15,16] For example, in the IBM quarterly econometric model of the U.S. economy, of the fourteen equations estimated by ordinary least squares on level time series data with no lagged dependent variables, the average Durbin–Watson statistic is 0.6. This implies that the average value of ρ in the equations is roughly $(2 - 0.6)/2 = 0.7$. All these specifications fail the Chow test miserably when the data are not pre-filtered (for some examples, see Section 10.4).[17]

It is also interesting to note that significant deviations of the distribution of S from $F(1, 48)$ do occur when ρ and ϕ are large in absolute value but opposite in sign. In these cases, the probability of type I error is reduced to significantly *below* 0.05, indeed practically to zero. While we lack precise information on the power function of the Chow test in the presence of serially correlated disturbances, one can only suspect that the power of the Chow test is seriously damaged for values of the parameters falling in these regions.

Table 10.3 presents the empirically calculated probability of type I error when one mistakenly compares S to the critical value of $F(1, 48)$ at the one percent level of significance ($=7.2$). Again the biases can be substantial. For example, when

Table 10.2 Empirical probability of type I error when $F_{0.05}$ (1, 48) = 4.04 is (mistakenly) assumed the critical value for S at the 5 % level

ϕ \ ρ	−0.9	−0.8	−0.7	−0.6	−0.5	−0.4	−0.3	−0.2	−0.1	0	0.1	0.2	0.3	0.4	0.5	0.6	0.7	0.8	0.9
−0.9	0.512	0.445	0.284	0.296	0.204	0.162	0.116	0.102	0.065	0.054	0.019	0.022	0.020	0.011	0.006	0.001	0.023	0.000	0.000
−0.8	0.632	0.406	0.339	0.170	0.183	0.143	0.138	0.094	0.060	0.052	0.037	0.027	0.010	0.012	0.002	0.000	0.002	0.000	0.000
−0.7	0.343	0.255	0.120	0.156	0.182	0.194	0.090	0.088	0.053	0.042	0.042	0.038	0.023	0.013	0.007	0.004	0.000	0.000	0.000
−0.6	0.257	0.336	0.261	0.139	0.129	0.063	0.102	0.089	0.075	0.041	0.026	0.035	0.025	0.022	0.010	0.006	0.033	0.006	0.002
−0.5	0.092	0.213	0.087	0.132	0.103	0.102	0.111	0.088	0.071	0.048	0.041	0.043	0.023	0.026	0.016	0.012	0.023	0.005	0.005
−0.4	0.081	0.056	0.132	0.154	0.097	0.114	0.075	0.056	0.072	0.046	0.052	0.043	0.036	0.016	0.016	0.014	0.056	0.004	0.002
−0.3	0.153	0.040	0.158	0.071	0.055	0.051	0.056	0.061	0.045	0.036	0.059	0.046	0.039	0.025	0.020	0.025	0.004	0.008	0.002
−0.2	0.010	0.178	0.083	0.108	0.075	0.039	0.053	0.064	0.047	0.039	0.048	0.049	0.045	0.034	0.062	0.047	0.069	0.009	0.086
−0.1	0.114	0.015	0.042	0.062	0.097	0.082	0.072	0.063	0.057	0.054	0.060	0.062	0.034	0.032	0.034	0.031	0.055	0.011	0.016
0	0.009	0.063	0.042	0.045	0.039	0.061	0.058	0.067	0.049	0.056	0.059	0.044	0.058	0.048	0.102	0.038	0.024	0.159	0.024
0.1	0.024	0.022	0.025	0.042	0.048	0.038	0.036	0.039	0.049	0.048	0.038	0.050	0.039	0.074	0.057	0.072	0.044	0.113	0.055
0.2	0.002	0.035	0.124	0.019	0.034	0.040	0.048	0.038	0.048	0.056	0.059	0.078	0.051	0.080	0.104	0.129	0.137	0.204	0.033
0.3	0.006	0.026	0.011	0.013	0.019	0.031	0.028	0.044	0.047	0.046	0.073	0.062	0.071	0.093	0.141	0.098	0.048	0.207	0.232
0.4	0.016	0.002	0.028	0.003	0.024	0.040	0.029	0.022	0.051	0.045	0.055	0.080	0.082	0.086	0.135	0.143	0.106	0.173	0.252
0.5	0.001	0.000	0.025	0.019	0.020	0.019	0.035	0.022	0.046	0.066	0.063	0.081	0.079	0.086	0.050	0.031	0.156	0.199	0.157
0.6	0.001	0.000	0.009	0.011	0.018	0.033	0.019	0.017	0.042	0.057	0.052	0.095	0.116	0.140	0.168	0.179	0.171	0.172	0.247
0.7	0.000	0.000	0.000	0.003	0.008	0.011	0.047	0.030	0.037	0.047	0.072	0.097	0.100	0.119	0.197	0.225	0.270	0.349	0.291
0.8	0.000	0.003	0.001	0.010	0.011	0.009	0.030	0.037	0.047	0.001	0.075	0.094	0.111	0.158	0.223	0.133	0.263	0.419	0.491
0.9	0.000	0.000	0.001	0.002	0.001	0.020	0.018	0.025	0.048	0.065	0.068	0.082	0.109	0.191	0.190	0.232	0.260	0.434	0.620

Table 10.3 Empirical probability of type I error when $F_{0.01}(1, 48) = 7.19$ is (mistakenly) assumed the critical value for S at the 1 % level

ϕ \ ρ	−0.9	−0.8	−0.7	−0.6	−0.5	−0.4	−0.3	−0.2	−0.1	0	0.1	0.2	0.3	0.4	0.5	0.6	0.7	0.8	0.9
−0.9	0.366	0.277	0.140	0.163	0.087	0.058	0.034	0.025	0.013	0.013	0.005	0.003	0.001	0.002	0.000	0.000	0.001	0.000	0.000
−0.8	0.513	0.264	0.196	0.063	0.068	0.053	0.037	0.031	0.016	0.011	0.006	0.004	0.000	0.000	0.000	0.000	0.000	0.000	0.000
−0.7	0.190	0.141	0.034	0.069	0.068	0.067	0.025	0.022	0.015	0.006	0.004	0.003	0.003	0.000	0.000	0.001	0.000	0.000	0.000
−0.6	0.141	0.191	0.101	0.038	0.049	0.016	0.025	0.025	0.016	0.010	0.001	0.005	0.003	0.002	0.003	0.000	0.007	0.000	0.000
−0.5	0.029	0.095	0.014	0.047	0.029	0.032	0.025	0.010	0.016	0.008	0.010	0.010	0.005	0.001	0.001	0.000	0.002	0.001	0.000
−0.4	0.018	0.012	0.042	0.055	0.033	0.037	0.019	0.013	0.019	0.007	0.008	0.004	0.004	0.000	0.003	0.000	0.005	0.000	0.001
−0.3	0.030	0.009	0.056	0.017	0.010	0.007	0.008	0.012	0.009	0.012	0.009	0.009	0.008	0.000	0.003	0.003	0.000	0.000	0.000
−0.2	0.003	0.064	0.028	0.021	0.024	0.012	0.012	0.010	0.009	0.004	0.008	0.010	0.006	0.003	0.020	0.007	0.013	0.000	0.007
−0.1	0.016	0.003	0.008	0.009	0.027	0.026	0.013	0.013	0.005	0.011	0.014	0.011	0.005	0.003	0.005	0.005	0.010	0.001	0.001
0	0.000	0.008	0.004	0.010	0.004	0.009	0.013	0.023	0.010	0.013	0.012	0.005	0.009	0.009	0.019	0.008	0.001	0.037	0.001
0.1	0.004	0.003	0.005	0.007	0.008	0.009	0.005	0.007	0.015	0.009	0.004	0.013	0.003	0.016	0.010	0.020	0.009	0.028	0.012
0.2	0.002	0.003	0.023	0.001	0.006	0.006	0.005	0.010	0.007	0.013	0.015	0.014	0.007	0.016	0.031	0.037	0.039	0.076	0.004
0.3	0.001	0.002	0.000	0.002	0.002	0.003	0.004	0.009	0.009	0.008	0.017	0.019	0.010	0.031	0.052	0.023	0.009	0.083	0.091
0.4	0.016	0.000	0.001	0.000	0.004	0.005	0.007	0.001	0.010	0.005	0.011	0.020	0.019	0.025	0.051	0.039	0.024	0.070	0.100
0.5	0.000	0.000	0.000	0.003	0.002	0.005	0.006	0.002	0.009	0.009	0.015	0.013	0.024	0.026	0.007	0.006	0.060	0.087	0.038
0.6	0.001	0.000	0.000	0.000	0.002	0.005	0.005	0.003	0.008	0.014	0.011	0.023	0.032	0.060	0.067	0.077	0.057	0.076	0.113
0.7	0.000	0.000	0.000	0.000	0.000	0.000	0.006	0.006	0.006	0.006	0.012	0.019	0.037	0.030	0.088	0.103	0.134	0.180	0.127
0.8	0.000	0.000	0.001	0.000	0.000	0.000	0.008	0.005	0.009	0.014	0.019	0.027	0.039	0.053	0.120	0.046	0.126	0.274	0.344
0.9	0.000	0.000	0.000	0.000	0.000	0.000	0.005	0.003	0.008	0.012	0.028	0.017	0.049	0.078	0.088	0.114	0.138	0.262	0.500

$\rho = \phi = 0.7$, the actual probability of type I error is larger than presumed by a factor of thirteen. There are, however, fewer cases in which these biases prove significant since the distributions of S and F become indistinguishable in their right-hand tails. Therefore, the significant deviations of $D_s(S = 7.2)$from $D_f(F = 7.2)$ occur only for the more extreme values of ρ and ϕ when they are similar in sign.[18]

An alternative way of depicting these results is to ask what is the actual critical value of S for various degrees of autocorrelation in the regressor and the residuals. These figures are presented for both the five percent and the one percent significance level in Tables 10.4 and 10.5 respectively. The results are self-explanatory. For positive values of ρ and ϕ, critical values from the presumed F distribution understate the true critical values of the test statistic. The degree of understatement can be quite substantial, and suggests that Chow tests should be approached with extreme caution when applied under such circumstances.

Other types of numerical experiments bear further examination. For example, in some unreported trials we have found evidence that the bias in the Chow test that occurs in small samples when ρ and ϕ are large is maximized when the sample is split precisely in the middle. This contrasts to the classical case in which, provided sufficient degrees of freedom exist to permit estimation over the two subperiods, the distribution of the test statistic is independent of the point of division. If this were indeed true, results presented here represent the worst possible cases. We hope to report on this issue later in more detail.

10.4 EXAMPLES FROM THE IBM QUARTERLY ECONOMETRIC MODEL

Both the theoretical considerations of Section 10.2 and the Monte Carlo experiments of Section 10.3 suggest that, in the presence of serially correlated errors, the Chow test may overstate the incidence of instability in regression equations. To get a better feel for the potential seriousness of the problem when there are several trended regressors, we have chosen some representative equations from the IBM quarterly econometric model of the U.S. economy and subjected them to Chow tests both before and after correction of the equations for first-order serial correlation by the Cochrane–Orcutt technique. The equations marked for consideration all sport very low Durbin–Watson statistics and, to simplify affairs, none includes lagged dependent variables. We do not argue that the equations are as well specified as might be possible. Furthermore, they are plagued by problems other than autocorrelation.[19] These difficulties have been ignored in our efforts to concentrate on the effect of autocorrelation on the Chow test.

Table 10.4 Empirical critical value of S at 5% significance level. The presumed 5% critical value is $F_{0.05}$ (1,48) = 4.04

ϕ \ ρ	−0.9	−0.8	−0.7	−0.6	−0.5	−0.4	−0.3	−0.2	−0.1	0	0.1	0.2	0.3	0.4	0.5	0.6	0.7	0.8	0.9
−0.9	26.4	22.3	11.9	14.5	9.7	8.0	6.2	5.3	4.5	4.1	3.0	2.9	2.6	1.9	1.7	1.0	2.8	0.9	0.6
−0.8	40.3	21.7	16.3	7.9	8.0	7.2	6.5	5.7	4.2	4.0	3.5	3.1	2.3	2.5	1.5	1.6	1.3	1.0	0.7
−0.7	15.0	11.9	6.1	8.0	8.5	8.3	5.4	5.1	4.1	3.7	3.6	3.3	3.0	2.3	1.8	1.9	1.5	1.3	0.8
−0.6	13.0	14.9	10.4	6.3	7.0	4.3	5.7	5.4	4.8	3.8	3.3	3.2	3.1	3.0	2.4	2.0	3.6	1.8	2.0
−0.5	5.5	9.9	5.0	7.0	5.6	5.8	5.3	5.0	4.6	3.9	3.5	3.6	2.8	3.0	2.4	2.1	2.3	2.1	2.0
−0.4	5.0	4.1	6.5	7.3	5.3	5.8	4.8	4.1	4.7	3.8	4.0	3.7	3.4	2.5	2.4	2.5	4.1	1.7	1.5
−0.3	6.3	3.5	7.3	4.8	4.2	4.0	4.1	4.4	3.7	3.5	4.1	3.8	3.6	3.0	2.9	2.9	2.0	2.3	1.5
−0.2	2.2	8.2	5.3	5.6	4.9	3.4	4.1	4.5	3.8	3.7	3.9	3.8	3.8	3.3	4.4	3.9	4.5	2.5	4.6
−0.1	5.2	2.3	3.5	4.4	5.2	5.1	4.8	4.4	4.0	4.1	4.2	4.2	3.3	2.9	3.3	3.0	4.2	2.6	2.8
0	2.4	4.3	3.5	3.6	3.4	4.3	4.5	4.6	3.9	4.2	4.3	3.8	4.2	3.8	5.4	3.4	2.8	6.5	2.9
0.1	3.2	2.6	2.8	3.5	3.9	3.7	3.5	3.6	3.8	3.8	3.4	3.9	3.4	5.0	4.2	4.8	3.8	5.5	4.1
0.2	1.6	3.4	5.5	2.6	3.4	3.4	3.9	3.5	3.9	4.1	4.2	4.8	4.0	5.0	5.5	6.4	6.6	8.8	3.4
0.3	2.2	3.2	2.2	2.4	2.7	3.3	3.2	3.8	3.8	3.9	4.7	4.3	4.4	5.8	7.2	5.8	3.8	9.3	9.3
0.4	2.5	1.6	3.1	1.8	2.9	3.4	3.2	3.0	4.0	3.8	4.1	5.2	5.1	4.9	7.2	6.6	5.7	8.0	9.3
0.5	1.1	1.2	2.7	2.6	2.9	2.6	3.5	3.0	3.7	4.3	4.5	4.9	5.6	5.3	3.9	3.2	7.5	8.8	6.5
0.6	1.7	1.8	2.1	2.7	2.8	3.3	2.8	2.7	3.6	4.1	4.0	5.2	5.8	7.6	8.0	8.4	7.5	8.4	10.6
0.7	1.1	1.0	1.3	1.7	2.0	2.5	3.6	3.2	3.3	3.9	4.4	5.0	6.0	6.1	9.3	10.3	12.5	14.3	10.5
0.8	0.9	1.8	1.2	2.2	2.5	1.9	3.1	3.4	3.9	4.6	4.8	5.5	6.4	7.3	10.9	7.0	11.3	20.5	29.6
0.9	0.4	0.7	1.0	1.5	1.6	2.7	2.3	2.8	3.7	4.4	5.0	4.8	7.0	9.1	9.7	10.7	12.0	21.9	48.5

Table 10.5 Empirical critical value of S at 1 % significance level. The presumed 1 % critical value is $F_{0.05}(1, 48) = 7.19$

ϕ \ ρ	−0.9	−0.8	−0.7	−0.6	−0.5	−0.4	−0.3	−0.2	−0.1	0	0.1	0.2	0.3	0.4	0.5	0.6	0.7	0.8	0.9
−0.9	41.4	43.0	17.8	25.9	16.5	12.3	10.0	9.3	7.6	7.3	5.4	4.8	4.6	4.0	3.2	1.9	5.0	1.7	1.0
−0.8	61.0	35.8	30.0	12.8	12.9	13.3	10.3	9.9	8.0	8.0	5.6	5.5	3.9	4.0	2.6	2.9	2.4	1.7	1.2
−0.7	24.6	18.2	11.2	15.0	14.1	15.0	10.0	9.6	7.6	6.4	6.0	5.6	4.7	4.6	3.5	2.7	2.7	2.2	1.4
−0.6	22.3	23.5	16.6	11.5	13.6	9.2	8.9	9.2	8.3	6.9	5.4	6.1	4.7	4.6	3.9	3.3	6.2	3.1	3.0
−0.5	10.4	16.7	8.1	12.0	9.8	10.6	8.9	6.8	8.0	6.8	6.8	6.9	5.2	4.8	4.4	4.1	4.6	3.4	3.0
−0.4	8.4	7.2	11.3	12.7	10.5	10.5	9.0	8.1	9.0	6.4	7.0	6.0	5.7	5.2	4.4	4.2	6.9	3.1	3.0
−0.3	9.7	7.0	12.5	9.6	7.1	6.0	6.7	7.7	6.9	7.2	6.2	7.0	6.6	5.3	4.6	5.6	3.4	3.8	2.6
−0.2	3.9	13.3	10.5	9.7	9.2	7.4	7.9	6.9	7.0	5.7	6.3	6.4	5.5	5.2	9.2	5.9	7.4	3.9	6.5
−0.1	7.9	5.0	6.5	6.3	9.9	9.5	7.5	7.6	6.1	7.3	8.0	7.1	6.1	5.6	6.0	5.4	6.6	4.1	4.3
0	3.8	4.3	6.3	3.6	6.1	4.3	7.6	4.6	7.1	4.2	7.2	5.9	7.0	7.1	8.7	6.2	4.7	9.9	4.6
0.1	6.0	5.0	5.8	6.4	6.2	7.0	5.6	6.6	7.8	6.8	6.2	7.7	5.4	8.3	7.1	9.1	6.6	9.2	7.6
0.2	2.8	5.5	8.5	4.8	5.3	6.6	6.2	7.0	6.4	7.8	7.9	7.9	6.4	8.1	10.5	10.6	11.2	13.9	5.7
0.3	3.7	5.4	4.0	4.1	5.3	5.3	5.7	7.0	6.8	7.0	7.6	7.9	7.1	9.9	12.4	10.2	6.5	13.3	14.3
0.4	4.2	2.6	5.3	3.1	5.3	5.7	6.0	4.9	7.1	6.2	7.4	8.4	8.3	9.0	13.0	12.3	10.6	13.7	13.3
0.5	2.1	2.0	4.9	4.7	5.1	4.8	6.2	5.0	6.6	7.1	7.7	8.2	8.8	10.0	6.7	6.2	13.9	13.9	10.1
0.6	2.5	3.0	3.7	4.0	5.1	5.8	5.4	5.1	5.9	8.0	7.2	9.4	9.9	15.7	13.7	13.8	12.9	14.0	17.6
0.7	1.7	1.9	2.4	3.0	3.4	4.1	6.3	5.4	6.2	6.5	7.5	8.3	10.2	10.7	15.0	17.0	19.6	23.4	19.5
0.8	1.4	2.8	2.1	3.9	4.1	3.6	6.4	6.4	6.7	7.8	8.0	9.1	12.5	12.6	17.2	13.4	18.8	32.2	47.0
0.9	0.8	1.4	2.0	2.7	2.9	4.6	4.9	5.3	6.6	8.1	8.8	8.9	11.8	16.3	17.0	20.0	23.3	33.0	71.8

Example 1 Average work week

In the IBM model, the average workweek (AWHPE) is a function of the rate of growth in private GNP (GNPPDOT) and a time trend (TREND):[20]

$$\text{AWHPE}_t = a_0 - a_1\text{GNPPDOT}_t - a_3\text{TREND}_t. \tag{38}$$

First, least squares regressions of (38) were estimated over the full sample period (1955 I–1973 IV) and over the two subperiods created by splitting the full sample after 1964 I.[21] Results of these regressions are summarized in the top panel of Table 10.6. The coefficients do vary from the earlier period to the later, and the calculated value of S used to test the hypothesis of stability is 26.4.[22] The corresponding critical values from the assumed F distributions are $F_{0.05}(3, 70) = 2.74$ and $F_{0.01}(3, 70) = 4.08$. Thus, specification (38) appears to fail the Chow test easily at both the five and the one percent significance level. However, when the test is performed by running the regressions on data transformed by the Cochrane–Orcutt method,[23] a very different picture emerges (Table 10.6, bottom panel). Again, the coefficients move about somewhat; but the value of the test statistic has fallen to an insignificant 0.59.[24]

Table 10.6 Estimates of specification (38) before and after autocorrelation correction*

	Least squares estimates		
	1955 I–1973 IV	1955 I–1963 IV	1964 I–1973 IV
a_0	40.340	39.930	42.680
a_1	8.990	8.680	4.240
a_2	−0.027	−0.020	−0.053
n	76.000	37.000	40.000
SE	0.332	0.254	0.206
SSR	8.020	2.200	1.560
DW	0.310	0.350	0.360
	Cochrane–Orcutt estimates		
	1955 I–1973 IV	1955 I–1963 IV	1964 I–1973 IV
a_0	40.450	40.080	41.610
a_1	3.070	4.150	1.480
a_2	−0.028	−0.021	−0.041
n	76.000	37.000	40.000
SE	0.125	0.135	0.115
SSR	1.150	0.620	0.490
DW	1.760	1.510	1.920
RHO	0.920	0.920	0.920

* n = sample size; SE = standard error; SSR = sum of squared residuals; DW = Durbin–Watson statistic; RHO = autocorrelation coefficient.

Example 2 Investment in producers' durables

IBM's specification for investment in producers' durable equipment (PDE) is:

$$PDE_t = b_1\left(0.125 \sum_{i=0}^{7} GNPP_{t-i}\right) + b_2\left(\frac{PPDE}{UNITC}\right)_t + b_3\left(\frac{CPAT}{PPFI}\right)_t + b_4 CUMFG_t \qquad (39)$$

where GNPP is private GNP, PPDE is the deflator for PDE, UNITC is unit labour costs, CPAT is after-tax corporate profits, PPFI is the deflator for business fixed investment (including structures), and CUMFG is the rate of capacity utilization in manufacturing. The same procedure described above was repeated, with the regressions appearing in Table 10.7. When the Chow test is performed using level data, the calculated test statistic is 19.3. This would easily lead to rejection of the hypothesis of stability at the one percent significance level if S was compared to $F_{0.01}(4, 68) = 3.61$. In the corrected equation, however, S drops to 2.84, which is no longer significant at the one percent level.

Table 10.7 Estimates of specification (39) before and after autocorrelation correction*

	Least squares estimates		
	1955 I–1973 IV	1955 I–1963 IV	1964 I–1973 IV
b_1	0.079	0.070	0.079
b_2	−50.330	−39.680	−65.800
b_3	0.097	−0.159	0.135
b_4	0.495	0.534	0.656
n	76.000	37.000	40.000
SE	1.540	1.110	1.060
SSR	171.800	40.800	39.560
DW	1.020	1.130	1.110
	Cochrane–Orcutt estimates		
	1955 I–1973 IV	1955 I–1963 IV	1964 I–1973 IV
b_1	0.079	0.066	0.07
b_2	−42.580	−30.100	−60.930
b_3	0.184	−0.007	0.196
b_4	0.350	0.368	0.583
n	76.000	37.000	40.000
SE	1.090	1.040	1.000
SSR	86.360	36.050	35.040
DW	2.020	1.960	2.280
RHO	0.720	0.720	0.720

* n = sample size; SE = standard error; SSR = sum of squared residuals; DW = Durbin–Watson statistic; RHO = autocorrelation coefficient.

Example 3 Wholesale price index for crude materials (less food)

The specification of this equation is:

$$\ln \frac{\text{PWCLF}_t}{0.25 \sum_{i=0}^{4} \text{PWCLF}_{t-i}} = c_0 + c_1 \ln \frac{\text{UNITCA}_t}{0.25 \sum_{i=0}^{4} \text{UNITC}_{t-i}} + c_2 \ln \frac{\text{GNP}_t}{0.25 \sum_{i=1}^{4} \text{GNP}_{t-1}} + c_3 \ln \frac{\text{PM}_t}{0.25 \sum_{i=1}^{4} \text{PM}_{t-1}} \tag{40}$$

where PWCLF is the producers' price index for crude materials (less food), UNITCA is unit labour costs plus indirect business taxes per unit of output, GNP is real gross national product, and PM is the import deflator. Results are shown in Table 10.8. Again, the specification, when estimated by ordinary least squares on level data, fails the Chow test easily ($S = 11.5$). After correction for autocorrelation, the hypothesis of stability can no longer be rejected at the five and one percent levels of significance ($S = 2.08$).

Table 10.8 Estimates of specification (40) before and after autocorrelation correction*

	Least squares estimates		
	1955 I–1973 IV	1955 I–1961 III	1961 IV–1973 IV
c_0	−0.079	−0.052	−0.028
c_1	0.710	1.430	0.876
c_2	1.113	2.250	0.633
c_3	0.679	−0.835	0.787
n	76.000	27.000	49.000
SE	0.026	0.021	0.020
SSR	0.047	0.011	0.017
DW	0.540	0.530	0.688
	Cochrane–Orcutt estimates		
	1955 I–1973 IV	1955 I–1961 III	1961 IV–1973 IV
c_0	−0.019	−0.023	−0.106
c_1	0.700	0.555	0.973
c_2	0.860	1.455	0.359
c_3	0.637	−0.116	0.642
n	76.000	27.000	49.000
SE	0.018	0.019	0.015
SSR	0.022	0.009	0.010
DW	1.520	2.000	1.490
RHO	0.740	0.740	0.740

* n = sample size; SE = standard error; SSR = sum of squared residuals; DW = Durbin–Watson statistic; RHO = autocorrelation coefficient.

10.5 CONCLUSIONS

The Chow test is potentially biased when the specification being tested is characterized by an error structure exhibiting first-order serial correlation. The magnitude and extent of the bias depends on the product-moment matrix of the regressors and on the extent of autocorrelation present in the errors. In Monte Carlo experiments applied to a simple one-variable model, the presence of autocorrelated residuals by itself did not appear to undermine seriously the usefulness of the Chow test. However, for values of key parameters not uncommon in time series work, the Chow test led to a systematic and often severe overstatement of the probabilities of rejecting the hypothesis of stability when it was in fact true. This tendency was born out in more complex examples taken from the IBM quarterly model of the U.S. economy.

The implications of this study are clear. Those wishing to make sophisticated statistical inferences about a model or a particular equation of a model should take extreme care that assumptions assumed to underlie the test in question are in fact true. In our case, the reliability of the Chow test as a diagnostic tool can be greatly enhanced by passing the data through the standard autoregressive transforming filter prior to estimation.

APPENDIX DATA DEFINITIONS AND SOURCES

Data for capacity utilization are tabulated by the Federal Reserve Board. All other data are compiled by the U.S. Department of Commerce. Actual records have been drawn from the computer listing supplied by Citibank of New York in conjunction with the National Bureau of Economic Research. Variables are seasonally adjusted. Flows are at annual rates.

AWHPE	Average hours worked per week by private employees.
BIT	Indirect business taxes; billions of dollars.
CPAT	Corporate profits after tax; billions of dollars.
CUMFG	Rate of capacity utilization in manufacturing (percent).
GNP	Gross national product; billions of 1972 dollars.
GNPP	Gross domestic private product; billions of 1972 dollars.
PGNPP	Implicit deflator for gross domestic private product; 1972 = 1.
PDE	Investment in producers' durable goods; billions of 1972 dollars.
PM	Implicit deflator for imports; 1972 = 1.
PPDE	Implicit deflator for investment in producers' durable goods; 1972 = 1.
PPFI	Implicit deflator for business fixed investment; 1972 = 1.
PWCLF	Producers' index for non-farm crude materials; 1972 = 1.
UNITC	Unit labour costs in the private sector; 1967 = 100.
UNITCA	= UNITC + (BIT/PGNPP × GNPP)).
TREND	Time trend; 1948 I = 1.

ACKNOWLEDGMENTS

We would like to thank Gregory Chow, Harry Eisenpress, and especially K. S. Sarma for their helpful comments and suggestions during the preparation of this paper. The authors, of course, retain sole responsibility for any errors.

In the discussion which followed the presentation of this paper, a very useful contribution came out from I. Consigliere. In her paper, which is included in the references, she uses an analytic approach. Some differences in the numerical results, probably, can be explained by the different random numbers techniques.

NOTES

[1] For the seminal discussion of the use of this test in econometric work, see Chow (1960). A useful clarificatory statement on the Chow test is found in Fisher (1970). A variety of alternative techniques for evaluating the stability of regression coefficients exists. For examples, see Quandt (1958, 1960), Brown *et al.* (1975), and Farley *et al.* (1975).
[2] These authors consider the case in which the variance of the residuals is fixed within each period, but differs from one period to another. More general forms of heteroskedasticity have not been analysed.
[3] In what follows, we restrict ourselves to discussion of the cases in which there are sufficient degrees of freedom in each subperiod to allow the desired estimation. Cases involving insufficient degrees of freedom are treated nicely by both Chow (1960) and Fisher (1970).
[4] Proofs of theorems on the distribution and independence of quadratic forms are found in Graybill (1961, Chapter 4).
[5] These assumptions are usual. See Theil (1971, Chapter 8).
[6] We assume this expectation exists. Existence is guaranteed if M^* is positive definite so that $\mathbf{u}'M^*\mathbf{u}$, which appears in the denominator of S_n, has no density at zero. In essence, we rule out 'perfect fits'.
[7] This will indeed be the case given our assumptions in (17) and (18), and for $|\rho| < 1$.
[8] See Theil (1971, p. 255).
[9] The Monte Carlo program was written by Ralph Pollock.
[10] In constructing x by (37b), an initial value is required. This value, x_{-l}, was chosen randomly from the same distribution as ψ. Subsequently, the first l observations of the sample were dropped, where $\phi^l < 0.01$. This guarantees that x_t, $t = 1, 2, \ldots, n$, is not much influenced by the initial seed of the data. A similar procedure is used for (37d).
[11] For expository purposes we here treat $d_s(S)$ and $d_f(F)$ as continuous densities.
[12] The Kolmogorov–Smirnov test is discussed in Fisz (1963, pp. 445–449).
[13] Tabled values of K_δ appear in Fisz (1963, p. 664).
[14] These findings are consistent with results reported earlier by Orcutt and Winokur (1969, p. 1). They studied a simple autoregressive model such as equation (37b) and concluded that 'use of the... Chi-square distribution as (the) approximate sampling distribution is verified for inference concerning... residual error variance.'
[15] We have not presented results for $\phi > 1$ since in this case expression (31) is no longer valid. This follows from the fact that trended data violates (17) and (18) (see Theil, 1971, pp. 363–364). In unreported experiments for which $\phi > 1$, we have found results even more extreme than those reported here.
[16] Exceptions occur when the equation includes a lagged dependent variable. As is well known, however, usual measures of autocorrelation are inappropriate in such cases.
[17] Additional examples from the IBM model are discussed by Corsi (1979).

[18] It is impossible to observe here reductions in the probability of type I error by amounts significant at the five percent level when judged by the Kolmogorov–Smirnov test. This follows from the fact that $\alpha - K_{0.05} = 0.01 - 0.043 = -0.033$, but S is bounded from below by zero.

[19] Data for the regressors used to explain business investment are extremely ill-conditioned when judged by the techniques developed by Belsley *et al.* (1980). Errors in the equation for investment and the average workweek are heteroskedastic as well as autocorrelated.

[20] Data definitions and sources are detailed in the Appendix.

[21] This split point, as well as others used below, was decided on by calculating Quandt's (1960) likelihood ratio for each possible point of division, and then picking the point that maximized the likelihood of isolating a shift in the regression. Strictly speaking, this methodology is contrary to the spirit of the Chow test, which posits *a priori* an hypothesis regarding when the split occurred. This raises questions about the correct degrees of freedom to be used in calculating the test statistic. We sidestep the issue here. Note, however, that the 'optimal' split point falls in the middle of the sample—a result alluded to earlier.

[22] The test statistic can be calculated by substituting the summary statistics from the table into (19).

[23] To simplify the exposition, we have assumed the same ρ for all periods. In any event, this hypothesis could not be rejected here or in the examples below.

[24] In the case of the transformed data, both the numerator and denominator of S must be adjusted to reflect the degree of freedom lost in the estimation of ρ.

REFERENCES

Belsley, D. A., Kuh, E., and Welsch, R. E. (1980). *Regression Diagnostics*, Wiley, New York.

Brown, R. L., Durbin, J., and Evans, J. M. (1975). 'Techniques for testing the constance of regression relationships over time.' *Journal of the Royal Statistical Society*, Series B, **37,** 149–163.

Chow, G. C. (1960). 'Tests of equality between sets of coefficients on two linear regressions.' *Econometrica*, **28,** 591–605.

Cochrane, D., and Orcutt, G. H. (1949). 'Application of least squares regressions to relationships containing auto-correlated error terms.' *Journal of the American Statistical Association*, **44,** 32–61.

Consigliere, I. (1981). 'The Chow test with serially correlated errors.' *Rivista Internazionale di Scienze Sociali*, **LXXXIX,** 125–137.

Corsi, P. (1979). 'Tests for stability of regression parameters: An application to some equations of the IBM model for the U.S.A.' IBM Scientific Center, Pisa, unpublished working paper.

Farley, J. U., Hinich, M. J., and McGuire, T. (1975). 'Some comparisons of tests for a shift in the slopes of a multivariate linear time series model.' *Journal of Econometrics*, **3,** 297–318.

Fisher, F. M. (1970). 'Tests of equality between sets of coefficients in two linear regressions: An expository note.' *Econometrica*, **38,** 361–365.

Fisz, M. (1963). *Probability Theory and Mathematical Statistics*, Wiley, New York.

Goldberger, A. S. (1964). *Econometric Theory*, Wiley, New York.

Graybill, F. A. (1961). *An Introduction to Linear Statistical Models*, McGraw–Hill, New York.

Jayatissa, W. A. (1977). 'Tests of equality between sets of coefficients in two linear regressions when disturbance variances are unequal.' *Econometrica*, **45,** 1291–1292.

Orcutt, G. H., and Winokur, H. S., Jr. (1969). 'First order autoregression: Inference, estimation and prediction.' *Econometrica*, **37**, 1–14.
Quandt, R. E. (1958). 'The estimation of the parameters of a linear regression obeying two separate regimes.' *Journal of the American Statistical Association*, **53**, 873–880.
Quandt, R. E. (1960). 'Tests of the hypothesis that a linear regression system obeys two separate regimes.' *Journal of the American Statistical Association*, **55**, 324–330.
Schmidt, P., and Sickles, R. (1977). 'Some further evidence on the use of the Chow test under heteroskedasticity.' *Econometrica*, **45**, 1293–1298.
Theil, H. (1971). *Principles of Econometrics*, Wiley, New York.
Toyoda, T. (1974). 'Use of the Chow test under heteroskedasticity.' *Econometrica*, **42**, 601–608.

Discussion

G. Gambetta
Università di Bologna

R. Orsi
Università di Modena

We thank the authors for having introduced a very interesting and fundamental problem: time-varying parameter models. Since one of the objectives of the symposium is to some extent to ascertain the state of the art about the major problems concerning the econometrics of macro-economic models, it seems to us that such an important topic deserves a more general discussion than that implied by the Corsi, Pollock, and Prakken paper.

The study of time-varying parameters is in fact a relatively new topic in econometric theory and practice and its treatment has not yet found its way into the standard econometric textbooks. Apart from some important exceptions (The *Annals of Economic and Social Measurement* devoted a whole issue to this subject in 1973 and more recently in 1975 there has been a deep discussion at The Royal Statistical Society on the fundamental paper by Brown, Durbin, and Evans), theoretical work and empirical applications are still scarce if compared to other more traditional subjects.

Actually there is a reason for that. The two 'natural' ways to handle the problem, that is to split the sample into subsamples or to build explicitly a more general model embodying parameter instability, stumble over the poor and scarce data which are in general available. However, the abrupt change which occurred in economic time series during the 1970's indicates that the comfortable and theoretically useful hypothesis of structural parameter constancy needs to be reconsidered.

Therefore our discussion will be as follows: first, some general considerations on the problem of testing structural changes; secondly, some more specific considerations on the Corsi, Pollock, and Prakken paper; and, thirdly, some interactions between modelling and testing structural parameter changes.

1. There are basically two types of sources that may be thought to be responsible for parameter variation:

(a) models in which the parameter vector is imagined to take on a different value in each period, with the consequence of a large number of possible parameter vectors, and in which the main interest is focused on modelling the parameter variations. Some comments on this part will follow at the end of our discussion;

(b) models in which there is a structural change in the sense of switching; in this case the parameter vector takes on a small number of different values and therefore the major interest is focused on locating the break points and appreciating the significance of the structural varations.

In a context of time-varying parameter models, perhaps more than in other cases, we have to take care of the influence of model misspecification on the hypothesis of no structural change. In such a situation, in fact, it is not always easy to distinguish between departure from null hypothesis concerning structural parameters and the changes in residual variance.

This raises the problem of what to do and how to proceed once one has found a structural variation in model parameters. Up to now the more natural answer to this question has been that of splitting the sample into subsamples for which the stability assumption regarding structural parameters continues to hold. In many cases this is an artificial way of facing the problem, and in any case we have to be sure that the observed parameter variation is not a consequence of the model misspecification.

One possible solution which we think of is that of specifying a sharp alternative hypothesis since in such a situation one can immediately be aware of the consequences of rejecting the null hypothesis of stability.

As a general consideration, anyway, we have to observe that stability tests do not seem to provide as high a power as would be desirable in inference, and so any action following the rejection of null hypothesis would have to be based on suitable prior information justifying it.

2. The Corsi, Pollock, and Prakken paper fixes its attention on the case (b) sketched above, where the structural change has the meaning of switching, with the further complicating condition of serially correlated errors.

We have to be very careful in considering the meaning of structural parameter changes in the presence of autocorrelated residuals. In fact this basic theoretical question arises in two different ways: in the first the structural change is simply a result, that is an artificial consequence, of the serial correlation that affects the model when it is specified over the whole period. The second way takes as fundamental the structural change itself which, if not taken into account in a model, possibly causes serially correlated errors. It seems to us quite obvious that a correct procedure for facing the problem of testing structural parameter variation in the presence of serial correlation cannot leave these considerations apart. In other words we have to be able to decide between one of these explanations for a significant result, that is to distinguish among the departures from the null hypothesis concerning the stability of structural parameters and those concerning the autocorrelation of residuals.

Any approach that decides upon a sequential order in this testing problem ought to be discussed and justified. In fact, in that it concerns the presence of autocorrelation in models defined over the whole period available, it should be mentioned that, for a given autocorrelation structure, a partitioning into submodels is always possible such that the autocorrelation disappears completely, only because the 'suitable' subdivision of the time interval in different sub-intervals has been reached. This is, of course, to be thought of as a limiting situation which is very difficult to handle and which would be classified in the framework of the approach (a) we sketched above. Nevertheless, it is possible to think of *ad hoc* partitionings of the period allowing the problem of serial autocorrelation to be overcome successfully. For a deeper discussion of the problem of finding the number of regimes which gives the 'best fit' to the data, see Guthery (1974) who considers a sort of piecewise regression approach using a dynamic program from cluster analysis, and Ertel and Fowlkes (1976) who develop plotting procedures for detecting changes in linear regression models and then use efficient algorithms for linear splines and piecewise regression.

So when one decides to handle the problem of autocorrelation and structural change hierarchically, reasons justifying the choice ought to be provided.

The authors conclude their paper by saying that the error autocorrelation causes an artificial departure from the hypothesis of structural stability, and they suggest, if the errors are serially correlated in the entire model, transforming the error structure term by the same autoregressive filter before applying the Chow test to the whole period. They assume the same autoregressive residual coefficient for the two subperiods, which, in turn, is identical for the whole period in the entire model. This way of filtering data cuts off all possibilities of having a different coefficient for the two subperiods. In general this does not seem to be a justifiable assumption because when a structural parameter change happens, we do not expect it to leave the autocorrelation coefficient unchanged.

Generally speaking, the problem of testing the structural change of parameters, when we are not certain that the usual independence assumption on the residuals holds, has to be thought of as a simultaneous test on parameter shifts and autocorrelation coefficients, permitting the rolling together of both types of hypotheses. Indeed, the error terms in structural equation models represent a kind of poorly understood effect, due to various sorts of misspecification. In such a situation a simultaneous treatment of parameters and errors seems quite natural, as on the other hand has been suggested by Quandt (1975) and Smith (1975).

A second point concerns the possibility of taking directly into account the effect of serial correlation. When residuals are serially correlated there will be, as the authors show, an asymptotic bias represented by $[\mathrm{tr}(\Sigma_{xx}^{-1}\tilde{\Sigma}_{xx}) - k]/k$. It would be reasonable to correct the test by a rough estimate of this bias, obtaining then an asymptotically unbiased test. This is in the same line as Cox (1975).

Except for these few considerations, we are in substantial agreement with the major points emphasized by the authors and we would simply add the following remarks.

2.1 The Corsi, Pollock, and Prakken approach uses a 'pseudo F test' for testing whether the relationship, represented by a linear regression model, remains stable in two periods of time, since the value of the break point j which divides the sample into two parts is not known or is not given exogenously. In fact the separating observation j is chosen by evaluating the likelihood ratio test criterion for each observation and then picking the one which maximizes the likelihood of isolating a shift in the model. With two regimes for a sample of size n, where it is not known whether the observations came from one regime or another, 2^n partitions are possible.

As pointed out by Quandt (1960) this procedure tends to make the value of the F test criterion larger than in the case where this point is chosen exogenously. Nevertheless, in the experiment reported by Goldfeld and Quandt (1976) the power of the pseudo F test seems to be sufficiently high.

Moreover, in empirical analysis it often happens that the likelihood function is flat, with the consequence that almost the same relative maximum value of the likelihood function is reached for a wide range of breaking points. In such a situation it is hard to decide, on an empirical basis only, when the split occurs. This difficulty will then condition all the subsequent inference performed with the Chow test. Conversely, in this situation it may be useful to compute the recursive residuals; these residuals, being a sequence of one period ahead prediction errors, will give information about the stability of parameters over time. Brown *et al.* (1975) suggest two tests based on recursive residuals; Cox (1975) in the discussion of their paper suggests a modification of the significance lines in the graph of CUSUM of squares of recursive residuals that takes into account the effects of serial correlation. Unfortunately the authors leave the alternative hypothesis deliberately vague and the power of their tests may be low against many alternatives. Garbade (1977) clearly gives prominence to this weakness, comparing the power of different methodologies for testing instability in the coefficients of a linear regression model.

It seems to us that a logical integration of the Chow test as discussed in the Corsi, Pollock, and Prakken paper is the CUSUM plot. In fact this procedure can be used for locating the structural break and subsequently the Chow test may be applied to provide a formal significance test for the structural shift.

2.2 For this problem it is relatively easy to derive posterior odds ratios permitting a joint test on the β and ρ coefficients simultaneously.

A Bayesian version of the Chow test statistic has been proposed by Zellner and

Siow (1978) and Zellner (1980). Nevertheless, these results cannot be applied directly in this context because of the further complication derived from knowing or not knowing the break point. In the case where this point is known the analysis based on coefficient invariance over time can be performed conditioned on such a point, more precisely using the values at the initial period and at the break point j as starting values for the two dynamic processes underlying the two separate regimes.

In the case where the truncation point is unknown it is necessary to specify a prior distribution on the separating point j. This distribution will be combined with the prior distribution on coefficients and with the data likelihood in order to have a posterior distribution from which it will be possible to get the posterior odds ratio.

This testing procedure can be performed using not only a diffuse prior p.d.f. but also on the basis of informative prior p.d.f. or of a prior odds ratio different from one. It would be given by prior probabilities associated with null hypothesis divided by prior probabilities associated with alternative hypothesis. Moreover, many posterior probabilities related to possible values of alternative hypotheses other than the null hypothesis can be evaluated. This knowledge permits one to take into account the power of the test against particular interesting alternatives.

Finally, if we can consider a loss function giving the consequences of errors in choosing between hypotheses, posterior probabilities can be employed to evaluate expected losses associated with different hypotheses in such a way that will permit the maximization of the expected loss. The critical value of the posterior odds ratio k_{01} in order to reject or to accept H_0 naturally depends on the loss function one chooses. If we choose a quadratic loss function, then the critical value is 1.

2.3 The empirical results presented in Tables 10.6 to 10.8 seem, to a certain extent, surprising. In fact, when the hypothesis of parameter constancy in the two subperiods is accepted, the difference of the estimated coefficients is too large to agree with an intuitive idea of constancy. See, for example, the results of Table 10.7 where coefficient b_3 shows opposite signs in the two subperiods. In such a situation the constancy hypothesis can be accepted only if in both subperiods the coefficients are not significantly different from zero. It is not possible to verify this assumption since the standard errors of the estimates are not reported.

3. In this part we consider briefly the way of modelling structural parameter changes using random parameter methods. This leads to a specification with errors on the individual coefficients which permits, in the meantime, a further justification for the presence of residuals in economic models. The more interesting implication of such a method of modelling is the possibilitiy of handling the problem of time-varying parameters with the resulting detection of departures from constancy of regression relationships over time in the domain of classical residual analysis.

Another possibility is that of re-specifying the model by introducing further parameters that are allowed to capture the continuous development involving changes in regression coefficients. This re-parametrization of the models permits the restatement of the basic assumption of constancy but may produce a substantially more complicated model.

In any case, the explicit modelling of parameter changes seems to be the only possibility of taking this problem into account within a context of simultaneous-equation models.

REFERENCES

Annals of Economic and Social Measurements, 1973, **2,** No. 4 (whole issue).

Brown, R. L., Durbin, J., and Evans, J. M. (1975). 'Techniques for testing the constancy of regression relationships over time.' *Journal of the Royal Statistical Society*, Series B, **37,** 149–162.

Cox, D. R. (1975). Discussion of the paper by Brown, Durbin, and Evans, *Journal of the Royal Statistical Society*, Series B, **37,** 163–164.

Ertel, J. E., and Fowlkes, B. (1976). 'Some algorithms for linear spline and piecewise multiple linear regression.' *Journal of the American Statistical Association*, **71,** 640–648.

Garbade, K. (1977). 'Two methods for examining the stability of regression coefficients.' *Journal of the American Statistical Association*, **72,** 54–63.

Goldfeld, S. M. and Quandt, R. E. (1976). 'Techniques for estimating switching regressions.' Ch. 1 in *Studies in Non-Linear Estimation*, Ballinger, Cambridge.

Guthery, S. B. (1974). 'Partition regression.' *Journal of the American Statistical Association*, **69,** 945–947.

Quandt, R. E. (1960). 'Tests of the hypothesis that a linear regression system obeys two separate regimes.' *Journal of the American Statistical Association*, **55,** 324–330.

Quandt, R. E. (1975). Discussion of the paper by Brown, Durbin, and Evans, *Journal of the Royal Statistical Society*, Series B, **37,** 183–184.

Smith, A. F. M. (1975). Discussion of the paper by Brown, Durbin, and Evans, *Journal of the Royal Statistical Society*, Series B, **37,** 175–177.

Zellner, A. (1980). 'Posterior odds ratios for regression hypotheses: general considerations and some specific results.' Paper presented at the *4th World Congress of the Econometric Society, Aix-en-Provence, August 28th–September 2nd.*

Zellner, A. and Siow, A. (1978). 'Uses of posterior odds ratios in econometrics with applications to hypotheses in regression analysis.' In A. Zellner (ed.), *Reports of the NBER-NSF Seminar on Bayesian Inference in Econometrics*, H. G. B. Alexander Research Foundation, Graduate School of Business, University of Chicago. pp. 227–228.

Evaluating the Reliability of Macro-economic Models
Edited by G. C. Chow and P. Corsi

CHAPTER 11

The Effects of Misspecification on Predictive Accuracy

R. C. Fair
Yale University

11.1 INTRODUCTION

This paper is concerned with the estimation of misspecification effects on predictive accuracy. In a recent study (Fair, 1980a) I have proposed a method for estimating the total uncertainty of a forecast from an econometric model: uncertainty due to (1) the error terms, (2) the coefficient estimates, (3) the exogenous variables, and (4) the possible misspecification of the model. The method allows one to estimate the uncertainty from each of these sources separately, and so it can be used to examine the effects of misspecification on predictive accuracy. The emphasis in this paper is on the misspecification effects. The method is reviewed in Section 11.2, and then misspecification effects for my model are examined in Section 11.3. Estimates of total predictive uncertainty for my model are presented in Section 11.4. Section 11.5 contains a brief conclusion.

The method can be applied to a model that is nonlinear in both variables and coefficients. The general model will be written as:

$$f_i(\mathbf{y}_t, \mathbf{x}_t, \boldsymbol{\alpha}_i) = u_{it}, \qquad i = 1, \ldots, n, \qquad t = 1, \ldots, T, \tag{1}$$

where $\mathbf{y}_t$ is an n-dimensional vector of endogenous variables, $\mathbf{x}_t$ is a vector of predetermined variables (including lagged endogenous variables), and $\boldsymbol{\alpha}_i$ is a vector of unknown coefficients. The first m equations are assumed to be stochastic, with the remaining u_{it} $(i = m + 1, \ldots, n)$ identically zero for all t. For expositional convenience the model will be assumed to be quarterly.

11.2 A REVIEW OF THE METHOD

The uncertainty of a model's forecast that is due to the error terms and coefficient estimates can be estimated by stochastic simulation, given an estimate of the distribution of the error terms and an estimate of the distribution of the coefficient estimates. Each 'trial' consists of draws of the error terms for each quarter of the forecast period and of the coefficients. Stochastic-simulation procedures are to some extent model specific, and for purposes of describing the method it is unnecessary to discuss the details of any particular procedure. The procedure that was followed for the results in this paper is discussed in Section 11.3. Let σ_{itk}^2 denote the variance of the forecast error for a k-quarter-ahead forecast of variable i from a simulation beginning in quarter t, and let $\tilde{\sigma}_{itk}^2$ denote the stochastic-simulation estimate of σ_{itk}^2.[1]

It is also possible to estimate by means of stochastic simulation the uncertainty of a model's forecast that is due to the uncertainty of the exogenous variables, given an assumption about the uncertainty of the exogenous variables themselves. There are two polar assumptions that can be made about the uncertainty of the exogenous variables. One is, of course, that there is no exogenous-variable uncertainty. The other is that the exogenous-variable forecasts are in some way as uncertain as the endogenous-variable forecasts. Under this second assumption one could, for example, estimate an autoregressive equation for each exogenous variable and add these equations to the model. This expanded model, which would have no exogenous variables, could then be used for the stochastic-simulation estimates of the variances. While the first assumption is clearly likely to underestimate exogenous-variable uncertainty in most applications, the second assumption is likely to overestimate it. This is particularly true for fiscal-policy variables in macro-econometric models, where government-budget data are usually quite useful for purposes of forecasting up to at least about eight quarters ahead. The best approximation is thus likely to lie somewhere in between these two assumptions.

The assumption that was made for the results in Fair (1980a) and for the results in Section 11.4 is in between the two polar assumptions. The procedure that was followed was to estimate an eighth-order autoregressive equation for each exogenous variable (including a constant and time in the equation) and then to take the estimated standard error from this regression as the estimate of the degree of uncertainty attached to forecasting the change in this variable for each quarter. This procedure ignores the uncertainty of the coefficient estimates in the autoregressive equations, which is one of the reasons it is not as extreme as the second polar assumption.

It is also unnecessary for purposes of describing the method to discuss the details of any particular assumption about exogenous-variable uncertainty. All that needs to be noted is that some assumptions must be made. If equations for the exogenous variables are not added to the model, but instead some in-between procedure is followed, then each stochastic-simulation trial consists of draws of error terms, coefficients, and exogenous-variable errors. If equations are added, then each trial consists of draws of error terms and coefficients from both the structural equations and the exogenous-variable equations. In either case, let $\tilde{\tilde{\sigma}}_{itk}^2$

denote the stochastic-simulation estimate of the variance of the forecast error that takes into account exogenous-variable uncertainty as well as uncertainty from the error terms and coefficients.

Estimating the uncertainty from the possible misspecification of the model is the most difficult and costly part of the method. It requires successive re-estimation and stochastic simulation of the model. It is based on a comparison of estimated variances computed by means of stochastic simulation with estimated variances computed from outside-sample forecast errors.

Consider for now stochastic simulation with respect to the structural error terms and coefficients only (no exogenous-variable uncertainty). Assume that the forecast period begins one quarter after the end of the estimation period, and call this quarter t. As noted above, from this stochastic simulation one obtains an estimate of the variance of the forecast error, $\tilde{\sigma}^2_{itk}$. One also obtains from this simulation an estimate of the *expected value* of the k-quarter-ahead forecast of variable i. Let $\tilde{\bar{y}}_{itk}$ denote this estimate. The difference between this estimate and the actual value, y_{it+k-1}, is the mean forecast error:[2]

$$\hat{\varepsilon}_{itk} = y_{it+k-1} - \tilde{\bar{y}}_{itk}. \tag{2}$$

If it is assumed that $\tilde{\bar{y}}_{itk}$ exactly equals the true expected value, $\bar{y}_{itk}$, then $\hat{\varepsilon}_{itk}$ in (2) is a sample draw from a distribution with a known mean of zero and variance σ^2_{itk}. The square of this error, $\hat{\varepsilon}^2_{itk}$, is thus under this assumption an unbiased estimate of σ^2_{itk}. One thus has two estimates of σ^2_{itk}: one computed from the mean forecast error and one computed by stochastic simulation. Let d_{itk} denote the difference between these two estimates:

$$d_{itk} = \hat{\varepsilon}^2_{itk} - \tilde{\sigma}^2_{itk}. \tag{3}$$

If it is further assumed that $\tilde{\sigma}^2_{itk}$ exactly equals the true value, then d_{itk} is the difference between the estimated variance based on the mean forecast error and the true variance. Therefore, under the two assumptions of no error in the stochastic-simulation estimates, the expected value of d_{itk} is zero.

The assumption of no stochastic-simulation error, i.e. $\tilde{\bar{y}}_{itk} = \bar{y}_{itk}$ and $\tilde{\sigma}^2_{itk} = \sigma^2_{itk}$, is obviously only approximately correct at best. Even with an infinite number of draws the assumption would not be correct because the draws are from estimated rather than known distributions. It does seem, however, that the error introduced by this assumption is likely to be small relative to the error introduced by the fact that some assumption must be made about the mean of the distribution of d_{itk}. Because of this, nothing more will be said about stochastic-simulation error. The emphasis instead is on the possible assumptions about the mean of the distribution of d_{itk}, given the assumption of no stochastic-simulation error.

The procedure just described uses a given estimation period and a given simulation period. Assume for sake of an example that one has data from quarter 1 through 100. The model can then be estimated through, say, quarter 70, with the forecast period beginning with quarter 71. Stochastic simulation for the forecast period will yield for each i and k a value of d_{i71k} in (3). The model can then be re-estimated through quarter 71, with the forecast period now beginning with quarter 72. Stochastic simulation for this forecast period will yield for each i and k a value of d_{i72k} in (3). This process can be repeated through the estimation period ending with quarter 99. For the one-period-ahead forecast ($k = 1$) the procedure will yield, for each variable i, 30 values of d_{it1} ($t = 71, \ldots, 100$); for the two-period-ahead forecast ($k = 2$) it will yield 29 values of d_{it2} ($t = 72, \ldots, 100$); and so on. If the assumption of no simulation error holds for all t, then the expected value of d_{itk} is zero for all t.

The discussion so far is based on the assumption that the model is correctly specified. Misspecification has two effects on d_{itk} in (3). First, if the model is misspecified, the estimated covariance matrices that are used for the stochastic simulation will not in general be unbiased estimates of the true covariance matrices. The estimated variances computed by means of stochastic simulation will thus in general be biased. Secondly, the estimated variances computed from the forecast errors will in general be biased estimates of the true variances. Since misspecification affects both estimates, the effect on d_{itk} is ambiguous. It is possible for misspecification to affect the two estimates in the same way and thus leave the expected value of the difference between them equal to zero. In general, however, this does not seem likely, and so one would not expect the expected value of d_{itk} to be zero for a misspecified model. The expected value may be negative rather than positive for a misspecified model, although in general it seems more likely that it will be positive. Because of the possibility of data mining, misspecification seems more likely to have a larger positive effect on the outside-sample forecast errors than on the (within-sample) estimated covariance matrices.

An examination of how the d_{itk} values change over time (for a given i and k) may reveal information about the strengths and weaknesses of the model that one would otherwise not have. This information may then be useful in future work on the model. The individual values may thus be of interest in their own right, besides their possible use in estimating total predictive uncertainty.

For the total uncertainty estimates some assumption has to be made about how misspecification affects the expected value of d_{itk}. For the results in Fair (1980a) it was assumed that the expected value of d_{itk} is constant across time: for a given i and k, misspecification was assumed to affect the mean of the distribution of d_{itk} in the same way for all t. Other possible assumptions are, of course, possible. One could, for example, assume that the mean of the distribution is a function of other variables. (A simple assumption in this respect is that the mean follows a linear time trend.) Given this assumption, the mean can be then estimated from a regression of d_{itk} on the variables. For the assumption of a constant mean, this regression is merely a regression on a constant (i.e. the estimated constant term is merely the mean of the d_{itk} values).[3] The predicted value from this regression for period t, denoted $\hat{d}_{itk}$, is then the estimated mean for period t.

An estimate of the total variance of the forecast error, denoted $\hat{\sigma}^2_{itk}$, is the sum of $\tilde{\tilde{\sigma}}^2_{itk}$—the stochastic-simulation estimate of the variance due to the error terms, coefficient estimates, and exogenous variables—and $\hat{d}_{itk}$:

$$\hat{\sigma}^2_{itk} = \tilde{\tilde{\sigma}}^2_{itk} + \hat{d}_{itk}. \tag{4}$$

Since the procedure in arriving at $\hat{\sigma}^2_{itk}$ takes into account the four main sources of uncertainty of a forecast, the values of $\hat{\sigma}^2_{itk}$ can be compared across models for a given *i*, *k*, and *t*. If, for example, one model has consistently smaller values of $\hat{\sigma}^2_{itk}$ than another, this would be fairly strong evidence for concluding that it is a more accurate model, i.e. a better approximation to the true structure.

This completes the outline of the method. It may be useful to review the main steps involved in computing $\hat{\sigma}^2_{itk}$ in (4). Assume that data are available for quarters 1 through T and that one is interested in estimating the uncertainty of an eight-quarter-ahead forecast that began in quarter $T+1$ (i.e. in computing $\hat{\sigma}^2_{itk}$ for $t = T+1$ and $k = 1,\ldots,8$). Given a base set of values for the exogenous variables for quarters $T+1$ through $T+8$, one can compute $\tilde{\tilde{\sigma}}^2_{itk}$ for $t = T+1$ and $k = 1,\ldots,8$ by means of stochastic simulation. Each trial consists of one eight-quarter dynamic simulation and requires draws of the error terms, coefficients, and exogenous-variable errors. These draws are based on the estimate of the model through quarter T. This is the relatively inexpensive part of the method. The expensive part consists of the successive re-estimation and stochastic simulation of the model that are needed in computing the d_{itk} values. In the above example, the model would be estimated 30 times and stochastically simulated 30 times in computing the d_{itk} values. After these values are computed for, say, quarters $T-r$ through T, then $\hat{d}_{itk}$ can be computed for $t = T+1$ and $k = 1,\ldots,8$ using whatever assumption has been made about the distribution of d_{itk}. This then allows $\hat{\sigma}^2_{itk}$ in (4) to be computed for $t = T+1$ and $k = 1,\ldots,8$.

In the successive re-estimation of the model, the first quarter of the estimation period may or may not be increased by one each time. The criterion that one should use in deciding this is to pick the procedure that seems likely to correspond to the chosen assumption about the distribution of d_{itk} being the best approximation to the truth. It is also possible to take the distance between the last quarter of the estimation period and the first quarter of the forecast period to be other than one, as was done above.

It is important to note that the above estimate of the mean of the d_{itk} distribution is not in general efficient because in general the error term in the d_{itk} regression is heteroskedastic. Even under the assumption of no misspecification, the variance of d_{itk} is not constant across time. Without further assumptions about the distribution of $\hat{\varepsilon}_{itk}$ in (2), there is little that can be done about improving the efficiency of the estimates. Litterman (1979) for some of his results assumes that $\hat{\varepsilon}_{itk}$ is $N(0, \sigma^2_{itk})$, and this allows him to estimate the mean of the d_{itk} distribution by maximum likelihood (pp. 63–64). The problem with this approach is that the assumption that $\hat{\varepsilon}_{itk}$ is normally distributed is not in general correct, and so it is not clear that Litterman's approach does in fact lead to more efficient estimates. This is still an open question.

11.3 CALCULATION AND ANALYSIS OF THE d_{itk} VALUES

I have used the method discussed in Section 11.2 to calculate d_{itk} values for my model (Fair, 1976, 1980b) for a forecast horizon of eight quarters. The model was estimated and stochastically simulated 44 times for these results. It may help in understanding the method to describe in some detail the steps that were involved in these calculations.

The model consists of 97 equations, 29 of which are stochastic, and has 183 unknown coefficients to estimate, including 12 first-order serial correlation coefficients. It is nonlinear in both variables and coefficients. The data base that was used for this study consists of observations from 1952 I through 1980 II, although the observations for 1980 II were preliminary and with one exception noted in Section 11.4 were not used for the results.

The first of the 44 estimation periods was 1954 I–1968 IV (60 observations). The coefficients were estimated by two-stage least squares (2SLS), and the covariance matrix of the coefficient estimates was computed. Let $\hat{\boldsymbol{\alpha}}$ denote the vector of coefficient estimates, and let $\hat{\boldsymbol{V}}$ denote the estimated covariance matrix.[4] Given the coefficient estimates, the covariance matrix of the error terms was estimated as $(1/60)\boldsymbol{E}\boldsymbol{E}'$, where $\boldsymbol{E}$ is the 29 × 60 matrix of values of the estimated error terms. Let $\hat{\boldsymbol{\Sigma}}$ denote this matrix. Given these estimates, stochastic simulation was then performed for the 1969 II–1971 I period (8 quarters).[5] Both the distribution of the error terms and the distribution of the coefficient estimates were assumed to be normal. Each trial consisted of a draw of the 29 error terms for each of the 8 quarters from the $N(0, \hat{\boldsymbol{\Sigma}})$ distribution and of a draw of the coefficients from the $N(\hat{\boldsymbol{\alpha}}, \hat{\boldsymbol{V}})$ distribution.[6] Each trial is a dynamic eight-quarter simulation. The actual values of the exogenous variables were used for these simulations. Assume that the quarters are numbered consecutively beginning with 1952 I, so that 1969 II, the first quarter of the simulation period, is quarter number 70. Let $\tilde{y}^j_{i70k}$ denote the value on the jth trial of the k-quarter-ahead prediction of variable i from the simulation beginning in quarter 70. For J trials, the estimate of the expected value of this variable, denoted $\tilde{\bar{y}}_{i70k}$, is:

$$\tilde{\bar{y}}_{i70k} = \frac{1}{J}\sum_{j=1}^{J} \tilde{y}^j_{i70k}. \tag{5}$$

The estimate of the variance of the forecast error, $\tilde{\sigma}^2_{i70k}$, is:

$$\tilde{\sigma}^2_{i70k} = \frac{1}{J}\sum_{j=1}^{J} (\tilde{y}^j_{i70k} - \tilde{\bar{y}}_{i70k})^2. \tag{6}$$

The number of trials used for these estimates was 25.[7] Values of $100(\tilde{\sigma}_{i70k}/\bar{\tilde{y}}_{i70k})$, $k = 1,\ldots,8$, for real GNP are presented in the first half of row 1 in Table 11.1. These values are the stochastic-simulation estimates of the standard errors of the forecast, expressed as a percentage of the forecast mean. Given $\bar{\tilde{y}}_{i70k}$, the mean forecast errors were next computed using (2). Values of $100(|\hat{\varepsilon}_{i70k}|/\bar{\tilde{y}}_{i70k})$, $k = 1,\ldots,8$, for real GNP are presented in the second half of row 1 in Table 11.1. These ratios are the estimates of the standard errors of the forecast based on the actual outside-sample forecast errors, again expressed as a percentage of the forecast mean.

The second estimation period was 1954 I–1969 I (61 observations), which differs from the first period by the addition of one quarter at the end. Note that the first quarter of the period was left unchanged. The coefficients were estimated by 2SLS for the period, and $\hat{V}$ and $\hat{\Sigma}$ were computed. Stochastic simulation was then performed for the 1969 III–1971 II period, yielding (for each variable i and $k = 1,\ldots,8$) values of $\bar{\tilde{y}}_{i71k}$ and $\tilde{\sigma}^2_{i71k}$. Given $\bar{\tilde{y}}_{i71k}$, the mean forecast errors were computed using (2). Values of $100(\tilde{\sigma}_{i71k}/\bar{\tilde{y}}_{i71k})$ and $100(|\hat{\varepsilon}_{i71k}|/\bar{\tilde{y}}_{i71k})$, $k = 1,\ldots,8$, for real GNP are presented in row 2 in Table 11.1.

The above process was repeated for the remaining 42 estimation periods. Since only data through 1980 I were used for the present results, the length of the simulation periods for the last seven sets of estimates was less than eight, as can be seen in Table 11.1. The last estimation period was 1954 I–1979 III (103 observations), and for this set of estimates the simulation period was merely one quarter, 1980 I, which is quarter number 113.

The results in Table 11.1 show that the stochastic-simulation estimates of the standard errors vary considerably across prediction periods (for a fixed k). Part of this variability can be explained by sampling error, since only 25 trials were used for each stochastic simulation. (Cost considerations prevented more trials from being performed.) This does not, however, appear to be the main cause of the variability. I re-ran a few of the 44 stochastic simulations using 250 trials, and in general the variability between the estimates based on 25 trials and those based on 250 trials was small relative to the variability across prediction periods. It thus appears that there is considerable variability of forecast-error variances across time (for a fixed k), at least for my model. This variability is due to different covariance matrices, different initial conditions (i.e. different lagged values of the endogenous and exogenous variables), and different values of the exogenous variables for the prediction periods.

It is possible from the results for the 44 periods to compute values of d_{itk} in (3) for each of the 97 endogenous variables for $k = 1,\ldots,8$. For $k = 1$, 44 values of d_{itk} can be computed ($t = 70,\ldots,113$). For $k = 2$, 43 values can be computed ($t = 71,\ldots,113$), and so on through $k = 8$ ($t = 77,\ldots,113$).

It is possible, as discussed in Section 11.2, to try to estimate equations explaining d_{itk} (for a fixed i and k). The explanatory variables in these equations would be variables that one felt had an effect on the degree of misspecification of

Table 11.1 Estimated standard errors for 44 estimation periods for real GNP. (Each simulation period begins two quarters after the end of the estimation period)

	Estimation period ending in		$100(\tilde{\sigma}_{itk}/\bar{\tilde{y}}_{itk})$								$100(\lvert\hat{\varepsilon}_{itk}\rvert/\bar{\tilde{y}}_{itk})$							
		k:	1	2	3	4	5	6	7	8	1	2	3	4	5	6	7	8
1	1968 IV		0.66	0.94	1.41	1.63	2.10	2.95	4.38	5.49	0.24	1.69	2.69	3.36	3.46	3.28	1.95	2.27
2	1969 I		0.77	1.23	1.71	2.01	2.31	3.28	4.04	4.48	0.94	1.40	1.92	1.78	1.34	0.17	0.56	0.32
3	II		0.68	0.93	1.13	1.34	1.82	2.03	2.68	3.29	0.30	1.02	1.37	1.66	0.55	1.61	1.56	1.28
4	III		0.70	0.94	1.10	1.34	1.58	1.78	2.21	2.34	0.61	0.49	0.81	0.24	1.01	1.33	1.35	1.39
5	IV		0.66	1.17	1.75	2.15	2.63	2.97	3.45	3.76	0.25	0.57	0.24	1.19	1.62	1.88	2.61	3.19
6	1970 I		0.80	1.07	1.01	1.33	1.59	1.80	1.85	2.19	1.10	0.49	1.91	2.10	2.26	2.66	2.95	4.24
7	II		0.68	0.82	1.18	1.86	2.23	2.78	3.05	3.40	0.85	0.58	1.49	1.66	2.52	3.38	5.03	5.18
8	III		0.69	1.21	1.75	2.07	2.41	2.44	2.35	2.43	1.58	2.49	2.74	3.29	3.22	4.34	4.15	3.72
9	IV		0.43	0.78	1.29	1.57	1.94	2.11	2.25	2.03	0.56	1.00	0.43	0.11	1.38	1.76	1.95	2.03
10	1971 I		0.70	1.30	1.67	1.75	2.12	2.52	2.90	3.06	0.22	0.16	0.59	1.91	2.06	2.10	2.45	1.38
11	II		0.74	1.36	1.82	2.13	2.32	2.41	2.90	3.31	0.60	1.49	3.17	3.82	4.47	5.10	3.98	3.80
12	III		0.76	0.97	1.19	1.59	1.91	1.98	2.21	2.69	0.42	1.96	2.56	3.26	3.94	3.18	3.57	4.05
13	IV		0.75	1.11	1.69	1.86	2.04	2.19	2.32	2.37	1.09	1.13	1.83	2.49	1.43	1.82	2.36	0.80
14	1972 I		0.52	0.72	1.06	1.38	1.40	1.71	2.18	2.98	0.26	0.71	1.43	0.83	1.20	1.69	0.20	0.99
15	II		0.58	0.91	1.17	1.31	1.24	1.40	1.82	2.27	0.35	1.04	0.16	0.43	0.66	1.25	0.87	0.77
16	III		0.51	0.70	1.06	1.37	1.91	2.39	3.12	4.29	0.54	0.40	0.34	0.01	1.52	1.23	0.97	1.80
17	IV		0.65	0.95	1.29	1.61	2.29	3.12	3.64	4.66	1.12	0.79	0.27	1.60	1.21	0.73	1.68	3.33
18	1973 I		0.53	0.87	1.25	1.66	2.33	3.02	4.17	5.37	0.32	0.53	2.50	2.15	1.91	2.51	3.67	1.26
19	II		0.48	0.88	1.45	2.25	2.67	3.16	3.41	3.47	0.20	1.73	1.20	1.24	2.35	4.30	2.80	1.99

20		III	0.66	1.12	1.59	1.99	2.13	2.45	2.87	3.29	1.54	1.35	1.05	2.31	4.45	2.85	2.10	1.84
21		IV	0.61	1.22	1.74	2.24	2.82	3.46	3.97	4.99	0.15	0.42	1.80	4.22	2.23	0.86	0.28	2.48
22	1974	I	0.77	1.13	1.38	1.87	1.95	2.20	2.25	2.86	0.08	1.06	2.79	1.00	0.41	0.73	3.11	3.79
23		II	0.87	1.36	2.06	2.58	2.88	3.09	3.97	4.72	0.12	1.30	1.53	3.28	3.86	7.26	9.12	9.91
24		III	0.72	1.15	1.94	2.30	2.46	3.04	3.38	3.42	1.58	0.78	2.55	3.62	6.34	7.47	7.59	7.81
25		IV	0.83	1.66	2.11	2.43	2.46	2.45	2.69	3.01	1.23	1.77	1.70	3.79	4.46	4.79	5.56	7.86
26	1975	I	0.90	1.49	2.02	2.41	3.07	3.17	3.53	3.62	0.23	0.93	0.75	1.14	1.13	1.76	3.03	2.72
27		II	1.01	1.51	2.18	2.18	2.05	2.19	2.22	2.28	0.64	0.88	0.72	0.05	0.40	0.57	0.02	0.09
28		III	0.69	1.07	1.44	1.84	2.12	2.32	2.32	2.48	1.57	1.55	1.14	1.07	2.36	1.75	1.76	0.96
29		IV	0.68	0.98	1.28	1.57	1.70	1.82	2.09	2.16	0.28	0.73	0.45	1.07	0.49	0.49	0.03	0.36
30	1976	I	0.74	1.07	1.20	1.64	1.56	1.57	1.43	1.54	0.71	1.08	0.18	0.94	0.74	1.25	1.53	0.51
31		II	0.80	1.27	1.40	1.40	1.63	1.86	1.80	2.02	0.01	1.17	0.53	0.79	0.01	0.77	0.19	0.53
32		III	0.56	0.89	1.30	1.48	1.59	1.85	1.74	1.71	1.27	0.67	0.79	0.37	1.08	0.37	0.75	0.70
33		IV	0.88	1.12	1.34	1.35	1.75	1.82	1.76	1.82	0.55	0.45	1.06	1.38	0.56	0.67	0.29	0.40
34	1977	I	0.74	1.49	1.57	1.45	1.54	1.56	1.23	1.25	0.06	0.78	1.05	0.26	0.78	0.75	1.04	1.83
35		II	0.68	0.89	1.17	1.46	1.70	1.79	2.05	2.37	0.19	0.55	0.54	0.21	0.44	0.29	0.56	0.83
36		III	0.57	0.89	1.20	1.56	1.67	1.87	1.92	1.99	0.36	0.47	0.28	0.61	0.34	0.14	0.40	1.09
37		IV	0.79	0.92	0.92	1.05	1.29	1.49	1.33	1.51	1.08	0.57	0.59	0.64	0.08	0.18	0.59	0.56
38	1978	I	0.59	1.10	1.04	1.31	1.44	1.54	1.40	—	0.06	0.45	0.38	0.32	0.29	0.93	0.93	—
39		II	0.49	0.92	0.99	1.16	1.46	1.44	—	—	0.69	0.50	0.13	0.23	0.53	0.64	—	—
40		III	0.62	0.67	1.06	1.09	1.29	—	—	—	0.28	0.31	0.06	0.40	0.28	—	—	—
41		IV	0.76	1.11	1.45	1.39	—	—	—	—	0.36	0.08	0.23	0.18	—	—	—	—
42	1979	I	0.47	0.96	1.18	—	—	—	—	—	0.02	0.49	0.20	—	—	—	—	—
43		II	0.70	0.93	—	—	—	—	—	—	0.48	0.28	—	—	—	—	—	—
44		III	0.63	—	—	—	—	—	—	—	0.72	—	—	—	—	—	—	—

the model. If, for example, one felt that the misspecification of the model was greater during periods of rapidly rising import prices, some variable measuring import prices or the rate of change of import prices could be tried as an explanatory variable. Another possibility would be to use as an explanatory variable a dummy variable that took on, say, a value of one in the quarters in which misspecification was considered greater and zero otherwise. If one felt that the degree of misspecification was changing smoothly over time, then a time trend could be tried as an explanatory variable to test this. The ordinary least squares estimates of these equations would not be efficient even if the correct explanatory variables were used because, as discussed in Section 11.2, the error terms in the equations are heteroskedastic. Nevertheless, the estimates might reveal useful information regarding the misspecification of the model.

No regressions of the above kind were in fact run for the results in this paper. Instead, values of d_{itk} were plotted and examined in a casual way to see if any systematic tendencies could be noted. Given the relative small number of observations (between 37 and 44) and the fact that there is little past experience examining values of this kind, it seemed best at this stage to take a less formal approach. For the plots for variables with trends, like real GNP, d_{itk} was normalized by the square of the forecast mean before being plotted. In other words, $d_{itk}/\tilde{\bar{y}}_{itk}^{2}$ was plotted instead of d_{itk}. (Remember that d_{itk} is in units of the variable squared.) With respect to the values in Table 11.1, $d_{itk}/\tilde{\bar{y}}_{itk}^{2}$ is for a given k the difference between the square of the value in the first half of a particular row and the square of the value in the second half of the row.

The plot for real GNP for the one-quarter-ahead forecast ($k = 1$) is presented in Figure 11.1. It is clear from this plot that there is no obvious pattern. The values are not obviously larger on average for one subperiod than for another, and there is no obvious trend in either direction. The four largest values are for 1971 I, 1974 I, 1975 I, and 1976 I. This can also be seen from the results in Table 11.1. The estimation period ended in 1970 III (row 8) for the simulation period beginning in 1971 I and, for this set of estimates, the absolute value of the one-quarter-ahead forecast error is large (1.58 percent). Likewise, the one-quarter-ahead errors in rows 20, 24, and 28 are large (1.54, 1.58, and 1.57 percent, respectively). 1971 I is a quarter following an automobile strike, and this probably accounts for the large value for this quarter. Although the other three quarters are in a period of rapidly rising U.S. import prices (due to rapidly rising oil and food prices and the weakness of the dollar), the fact that the values for these three quarters are not surrounded by other large values considerably lessens the evidence in favour of the hypothesis that the misspecification of the model was greater during this period.

Similar 'nonsystematic' plots were obtained for other variables in the model. Plots are presented in Figures 11.2–11.6 for five other variables (for $k = 1$): the GNP deflator, the unemployment rate, the wage rate, the bill rate, and the money supply. As can be seen, these plots show no real systematic tendencies. A partial

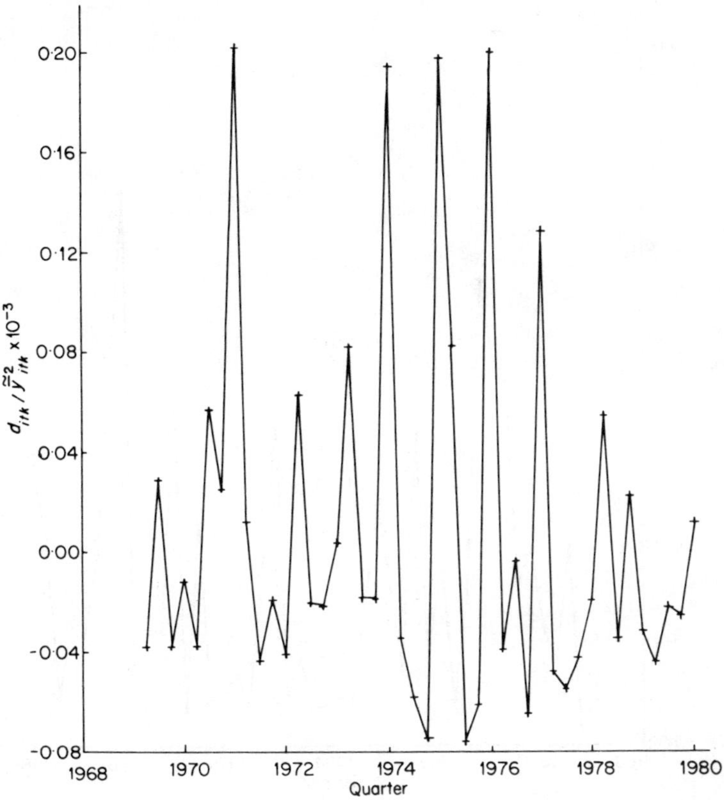

Figure 11.1 Real GNP one quarter ahead ($k = 1$). 44 observations: 1969 II–1980 I

exception to this is the plot for the bill rate, where the values for the last two quarters are large. If there was a substantial change in U.S. monetary policy following the October 6, 1979, announcement of the Federal Reserve, then one would expect the bill-rate equation in the model, which is meant to explain the behaviour of the Fed, to be misspecified more in 1979 IV and 1980 I than otherwise. This appears to be the case from the plot in Figure 11.5. This issue of the possible change in Fed behaviour is discussed in detail in Fair (1981).

Plots of d_{itk} or $d_{itk}/\tilde{\tilde{y}}^2_{itk}$ for values of k greater than one also showed no systematic tendencies except for a tendency for some of the series to be serially correlated for values of k greater than about four or five. This can be explained as follows. If, say, quarter 85 is a difficult quarter to predict, perhaps because of a large unexplained shock in the quarter, then a dynamic simulation that runs through this quarter may also do poorly in predicting quarters 86 and beyond. In other words, the simulation may get thrown off by the bad prediction in quarter 85. This means, for example, that five-quarter-ahead forecasts for quarters 85, 86,

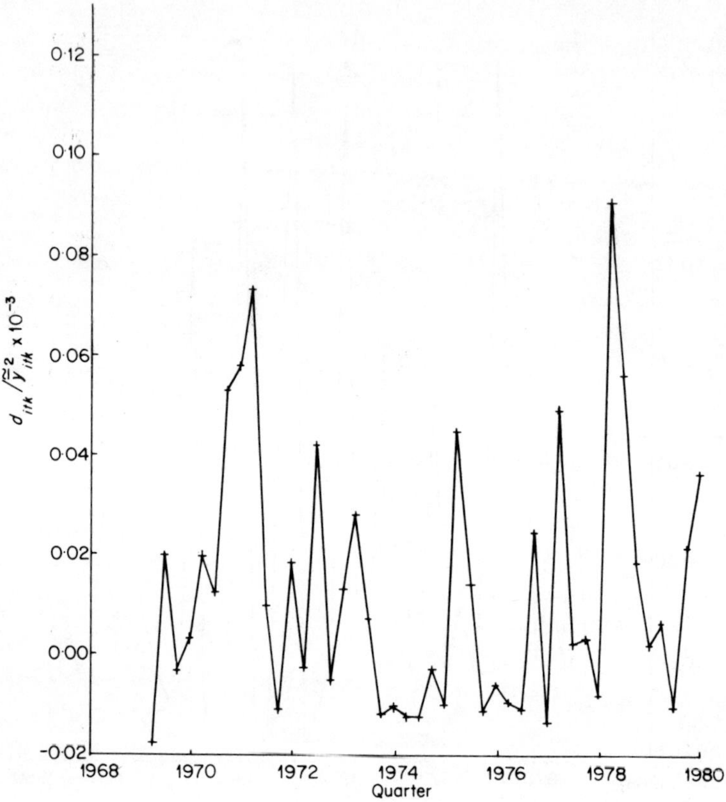

Figure 11.2 GNP deflator one quarter ahead ($k = 1$). 44 observations: 1969 II–1980 I

87, 88, and 89 may all be on average poor, thus implying large values for $\hat{\varepsilon}^2_{itk}$ ($k = 5$ and $t = 85, \ldots, 89$). The shock in quarter 85 will have no effect on the stochastic-simulation estimates of the variances, since these are not based on the actual data for the endogenous variables for this quarter, and so the large values of the outside-sample errors imply large values of d_{itk}. In this way, serial correlation may be introduced into the d_{itk} series for values of k greater than one.

My impression from examining all the plots is that the misspecification of the model does not appear to have changed over time or to have been different in any subperiods. To give one final example of these plots, $d_{itk}/\tilde{\bar{y}}^2_{itk}$ for real GNP for $k = 8$ is plotted in Figure 11.7. The values for 1976 III, 1976 IV, and 1977 I are large, but otherwise there is nothing unusual. The values for these three quarters are from simulations beginning in 1974 IV, 1975 I, and 1975 II, the period of rapidly rising U.S. import prices. As can be seen from rows 23, 24, and 25 in Table 11.1, the outside-sample errors for these three simulations are generally large. This pattern does not persist beyond row 25 (i.e. beyond 1977 I in Figure 11.7), and so one would probably not conclude from Figure 11.7 that the misspecification of the model changed in this period.

The fact that the misspecification of the model does not appear to have changed over time is not in itself encouraging regarding the accuracy of the model. The misspecification may in fact be quite large, even though unchanging, and have a large effect on total forecasting uncertainty. What is encouraging about the results is that the assumption of a constant mean for the d_{itk} distribution (for a fixed i and k) seems to be a reasonable approximation.[8] Given this assumption, it is possible to estimate the effect of misspecification on total uncertainty, and this is done in the next section.

11.4 ESTIMATION OF TOTAL UNCERTAINTY

The estimates of total predictive uncertainty for the period 1980 III–1982 IV are presented in Table 11.2 for six variables. The steps that were involved in obtaining

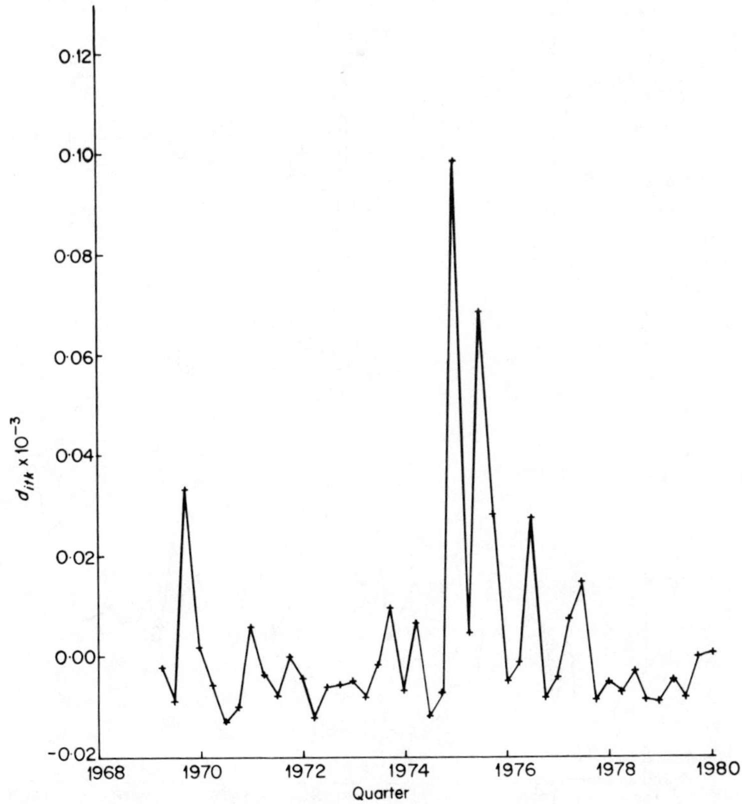

Figure 11.3 Unemployment rate one quarter ahead ($k = 1$). 44 observations: 1969 II–1980 I

these results will first be explained, and then the results themselves will be briefly discussed.

Remember that the data base for this study consists of observations from 1952 I through 1980 II, although the data for 1980 II are preliminary. The last of the 44 estimation periods used for the results in Section III was 1954 I–1979 III. For the results in Table 11.2 the model was re-estimated through 1980 I, i.e. for the 1954 I–1980 I period.[9] The simulation period was chosen to be 1980 III–1982 IV. The values for 1980 II were used as initial conditions for the simulations, although, as just noted, they were not used in the estimation. The values of the exogenous variables for the simulation period had to be guessed. The values that were used for this purpose were values that I used in August 1980 to make a forecast with the model. For future reference, these values will be called 'base' values.

Given the estimates of the coefficients and of the covariance matrices and given the exogenous-variable values, the uncertainty from the error terms and coefficient estimates was computed by means of stochastic simulation. These

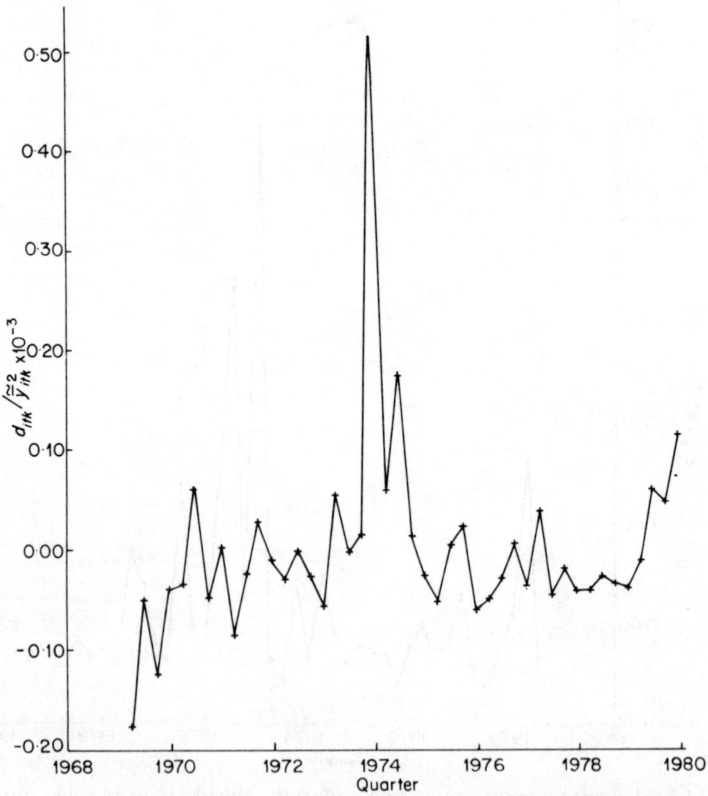

Figure 11.4 Wage rate one quarter ahead ($k = 1$). 44 observations: 1969 II–1980 I

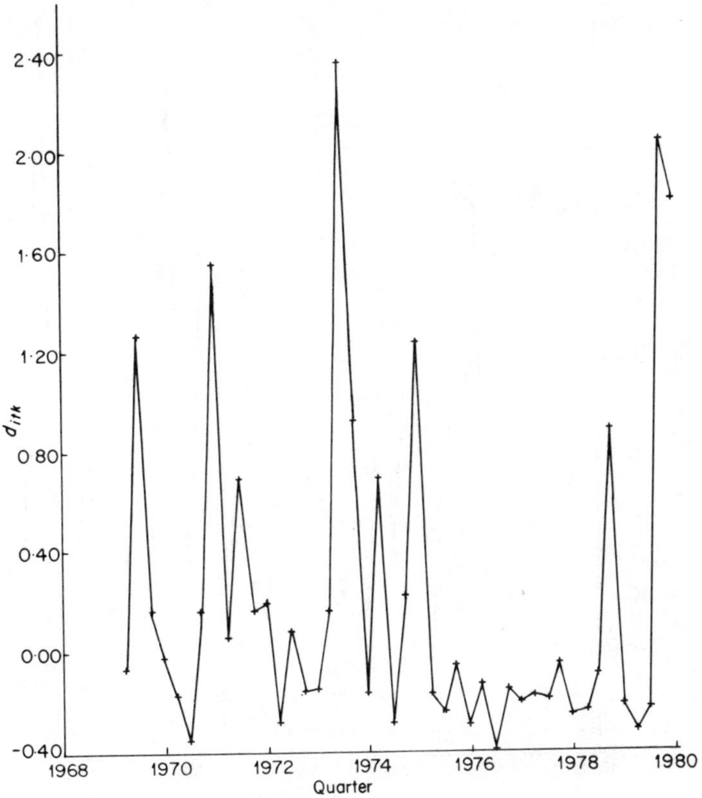

Figure 11.5 Bill rate one quarter ahead ($k = 1$). 44 observations: 1969 II–1980 I

results are presented in the *a* and *b* rows in Table 11.2. For the *a*-row results, only draws from the distribution of the error terms were made, whereas for the *b*-row results draws from both the distribution of the error terms and the distribution of the coefficient estimates were made. The number of trials used for each of these two stochastic simulations was 250.

As noted in Section 11.2, for the estimates of exogenous-variable uncertainty an eighth-order autoregressive equation for each exogenous variable (including a constant and time in the equation) was estimated. This was done for the 60 nontrivial exogenous variables in the model. The estimation period was 1954 II–1980 I. For each exogenous variable the estimated standard error from this regression was used for the estimate of the degree of uncertainty attached to forecasting the change in the variable for each quarter. Given these estimates and given the base values of the exogenous variables, alternative values of the exogenous variables can be drawn for the stochastic-simulation trials.[10] The results of stochastic simulation with respect to the error terms, coefficients, and

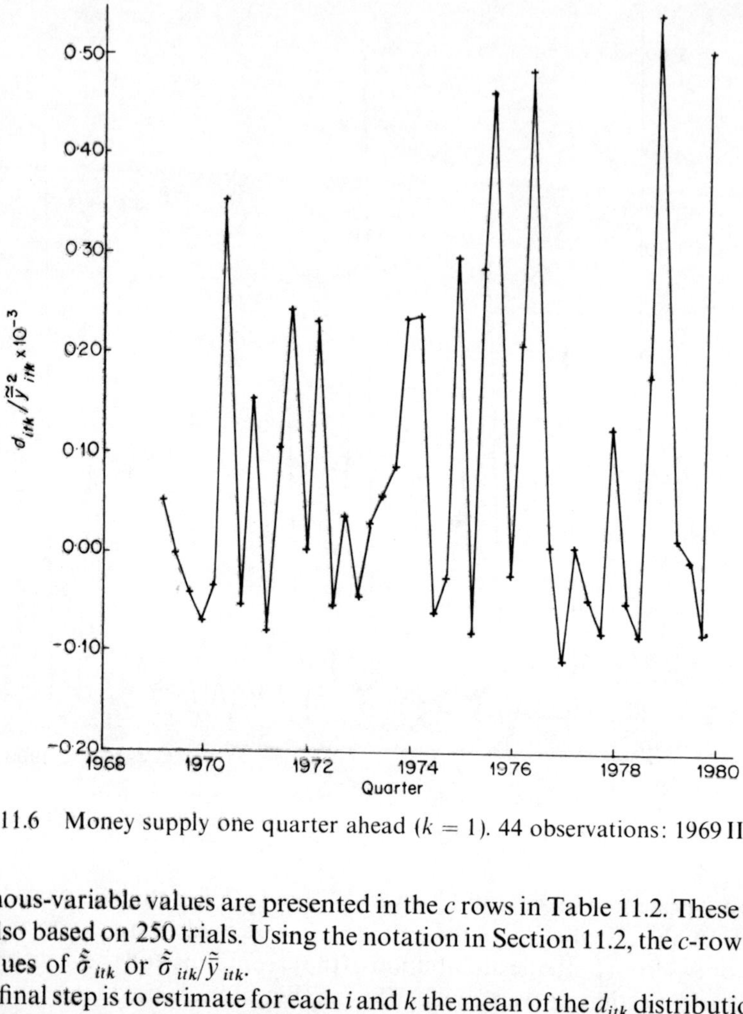

Figure 11.6 Money supply one quarter ahead ($k = 1$). 44 observations: 1969 II–1980 I

exogenous-variable values are presented in the c rows in Table 11.2. These results were also based on 250 trials. Using the notation in Section 11.2, the c-row values are values of $\tilde{\tilde{\sigma}}_{itk}$ or $\tilde{\tilde{\sigma}}_{itk}/\bar{\tilde{y}}_{itk}$.

The final step is to estimate for each i and k the mean of the d_{itk} distribution, $\hat{d}_{itk}$, and then use equation (4) to compute the estimate of the total variance of the forecast error, $\hat{\sigma}^2_{itk}$. Given the assumption that the mean of the d_{itk} is constant, $\hat{d}_{itk}$ is for each i and k merely the mean of the d_{itk} values.[11] From the results in Section 11.3, these means can be computed for each i and k. For $k = 1$, there are 44 observations; for $k = 2$, there are 43 observations; and so on. These means were calculated, and $\hat{\sigma}^2_{itk}$ in (4) was computed. The values in the d rows in Table 11.2 are the square roots of $\hat{\sigma}^2_{itk}$.[12] Examining the differences between the d- and c-row values in Table 11.2 is a way of examining the effects of misspecifications on the predictive accuracy of the model.

The results in Table 11.2 are fairly self explanatory, although a few features should be mentioned. Note first that some of the c-row values are less than the

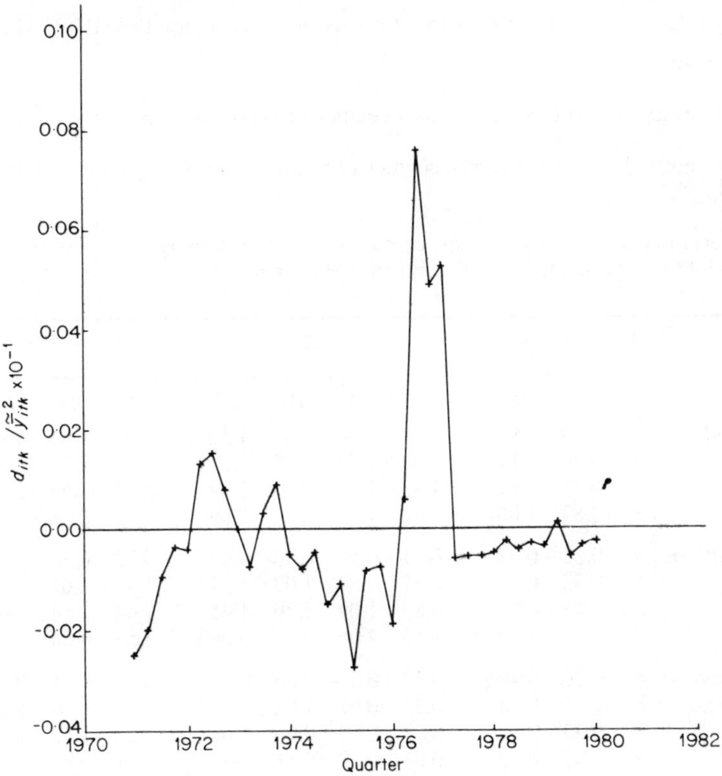

Figure 11.7 Real GNP eight quarters ahead ($k = 8$). 37 observations: 1971 I–1980 I

corresponding b-row values. Although some of this may be due to sampling error, there is no requirement that each c-row value be larger than the corresponding b-row value. In the present model there is a tendency for more variability of prices to be associated with less variability of real GNP and related real variables. One of the most important and uncertain exogenous variables in the model is the price of imports, and this variable has its major impact on prices. Adding exogenous-variable uncertainty thus increases the variability of prices, and leads, as in row c in Table 11.2 for the GNP deflator, to increased predictive uncertainty for prices. This increased variability in prices leads, other things being equal, to decreased variability (and thus decreased predictive uncertainty) in real GNP and related real variables. There are also undoubtedly other offset effects like this. The net result of these and other effects may be that for some variables adding exogenous-variable uncertainty lessens predictive uncertainty.

Note also that some of the d-row values in Table 11.2 are less than the corresponding c-row values. As discussed in Section 11.2, the mean of the d_{itk}

Table 11.2 Estimated standard errors of forecasts for 1980 III–1982 IV

a = uncertainty due to error terms.

b = uncertainty due to error terms and coefficient estimates—$\tilde{\sigma}_{itk}$ or $\tilde{\sigma}_{itk}/\bar{\tilde{y}}_{itk}$.

c = uncertainty due to error terms, coefficient estimates, and exogenous variables—$\tilde{\tilde{\sigma}}_{itk}$ or $\tilde{\tilde{\sigma}}_{itk}/\bar{\tilde{\tilde{y}}}_{itk}$.

d = uncertainty due to error terms, coefficient estimates, exogenous variables, and the possible misspecification of the model—$\hat{\sigma}_{itk}$ or $\hat{\sigma}_{itk}/\bar{\tilde{y}}_{itk}$.

		1980		1981				1982			
		III	IV	I	II	III	IV	I	II	III	IV
Real GNP	*a*	0.59	0.96	1.08	1.20	1.44	1.52	1.54	1.55	1.48	1.48
	b	0.70	1.11	1.43	1.77	1.99	2.15	2.25	2.35	2.46	2.48
	c	0.77	1.11	1.43	1.69	2.02	2.34	2.63	2.68	2.78	2.93
	d	0.82	1.06	1.42	1.37	2.27	2.69	2.89	2.78		
GNP deflator	*a*	0.32	0.43	0.51	0.58	0.60	0.64	0.72	0.76	0.82	0.85
	b	0.32	0.46	0.67	0.84	1.03	1.22	1.43	1.61	1.77	1.94
	c	0.46	0.67	0.89	1.09	1.26	1.45	1.64	1.84	2.00	2.19
	d	0.58	1.03	1.53	2.06	2.56	3.06	3.58	4.04		
Unemployment rate	*a*	0.26	0.40	0.52	0.58	0.66	0.74	0.82	0.85	0.89	0.92
	b	0.33	0.54	0.75	0.91	1.08	1.13	1.18	1.24	1.28	1.36
	c	0.33	0.52	0.67	0.79	0.96	1.08	1.20	1.32	1.39	1.50
	d	0.37	0.53	0.61	0.67	0.81	0.87	0.91	0.91		
Wage rate	*a*	0.58	0.78	0.99	1.08	1.19	1.30	1.36	1.42	1.44	1.51
	b	0.65	1.05	1.40	1.73	2.06	2.33	2.63	2.86	3.12	3.38
	c	0.71	1.08	1.46	1.78	2.04	2.38	2.66	2.94	3.27	3.49
	d	0.71	1.23	1.80	2.37	3.03	3.67	4.33	4.92		
Bill rate	*a*	0.46	0.67	0.82	0.93	0.97	1.00	1.03	1.10	1.20	1.23
	b	0.55	0.84	1.07	1.20	1.38	1.52	1.64	1.82	1.95	2.06
	c	0.54	0.80	0.99	1.14	1.29	1.40	1.51	1.63	1.72	1.79
	d	0.72	1.08	1.18	1.31	1.49	1.61	1.69	1.75		
Money supply	*a*	0.83	1.09	1.31	1.46	1.62	1.79	1.86	1.95	2.04	2.06
	b	0.94	1.28	1.63	2.05	2.29	2.53	2.77	3.12	3.33	3.63
	c	0.92	1.33	1.67	1.99	2.39	2.71	3.13	3.47	3.86	4.28
	d	1.32	2.03	2.64	3.30	4.10	4.70	5.41	6.21		

Estimation period for a, b, c calculations: 1954 I–1980 I.

d-row values based on 44 sets of estimates of the model.

Units are percentage points.

The standard errors are divided by $\bar{\tilde{y}}_{itk}$ except for the unemployment rate and the bill rate.

distribution may be negative for a misspecified model, although in most cases this does not seem likely. There are a few cases in Table 11.2 where this is true, although in general the estimated means are positive.

The results in Table 11.2 are an update of the results in Table 2 in Fair (1980a). The previous results were based on 35 sets of estimates of the model, as opposed to 44 here. The new results are quite close to the old; there appear to be no major changes in the predictive uncertainty of the model by the addition of 9 more quarters. For a user of the model the results in Table 11.2 can be used to gauge how much confidence to place on any given forecast from the model.

It should finally be noted that because the d-row values account for all four sources of uncertainty, they can be used to make accuracy comparisons across models. I have used the method for this purpose in Fair (1979), where four models are compared. The hope is that over time the method can be used to eliminate less accurate models.

11.5 CONCLUSION

The emphasis in this paper has been on estimating the effects of misspecification on predictive accuracy. For a correctly specified model the expected value of the difference between a forecast-error variance estimated by stochastic simulation and by an outside-sample forecast error is zero (ignoring simulation error). For a misspecified model the expected value is unlikely to be zero, and so examining the differences between these two estimates is a way of examining the effects of misspecification. The examination of the differences for my model in Section 11.3 did not reveal any evidence that the degree of misspecification of the model was changing over time or was different for different subperiods. This implies that the assumption that the mean of the distribution of the differences (for a given variable and horizon of the forecast) is constant across time may be a fairly good approximation. Given this assumption, it is possible to estimate the effects of misspecification on predictive accuracy, and this was done in Section 11.4.

The approach taken in this paper is one of estimation rather than hypothesis testing. The implicit premise is that misspecification exists and so must be accounted for in some way. If more were known about the distribution of the differences, it might be possible to test the hypothesis of no misspecification. As noted in Section 11.2, Litterman (1979) has made some progress in this area, although his results are based on a strong assumption about the distribution of the outside-sample forecast errors. It is clearly an open question as to how much can be learned about the distribution of the differences. If, however, most models are misspecified, as I believe is likely to be the case, then testing the hypothesis of no misspecification is of less importance than trying to estimate the effects of misspecification. Given an assumption about the mean of the distribution of the differences, the method discussed in this paper does allow this to be done.

NOTES

[1] Note that it is implicitly assumed here that the variances of the forecast errors exist. For some estimation techniques this is not always the case. If in a given application the variances do not exist, then one should estimate other measures of dispersion of the distribution, such as the interquartile range or mean absolute deviation.
[2] Note that t denotes the first quarter of the simulation, so that $\tilde{\bar{y}}_{itk}$ is the estimated expected value for quarter $t + k - 1$.
[3] For the results in Fair (1980a) a slightly different assumption than that of a constant mean was made for variables with trends. For these variables it was assumed that the mean of d_{itk} is proportional to $\tilde{\bar{y}}^2_{itk}$, i.e. that the mean of $d_{itk}/\tilde{\bar{y}}^2_{itk}$ is constant across time.
[4] There are a few dummy variables in the model that are not relevant for the early estimation periods, which means that there are slightly fewer than 183 coefficients to estimate for the early periods. For the first estimation period, for example, there are 170 coefficients to estimate. Although the covariance matrix of the 2SLS coefficient estimates is not block diagonal (see Fair and Parke, 1980, p. 273), for purposes of the results in this section only the diagonal blocks of $\hat{V}$ were computed. It is fairly expensive to compute the off-diagonal blocks, and this would have to have been done 44 times. Instead, the off-diagonal blocks were taken to be zero.
[5] Note that there is a one quarter gap between the end of the estimation period and the beginning of the simulation period. In practice the data for the most recent quarter are usually preliminary, and in my work I use these data as initial conditions for a forecast but not as observations for estimation. The procedure in this section is consistent with this practice.
[6] The draws were performed as follows. Let $\mathbf{u}_t^*$ denote a particular draw of the 29 error terms for quarter t from the $N(0, \hat{\mathbf{\Sigma}})$ distribution. $\hat{\mathbf{\Sigma}}$ was factored into $\boldsymbol{PP}'$, and then $\mathbf{u}_t^*$ was computed as $\boldsymbol{P}\mathbf{e}$, where $\mathbf{e}$ is a 29×1 vector of standard normal draws. Since $\boldsymbol{E}\mathbf{ee}' = \boldsymbol{I}$, then $\boldsymbol{E}\mathbf{u}_t^*\mathbf{u}_t^{*\prime} = \boldsymbol{EP}\mathbf{ee}'\boldsymbol{P}' = \hat{\mathbf{\Sigma}}$, which is as desired. $\mathbf{u}_t^*$ was drawn for each of the eight quarters. Let $\boldsymbol{\alpha}^*$ denote a particular draw of the coefficients from the $N(\hat{\boldsymbol{\alpha}}, \hat{\boldsymbol{V}})$ distribution. $\hat{\boldsymbol{V}}$ was factored into $\boldsymbol{PP}'$, and then $\boldsymbol{\alpha}^*$ was computed as $\hat{\boldsymbol{\alpha}} + \boldsymbol{P}\mathbf{e}$, where $\mathbf{e}$ is a vector of standard normal draws with dimension equal to the number of coefficients. Since $\boldsymbol{E}\mathbf{ee}' = \boldsymbol{I}$, then $\boldsymbol{E}(\boldsymbol{\alpha}^* - \hat{\boldsymbol{\alpha}})\,(\hat{\boldsymbol{\alpha}} - \hat{\boldsymbol{\alpha}})' = \boldsymbol{EP}\mathbf{ee}'\boldsymbol{P}' = \hat{\boldsymbol{V}}$, which is as desired.
[7] The number of trials for the other 43 stochastic simulations was also 25. For a few of the 25×44 trials the solution algorithm failed, and in these cases the trials were merely skipped. This procedure is likely to introduce a downward bias in the stochastic-simulation estimates of the variances, since the algorithm presumably failed because of an extreme draw. In most, if not all, of these cases it is likely that a solution could have been obtained had the solution algorithm been appropriately damped. The number of failures was fairly small, and so this bias is not likely to be very large.
[8] For variables with trends the assumption is that the mean of d_{itk} is proportional to $\tilde{\bar{y}}^2_{itk}$. See Note 3.
[9] For this set of estimates the covariance matrix of the 2SLS coefficient estimates was not taken to be block diagonal, but was instead estimated using formula (4), p. 273 in Fair and Parke (1980).
[10] See Fair (1980a), pp. 374–375, for a detailed discussion of the procedure that was used to draw the exogenous-variable values.
[11] In this case no t subscript is really needed for $\hat{d}_{itk}$, since it is not a function of t.
[12] For variables with trends the mean of the $d_{itk}/\tilde{\bar{y}}^2_{itk}$ values was calculated (for a given i and k) and this mean was added to $\tilde{\bar{\sigma}}^2_{itk}/\tilde{\bar{y}}^2_{itk}$ to yield a value of $\hat{\sigma}^2_{itk}/\tilde{\bar{y}}^2_{itk}$. The d-row values in Table 11.2 for these variables are the square roots of $\hat{\sigma}^2_{itk}/\tilde{\bar{y}}^2_{itk}$.

REFERENCES

Fair, R. C. (1976). *A Model of Macroeconomic Activity. Volume II: The Empirical Model*, Ballinger, Cambridge.

Fair, R. C. (1979). 'An analysis of the accuracy of four macro-econometric models.' *Journal of Political Economy*, **87**, 701–718.

Fair, R. C. (1980a). 'Estimating the expected predictive accuracy of econometric models.' *International Economic Review*, **21**, 355–378.

Fair, R. C. (1980b). 'The Fair model as of August 1, 1980.' Yale University, mimeo.

Fair, R. C. (1981). 'Estimated effects of the October 1979 change in monetary policy on the 1980 economy.' *American Economic Review*, **71**, 160–165.

Fair, R. C., and Parke, W. R. (1980). 'Full-information estimates of a nonlinear macro-econometric model.' *Journal of Econometrics*, **13**, 269–291.

Litterman, R. B. (1979). 'Techniques of forecasting using vector autoregression.' Federal Reserve Bank of Minneapolis, Working Paper No. 115.

Discussion

M. GRASSINI
Università di Firenze

I will begin my comment on Fair's paper by quoting the following sentence: 'It is clear that the method relies heavily on the use of stochastic simulation, but it can be explained without going into the simulation procedure.'

In my own view, however, a simulation procedure can and must be considered. A good reason for this is that Fair's results rest heavily on his methodology. Other papers — at least one — to be presented at this meeting are devoted precisely to those aspects of the question indirectly connected with the simulation procedure adopted. Evidence of the impact of outliers on the computed values and on the tendencies shown by the main statistics considered provides a useful contribution to the evaluation of the results.

Here I wish to say a few words on what I believe is the main topic of the paper, the *d*-statistic. First of all, on the procedure adopted for computing it, and secondly on the use of the statistic.

The estimation of misspecification is based upon the difference between the estimated variances based on the *mean forecast error* $(y - \bar{\tilde{y}})$ and the *'true' variance* computed through stochastic simulation. That is to say, *the variance of the forecast error*. Since Fair's model is specified as having knowledge of 'past-history' up to today, it seems that misspecification is considered to be not only a characteristic of the model, but a constant of it, a kind of original sin which one cannot just take into account in passing.

I think that the *d*-statistic must first be considered an indicator of misspecification and then used, when its value becomes unacceptable, to revise the model; the decision as to the level at which it begins to provide strong evidence of misspecification belongs to the field of the criteria for evaluating econometric models. This is the area to which the d-statistic properly belongs and in which it can be used conceptually; and in fact it has been, even if there is no evidence of the 'past' use of the d-statistic in revising the model. At least indirectly, we can detect when a model is undergoing a specification process through a subset of the exogenous variables—namely the dummy variables—which, as is well known, increase in number as the updating of a model proceeds. Now explanatory variables, including dummies, and different analytical specifications of equations occur when indicators such as the d-statistic give strong evidence of the presence of misspecification. At this point it becomes important to work out the procedure which links the misspecification indicator to the main sources of misspecification present in the model.

Further, it must be noted that d is based upon a *not strictly outside-sample forecasting*. In fact, the estimated model is specified when the sample has, for instance, size $t = 100$ and is then used to produce the misspecification component of the forecast error as the sample period end is $t = 60$. To this end, all the information contained in the available data is used. It is not certain at this point whether the model 'outside-sample' accuracy computed for $t = 61$–100 will hold in the future. If it does not, the model will be revised. It thus seems that the importance of the d-statistic is found more in its use for increasing the reliability of an econometric model than for measuring the total uncertainty of forecast errors.

In any case, the d-statistic is a measure of misspecification according to Fair's approach. It is thus worthwhile commenting on its use and components. The detailed representation of the results of the simulation experiments for the real GNP variable in Table 11.1 can be taken, as I have done, as an invitation to take a closer look at the components of d in order to analyse the meaning of this measure of forecasting accuracy.

First of all, one may observe that from the estimation period ending in 1968 IV up to the period ending in 1979 III, the sample size shows an increase of about 67 %, which is so remarkable as to lead one to expect some effect on the stability of the coefficient estimate. In general, such an increase in sample size should reduce, given no misspecification error, the variance of the forecasting error, at least in part, because of the decrease in uncertainty in coefficient estimates. Nonlinearities make this guess rather ambiguous. Anyway, we may take a look at the tendencies of the standard errors of the forecast presented on the left-hand side of Table 11.1. Using these figures, a 'mean' value for the standard error of the forecast has been computed and reported in Table 11.3 considering the first N values, for $N = 10, 20, 37$ for the different k's (the quarters ahead).

As long as the 'mean' standard error of the forecast is meaningful in detecting tendencies in the model's forecasting accuracy, at least for real GNP, we may note that the model does better for quarters in the second year (as the sample size increases) while it is a little shortsighted for the first year.

Table 11.3

	'Mean' standard error of the forecast		
k	N: 10	20	37
1	0.683	0.656	0.707
2	1.053	1.016	1.108
3	1.428	1.404	1.492
4	1.731	1.737	1.798
5	2.098	2.082	2.081
6	2.516	2.483	2.396
7	3.020	2.984	2.766
8	3.411	3.508	3.194

Furthermore, given the assumption used, it is possible to look at the d-statistic components in a different way. This may indeed be more suitable for evaluating the predictive accuracy of a model.

If we have

$$\hat{\varepsilon} = y - \tilde{\bar{y}}$$

and it is assumed that

$\tilde{\bar{y}}$ exactly equals the true expected value $\bar{y}$

$\tilde{\sigma}^2$ exactly equals the true value σ^2

and, under no misspecification error, the mean forecast error is such that $E(\hat{\varepsilon}) = 0$ and $E(\hat{\varepsilon}^2) = \sigma^2$, instead of the difference between the two estimates of σ^2 (one computed from the mean forecast error and one computed by stochastic simulation), we can work with the ratio

$$\frac{\hat{\varepsilon}}{\sigma}$$

which, under the above assumptions, has zero mean and a variance of 1. Without enlarging the set of assumptions concerning the mean forecast error, it is possible to work with a kind of χ^2 or, if we prefer to remain within the spirit of the d-statistic, with the mean value of the square of the ratio.

The indicators in Table 11.4 have been computed from the figures in Table 11.1.

If, on the other hand, we prefer to accept the normality assumption on the mean forecast error, column (3) is a χ^2 with the degrees of freedom of column (2); the hypothesis of misspecification error on the model, at least for the real GNP forecast over all the quarters considered, should, broadly speaking, be rejected.

If this normality assumption must be avoided we can restrict our attention to column (4). Here, even if there are no boundaries to evaluate if the departure from 1 is large, the figures seem regular enough to justify the conclusion that the

Table 11.4

(1) Quarters ahead	(2) Numbers of forecasts	(3) $\Sigma_i(\hat{\varepsilon}_i/\tilde{\sigma}_i)^2$	(4) (3)/(2)
1	44	52.90	1.20
2	43	39.99	0.92
3	42	42.31	1.00
4	41	41.89	1.02
5	40	41.93	1.05
6	39	43.17	1.11
7	38	40.07	1.05
8	37	38.61	1.04

misspecification of the model does not appear to be relevant with respect to the total uncertainty due to the other sources.

In order to extend our attention to other endogenous variables in the model, the *d*-statistic can be computed separately, using the figures in Table 11.2. From rows *c* and *d* it is easy to work out the mean values of *d*'s; their square roots are plotted in Figure 11.8. These values are not comparable with the ones computed for real GNP since they include uncertainty due to exogenous variables. In any case, it is easy to recognize a strong relationship between the values of column (4) in the previous table and the plot of the real GNP *d*-statistic. At least for this variable, the impact of uncertainty due to exogenous variables does not alter the tendency of the total uncertainty due to error terms and coefficient estimates. But even when analysing rows *b* and *c*, uncertainty due to exogenous variables appears to be a minor source of the standard error of forecast for all the variables.

Confining ourselves to the six endogenous variables considered in the paper, it is possible to divide those into two groups: on the one hand we have real GNP, unemployment rate, and bill rate; on the other hand the GNP deflator, wage rate, and money supply. For the first group it is possible to assert that the model does not reveal any evidence of misspecification; for the second group it is hard to say that misspecification does not exist. The nature of the *d*-statistic does not permit a rigorous decision. What can be achieved is a comparison between different models using one of these as a control experiment. Indeed, this procedure has been followed by Fair in a previous article in which the model is compared with a set of equations in which each endogenous variable is regressed on a constant, time, and its first eight lagged values. This model is particularly suited for forecasting purposes. This kind of a comparison using an indicator of misspecification, if not a test, may be a procedure for evaluating how far theory has been useful in the specification of a model. Using a control model which is an example of 'measurement without theory' we can analyse whether we have been

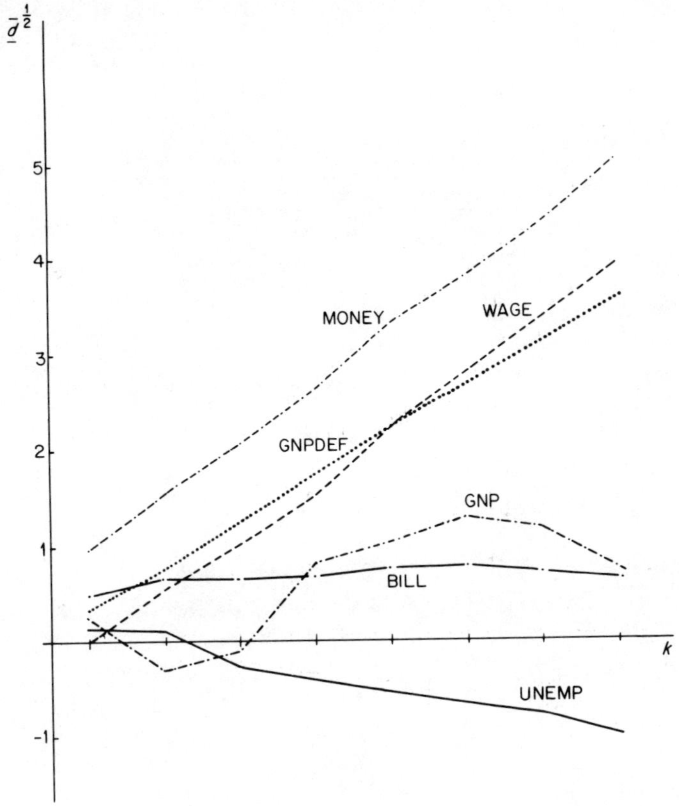

Figure 11.8

able to do better with a given theory. If not, we have a negative measure of its coherence with real life which remains valid even if the theory itself is considered a cornerstone in our reasoning.

Evaluating the Reliability of Macro-economic Models
Edited by G. C. Chow and P. Corsi

CHAPTER 12

Model Validation and Forecast Comparisons: Theoretical and Practical Considerations

M. SALMON
University of Warwick
K. F. WALLIS
University of Warwick

12.1 INTRODUCTION

Most macro-econometric models are built with the object, wholly or partly, of providing forecasts. The term 'forecast' covers three rather distinct types of exercise:

(a) genuine *ex-ante* forecasts, in which the model user predicts the actual future development of the economy, and for which projected future values of input variables must be supplied;
(b) *ex-post* forecasts, in which the model user eliminates the effects of error in the projections of the input variables by calculating 'forecasts' over some period in the recent past, given the actual observed values of the input variables;
(c) hypothetical forecasting or policy analysis exercises, in which the model user estimates the response of the economy to alternative scenarios, that is, to alternative values of policy instruments or to different kinds of exogenous shock.

In each case there is interest in evaluating the results of the forecasting exercise, not only for its own sake but also to provide information that is useful in model validation, that is, in checking the specification of the model. Of course, the various forecasting exercises and their respective evaluations are not necessarily independent of one another, for example it is often said that in order to be useful in policy analysis a model should have a good real-world forecasting record over a period that was not part of the estimation period, so that it might also be expected to provide 'good' estimates of responses to policy changes.

As elements of the evaluation process we identify for further discussion three main types of forecast comparison:

(a) comparison of the forecasts of a single model with actual outcomes;
(b) comparison of the forecasts of an econometric model with those obtained by ostensibly different methods, such as statistical time series ('Box–Jenkins') methods;
(c) comparison of the forecasts of a number of different macro-econometric models.

Theoretical and practical aspects of these comparisons are discussed in Sections 12.2–12.4. In general this discussion is set in the context of standard linear textbook models, and in Section 12.5 we discuss further issues that arise from the nonlinearity of practical models. Section 12.6 deals with structural change, and Section 12.7 contains concluding comments.

The practical use of model-based forecasts is in decision-making, and in principle the evaluation of a model and its forecasts should be associated with the loss function relevant to the particular objective. In practice this does not feature in the literature, since decision makers and the users of forecasts seldom discuss such matters, at least not in public. As a result models are generally evaluated by the model builders themselves and their econometric critics, in rather general terms, using statistical criteria that seem reasonable but are seldom rigorously justified. Model builders typically report a range of criteria, perhaps in the hope that a particular model user will find therein the information needed for a particular decision problem. That models are built to achieve different objectives is clear from their different sizes and their coverage of different markets in the economy. Thus a different loss function is implicit in each model, occasionally made more explicit as, for example, when a model is given a specific control orientation (Wall *et al.*, 1975). In the absence of a completely explicit specification of a loss function, our own discussion is concerned with some of the various general criteria that are employed.

12.2 COMPARING A SINGLE MODEL'S FORECASTS WITH ACTUALITY

We begin by assuming a linear simultaneous-equations model, describing the relations between the elements of a vector of current endogenous variables $\mathbf{y}_t$ and a vector of predetermined variables $\mathbf{z}_t$, and of which the reduced form can be written

$$\mathbf{y}_t = \mathbf{\Pi z}_t + \mathbf{v}_t.$$

Given estimates of the coefficients, $\hat{\boldsymbol{\Pi}}$, based on a sample period $t = 1, \ldots, T$, and projections of the predetermined variables, $\hat{\mathbf{z}}_{T+j}$, for a forecast period $t = T+1, T+2, \ldots, T+h$, *ex-ante* forecasts are given as

$$\hat{\mathbf{y}}_{T+j} = \hat{\boldsymbol{\Pi}}\hat{\mathbf{z}}_{T+j}, \qquad j = 1, 2, \ldots, h.$$

For a correctly-specified model, the corresponding actual values are given as

$$\mathbf{y}_{T+j} = \boldsymbol{\Pi}\mathbf{z}_{T+j} + \mathbf{v}_{T+j},$$

and in this event the forecast error can be written as

$$\mathbf{y}_{T+j} - \hat{\mathbf{y}}_{T+j} = \hat{\boldsymbol{\Pi}}(\mathbf{z}_{T+j} - \hat{\mathbf{z}}_{T+j}) - (\hat{\boldsymbol{\Pi}} - \boldsymbol{\Pi})\mathbf{z}_{T+j} + \mathbf{v}_{T+j}.$$

This expression breaks down the forecast error into three components.

First, projections of the predetermined variables are unlikely to be exact, and the error in these projections, $\mathbf{z}_{T+j} - \hat{\mathbf{z}}_{T+j}$, contributes to the overall *ex-ante* forecast error. Secondly, the coefficient estimates $\hat{\boldsymbol{\Pi}}$ based on the sample-period information differ from the true values $\boldsymbol{\Pi}$. Finally, the random disturbances $\mathbf{v}_{T+j}$ occurring in the forecast period affect the outcome, the above equation for $\hat{\mathbf{y}}_{T+j}$ having assumed that the optimal forecast of these disturbances is their unconditional mean value of zero. In practice this might be modified either given evidence that the disturbances are autocorrelated, so that earlier residuals are helpful in forecasting later disturbances, or given information about extraneous influences likely to impinge on the model in the forecast period but not explicitly incorporated in the original specification. This last possibility occurs frequently in practical forecasting exercises, since good information about changes in legislation, institutional arrangements both foreign and domestic, labour contracts, and so forth is often available and incorporated into *ex-ante* forecasts as predictions of residuals, equivalently handled as adjustments to the intercept terms of the appropriate equations. The success of these adjustments reflects the skill and judgment of the model user, hence their evaluation contributes little to model validation. However, a persistent need for modifications to an estimated equation, perhaps with similar justifications being offered from one period to the next, would suggest that an important explanatory variable had been omitted from the original specification. In the absence of a complete re-specification, the construction of simple statistical models for the residuals might provide a short-run, but second-best, solution (compare Surrey and Ormerod, 1977).

The first component of the forecast error results from errors in the projections of the predetermined variables, and in dynamic models further possibilities arise by distinguishing between lagged endogenous and exogenous variables. We partition $\mathbf{z}_t$, the vector of predetermined variables, into subvectors $\mathbf{y}_{t-1}$ and $\mathbf{x}_t$, taking the case of one-period lagged endogenous variables for simplicity. Partitioning the reduced form conformably we have

$$\mathbf{y}_t = \boldsymbol{\Pi}_1\mathbf{y}_{t-1} + \boldsymbol{\Pi}_2\mathbf{x}_t + \mathbf{v}_t.$$

In *ex-ante* forecasting one period ahead, only the exogenous variables contribute to the errors in projecting predetermined variables since $\mathbf{y}_T$ is known, and the forecast is given by

$$\hat{\mathbf{y}}_{T+1} = \hat{\mathbf{\Pi}}_1\mathbf{y}_T + \hat{\mathbf{\Pi}}_2\hat{\mathbf{x}}_{T+1}.$$

In forecasting further ahead, the model generates its own lagged endogenous variables, and the sequence of forecasts is given by

$$\hat{\mathbf{y}}_{T+j} = \hat{\mathbf{\Pi}}_1\hat{\mathbf{y}}_{T+j-1} + \hat{\mathbf{\Pi}}_2\,\hat{\mathbf{x}}_{T+j}, \qquad j = 2, 3, \ldots, h.$$

which reverts to the general expression given above.

Errors in the projections of exogenous variables, by definition formed outside the model, also reflect the skill of the model user rather than that of the model builder. When the model forecasts are compared to the actual outcomes after the event, as in studies of forecasters' 'track records' (for example, Osborn and Teal, 1979), this contribution can be eliminated by considering *ex-post* forecasts. These are based on the actual realized values of $\mathbf{z}_{T+j}$, and are given by

$$\tilde{\mathbf{y}}_{T+j} = \hat{\mathbf{\Pi}}\mathbf{z}_{T+j} = \hat{\mathbf{\Pi}}_1\mathbf{y}_{T+j-1} + \hat{\mathbf{\Pi}}_2\mathbf{x}_{T+j}, \qquad j = 1, 2, \ldots, h.$$

Ex-post forecasts can be calculated as part of an evaluation of the model's genuine forecasting performance, or as a check on the model's structural stability carried out immediately after specification and estimation by holding back from the estimation period a subsample of h observations specifically for this purpose. Assuming that the data are truly generated by the given linear model, the *ex-post* forecast errors have two components:

$$\mathbf{y}_{T+j} - \tilde{\mathbf{y}}_{T+j} = \mathbf{v}_{T+j} - (\hat{\mathbf{\Pi}} - \mathbf{\Pi})\mathbf{z}_{T+j}, \qquad j = 1, 2, \ldots, h.$$

Study of the absolute magnitudes of these errors may be informative, in the light of the known development of the economy, but in the absence of a standard of measurement, such a study is of limited usefulness. A standard of comparison is provided by an estimate of the variance of these errors, based on the estimated variances of disturbances and coefficient estimates, obtained as a by-product of the sample-period estimation process. Clearly *ex-post* forecasts can be calculated *within* the estimation period,

$$\tilde{\mathbf{y}}_t = \hat{\mathbf{\Pi}}\mathbf{z}_t, \qquad t = 1, \ldots, T,$$

and estimates of the variance of the forecast errors for the period $t = T + 1, \ldots, T + h$ are in effect based on the variance of the *ex-post* forecast errors or residuals $\mathbf{y}_t - \tilde{\mathbf{y}}_t$ in the period $t = 1, \ldots, T$. Formal tests are available for comparing this estimated forecast error variance with the actual mean squared error of the forecasts (Christ, 1966, Ch.X.7; Dhrymes *et al.*, 1972; Hendry, 1974), and, if the latter is not significantly greater than the former, the model passes its structural stability test. (Using stochastic simulation methods, Fair (1980) provides analogous estimates of the forecast error variance for nonlinear models.) Note, however, that there is no statistical theory available for the case in which the forecasts sequentially generate their own lagged values, as follows:

$$\mathbf{y}^*_{T+j} = \hat{\mathbf{\Pi}}_1 \mathbf{y}^*_{T+j-1} + \hat{\mathbf{\Pi}}_2 \mathbf{x}_{T+j} \qquad j = 1, 2, \ldots, h.$$

In this case forecast errors typically cumulate, and while various plots can be informative, in particular for checking that the forecasts do not 'drift', the theory of standard CUSUM techniques does not cover models with lagged endogenous variables (Brown *et al.*, 1975). A further possibility, given forecasts calculated over a suitably long period, is to compare the properties of the forecasts to actuality through the National Bureau of Economic Research business cycle methodology, that is, by considering whether the forecasts reproduce actual behaviour in terms of such features as the length of cycles, the coincidence of turning points, and the lead–lag relations of the variables to one another and to the reference cycle.

If the model fails its structural stability test, then re-specification is indicated. However, such tests are not very powerful, since specification errors also affect the sample-period estimates of the model's behaviour. For example, omitting a relevant explanatory variable increases the residual variance of an equation and biases its coefficients, hence it is not necessarily the case that forecasts from the misspecified equation have mean squared error greater than that anticipated on the basis of (erroneous) sample-period calculations. Indeed, if the behaviour of the variables is unchanged, the forecast-period estimates will be equally erroneous as the sample-period estimates. Thus forecast periods in which the behaviour of exogenous variables is substantially different from that in the sample period provide particularly informative comparisons which may lead to improved specification, as in the case of the aggregate consumption function following the high inflation of the early 1970's (Wallis, 1979, Ch. 1). In effect, the hypothesis being tested in structural stability tests is that the model's explanation of the variables is equally good in the sample and forecast periods, and no absolute measure of the quality of that explanation is provided.

In sum, the general problem in evaluating a single set of forecasts is that no absolute standard, such as an estimate of the minimum forecast error variance that can be achieved, is available. These difficulties have led to econometric forecasts being evaluated relative to forecasts produced by other means, or to forecast comparisons being conducted across different models, in order to gain an impression of their relative merits. These are discussed in turn in the next two sections.

12.3 COMPARING FORECASTS FROM ECONOMETRIC AND 'NON-ECONOMETRIC' REPRESENTATIONS

In the absence of an absolute standard, the forecast performance of an econometric model has often been evaluated relative to the performance of some simpler forecasting rules. In the words of Cooper (1972, pp. 828–829):

> Comparing an econometric to a naive method of forecasting supplies a technique for assessing the economic information contained in an econometric model. The defining characteristic of a 'naive' forecasting method is that it depends exclusively on purely statistical properties of economic time series, such as trend, past levels, or past changes. A naive method does not incorporate any economic information... Forecasts made by naive methods are then compared with forecasts made by other methods. Forecasting methods that cannot do better than a purely mechanical one should be discarded.

That progress has occurred since the early development of econometric models is clear from the fact that the forecasting methods against which the models have been compared have gradually become less naive. Initially 'no-change' ($\hat{y}_{T+1} = y_T$) or 'same-change' ($\hat{y}_{T+1} - y_T = y_T - y_{T-1}$) forecasting rules were employed. Subsequently autoregressive models of the form

$$y_t = \phi_1 y_{t-1} + \phi_2 y_{t-2} + \cdots + \phi_p y_{t-p} + \varepsilon_t$$

fitted to individual endogenous variables were used to generate forecasts. Finally there have been applications of the ARIMA models of Box and Jenkins (1970), possibly in their seasonal form, that is,

$$\phi(L)\Phi(L^s)\Delta^d\Delta_s^D y_t = \theta(L)\Theta(L^s)\varepsilon_t$$

where L is the lag operator, the first factors on each side are polynomials in L, the second factors on each side are polynomials in L^s, s is the number of seasons per year, $\Delta = 1 - L$, and $\Delta_s = 1 - L^s$. Nelson (1972) compares the FRB–MIT–PENN model against ARIMA models for certain endogenous variables, and finds that in within-sample comparisons the econometric model was ahead, whereas outside the sample the 'pure time-series' models had smaller forecast errors. In this section we challenge the idea that 'purely statistical' models for endogenous variables provide an independent check on the econometric model, and more generally consider the relations among the various representations of a model that might be used for forecasting and other purposes (Prothero and Wallis, 1976; Wallis, 1977; Zellner and Palm, 1974).

A linear dynamic econometric model, explaining the behaviour of a vector of endogenous variables $\mathbf{y}_t$ in terms of a vector of exogenous variables $\mathbf{x}_t$ and a vector of disturbances $\mathbf{u}_t$, may be written in *structural form* as

$$\boldsymbol{B}(L)\mathbf{y}_t + \boldsymbol{C}(L)\mathbf{x}_t = \mathbf{u}_t$$

where $\boldsymbol{B}(L)$ and $\boldsymbol{C}(L)$ are matrices of polynomials in the lag operator, viz.

$$\boldsymbol{B}(L) = \boldsymbol{B}_0 + \boldsymbol{B}_1 L + \ldots + \boldsymbol{B}_r L^r, \qquad \boldsymbol{C}(L) = \boldsymbol{C}_0 + \boldsymbol{C}_1 L + \ldots + \boldsymbol{C}_s L^s.$$

Usually $\boldsymbol{B}_0 \neq \boldsymbol{I}$, hence there is 'instantaneous coupling' between the endogenous (output) variables. This is removed in the *reduced form*, which expresses each endogenous variable as a function of predetermined (exogenous plus lagged endogenous) variables, as follows:

$$\mathbf{y}_t = -\boldsymbol{B}_0^{-1}\{\boldsymbol{B}_1\mathbf{y}_{t-1} + \cdots + \boldsymbol{B}_r\mathbf{y}_{t-r} + \boldsymbol{C}(L)\mathbf{x}_t\} + \boldsymbol{B}_0^{-1}\mathbf{u}_t.$$

The present formulation generalizes the reduced form used in the previous section by including higher-order lags of both endogenous and exogenous variables. It also makes explicit the dependence of reduced form coefficients (the $\boldsymbol{\Pi}$-matrices, in the previous section) on structural parameters.

An alternative solution of the structural form is obtained by multiplying through by the inverse, not of $\boldsymbol{B}_0$, but of $\boldsymbol{B}(L)$ (under appropriate stability conditions). The result is the *final form*

$$\mathbf{y}_t = -\boldsymbol{B}(L)^{-1}\boldsymbol{C}(L)\mathbf{x}_t + \boldsymbol{B}(L)^{-1}\mathbf{u}_t,$$

in which each endogenous variable is expressed as an infinite distributed lag function of the exogenous variables, together with an error term that is a moving average of the original structural disturbances. The coefficients in the expansion of $\boldsymbol{B}(L)^{-1}\boldsymbol{C}(L)$ provide *dynamic multipliers*, describing the response of y_{it} to a unit shock in $x_{j,t-l}$. In empirical work the infinite distributed lag is generally approximated by a ratio of finite-degree polynomials in L, but in the present context an explicit expression is obtained by writing $\boldsymbol{B}(L)^{-1} = \boldsymbol{b}(L)/|\boldsymbol{B}(L)|$, where $\boldsymbol{b}(L)$ is the adjoint matrix of $\boldsymbol{B}(L)$ and $|\boldsymbol{B}(L)|$ the determinant. Thus the final form may be written

$$\mathbf{y}_t = \frac{-\boldsymbol{b}(L)\boldsymbol{C}(L)}{|\boldsymbol{B}(L)|}\mathbf{x}_t + \frac{\boldsymbol{b}(L)}{|\boldsymbol{B}(L)|}\mathbf{u}_t,$$

giving a set of multi-input 'transfer function' equations. Multiplying through by $|\boldsymbol{B}(L)|$, we obtain a further representation known as the *final equations* (Tinbergen, 1939; Goldberger, 1959):

$$|\boldsymbol{B}(L)|\mathbf{y}_t = -\boldsymbol{b}(L)\boldsymbol{C}(L)\mathbf{x}_t + \boldsymbol{b}(L)\mathbf{u}_t.$$

Since $|\boldsymbol{B}(L)|$ is a scalar polynomial, each final equation relates a given endogenous variable to its own past values and to the exogenous variables, current and past, but to no other endogenous variable, current or past. In effect, the dynamic interrelations with other endogenous variables have been solved out. The interesting property of this representation is that the autoregressive operator $|\boldsymbol{B}(L)|$ is common to all endogenous variables (unless, as noted by Goldberger, the model is decomposable, for this results in cancellation of common factors across some of the final equations). Thus the characteristic dynamic behaviour of the endogenous variables could, in principle, be studied by considering a single endogenous variable or, more abstractly, the common characteristic polynomial $|\boldsymbol{B}(L)|$.

To obtain a further representation, we add an assumption about the data generation process of the exogenous variables, namely that this can be represented as the vector ARMA process

$$\boldsymbol{G}(L)\mathbf{x}_t = \boldsymbol{H}(L)\boldsymbol{\eta}_t,$$

where $\boldsymbol{\eta}_t$ is a vector white noise process. The complete model of the data generation process of the observable variables can then be written

$$\begin{bmatrix} \boldsymbol{G}(L) & \mathbf{0} \\ \boldsymbol{C}(L) & \boldsymbol{B}(L) \end{bmatrix} \begin{bmatrix} \mathbf{x}_t \\ \mathbf{y}_t \end{bmatrix} = \begin{bmatrix} \boldsymbol{H}(L)\boldsymbol{\eta}_t \\ A(L)\boldsymbol{\xi}_t \end{bmatrix}$$

where $\mathbf{u}_t$ is assumed to have a vector moving average representation. (If $\mathbf{u}_t$ is non-autocorrelated, only the leading coefficient matrix A_0 is nonzero. If a vector ARMA representation is alternatively assumed, then it is postulated that the autoregressive operator has been multiplied through and incorporated in $\boldsymbol{B}(L)$ and $\boldsymbol{C}(L)$.) On multiplying through by the inverse of the matrix on the left-hand side, defined as its adjoint matrix divided by its determinant, as in the previous paragraph, we obtain 'final equations' for $\mathbf{y}_t$ of the form

$$\phi(L)\mathbf{y}_t = \boldsymbol{F}_1(L)\boldsymbol{\eta}_t + \boldsymbol{F}_2(L)\boldsymbol{\xi}_t,$$

where $\phi(L) = |\boldsymbol{G}(L)| \times |\boldsymbol{B}(L)|$, and $\boldsymbol{F}_1(L)$ and $\boldsymbol{F}_2(L)$ are defined in terms of the original matrices and their adjoints. Thus a typical element y_{it} is expressed in terms of a finite number of its own past values and a composite error term which is the sum of a number of separate moving average processes. By a result in time series theory this error term has a representation as a moving average of a single white noise process, ε_{it} say, and so we have a *univariate ARMA model* for each y_{it}, of the form

$$\phi(L)y_{it} = \theta_i(L)\varepsilon_{it}.$$

We can thus interpret this ARMA time series equation for an endogenous variable of an econometric model as an alternative solution form, that is, an implication of the model. A further implication of this development is that the ε-processes for different endogenous variables are cross-correlated, and so joint estimation of the time series models for a number of variables yields a gain in efficiency. A multiple time series modelling strategy based on the connections among the representations described in this paragraph is developed by Chan and Wallis (1978).

It is interesting to note that a further member of this sequence of alternative representations of the same structural model is the *state space representation* favoured in other disciplines. Thus forecasts generated from the Kalman filter via a state space econometric model may be seen as the application of a common statistical principle to an equivalent representation of the same structure. This equivalence is obtained by rewriting either the structural econometric model or the equivalent ARMA representation in state space form. The system of equations

$$\begin{aligned} \mathbf{w}_{t+1} &= \boldsymbol{D}\mathbf{w}_t + \boldsymbol{E}\mathbf{x}_t + \boldsymbol{\varepsilon}_{1t} \\ \mathbf{y}_t &= \boldsymbol{J}\mathbf{w}_t + \boldsymbol{\varepsilon}_{2t} \end{aligned}$$

is known as a *state space model.* The matrices $\boldsymbol{D}$, $\boldsymbol{E}$ and $\boldsymbol{J}$ are constants, not polynomials in L, since the vector of state variables, $\mathbf{w}_t$, incorporates all relevant lags explicitly. The concept of the *state* may be defined either as the minimal set of variables, knowledge of which is necessary for prediction of the future (apart from exogenous inputs) or alternatively, and more rigorously, as a basis for the predictor space. It can then be seen as a rather fundamental form in which our previous representations may be expressed. A simple transformation allows the above equations to be rewritten as

$$\mathbf{y}_t = \boldsymbol{J}(\boldsymbol{I} - \boldsymbol{D}L)^{-1}\boldsymbol{E}L\mathbf{x}_t + \boldsymbol{K}(L)\boldsymbol{\varepsilon}_t,$$

which corresponds to our earlier final form representation, but with a different set of parametric restrictions. Many ramifications of this equivalence are developed by Akaike (1974a) and Hannan (1979). It is interesting to note that in general there is not a unique state space representation, and while the structural econometric model leads to one form, the vector ARMA model leads to another. Akaike (1974a) demonstrates the statistical equivalence of the various state space forms.

The relations among these alternative representations raise a number of questions. First, since they are mathematically equivalent, the application of a common statistical approach to the different representations of a given model can only yield different answers if the various representations impose different restrictions on the statistical method, or have different requirements in statistical implementation. The choice of a particular representation that is most appropriate for a given statistical application is often clear, but the choice remains between deriving this representation from an estimated structural form, so that any implied restrictions are imposed and the equivalence of the representation is guaranteed, or obtaining it empirically, perhaps relying on the above development for part of the specification but relying on the data for the remainder.

Economists find the structural form, with its explicit statement of different economic agents' autonomous behaviour, accounting identities, technical relations, and so forth, to be the most convenient framework in which to consider questions of economic theory and on which to impose the resulting restrictions. But to obtain forecasts of the endogenous variables the structural form is transformed to the reduced form as above, and in practice estimates of the reduced form coefficients are obtained from estimates of the structural parameters, rather than directly from (unrestricted) regressions of each endogenous variable on the predetermined variables. Although the directly-estimated reduced form equations have smaller sample-period residual sums of squares, the argument for preferring the 'solved out' or derived (and hence restricted) reduced form equations is that they forecast better if the (typically *over*-identifying) prior restrictions incorporated in the specification of the matrices $\boldsymbol{B}$ and $\boldsymbol{C}$ are correct. This is an argument about *asymptotic* efficiency, however, which cannot be immediately applied to a finite-sample situation, since it is known that the derived reduced form coefficients based on the commonly-used 2SLS and 3SLS structural estimators possess no integral moments (McCarthy, 1972; Sargan, 1976). This suggests that criteria other than mean squared error should be used, and that forecasts might occasionally be very poor when an estimated $\boldsymbol{B}$-matrix is nearly singular.

The implied final form and final equations can also be derived readily from an estimated structural form, and in practice dynamic multipliers and/or the properties of the characteristic polynomial are frequently reported. However, it is again possible to ignore the structural form and estimate these directly, with the only restriction being a prior classification of endogenous and exogenous variables, the detailed dynamic specification being data-based.

The same arguments apply to the consideration of univariate ARMA representations, except that in this case an additional assumption has been made, namely that the exogenous variables satisfy a vector ARMA process. On incorporating this assumption the 'pure time series' representation of an endogenous variable that is implied by an estimated structure can be derived. However, in the last stage of this derivation we construct a moving average error term, with a single innovation process, that is observationally equivalent to the sum of a number of such series, and so the 'structural' information on the separate series is lost, and in consequence the implied time series representation gives less efficient forecasts than the econometric model. In the formal framework of this section, *ex-ante* forecasts of a given endogenous variable are obtained from the reduced form, with forecasts of the exogenous variables being obtained from the vector ARMA model: it can be shown, following Pierce (1975), that such *ex-ante* forecasts have smaller mean squared error than forecasts from the implied univariate ARMA models. Again, in contrast to this derivation, a univariate ARMA model for an endogenous variable, to be used in forecast comparisons with the structural model, can be obtained directly from the data, using the 'model identification' and diagnostic devices developed by Box and Jenkins and others. It is commonly said that such models 'let the data speak for themselves', and so they qualify as 'naive' models in the sense of the quotation at the beginning of this section. Usually the degrees of the autoregressive and moving average operators in empirical ARMA models are substantially less than those implied by the formal derivation, since $|\boldsymbol{B}(L)|$ is typically of high degree, and so in practice there is some conflict between the theoretical and empirical models. Statistical reasons for this are discussed in Wallis (1977), and more general explanations for this disagreement between, in effect, two different approximations to reality are discussed below.

The foregoing analysis shows that there are difficulties in interpreting the univariate ARMA model as an independent check on the econometric model, in terms of forecast or any other comparison. The theoretical derivation of the ARMA model from a given structural form does not in general result in restrictions on its parametrization that could provide the basis of a formal test. The structural form implies the existence of various alternative representations, of which the univariate ARMA model is one, but a given ARMA model is consistent with a number of different structures. Perhaps for this reason, the implied ARMA model is seldom derived (although other difficulties arise in practical models, discussed below) and in practice the comparison simply rests on the relative forecasting ability of the structural model and the data-based ARMA model. Since the data used in empirical specification and estimation of the two forms are the same, their forecasts, forecast errors, and resulting summary measures are not statistically independent, hence a formal test cannot be based on a direct comparison of the two forecast error variances, for example. An alternative test of (one-step ahead) forecast errors is presented by Granger and Newbold (1977, p. 281), who in addition describe (p. 283) tests based on combinations of the two forecasts, also considered by Nelson (1972). However, it is impossible in practice to be sure that the two models are not simply two different representations of the same structure. Different forecast properties may indicate that they *are* two different approximations to reality, or that the two different representations of the same structure are affected in different ways by the requirements of the statistical method in each case. It is difficult to compare models at different points in the sequence of alternative representations, and it cannot be maintained that, from their forecast properties alone, the pure time series models provide an independent check on structural econometric models.

However, practical forecast comparisons have often tended to suggest that for a number of variables the empirical time series representations have the better forecasting performance. This result is in conflict with the theoretical result that forecasts based on the implied time series representation have larger mean squared error than those based on the structural econometric model. How can this discrepancy be rationalized? The equivalence of the alternative representations rests on a number of assumptions, few of which may be valid in practice. The implications of the assumption of a *linear* model are examined more generally in Section 12.5. The impact of parameter estimation errors may be different in different representations, but although little is known about this, it is clear that their contribution to forecast error variance is of relatively small order of magnitude. The vector ARMA process assumed for the exogenous variables may not be a good approximation, since the variables classified as exogenous in macro-econometric models often exhibit jumps and discontinuities. Indeed, a number of dummy variables (indicator variables) are often included among the exogenous variables, and while these can be appropriately treated in the model-based forecasts, one would expect that the neglect of such discontinuities in univariate ARMA modelling (unless taken into account by what is termed 'intervention analysis' in the time series literature) would work to the disadvantage of the purely statistical forecasts. More generally, however, the model is assumed to be correctly specified, and in practice one doubts this assumption particularly insofar as the dynamic and stochastic specification of large models is concerned. In these areas there is little guidance from economic theory, and one suspects that, taking a large model equation-by-equation, relatively less systematic attention is given to these matters than when a time series model is identified for a single endogenous variable, for it is precisely the dynamic and stochastic aspects of the behaviour of the variables that such models emphasize. Rather than providing an independent post-construction check on an econometric model, comparisons with time series models represent a useful diagnostic device during model-building; moreover, attention should not be limited to a comparison of forecast variances, since a comparison of the dynamic specifications of the various representations yields valuable information about their adequacy.

12.4 COMPARISONS ACROSS MACRO-ECONOMETRIC MODELS

An alternative response to the absence of an absolute standard of forecasting performance against which to assess a single econometric model has been to turn to comparisons across a number of models of a national economy. Three related aspects of the different models have been compared:

(a) pure forecasting ability, based on the mean squared error of forecasts over a post-model-building period;
(b) policy multipliers, through simulation or hypothetical forecasts;
(c) dynamic properties, stability, and cyclical behaviour, through stochastic simulation or spectral analysis.

For U.S. examples of (a) and (b) see Christ (1975) and Fromm and Klein (1976), while for the U.K. see Laury *et al.* (1978); for (c) see Howrey (1972). The validation of a single model as an approximation to reality is not an objective of these exercises; instead models are compared in a rather general, descriptive manner. Thus few strong conclusions have been drawn, although outliers are occasionally detected. We first discuss the statistical foundations, or lack thereof, of these comparisons, in general taking the three types of exercise together, since they have certain essential similarities. These similarities become clear in our subsequent discussion of the experimental design aspects of the comparisons.

It is apparent that a complete statistical theory for a formal selection between competing large-scale dynamic models, seen as non-nested hypotheses, is not available. This was noted by Dhrymes *et al.* (1972), and although progress has been made, for example by Pesaran and Deaton (1978) and Davidson and MacKinnon (1981), as yet it remains the case. An alternative approach rests on establishing distance measures for the alternative models from the true probability process: the model that minimizes this distance is then considered to be the best available, but again this is in practice a relative comparison and an absolute measure of the 'quality' of the chosen model is not provided. These notions underlie recent developments using information criteria (Akaike, 1974b; Sawa, 1978) and the method of support (Edwards, 1972), and relieve objections to the use of significance tests. While these methods are related to estimation of the predictive distribution, and a formal equivalence between Akaike's information criterion and Amemiya's prediction criterion can be shown (Amemiya, 1980), extensions from the linear regression context to large-scale model validation via forecast comparisons are awaited.

It is also clear that the choice of economic structure differs between models, with a different loss function implicit in each one, as already noted. The most obvious manifestations is the differing size of models, which results in certain variables being variously treated as endogenous or exogenous, although differences in the classification of variables can arise for other reasons. The type of policy objective to be considered clearly influences the level of disaggregation and size of the model. The main reason for the increasing size of models, the Treasury model of the U.K. economy having some 500 equations, is the need to model the channels through which various policy instruments affect the economy, and in practice the number of available instruments is large. The tax system involves a large number of different rates and allowances, and monetary and interest rate policy works through many channels. To describe the differential impact of particular measures on particular groups or sectors of the economy or particular types of expenditure a full account of these impacts is required. Of course to forecast broad aggregates a smaller, more aggregated model might suffice. However, in forecast comparisons the fact that the larger model provides information on a number of matters about which the smaller model has nothing to say is usually neglected, there being no loss function specified. *Ex-post* forecast comparisons clearly give an advantage to models that treat a variable that is difficult to forecast as exogenous, and this can be eliminated to some extent by basing the comparison on *ex-ante* forecasts. But comparing models augmented by their forecasting rules for exogenous variables may distort the appraisal of different models that are designed to serve different ends.

The specification of a particular model may also be influenced by the statistical method employed, the sample period, the level of temporal aggregation, any pre-filtering of the data, and an emphasis on one or another of the alternative representations discussed in the previous section. The particular objective will lead a model builder to make a careful choice under each of these headings, and Cooper's (1972) attempt to compare various models on a standardized basis by re-estimating them mechanically on a consistent body of data has been criticized by Howrey *et al.* (1974) for its neglect of this ('tender loving') care.

An important feature both in model specification and in elucidation of the model's properties is the nature of the input characteristics, given not only by the choice of variables to be treated as exogenous but also by their intrinsic behaviour: together we term these the *input topology*. The specification of the model reflects the sample input topology in a number of ways. Clearly the model cannot capture the economy's response to a signal that is scarcely present in the input. Further, the specification of lag polynomials is typically data-based, and so reflects the sample input topology rather than a prior theoretical view of the dynamics. However, almost no systematic examination of the nature of the inputs that characterize the model during the sample period is carried out. Such an examination would provide useful preliminary information in a model comparison exercise, providing guidelines as to possible uses of the model and an indication of the frequency range over which the model may be reliable.

The input topology in the forecast period or experimental situation is the distinguishing feature of the three types of comparison outlined at the beginning of this section. In principle, comparisons across models of forecasts, policy multiplier' paths, or cyclical behaviour in stochastic simulation, provided that there is no unequal injection of the skill and judgment of the model user, yield partial information on essentially the same characteristic of the models, namely the map of their dynamic properties. The question is one of experimental design, since the three exercises differ only in input topology: a forecast comparison is based on those inputs that are economically meaningful in the particular forecast period, a multiplier comparison is typically based on unit impulse or unit step change inputs, and stochastic simulation comparisons usually study the response to a white noise, random input. It is potentially confusing that different conclusions about the relative merits of various models may be drawn from these different exercises, and there is room for an analysis that fully explores the dynamic response of alternative models in an objective manner, the crucial aspect being the design of the input signal.

The characteristic polynomial $|\boldsymbol{B}(L)|$ determines the dynamic behaviour of the model, as noted in the previous section. In transfer function analysis, the positioning of the roots of the characteristic polynomial, or poles, determines the stability, speed of response, and cyclical behaviour of the system. The eigenvalues of the system provide precisely the same information. Writing the polynomial $|\boldsymbol{B}(z)|$ as

$$(z - \lambda_1)(z - \lambda_2)(z - \lambda_3)\ldots(z - \lambda_n)$$

where the poles are $\lambda_1, \lambda_2, \ldots, \lambda_n$, the dynamic behaviour of the system may be seen in the frequency domain to be composed of the product of terms, each resonant at a particular frequency determined by the position of the particular pole or eigenvalue. In designing an input signal we would wish to ensure that the input was 'rich enough' in frequency terms to draw behaviour in the output from each of these poles. A badly designed input will not 'excite' all the possible modes of behaviour in a model. In comparative studies the possibility exists that an input signal, apparently well justified on economic criteria, may excite different modes of behaviour in different models, or a particular mode of behaviour to a different extent. Of the three types of comparative exercise, the pure forecast comparison is potentially the most deficient in this respect. A full frequency response analysis, objectively designed to determine the values of the poles in the characteristic polynomial, may avoid these difficulties. In addition, although we are free to choose between the 'equivalent' information provided by analysis in either the time or frequency domain, there are situations in which vital aspects of the dynamic response may be more apparent in one form rather than the other. For example, it is difficult to detect, in the time domain, differences between models that are frequency dependent, such as might arise from varying attitudes to the use of seasonally filtered data or differing emphasis on short term rather than medium term responses. Thus relaxing the existing relative neglect of frequency based comparisons *across* econometric models may result in substantial gains in the systematic evaluation of these models.

An input signal, as the final form or final equations make clear, may stimulate the system either via the exogenous variables or via the disturbances, often with different economic interpretations. However, these relations also show that for dynamic analysis the only distinction lies in the different lag polynomials applied to the input, which alter the characteristics of an otherwise standard input, and may result in the observation of apparently different dynamic responses. For example, in the classic study by Adelman and Adelman (1959), white noise disturbances generated cycles at business-cycle frequencies, while white noise innovations in exogenous variables did not. It is noted above that information on the sample input topology would be useful in model comparisons: if no evidence of cycles is found in the 'unforced' behaviour of a system, but cycles are present in the input topology and these induce cycles in the endogenous variables, it is important to say why.

A final question is whether the white noise input, which is potentially exciting at each frequency of the dynamic response, is an optimal input signal. The recent literature on the experimental design of dynamic systems (Goodwin and Payne, 1977; Zarrop, 1980) suggests that it may not be so. If an optimum is defined as a maximum of some scalar function of the Fisher information matrix, it appears that a finite number of discrete frequency components is preferable to white noise when estimating the parameters of a dynamic regression. The problem with a white noise input is that it enhances noise at irrelevant frequencies. A physical analogy suggested to us is that of determining the resonant frequency of an organ pipe: a sequence of tuning forks, each of a particular pitch, offers a better prospect of finding the frequency than white noise forced into the other end of the pipe! Of course this is essentially an argument about efficiency in estimation, which may not necessarily override other advantages of white noise, such as ease of interpretation. With a white noise input, the transfer function of the dynamic response is directly proportional to the output spectrum, although in practice output spectra from different models are not readily distinguishable from one another—the 'typical spectral shape' predominates. The cross-spectrum yields information about the separate gain and phase shift components of the frequency response function, again easily calculated and giving information across the full frequency range if a white noise input is used. The information on gain and phase may be combined in the Nyquist diagram, which has proved a useful tool in the physical sciences and might be fruitfully employed in econometrics in general, and in model comparisons in particular.

12.5 NONLINEARITY

Most practical econometric models are nonlinear, and in this section we examine how this affects the various procedures for comparing models, discussed in the preceding sections in an entirely linear context. We first consider statistical consequences of nonlinearity, and then consider its impact on the forecast comparison exercises discussed in Sections 12.2–12.4.

12.5.1 Statistical implications of nonlinearity

The nonlinear system may be written in *structural form* as

$$\mathbf{f}(\mathbf{y}_t, \mathbf{z}_t; \boldsymbol{\theta}) = \mathbf{u}_t,$$

where $\mathbf{f}$ is a vector of functions, having as many elements as the vector $\mathbf{y}_t$, and θ is a vector of parameters. We assume that this implicitly defines a single inverse relationship giving the solution

$$\mathbf{y}_t = \mathbf{g}(\mathbf{u}_t, \mathbf{z}_t; \boldsymbol{\theta}),$$

valid for relevant z-values, analogous to the reduced form in the linear case. Typically an explicit analytic solution does not exist, and the structural equations are solved numerically. The *conditional expectation* of the endogenous variables is written

$$E(\mathbf{y}_t) = E\{\mathbf{g}(\mathbf{u}_t, \mathbf{z}_t; \boldsymbol{\theta})\} = \mathbf{h}(\mathbf{z}_t, \boldsymbol{\theta}).$$

Since the expected value of a nonlinear function of a random variable is not in general equal to the nonlinear function of the expected value of the random variable, it is generally the case that

$$\mathbf{h}(\mathbf{z}_t, \boldsymbol{\theta}) \neq \mathbf{g}(\mathbf{0}, \mathbf{z}_t; \boldsymbol{\theta}).$$

The right-hand side is termed the *deterministic solution*. It is the solution for $\mathbf{y}_t$ of the equations $\mathbf{f}(\mathbf{y}_t, \mathbf{z}_t; \boldsymbol{\theta}) = \mathbf{0}$, but unlike the linear case it is not equal to the conditional expectation of $\mathbf{y}_t$, which is what is required in forecasting exercises. However, the conditional expectation can be estimated by stochastic simulation, and a common measure of the (stochastic) importance of nonlinearity is given by the deviation of the deterministic solution from the mean of replicated stochastic simulations. A sizable discrepancy may have serious implications. First, it implies that, to avoid serious biases, policy analysis should be conducted via stochastic simulation rather than, as is commonplace, deterministic solution, and this considerably increases the computational burden. Secondly, many estimation methods rest on the use of the conditional expectations of the endogenous variables, and if these are not correctly calculated in the nonlinear model the properties of the estimation method will be adversely affected. Notice that it is only nonlinearity between the endogenous variables that is our present concern; nonlinearity among exogenous variables has important but as yet unexplored implications for experimental design.

Most examinations of the stochastic importance of nonlinearity carried out as described above have in fact found relatively little difference between the deterministic solution and the mean of replicated stochastic simulations. This has provided some confidence in the existing practice of deterministic forecasting and a general impression that nonlinearity is not of major concern. However, we argue below that this is a dangerous position to take for a number of reasons.

First, the specification of most models is biased towards linearity through the statistical techniques used in both estimation and specification tests. The estimation method used to determine the specification of most large models is still ordinary least squares. Through its neglect of the simultaneity problem the OLS estimator also ignores the stochastic importance of nonlinearity. Moreover the linear-in-parameter constraint can in fact be a serious restriction when a conditional expectation is a general nonlinear function of the parameters and the conditioning variables. This point is best seen by viewing the question of model estimation *and specification* as one of optimal signal extraction. In this case the optimal estimate of both functional form and parameters would be obtained by orthogonal projection on the conditioning variable set. Thus the conditional expectation of the variable defines both the optimal functional form and then, perhaps in a separate exercise, the optimal parameter estimates. However, in practice, the functional form is invariably predetermined and only the parameter values are determined by an orthogonal projection operation, on the assumption that the functional form is true. The restriction imposed by ordinary least squares and most other minimum distance methods in econometrics is that the functional form be a linear combination of possibly nonlinear functions of the variables. It is unlikely in general that this linear-in-parameter model will coincide with the nonlinear expression for the conditional expectation, $\mathbf{h}(\mathbf{z}_t, \boldsymbol{\theta})$, although it may perhaps be justified as a linearization via a Taylor series expansion. Notice that this point is equally applicable to the nonlinear simultaneous-equations estimators such as nonlinear two-stage least squares when applied to models where the linear-in-parameter assumption is maintained. Further, most of the common summary statistics are in effect linear measures: R^2 is a measure of linear correlation, and the Durbin–Watson statistic tests a linear first-order autoregression. Hence their use also leads to models that are biased towards linearity.

A second reason for believing that this approach to the measurement of nonlinearity is flawed is provided by Mariano and Brown (1980). In a theoretical examination, through asymptotic expansions for the first two prediction moments of a nonlinear model, they find that the leading term in the asymptotic prediction bias in the deterministic solution may be decomposed into two terms, one due to possible inconsistencies in the parameter estimates and the other due to the nonlinearity. The leading term for a stochastic simulation depends only on potentially inconsistent parameter estimates. Thus from this point of view the neglect of simultaneity in a deterministic solution is of the same order of magnitude as the neglect of the stochastic importance of nonlinearity. A second important observation that follows from their work is that if inconsistent parameter estimates are used when comparing deterministic and stochastic simulations then it is impossible to separate the effects of nonlinearity from the use of inconsistent parameter estimates. Thus the fact that the simulation exercises may have found little difference between deterministic and stochastic simulations may either imply that the stochastic effects of nonlinearity are weak or, as has usually been the case, that inconsistent parameter estimates have been employed. They also suggest that the use of nonstochastic simulations in specification searches may lead the model builder away from the true specification to one that performs better in deterministic simulations.

In this context we note the results of Fair and Parke (1980). In their examination of alternative estimators in the context of a nonlinear model they find that certain policy multipliers that follow from the use of ordinary least squares deviate from a relatively uniform set of multipliers obtained from nonlinear simultaneous estimators. As discussed above this could be due either to a neglect of simultaneity or to a neglect of the stochastic importance of nonlinearity on behalf of the OLS estimator.

In Section 12.3 we discussed a hierarchy of alternative representations of a structure within the linear framework. When the original structure is actually nonlinear then it is difficult to exploit these equivalences in practice, hence the importance in the nonlinear case of our earlier statement that a common statistical principle may not give equivalent results when applied to apparently equivalent mathematical representations if they impose different restrictions on the statistical method. This not only applies to our foregoing discussion of the difficulties of estimating a conditional expectation correctly in a nonlinear model, but becomes particularly important when we attempt to compare different representations of what may be the same structure, such as with the forecasts of a structural econometric model and the forecasts from an ARMA model. In this case the most obvious distinction is that these comparisons are with a *nonlinear* model (although typically examined through deterministic simulation) and a *linear* time series model. Thus we are immediately assured that the two competing representations must be supporting different approximations to reality, although it is possible that the linear time series model is representing a linearization of some underlying nonlinear time series representation. Evidence to this effect may already exist given that the forecast performance of the linear time series representations tends to decay faster than that from the nonlinear structural models. Thus the linear ARMA representations are perhaps only *locally* justified in reality, because the Jacobian of the transformation from the unobserved disturbances to the observed endogenous variables is not constant in a nonlinear system.

12.5.2 Forecast comparisons in the context of nonlinearity

Nonlinearity also invalidates many of the alternative methods of forecast comparison discussed in Section 12.4. The reason has already been mentioned: the Jacobian of a nonlinear transformation is not a constant function throughout the sample. Thus policy multipliers and empirical spectra are not uniquely defined and eigenvalues do not exist in the same sense, since they are aspects of a linear algebra. It is surprising that this fact has been so readily disregarded, particularly in comparisons of policy multiplier paths. Although such exercises still do provide comparative information their generality is substantially weakened. Perhaps in an attempt to avoid this problem various linearizations have been adopted. The question then is how relevant are these linearized models to policy analysis and forecast comparisons.

The first type of linearization follows from a retention of only the first terms in a Taylor series expansion of the nonlinear model around some point, perhaps the sample mean values of the variables. This could of course be generalized to successive linearizations around a number of points, which would in effect give a number of models, one for each linearization point. Once linearized the properties of the submodels could be analysed in exactly the manner discussed in the first part of this paper. However, since the act of linearization has different effects on the different models it is virtually impossible to gain unambiguous comparisons of the underlying models in this way. A second form of linearization that has been discussed in the literature (Bowden, 1974; Aoki, 1980) but does not appear to have been applied in practice is a linearization around a particular form of behaviour or state, rather than around a point. This approach suggests that rather than somewhat arbitrarily choosing a point about which to linearize, a better choice is to ensure that the resulting set of linearized submodels at least uniformly coincides with common behaviour, for example, by collecting all the upswings of a business cycle into one model and all the downswings into another. A third type of linearization arises from our preceding discussion of the conditional expectation of nonlinear models. By stochastically simulating the nonlinear model and averaging the results of successive replications we obtain a conditional expectation data series that reflects the dynamic structure of the model. A linearization may then be constructed by modelling this simulation output series using linear time series techniques. Since the resulting model captures the linear component of the total response of the nonlinear model we may now directly observe the degree of nonlinearity by measuring the relative size of the residual in the time series model, perhaps through R^2, an opportunity not directly available in the preceding linearizations. Thus this exercise provides a linearization around the conditional expectation which could be analysed using the linear techniques discussed above, and further, the properties of the nonlinear component may be examined by an analysis of the residual series.

Approaches to separating the linear and nonlinear responses are well-founded mathematically in terms of a Volterra series expansion (Priestley, 1981). If x_t and y_t denote scalar input and output variables related through a nonlinear relation

$$y_t = f(y_{t-j}, x_{t-l}) \qquad \text{for} \quad j, l \geqslant 0$$

then, under certain conditions, we may write the relation in the form:

$$y_t = \sum_{\tau_1=0}^{\infty} g_1(\tau)x_{t-\tau_1} + \sum_{\tau_1=0}^{\infty}\sum_{\tau_2=0}^{\infty} g_2(\tau_1, \tau_2)x_{t-\tau_1}x_{t-\tau_2} + \text{higher-order terms.}$$

This is known as a Volterra expansion and the functions g_i corresponding to higher-order transfer functions are known as the Volterra kernels. The linearization we have suggested may then be seen as an attempt to estimate the first term, or the linear response component of this expansion, and thereby to enable the collective properties of the higher-order, nonlinear response components to be examined through the resulting residual.

Table 12.1 illustrates this approach to the measurement of the relative importance of nonlinearity. In this example the GDP–government expenditure link of the Australian NIF7 model has been examined through a white noise input applied to government expenditure, x. The observed GDP simulation output, y, was then modelled using standard linear time series techniques, and the exercise repeated for different levels of variance in the white noise input. Thus we measure the scale change effects of nonlinearity, as considered by Zellner and Peck (1973). Two results stand out: first the constancy of the linear representation (i.e. $g_1(\tau)$) under the increasing scale of the government expenditure level, and secondly the decreasing R^2 indicating, not surprisingly, that the nonlinear effect is becoming more important.

Shocking the exogenous variables in the nonlinear model directly, as in the example, may give some guidance as to the degree of nonlinearity in particular

Table 12.1 Model: $y_t = a_1 y_{t-1} + b_0 x_t$ + remainder

Scale change $\alpha(\sigma)$	a_1	b_0	Long run multiplier	Time constant	R^2
10	−0.542	0.739	1.61	1.63	0.710
5	−0.534	0.762	1.59	1.63	0.889
2	−0.537	0.761	1.61	1.64	0.897
1	−0.529	0.764	1.57	1.62	0.901
0.5	−0.538	0.752	1.61	1.63	0.904
0.1	−0.525	0.761	1.55	1.60	0.909

channels, but does not provide a linearization around the conditional expectation. One solution would be to shock simultaneously both the exogenous channels of interest and the stochastic terms in the nonlinear equations. The resulting output from the stochastic simulations could then be modelled as a system of linear multi-input multi-output transfer functions and would again provide a linearization around the conditional expectation. This latter suggestion seems to provide a number of practical advantages for model comparison, policy calculations, and the systematic study of nonlinearity in the residuals.

12.6 STRUCTURAL CHANGE

Different linearizations of a nonlinear model, applicable over different ranges of behaviour as discussed in the previous section, may appear to exhibit structural change whether or not the underlying model is stable. More generally a model, linear or not, that is characterized by a particular sample period may appear to break down when the range of behaviour over which it is expected to operate changes from that over which it was specified. We have assumed throughout this paper that there is a unique and stable structure that the model builder is attempting first to capture and then to validate through forecast comparisons. In the absence of such a stable structure most econometric analysis, including forecast comparisons, breaks down. A number of attacks have recently been made on this concept of a stable economic structure, and they are examined in this section. We consider first the question of structural change in the absence of rational expectations, and then the argument derived from the 'Lucas critique' concerning the stability, in the face of rational expectations, of the 'laws of motion' that govern economic behaviour. Salmon (1980) examines the impact of these arguments on modelling practice.

We begin by distinguishing two types of structural shift, namely a change in the behavioural basis for economic decisions and a change in the institutional structure. Clearly, over an historical period changing opportunity sets alter observed consumption behaviour; however, it is most probable that this occurs within the framework of a constant structure of tastes. Again, over time this structure of preferences, defined by basic tastes, is itself subject to change as completely new economic environments evolve. However, this type of fundamental change in the economy, and consequently tastes, will occur over a substantially longer period than our econometric models are covering. Thus we may be assured in applied econometrics of a fundamental constancy in the parameters that define the tastes and perhaps the technology of the observed economic system and hence of the constancy of the fundamental 'laws of motion' of the economy. When we consider how econometric models appear to break down and fail to predict as the institutional structure in which they are defined changes, we are at first sight led to question the preceding argument for constancy. However, the reason why we fail to observe constancy is simply a reflection of the level of approximation to reality of the macro model. Given our constancy premise, there exists a metamodel defined by the constant parameters of taste, technology, etc. that would also define uniquely the reaction of the economic agent to any outside stimulus. This model of course is bound to be highly complicated and well beyond the reach of the economist given his limited knowledge of economic behaviour and restricted data sets. So the reason that we observe variation following an institutional change is that the approximate model has been specified at a level such as to prevent it from accommodating the change. In addition, model specification is usually dependent on one particular sample, and any information that may have been available in that sample on behaviour in the new circumstances may not have been sufficient to enable the specification of a more general model to have been detected, or even thought necessary. Thus structural shift in this sense provides *prima facie* evidence of misspecification and an opportunity to use the new information to determine a better specification.

In sum, when the economic structure is supposed to have changed in the forecast period, compared with the sample specification, then it is only reasonable to assume that the 'new' behaviour could have been identified beforehand if a suitable signal was present in the estimation period. The fact that we do observe apparent structural breakdowns does not necessarily imply that the underlying structure is not constant. It may, however, mean that we should develop new techniques for examining the information within an available sample (Salmon, 1980).

Let us now turn to the question of the effect of rational expectations on the preceding arguments. Lucas (1976) criticizes the standard use of policy simulation to compare the effects of alternative policy rules on the grounds that the 'structure' of econometric models is not invariant to changes in policy. The models contain behavioural relations derived from the optimal decision rules of economic agents, based in part on their expectations of the future movements of relevant variables. Changes in the nature of these movements are said to cause changes in the optimal decision rules, hence 'any change in policy will systematically alter the structure of econometric models' (p. 41). Prescott (1977) also supports the view that the 'laws of motion' of the economy cannot by 'policy invariant'. It is important to distinguish in this debate the role of a change in government policy, seen as a shifting institutional structure in the sense of the preceding discussion, from the presence of rational expectations in the model.

Consider first a change in government policy that impinges on the economic agent's consumption choice. Economic theory postulates that the consumption decision is based on the optimization of a utility function, the form of which is determined by tastes and other basic motives for economic behaviour. These basic or instinctive motives could be seen to determine the functional form and any parameters in this utility function. The premise of constancy argues that these are intrinsically fixed by definition of the uniqueness (or more correctly the existence) of an individual. When the utility function is then optimized there will be a one-to-one relation, in the sense of structural constancy, between the utility function and the derived reaction function, which the econometrician observes in the aggregate as the consumption function. The situation is exactly that of any other, perhaps exogenous, structural change in the economy. To suggest that government policy causes structural variation in the agent's *true* reaction function must imply a change in, and hence previous inadequacy of, the utility function of the economic agent. However, this effectively denies the existence of such an agent given the premise of constancy. Once again, the reasons why the econometrician may observe variation are either that the approximate model is too naive, in that it fails to model appropriately the true reaction function, or that the sample information was insufficient to identify that particular mode of behaviour.

The Lucas critique can then be seen as a criticism of the commonplace confounding of two sources of dynamics: the economic structure, incorporating decision rules in which expectations appear, and secondly the expectation formation process, which in many cases will reflect the stochastic structure of exogenous variables. Wallis (1980) argues that these should be, and can be, kept separate, and suggests ways of achieving this. If this is done, the traditional view of econometric policy evaluation can be reasserted. What is not traditional is the resulting emphasis on the modelling of information flows, decision sequences, and the expectation formation process in general. Nevertheless, the notion of an *economic* structure that results is entirely consistent with preceding arguments for stability.

When we move on to consider expectations about government policy instruments we must first determine how these obviously varying expectations are formed. We may apparently once again confront an argument concerning structural variation, since it is frequently suggested that different political parties have different basic motives, leading to variation in endogenized government reaction functions. Notice that this variation should only be observed in the equations explaining government behaviour and *not* elsewhere in the model. However, even here it is possible to make a wider case regarding uniformity in the role and motives of all governments and the population they serve, although clearly the successful modelling of government behaviour is much further from our grasp. Indeed, the basic premise of constancy may well not carry over so readily in this case given the particular temporal structure of governmental power.

Thus in conclusion we suggest that the weight of the Lucas critique bears simply on the suggestion that models, by way of being correctly specified, should include rational expectations terms. There seems to be little strength in the argument that the economic environment is not constant; what may be required, however, are more informative statistical techniques to indicate the type of model we may (or may not) have specified.

12.7 CONCLUSION

Many of our suggestions and conclusions have been mentioned in passing in our discussion of theoretical and practical aspects of model validation and forecast comparisons. Here we restate briefly some points that readers might find the most controversial.

(1) To evaluate a model in an absolute sense requires the specification of a loss function. In its absence, only relative statements can be made.

(2) Acceptance of the null hypothesis in a post-sample parameter stability test implies that the degree of misspecification does not differ in the sample and forecast periods, and not that it is small.

(3) The theoretical equivalence between different representations of a given model may be difficult to realize in practice. Evidence that different representations have different forecast properties is *by itself* difficult to interpret.

(4) Most of the methods of comparison we have discussed are attempts to map the dynamic properties of a model. Frequency response analysis, perhaps using Nyquist plots, appears to have some advantages. The experimental design of inputs requires further attention, and in the meantime the use of discrete sinusoidal inputs appears to merit investigation. (In discussing Howrey (1972), Holt makes a similar suggestion, without any argument.)

(5) Nonlinearity disrupts many of the techniques developed for linear models. Practical models may be seriously biased towards linearity, and the degree of nonlinearity underestimated. The use of linearization around the conditional expectation should be explored.

(6) The 'Lucas critique' does not halt the search for constant economic structures, nor does it require fundamental change in simulation philosophy, once rational expectations terms have been correctly incorporated where necessary.

NOTE

[1] The helpful comments of Peter Burridge are gratefully acknowledged. This research was supported by a grant from the Social Science Research Council.

REFERENCES

Adelman, I., and Adelman, F. L. (1959). 'The dynamic properties of the Klein–Goldberger model.' *Econometrica*, **27**, 597–625.

Akaike, H. (1974a). 'Markovian representation of stochastic processes and its application to the analysis of autoregressive moving average processes.' *Annals of the Institute of Statistical Mathematics*, **26**, 363–387.

Akaike, H. (1974b). 'A new look at the statistical model identification.' *IEEE Transactions on Automatic Control*, **AC-19**, 716–723.

Amemiya, T. (1980). 'Selection of regressors.' *International Economic Review*, **21**, 331–354.

Aoki, M. (1980). 'Note on comparative dynamic analysis.' *Econometrica*, **48**, 1319–1325.

Bowden, R. J. (1974). 'Non-linearity and non-stationarity in dynamic econometric models.' *Review of Economic Studies*, **41**, 173–179.

Box, G. E. P., and Jenkins, G. M. (1970). *Time Series Analysis, Forecasting and Control*, Holden-Day, San Francisco.

Brown, R. L., Durbin, J., and Evans, J. M. (1975). 'Techniques for testing the constancy of regression relationships over time (with discussion).' *Journal of the Royal Statistical Society*, Series B, **37**, 149–192.

Chan, W. Y. T., and Wallis, K. F. (1978). 'Multiple time series modelling: another look at the mink–muskrat interaction.' *Applied Statistics*, **27**, 168–175.

Christ, C. F. (1966). *Econometric Models and Methods*, Wiley, New York.

Christ, C. F. (1975). 'Judging the performance of econometric models of the U.S. economy.' *International Economic Review*, **16**, 54–74.

Cooper, R. L. (1972). 'The predictive performance of quarterly econometric models of the United States.' In B. G. Hickman (Ed.), *Econometric Models of Cyclical Behavior*, Columbia University Press (for the National Bureau of Economic Research), New York. pp. 813–926.

Davidson, R., and MacKinnon, J. G. (1981). 'Several tests for model specification in the presence of alternative hypotheses.' *Econometrica*, **49**, 781–793.

Dhrymes, P. J., *et al.* (1972). 'Criteria for evaluation of econometric models.' *Annals of Economic and Social Measurement*, **1**, 291–324.

Edwards, A. W. F. (1972). *Likelihood*, Cambridge University Press, Cambridge.

Fair, R. C. (1980). 'Estimating the expected predictive accuracy of econometric models.' *International Economic Review*, **21**, 355–378.

Fair, R. C., and Parke, W. R. (1980). 'Full-information estimates of a nonlinear macroeconometric model.' *Journal of Econometrics*, **13**, 269–291.

Fromm, G., and Klein, L. R. (1976). 'The NBER/NSF model comparison seminar: An analysis of results.' *Annals of Economic and Social Measurement*, **5**, 1–28.

Goldberger, A. S. (1959). *Impact Multipliers and Dynamic Properties of the Klein–Goldberger Model*, North-Holland, Amsterdam.

Goodwin, G. C., and Payne, R. L. (1977). *Dynamic System Identification, Experiment Design and Data Analysis*, Academic Press, New York.

Granger, C. W. J., and Newbold, P. (1977). *Forecasting Economic Time Series*, Academic Press, New York.

Hannan, E. J. (1979). 'The statistical theory of linear systems,' In P. N. Krishnaiah (Ed.), *Developments in Statistics*, Volume 2, Academic Press, New York. pp. 83–121.

Hendry, D. F. (1974). 'Stochastic specification in an aggregate demand model of the United Kingdom.' *Econometrica*, **42,** 559–578.

Howrey, E. P. (1972). 'Dynamic properties of a condensed version of the Wharton model.' In B. G. Hickman (Ed.), *Econometric Models of Cyclical Behavior*, Columbia University Press (for the National Bureau of Economic Research), New York. pp. 601–663.

Howrey, E. P., Klein, L. R., and McCarthy, M. D. (1974). 'Notes on testing the predictive performance of econometric models.' *International Economic Review*, **15,** 366–383.

Laury, J. S. E., Lewis, G. R., and Ormerod, P. A. (1978). 'Properties of macro-economic models of the U.K. economy: A comparative study.' *National Institute Economic Review*, **83,** 52–72.

Lucas, R. E. Jr. (1976) 'Econometric policy evaluation: A critique.' In K. Brunner and A. H. Meltzer (Eds), *The Phillips Curve and Labor Markets*, (Carnegie–Rochester Conference Series on Public Policy, Volume 1) North-Holland, Amsterdam. pp. 19–46.

Mariano, R. S., and Brown, B. W. (1980). 'Asymptotic behavior of predictors in a nonlinear simultaneous system.' University of Pennsylvania, The Wharton School, Discussion paper No. 410.

McCarthy, M. D. (1972). 'A note on the forecasting properties of two stage least squares restricted reduced forms — the finite sample case.' *International Economic Review*, **13,** 757–761.

Nelson, C. R. (1972). 'The prediction performance of the FRB–MIT–PENN model of the U.S. economy.' *American Economic Review*, **62,** 902–917.

Osborn, D. R., and Teal, F. (1979). 'An assessment and comparison of two NIESR econometric model forecasts.' *National Institute Economic Review*, **88,** 50–62.

Pesaran, M. H., and Deaton, A. S. (1978). 'Testing non-nested nonlinear regression models.' *Econometrica*, **46,** 677–694.

Pierce, D. A. (1975). 'Forecasting in dynamic models with stochastic regressors.' *Journal of Econometrics*, **3,** 349–374.

Prescott, E. C. (1977). 'Should control theory be used for economic stabilization?' In K. Brunner and A. H. Meltzer (Eds), *Optimal Policies, Control Theory and Technological Exports*, (Carnegie–Rochester Conference Series on Public Policy, Volume 7). North-Holland, Amsterdam, pp. 13–38.

Priestley, M. B., (1981). *Spectral Analysis and Time Series*, Academic Press, London.

Prothero, D. L., and Wallis, K. F. (1976). 'Modelling macroeconomic time series (with discussion).' *Journal of the Royal Statistical Society*, Series A, **139,** 468–500.

Salmon, M. (1980). 'Structural constancy and model selection.' University of Warwick, Department of Economics, unpublished paper.

Sargan, J. D. (1976). 'The existence of the moments of estimated reduced form coefficients.' London School of Economics, Econometrics Programme Discussion Paper A6.

Sawa, T. (1978). 'Information criteria for discriminating among alternative regression models.' *Econometrica*, **46,** 1273–1292.

Surrey, M. J. C., and Ormerod, P. A. (1977). 'Formal and informal aspects of forecasting with an econometric model.' *National Institute Economic Review*, **81,** 67–71.

Tinbergen, J. (1939). *Statistical Testing of Business-Cycle Theories, II: Business Cycles in the U.S.A., 1919–1932*, League of Nations, Geneva.

Wall, K. D., Preston, A. J., Bray, J. W., and Peston, M. H. (1975). 'Estimates of a simple control model of the U.K. economy.' In G. A. Renton (Ed.), *Modelling the Economy*, Heinemann, London. pp. 398–446.

Wallis, K. F. (1977). 'Multiple time series analysis and the final form of econometric models.' *Econometrica*, **45,** 1481–1497.

Wallis, K. F. (1979). *Topics in Applied Econometrics*, 2nd Ed. Blackwell, Oxford.

Wallis, K. F. (1980). 'Econometric implications of the rational expectations hypothesis.' *Econometrica*, **48**, 49–73.

Zarrop, M. B. (1980). *Optimal Experiment Design for Dynamic System Identification*, Springer Verlag, Berlin.

Zellner, A., and Palm, F. (1974). 'Time-series analysis and simultaneous equation econometric models.' *Journal of Econometrics*, **2**, 17–54.

Zellner, A., and Peck, S. C. (1973). 'Simulation experiments with a quarterly macro-econometric model of the U.S. economy.' In A. A. Powell and R. A. Williams (Eds), *Econometric Studies of Macro and Monetary Relations*, North-Holland, Amsterdam. pp. 149–168.

Discussion

M. NERLOVE
Northwestern University, Evanston

It is always a pleasure to discuss a paper authored or co-authored by Kenneth Wallis, because one always learns a great deal. But it is also a difficult task since it is not easy to find things to criticize. Rather than attempt an extended critique, I propose to amplify and emphasize some of the points made by Salmon and Wallis.

The question addressed by the authors is: 'To what extent is forecasting a useful method of evaluating the validity, reliability, and utility of a macro-econometric model?' Since one of the primary purposes of econometric modelling is to forecast—the results of policy changes, variations in exogenous variables, the effects of structural changes—or simply to extrapolate on the basis of the model's dynamic structure, it is natural to evaluate a model by criteria related to various forecasts that may be derived from it. One must exercise extreme care, however, and Salmon and Wallis draw our attention to the difficulties inherent in using forecasting criteria to judge the validity of an econometric model.

Perhaps the most important point, but also the most obvious, is that models are clearly designed with various purposes in mind. In principle, a model is a precise description of underlying economic reality, i.e. of the mechanism that determines the values of some collection of economic variables. These variables, measured by line items in the national accounts, price indices, surveys, etc., are clearly themselves constructs and abstractions. Econometric models, which relate such variables, are equally abstractions from, and simplifications of, underlying economic reality (although, as Arnold Zellner pointed out in the Discussion following Chapter 7, this does not necessarily mean the more complex the model the better it may be able to represent the underlying reality). The trend is to ever larger and more complex models, but, even so, they remain drastic simplifications and approximations. There is no one way to represent reality by a model: a model's form and structure will be dictated by data availability and the purposes of the model builder. In particular, the purposes to which the forecasts of a model are to be put should play an important role in how the model is judged. As Salmon and Wallis point out, without a decision-making framework the evaluation of models and forecasts cannot be made rigorous. Yet those who build models and evaluate them are not always the same as those who use the forecasts or other output from the models. In a classic paper on Bayesian statistics written some years ago, Clifford Hildreth called this the problem of the 'remote client.'

One solution, as pointed out by Zellner in his discussion, is to invent a client, for example a representative firm maximizing profits, making use of GNP, price level, and other forecasts, within a well-defined decision framework with a specific loss function. In the absence of such a 'client', however, one typically falls back on rather general criteria. Depending on one's point of view, it is possible to find *any* such criteria unsatisfactory. Salmon and Wallis do not resolve this difficult issue, but rather discuss a variety of general criteria in relation to different kinds of comparisons:

1. Comparisons of a given model's forecasts with actual future realizations of the variables the model is supposed to explain.
2. Comparisons of forecasts from an econometric model with those from non-econometric models, e.g. pure time series models. An early example of such a comparison was that done by Carl Christ, who compared forecasts from Klein's first two models with what he called naive models.
3. Comparisons of forecasts and other characteristics across different macro-econometric models, particularly with respect to dynamic properties and structural change.

Finally, Salmon and Wallis take up in detail the issues of nonlinearity, structural change, and the Lucas–Prescott challenge to all econometric model building, a challenge based on the theory of rational expectations.

Salmon and Wallis, following Fair, separate the forecast errors from a linear static model, into three parts: (a) errors in forecasting exogenous variables; (b) errors in estimating the parameters of the model including those caused by structural change and misspecification; (c) stochastic elements inherent in the model. Lags and other dynamic characteristics complicate comparisons, since forecast errors now depend on how far into the future such comparisons are made. Because errors in forecasting exogenous variables and accumulation of forecast errors are sometimes supposed to result in unfair comparisons (note an implicit loss function and decision problem in such a supposition), very often only *ex post* forecasts are compared. Such a comparison is then simply a question of whether some new observations belong to the same population characterized by the structure estimated from another group of observations.

Comparisons of *ex post* forecasts are frequently carried out, as Salmon and

Wallis remark without comment, '...immediately after specification and estimation by holding back from the estimation period a subsample of...observations specifically for this purpose.' Although very common, this is certainly a perilous procedure: if one does this repeatedly in a serious fashion to revise the model, it would, first, amount to an inefficient use of all of the data to estimate and specify the model, and, secondly, give undue weight to the subsample selected for *ex post* forecast comparisons. Fair, who stresses the importance of forecast comparisons, is well aware of this difficulty and calls it a subtle form of data mining. There are clearly some loss functions and decision problems for which the procedure would, in fact, be a good approximation to the appropriate evaluation of the model.

Recent developments in time series analysis have led to much more elaborate forms of Christ's original naive models. In particular, in comparing forecasts of econometric models with non-econometric methods of forecasting, we can now consider the broad class of vector ARMA or ARIMA models. The main point made by Salmon and Wallis is that such naive models do not provide an independent test of an econometric model because the final form of such a model is also a vector ARMA or ARIMA model provided that the exogenous variables can be characterized by ARMA or ARIMA models. They state that an ARIMA model is an implication of an econometric model. But direct estimation of an implied ARIMA model presumably gives less efficient forecasts than an estimated econometric model since the former neglects much of the structural information contained in the latter. With respect to the Salmon–Wallis position I would like to make four points.

First, it is difficult to believe that *all* exogenous variables can be assumed to follow an ARMA or ARIMA process, for example changes in tax policy. However, one may introduce such variables separately and model the deviations or residuals by an ARMA process. This is a natural extension of the Salmon–Wallis position. Since, in general, there will not be enough policy variables to identify an underlying econometric model, the fact that some exogenous variables cannot be represented by ARMA models does not vitiate the conclusion that the modified form of an ARMA process is an implication of the econometric model but not *vice versa*.

Secondly, given the dynamic structure of the model and the ARMA processes that generate the exogenous variables, there are restrictions on the class of ARMA models consistent with the underlying econometric model. This leads to some interesting methods for comparing and evaluating econometric models by their time series properties.

Thirdly, in practice, an adequately fitting ARIMA model, apart from the restrictions implied by an underlying econometric model, will be much simpler than the model implied by any moderately complex econometric model. This is because most econometric models contain many, perhaps erroneously specified, lags in the endogenous variables. Thus, there is still scope for checking the forecasts or the stochastic dynamic properties of an econometric model against a good-fitting ARIMA model estimated from the same data.

Fourthly, that the final form of an econometric model is an ARIMA model holds for linear models with Gaussian disturbances. Since most econometric models are highly nonlinear, however, it is not clear whether a sufficiently good linear approximation exists that would lead to a similar conclusion.

In making comparisons across different econometric models, one is generally handicapped by the fact that the models are not estimated with consistent bodies of data or for the same time periods. Moreover, the models do not usually explain the same group of endogenous variables. Leaving aside such formidable difficulties, Salmon and Wallis note that all types of comparisons, forecasts, policy multipliers, and time series properties amount simply to a comparison of time series properties and depend upon the input series assumed for the exogenous variables. Following a suggestion made by Holt, Salmon and Wallis recommend looking at the frequency response function for each model at a finite number of frequencies. This amounts to assuming sinusoidal exogenous inputs at a fixed number of discrete frequencies. They also argue that examination of the spectral shapes of endogenous variables implied by a model for white noise exogenous inputs is not helpful because the spectral shapes are not easy to distinguish. I would comment, first, that in practice spectral shapes are easier to compare and often more different than Salmon and Wallis suppose. On the other hand, what limited experience I have had suggests that frequency response functions are more difficult to interpret in practice because of the poor statistical properties of estimates of their parameters. However, examination of the response functions at a finite, and presumably small, number of frequencies may greatly help to resolve such problems. Moreover, when the model is nonlinear, an analytical solution for the frequency response is not possible; in this case, simulation at a relatively few frequencies may facilitate comparisons. When the model is nonlinear, however, the rationale for the Holt suggestion no longer holds nor is it possible to specify what the frequencies are at which optimal comparisons should be made. It is clear that experience with Holt's recommendation is necessary before one can pass judgment.

Issues associated with nonlinearity have been mentioned several times. Salmon and Wallis devote a lengthy section of their paper to these and related problems. Their principal conclusions are that there is a general bias towards linearity in model estimation and formulation and that the use of the deterministic solution to a nonlinear econometric model for model comparisons and forecasting may be highly misleading.

The reason for the last point is well known: the expected value of a nonlinear function is not the same as the function of the expected value. Application of this simple result to the problems of model comparison and forecasting is novel and significant. For such purposes, Salmon and Wallis suggest that linearizing the model around the conditional means of the endogenous variables will provide a better approximation than the deterministic solution, but their case is not empirically documented. The supposed bias towards linearity rests primarily on the fact that least-squares methods are frequently used in the search for the correct model specification. That most macro-econometric models are highly *non*linear does not contradict the Salmon–Wallis position, however, since most of the nonlinearity is introduced *a priori* and is not tested.

The final section of the paper, on structural change, is perhaps the most controversial. The chief issue here is what are the effects of changes in government policies, particularly if economic agents have rational expectations, as in the criticism by Lucas and Prescott of all econometric modelling. With respect to this problem, as Salmon and Wallis point out, if the correct reaction functions are included in the model, there is no reason in principle that the fact that economic agents respond to policies based on variables endogenous to the model (including their own behaviour) is enough to destroy the possibility of modelling and forecasting. The point was made long ago in another context by Modigliani and Grunberg. They used a fixed point theorem to demonstrate the possibility of making a correct forecast of a variable determined in part by the behaviour of agents who respond to the forecast. Clearly, if one knows the relation between the forecast and the behaviour being forecast, it is always possible to construct a self-fulfilling prophecy.

One problem in the incorporation of such reaction functions was pointed out by Salmon in his response to the discussants: the information sets available to the econometrician and to the agents whose behaviour is being modelled may be quite different. Another difficulty is whether government policies are sufficiently consistently determined to allow the incorporation and estimation of stable reaction functions. It is difficult to argue with the principle that there must be some metamodel within which what are structural changes in one model are now endogenous in the corresponding metamodel. The trouble is in practice. Although there have been a few notably successful attempts to model the behaviour of policy-makers, not only are the information sets available to policy makers, economic agents, and econometricians different, but the behaviour of governments seems to be inherently more unstable and unpredictable than that of markets. To the extent that this is true, the more difficult it will be to incorporate the correct reaction functions into a model. On the other hand, the more unpredictable the behaviour of governments, the better the approximation of treating policy variables as exogenous and the less the need to take into account the reactions of economic agents to the current values of such policy variables.

Evaluating the Reliability of Macro-economic Models
Edited by G. C. Chow and P. Corsi

CHAPTER 13

Evaluating Forecast Uncertainty due to Errors in Estimated Coefficients: Empirical Comparison of Alternative Methods

C. BIANCHI[1]
Centro Scientifico IBM, Pisa
G. CALZOLARI
Centro Scientifico IBM, Pisa

13.1 INTRODUCTION

Forecasts produced by structural econometric models are subject to several sources of error; some of these are, for example, the random disturbance term of each stochastic equation, errors in estimated coefficients, errors in forecasts of exogenous variables, errors in preliminary data (before the final revisions become available), and possible misspecification of the model. Several analytical, empirical, numerical, and Monte Carlo methods have been proposed in the econometric literature for estimating the contribution to forecast errors of some or all of these error sources.[2]

This paper will be concerned with the contribution to forecast errors of errors in the estimated structural coefficients. Its main purpose is to perform, on several 'real world' models, an empirical comparison of alternative techniques available in the literature for this purpose.

For all models, the comparison will be performed in the case of one-period forecasts, outside the sample used for estimating the structural coefficients, under the assumptions of perfect knowledge of the predetermined variables and correct specification of the model structure; in other words, forecasts conditional on the predetermined variables and the model's specification. What remains is a forecast error that depends on the structural disturbances and on the coefficient estimates only. These two components, under general assumptions, are independent when forecasting outside the sample period, so that their statistical properties can be studied separately.

The statistical techniques available for this purpose include explicit analytical formulae, but these are applicable to linear models only; furthermore, in the cases in which they are applicable, several computational difficulties are involved, so that, in empirical applications for real world nonlinear models, one must resort to simulation techniques.

Stochastic simulation is usually used for estimating the component due to the error terms, obtaining the so-called 'reduced form' variance.

Stochastic and analytic simulation techniques are used for the estimation of the component due to the coefficient estimates. In this paper, the empirical results obtained with three alternative methods will be discussed. These three methods, briefly described in Section 13.4, are discussed in detail in Schink (1971), Fair (1980), and Bianchi and Calzolari (1980).

The methods of Schink (1971) and of Fair (1980) perform a number of stochastic simulation runs, in each run starting from a set of different structural coefficients, and they differ in the way in which the 'new' coefficients are obtained. Hence, even if they could be considered as belonging to the same area (i.e. stochastic simulation with respect to the coefficient estimates), they are substantially different. In order to avoid misunderstanding in the present paper, they will be referred to in the following way:

— 'Stochastic simulation and re-estimation', for the method of Schink (1971), where the analysis of the forecast error is performed starting from the covariance matrix of the structural form disturbances; each run of stochastic simulation with respect to the error terms supplies a new pseudo-sample for the endogenous variables and the new set of structural coefficients is obtained by re-estimating the model.
— 'Monte Carlo on coefficients' for the method of Fair (1980), where the new set of structural coefficients is generated by random sampling from the covariance matrix of the structural coefficients.
— The last method, by Bianchi and Calzolari (1980), will be referred to as 'analytic simulation on coefficients'.

13.2 NOTATION AND ASSUMPTIONS

Even though the purpose of this paper is to compare algorithms applicable to nonlinear models, it is useful to give some consideration to the case of a linear simultaneous-equations system. For this reason, notation will be introduced in this section both for linear and nonlinear models.

A general structural econometric model, linear or nonlinear in the variables as well as in the coefficients (including coefficient restrictions), can be represented as

$$\mathbf{f}(\mathbf{y}_t, \mathbf{x}_t, \mathbf{a}) = \mathbf{u}_t \qquad t = 1, 2, \ldots, T \tag{2.1}$$

where:

$\mathbf{f}' = (f_1, f_2, \ldots, f_m)$ is a vector of functional operators, continuously differentiable with respect to the elements of $\mathbf{y}$, $\mathbf{x}$, and $\mathbf{a}$; $\mathbf{y}_t' = (y_{1t}, y_{2t}, \ldots, y_{mt})$ and $\mathbf{x}_t' = (x_{1t}, x_{2t}, \ldots, x_{nt})$ are the vectors of endogenous and predetermined variables at time $t = 1, 2, \ldots, T$; $\mathbf{a}' = (a_1, a_2, \ldots, a_s)$ is the vector of the structural coefficients to be estimated (all the other known coefficients of the model are excluded from this vector and included in the functional operators); $\mathbf{u}_t' = (u_{1t}, u_{2t}, \ldots, u_{mt})$ is the vector of structural stochastic disturbances at time t, having zero mean and independently and identically distributed over time, with finite covariance matrix and independent of all the predetermined variables.

If the model is linear, its structural form can be represented as:

$$\boldsymbol{A}\mathbf{y}_t + \boldsymbol{B}\mathbf{x}_t = \mathbf{u}_t \qquad t = 1, 2, \ldots, T \tag{2.2}$$

In this case $\boldsymbol{A}$ and $\boldsymbol{B}$ are, respectively, $(m \times m)$ and $(m \times n)$ matrices of structural coefficients, including coefficients known *a priori*, such as zeros, ones, etc; the vector $\mathbf{a}$, therefore, will contain a subset of the elements of $\boldsymbol{A}$ and $\boldsymbol{B}$.

It is worth observing that the hypothesis on the structural disturbances, which are supposed to be independently distributed over time (serial independence), is indispensable for the derivation of the results in Section 13.3; it would be restrictive if the analysis were confined to linear models, but is less restrictive in the more general context of nonlinear models. In fact if, for example, the structural disturbances of the ith equation are assumed to be first-order serial correlated, i.e.

$$y_{it} + a_k x_{jt} = v_t \qquad v_t = \rho v_{t-1} + u_t \tag{2.3}$$

then the equation can be simply rewritten in the form

$$y_{it} - \rho y_{it-1} + a_k x_{jt} - \rho a_k x_{jt-1} = u_t \tag{2.4}$$

so that the equation becomes nonlinear in the coefficients, but no longer violates the above assumptions. In other words, serial correlation of any order is allowed, provided that the structural model is transformed leaving correlation-free disturbances.

The distribution function of the disturbances $\mathbf{u}_t$ must be specified in all the experiments that involve stochastic simulation. In all the experiments hereafter described, it will be assumed multivariate normal:

$$\mathbf{u}_t \sim N(0, \Sigma). \tag{2.5}$$

In the experiments which involve Monte Carlo or analytic simulation on coefficients, an estimate of the covariance matrix of the structural coefficients is also required. Such an estimate is a standard by-product of system estimation methods, like three-stage least squares (3SLS), full information maximum likelihood (FIML), or full information instrumental variables efficient (FIVE). If limited information methods are used, the derivation of an estimate of the full covariance matrix of the structural coefficients generally requires some additional computations beyond those usually involved in the estimation of the structural coefficients. Since most of our experiments have been performed using limited information instrumental variables efficient estimates (LIVE) or two-stage least squares (with principal components), reference is made to Brundy and Jorgenson (1971, p. 215) and to Theil (1971, p. 500) for the construction of the coefficients' covariance matrix.

However, it is more appropriate to call such a matrix an estimated asymptotic covariance matrix. In fact, under general assumptions, the classical estimation methods for systems of simultaneous equations first of all provide an estimate of the structural coefficients, $\hat{\mathbf{a}}$, such that $\sqrt{T}(\hat{\mathbf{a}} - \mathbf{a})$ has asymptotically a multinormal distribution with zero means and finite covariance matrix. They then provide a consistent estimate of this covariance matrix divided by the actual sample period length. This point is well known and described in econometric textbooks (see, for example, Christ, 1966, p. 379; Schmidt, 1976, p. 254; or Theil, 1971, p. 378 for a detailed discussion). Nevertheless, it has been noted because the difference between two of the three methods considered later in this paper lies mainly in the different treatment given to this covariance matrix, or, more precisely, in a different choice of the stage where the asymptotic estimate is interpreted as an approximation of the small sample estimate. This point will be clarified below.

The covariance matrix of structural coefficients will be denoted by $\mathbf{\Psi}$; more exactly we suppose that, asymptotically,

$$\sqrt{T}(\hat{\mathbf{a}} - \mathbf{a}) \sim N(0, \mathbf{\Psi}) \tag{2.6}$$

and that, if T is the actual sample period length, the available estimated matrix is $\hat{\mathbf{\Psi}}/T$, where $\hat{\mathbf{\Psi}}$ is a consistent estimate of $\mathbf{\Psi}$.

There are difficulties in proving that equation (2.6) holds when the nonlinear model includes lagged endogenous variables among the predetermined variables. In some sense, however, this work starts after structural estimation problems have been solved, for example by assuming as reasonable the considerations in Gallant (1977, pp. 73–74) and Hatanaka (1978, fn. 8).

13.3 DECOMPOSITION OF THE FORECAST ERRORS

It is usually assumed that a simultaneous-equation system like (2.1) uniquely defines the values of the elements of $\mathbf{y}_t$ once values for the coefficients, the predetermined variables, and the disturbance terms are given (at least in some range); in the case of the linear model (2.2) this is equivalent to assuming nonsingularity of the matrix A. This means that the structural form equations (2.1) implicitly define a system of reduced form equations

$$\mathbf{y}_t = \mathbf{y}(\mathbf{x}_t, \mathbf{a}, \mathbf{u}_t) \tag{3.1}$$

where the vector of functional operators $\mathbf{y}$ is generally unknown in the case of nonlinear models.

If the model is linear, equation (3.1) simply becomes

$$\mathbf{y}_t = \mathbf{\Pi}\mathbf{x}_t + \mathbf{v}_t \qquad \mathbf{\Pi} = -A^{-1}B \qquad \mathbf{v}_t = A^{-1}\mathbf{u}_t. \tag{3.2}$$

Let $\hat{\mathbf{a}}$ be an estimate of the vector $\mathbf{a}$, as described in Section 13.2, obtained by using the data for $\mathbf{y}_t$ and $\mathbf{x}_t$ in the sample period $t = 1, 2, \ldots, T$, and let h be the forecast period, not belonging to $1, 2, \ldots, T$. Under the assumption of serial independence, the disturbances at time h, $\mathbf{u}_h$, are independent of the disturbance terms in the sample period and, therefore, $\mathbf{u}_h$ and $\hat{\mathbf{a}}$ are two independent random variables.

The usual forecast supplied by the model is obtained by inserting, in the structural form equations (2.1), the estimated vector $\hat{\mathbf{a}}$ and the values of the predetermined variables $\mathbf{x}_h$ (supposed exact, for the purposes of this paper, as already observed), dropping the disturbance term, and solving the resulting system

$$\mathbf{f}(\hat{\mathbf{y}}_h, \mathbf{x}_h, \hat{\mathbf{a}}) = \mathbf{0} \tag{3.3}$$

by means of some numerical method. In terms of the (unknown) reduced form, this means that the vector of forecasts at time h can be represented as

$$\hat{\mathbf{y}}_h = \mathbf{y}(\mathbf{x}_h, \hat{\mathbf{a}}, \mathbf{0}). \tag{3.4}$$

The vector of the 'true' values of endogenous variables in the forecast period can be represented, using the reduced form notation, as

$$\mathbf{y}_h = \mathbf{y}(\mathbf{x}_h, \mathbf{a}, \mathbf{u}_h). \tag{3.5}$$

The vector of forecast errors is the difference between $\hat{\mathbf{y}}_h$ and $\mathbf{y}_h$. It is now convenient to introduce an auxiliary vector, $\bar{\mathbf{y}}_h$, defined as the vector of forecasts that would be produced by the model if the structural coefficients were known with certainty; in other words $\bar{\mathbf{y}}_h$ is the solution of the model free of errors at time h:

$$\mathbf{f}(\bar{\mathbf{y}}_h, \mathbf{x}_h, \mathbf{a}) = \mathbf{0} \tag{3.6}$$

that is, with reduced form notation,

$$\bar{\mathbf{y}}_h = \mathbf{y}(\mathbf{x}_h, \mathbf{a}, \mathbf{0}). \tag{3.7}$$

Returning to the vector of forecast errors, we now have

$$\begin{aligned}\hat{\mathbf{y}}_h - \mathbf{y}_h &= [\hat{\mathbf{y}}_h - \bar{\mathbf{y}}_h] + [\bar{\mathbf{y}}_h - \mathbf{y}_h] \\ &= [\mathbf{y}(\mathbf{x}_h, \hat{\mathbf{a}}, \mathbf{0}) - \mathbf{y}(\mathbf{x}_h, \mathbf{a}, \mathbf{0})] + [\mathbf{y}(\mathbf{x}_h, \mathbf{a}, \mathbf{0}) - \mathbf{y}(\mathbf{x}_h, \mathbf{a}, \mathbf{u}_h)].\end{aligned} \tag{3.8}$$

In the case of a linear model, equation (3.8) assumes the well-known form

$$\begin{aligned}\hat{\mathbf{y}}_h - \mathbf{y}_h &= [\hat{\mathbf{\Pi}}\mathbf{x}_h - \mathbf{\Pi}\mathbf{x}_h] + [\mathbf{\Pi}\mathbf{x}_h - (\mathbf{\Pi}\mathbf{x}_h + \mathbf{v}_h)] \\ &= [\hat{\mathbf{\Pi}} - \mathbf{\Pi}]\mathbf{x}_h - A^{-1}\mathbf{u}_h.\end{aligned} \tag{3.9}$$

In both cases, the vector of forecast errors is the sum of two random vectors: the first is a function of several variables, among which only the vector of estimated coefficients, $\hat{\mathbf{a}}$, is random; the second is also a function of several variables, among which only the vector of structural disturbances, $\mathbf{u}_h$, is random. Since, by assumption, $\hat{\mathbf{a}}$ and $\mathbf{u}_h$ are independent, so also are the two components of the vector of forecast errors.

Therefore the two components can be separately analysed and, in particular, an estimate of the variances of the forecast errors can be obtained by summing the estimated variances of the two components.

What we have stated above is not exactly true if lagged endogenous variables are present among the predetermined variables; in this case, in fact, the two terms of the sum are both functions of the (random) lagged endogenous variables. The above considerations, however, still hold 'conditional' on a given value of the lagged endogenous variables (for example, it could be the historical value, in the case of one-period forecasts).

There is substantial agreement about the methods of analysing the component $(\bar{\mathbf{y}}_h - \mathbf{y}_h)$, which is a function of the random structural disturbances; in most papers that deal with this problem, stochastic simulation is proposed as the basic computational method. By means of replicated solutions of the model, each time introducing a vector of pseudo-random disturbances in place of $\mathbf{u}_h$, it is possible to compute approximate values of the conditional means and variances of the elements of $(\bar{\mathbf{y}}_h - \mathbf{y}_h)$. The approximation improves, usually, as the number of replications increases; if finite moments of the first two orders exist, a very high number of replications would lead, in practice, to the exact values of means and variances, if the parameters of the model (the vector $\mathbf{a}$ and the covariance matrix of the structural disturbances) were known with certainty.

As, however, we are assuming only estimates of these parameters, stochastic simulation will lead to an estimate of the means and variances of the elements of $(\bar{\mathbf{y}}_h - \mathbf{y}_h)$ (a consistent estimate, in particular, if the available estimate of the structural form parameters is consistent).[3]

Of course, if the model is linear, the mean of this component is zero and the covariance matrix of its elements is

$$A^{-1}\Sigma(A^{-1})' \tag{3.10}$$

if Σ is the covariance matrix of $\mathbf{u}_h$; the estimated covariance matrix is

$$\hat{A}^{-1}\hat{\Sigma}(\hat{A}^{-1})'. \tag{3.11}$$

Since, as already mentioned, this method is widely accepted, it is unnecessary to go into further detail.

The rest of the paper will deal only with the other component, for which the literature presents methods that differ from one another both computationally and conceptually. To be more precise, in the works by Schink (1971) and Fair (1980), numerical results are not presented for this component by itself (as it is, for example, in Bianchi and Calzolari, 1980), but directly for the complete forecast error due to the two error sources together. However, since our assumptions allow us to separate the two components, the analysis of the first component by itself should allow us to compare in detail the empirical results obtained with the different methods.

Finally it must be pointed out that the decomposition of the forecast errors outlined in this section is not confined to the case of forecasts obtained by means of one-step (or static) simulation, but could be extended to the case of conditional forecasts obtained by dynamic simulation (always outside the sample estimation period). Since, however, we are not going to present, in this paper, results related to the forecast errors in dynamic simulation, this problem will not be discussed further. For a detailed analytical treatment of this problem in the case of linear models, reference can be made to Schmidt (1974).

13.4 THREE METHODS FOR ANALYSING THE COMPONENT OF FORECAST ERRORS DUE TO ERRORS IN THE ESTIMATED COEFFICIENTS

Three different methods for analysing the component $(\hat{\mathbf{y}}_h - \bar{\mathbf{y}}_h)$ are briefly described in this section. They will be referred to as:

—Stochastic simulation and re-estimation.

—Monte Carlo on coefficients.

—Analytic simulation on coefficients.

It will be clear that not only are there technical differences in the computational algorithms, but there are some basic conceptual differences among the methods.

Stochastic simulation and re-estimation tries to deal with the 'small sample' distribution of $(\hat{\mathbf{y}}_h - \bar{\mathbf{y}}_h)$ directly.

Monte Carlo on coefficients starts from the estimate of the asymptotic covariance matrix of the structural coefficients, treats this matrix as an approximation of the small-sample covariance matrix of the coefficients, and derives the consequences of this assumption on $(\hat{\mathbf{y}}_h - \bar{\mathbf{y}}_h)$.

Analytic simulation on coefficients also starts from the estimated asymptotic covariance matrix of the structural coefficients and derives the asymptotic covariance matrix of $(\hat{\mathbf{y}}_h - \bar{\mathbf{y}}_h)$; only after this computation is performed is the resulting matrix interpreted as an approximation of the small-sample covariance matrix of $(\hat{\mathbf{y}}_h - \bar{\mathbf{y}}_h)$. In some sense, with respect to Monte Carlo on coefficients, the approximation is performed at a later stage.

From a purely empirical point of view, however, all methods lead to the same information, i.e. an estimated covariance matrix of the given component of forecast errors.

13.4.1 Stochastic simulation and re-estimation

This method can be summarized as follows (see Schink, 1971, for more details). Let $\hat{\Sigma}$ be the available estimate of the covariance matrix of the structural disturbances.

1. T vectors of pseudo-random numbers, $\tilde{\mathbf{u}}_t$, $t = 1, 2, \ldots, T$ (each of which having multinormal distribution, zero means, and covariance matrix equal to the available $\hat{\Sigma}$), are generated. The method of Nagar (1969) can be applied if $\hat{\Sigma}$ is positive definite; otherwise, the method by McCarthy (1972a) can be used.
2. The vectors $\tilde{\mathbf{u}}_t$ are inserted into the model, where the structural coefficients are maintained fixed at their originally estimated values, and the model is solved over all the sample period, obtaining for the endogenous variables the vectors $\tilde{\mathbf{y}}_t$, $t = 1, 2, \ldots, T$.
3. The vectors $\tilde{\mathbf{y}}_t$ are treated as a new set of observations of the endogenous variables and are used to re-estimate the model, thus obtaining a new vector, $\tilde{\mathbf{a}}$, of pseudo-estimated coefficients (or new matrices $\tilde{\boldsymbol{A}}$ and $\tilde{\boldsymbol{B}}$ if the model is linear).
4. The coefficients $\tilde{\mathbf{a}}$ are inserted into the model to produce, via deterministic solution, a vector of pseudo-forecasts at time h, $\tilde{\mathbf{y}}_h$.

The process is repeated from step 1 to 4 and the desired results follow from the computation of the sample variances of the elements of all the $\tilde{\mathbf{y}}_h$ computed in the various replications.

Some complications arise from the treatment of lagged endogenous variables in the simulation phase (in other words simulation can be static or dynamic) and in the re-estimation phase (they can be maintained 'static', i.e. fixed at some given (historical) value, or their simulation value can be chosen). This problem is discussed in Schink (1971, pp. 101–108); in all the experiments here performed the static–static combination has been adopted.

This method is frequently used in the literature to derive small-sample distributions of estimators for simultaneous-equation systems when analytical methods are not available The main theoretical limitation is in the possible nonexistence of finite moments in the small-sample distribution of the structural form or reduced form coefficients (these last directly related to forecasts); this topic is discussed, for example, in Dhrymes (1970, p. 182), McCarthy (1972b), Sargan (1976), and Mariano (1980).

As pointed out in McCarthy (1972b, p. 761), '.... it should be noted that the non-existence of moments has some implications for those engaged Monte Carlo studies. Outliers can be expected. Computation of mean squared forecast errors and the mean squared errors of the restricted reduced form coefficient estimates will not converge as the number Monte Carlo runs increases. These computations really will not yield meaningful information. Throwing out the outliers in making these calculations is also of questionable value. What is accomplished by throwing them out?...'.

Whether the nonconvergence of this method is a purely theoretical problem or, on the contrary, is an actual problem for real world models will be clear from the examples in Sections 13.5 and 13.6.

13.4.2 Monte Carlo on coefficients

This method can be summarized as follows. Let $\hat{\mathbf{\Psi}}/T$ be the available estimate of the covariance matrix of the structural coefficients $\hat{\mathbf{a}}$.

1. A vector $\tilde{\mathbf{a}}$ of pseudo-random numbers, with mean $\hat{\mathbf{a}}$ and covariance matrix $\hat{\mathbf{\Psi}}/T$, is generated.
2. The pseudo-random coefficients vector $\tilde{\mathbf{a}}$ replaces the original estimates $\hat{\mathbf{a}}$ and the model is solved deterministically in the forecast period h, obtaining the vector of pseudo-forecasts $\tilde{\mathbf{y}}_h$.

The process is repeated from step 1 to 2 and the desired results follow from the computation of the sample variances of the elements of all the $\tilde{\mathbf{y}}_h$ computed in the various replications.

A difficulty may arise in the generation of the pseudo-random vectors $\tilde{\mathbf{a}}$. The usual generation methods are, in fact, based on Choleski triangularization of the matrix $\hat{\mathbf{\Psi}}/T$ (see Cooper and Fischer, 1974, or Nagar, 1969, for example) and this is possible only if such a matrix is positive definite. Unfortunately, this is not always the case. For example when, in a large-scale model, the length of the time series does not allow the application of system estimation methods, the matrix $\hat{\mathbf{\Psi}}/T$ must be built block by block (see, for example, Brundy and Jorgenson, 1971, p. 215, for LIVE estimates) and it is not necessarily of full rank. In this case the generation of the pseudo-random coefficients vectors $\tilde{\mathbf{a}}$ should pass through the generation of shorter vectors with full rank covariance matrix (see, for example, Rao, 1965, pp. 498–501) with some additional computational difficulties.

This problem clearly does not arise if only the diagonal blocks of the $\hat{\mathbf{\Psi}}/T$ matrix are taken into account, as in the work of Cooper and Fischer (1974), Haitovsky and Wallace (1972), and Fair (1980). In the experiments that will be described in the following sections, the complete matrix $\hat{\mathbf{\Psi}}/T$ will be taken into account whenever possible, otherwise only its diagonal blocks will be used. It must, however, be pointed out that all the experiments performed with the complete $\hat{\mathbf{\Psi}}/T$ matrix have also been repeated with the diagonal blocks only, usually obtaining quite similar results (a similar conclusion is in Bianchi *et al.*, 1981).

With respect to stochastic simulation and re-estimation this method seems to be more sensitive to outliers, so that a kind of 'instability' in the convergence of the Monte Carlo process has been encountered more often; examples are given in Section 13.6 and more details on the problem of outliers are given in Section 13.6.5.

13.4.3 Analytic simulation on coefficients

This method, described in detail in Bianchi and Calzolari (1980), is an extension to nonlinear models of the fully analytical method developed for linear models by Goldberger *et al.* (1961).

The method relies on the property, well known in large-sample theory (see, for example, Rao, 1965, p. 322), that asymptotic normality of sample statistics can be maintained through transformations, even nonlinear, provided they are continuous and differentiable.

If we assume that, as T increases, asymptotically

$$\sqrt{T}(\hat{\mathbf{a}} - \mathbf{a}) \sim N(0, \mathbf{\Psi}) \tag{4.3.1}$$

(and $\hat{\mathbf{\Psi}}$ is a consistent estimate of $\mathbf{\Psi}$) then, asymptotically,

$$\sqrt{T}(\hat{\mathbf{y}}_h - \bar{\mathbf{y}}_h) = \sqrt{T}\,[\mathbf{y}(\mathbf{x}_h, \hat{\mathbf{a}}, \mathbf{0}) - \mathbf{y}(\mathbf{x}_h, \mathbf{a}, \mathbf{0})] \sim N(0, \boldsymbol{G}_h \mathbf{\Psi} \boldsymbol{G}_h') \tag{4.3.2}$$

where $\boldsymbol{G}_h$ is the $(m \times s)$ matrix of first-order partial derivatives of the elements of $\mathbf{y}$ with respect to the elements of $\mathbf{a}$, computed at the point $(\mathbf{x}_h, \mathbf{a}, \mathbf{0})$.

If the computation is performed at the point $(\mathbf{x}_h, \hat{\mathbf{a}}, \mathbf{0})$ and $\hat{\mathbf{\Psi}}$ is used in equation (4.3.2), then $\hat{\boldsymbol{G}}_h \hat{\mathbf{\Psi}} \hat{\boldsymbol{G}}_h'$ is a consistent estimate of $\boldsymbol{G}_h \mathbf{\Psi} \boldsymbol{G}_h'$; the division by the sample period length, T, leads to the result we are looking for, the estimate of the covariance matrix of a multinormal distribution which approximates the small sample distribution of the random vector $(\hat{\mathbf{y}}_h - \bar{\mathbf{y}}_h)$.

Continuity and differentiability of the elements of the (unknown) vector of reduced form functional operators $\mathbf{y}$ is ensured by the implicit function theorem, which also provides the way of computing the partial derivatives

$$\frac{\partial \mathbf{y}}{\partial \mathbf{a}'} = -\left(\frac{\partial \mathbf{f}}{\partial \mathbf{y}'}\right)^{-1}\left(\frac{\partial \mathbf{f}}{\partial \mathbf{a}'}\right) \tag{4.3.3}$$

where the derivatives of the structural form operators vector $\mathbf{f}$ (known) can be also analytically computed, once the deterministic solution of the model at time h is known.

For medium- or large-scale models it can be more convenient to perform the computation of the above derivatives with numerical methods (finite differences), rather than analytically; this criterion has been followed for all the models used here, with the exception of the Klein-I model, where both analytical and numerical derivation has been performed (of course, with coincident results).

If the model is linear, recalling equation (3.9) and making use of the formula proposed in Nissen (1968), the above method can be made more explicit as follows:

$$\begin{aligned}\sqrt{T}(\hat{\mathbf{y}}_h - \bar{\mathbf{y}}_h) &= \sqrt{T}(\hat{\mathbf{\Pi}} - \mathbf{\Pi})\mathbf{x}_h = \sqrt{T}\,\mathrm{vec}\,[\boldsymbol{I}(\hat{\mathbf{\Pi}} - \mathbf{\Pi})\mathbf{x}_h] \\ &= \sqrt{T}(\mathbf{x}_h' \otimes \boldsymbol{I})\,\mathrm{vec}(\hat{\mathbf{\Pi}} - \mathbf{\Pi})\end{aligned} \tag{4.3.4}$$

where $\boldsymbol{I}$ is the $(m \times m)$ unit matrix.

Equation (4.3.4) represents a linear combination of the elements of $(\hat{\Pi} - \Pi)$ with fixed coefficients, so that the asymptotic covariance matrix of $\sqrt{T}(\hat{\mathbf{y}}_h - \bar{\mathbf{y}}_h)$ can be computed with no difficulty as soon as the asymptotic covariance matrix of $\sqrt{T}\,\text{vec}(\hat{\Pi} - \Pi)$ has been computed, and this can be done with the methods proposed by Goldberger *et al.* (1961) or Dhrymes (1973).

13.5 FIRST SET OF EXAMPLES

This section is concerned with the numerical results obtained from experiments performed on three nonlinear models, plus the linear Klein-I model. Some general considerations hold for all the experiments and must be taken into account for a clear understanding of the tables of results.

1. For all the models, forecasts are related to the first period (year or quarter) outside the sample estimation period.
2. In all the tables, the first numerical column displays the forecast values of some of the main endogenous variables of the model.
3. Analytic simulation on coefficients, not being a Monte Carlo method, leads to results that are not affected by simulation sampling errors. Only minor changes can be expected from the third decimal digit, due to approximations in the numerical computation (for example due to the choice of the finite increments to compute the derivatives). The estimated standard errors of the component of the forecast errors under consideration, computed with this method, are displayed in the second column of each table.
4. Results based on stochastic simulation and re-estimation have been obtained with a number of replications varying from 100 to 1000 and are, therefore, affected by the sampling variability characteristic of Monte Carlo methods. In no case, however, have significant changes in the results been observed after the first 40 or 50 replications.
5. What has just been observed for stochastic simulation and re-estimation means also that in no case has the generation of outliers produced any kind of 'instability' in the computed sample moments (at least up to the second order). The standard errors of the component of the forecast error under consideration, computed with this method, are displayed in column 3 of each table.
6. Also for the Monte Carlo on coefficients method, no problem of 'stability' in the computation of sample variances has been encountered for any of the models used in this section; in other words, no trouble due to outliers has been encountered. The results (standard errors of the component of the forecast error under consideration), all obtained with 1000 replications, are displayed in the fourth column of each table.
7. The last column (fifth) on the right-hand side of each table displays the reduced form standard errors, i.e. the standard errors of that component of the

forecast errors which is not treated in detail in this paper. They are displayed only for the sake of completeness. In Section 13.3, we observe that the standard error of the (complete) forecast error can be obtained, for each variable, by taking the square root of the sum of the square of the values in column 5 and columns 2, 3, or 4 (according to the method adopted).

8. For all the models in this section, the results obtained with the three different methods (columns 2, 3, and 4) are quite similar, but this statement is not of general validity, as will be clear from the examples of Section 13.6.

13.5.1 Klein-I model: LIVE estimates 1921–1941

The model proposed in Klein (1950) consists of three stochastic plus three definitional equations; there are 12 estimated coefficients, 4 for each equation. Estimation has been performed with the limited information instrumental variables efficient method proposed in Brundy and Jorgenson (1971), on the sample period 1921–1941. Forecasts are related to year 1948, using, for the predetermined variables, the values in Goldberger *et al.* (1961) (Table 13.1).

Table 13.1 Klein-I model: LIVE estimates 1921–1941. One-period forecasts at 1948

	(1)	(2)	(3)	(4)	(5)
C	78.1	1.5	1.7	1.7	2.0
I	9.22	0.91	0.91	1.2	1.4
W_1	59.8	1.2	1.4	1.4	1.7
Y	95.5	2.3	2.4	2.8	3.3
P	27.0	1.4	1.4	1.7	1.9
K	207.0	0.91	0.91	1.2	1.4

Glossary

C = Consumption
I = Net investment
W_1 = Private wage bill
Y = National income
P = Profits
K = End-of-year capital stock

13.5.2 ISPE model of Italian economy

The nonlinear model analysed in this section is an annual model of the Italian economy developed by a team led by ISPE (Istituto Studi Programmazione Economica).

The model, originally described in Sartori (1978), consists of 19 stochastic plus 15 definitional equations; there are 75 estimated coefficients. It has been re-estimated for the period 1955–1976 using limited information instrumental variables efficient method (LIVE) (Table 13.2).

The name LIVE has been maintained since the estimation method is exactly the method of Brundy and Jorgenson (1971), but it must be recalled that instrumental variables estimates are generally not efficient when applied to nonlinear models; the problem is discussed in Amemiya (1977) and Hatanaka (1978).

The results in column 2 (analytic simulation) and 4 (Monte Carlo on coefficients) have been obtained with the complete covariance matrix of coefficients.

Table 13.2 ISPE model of Italian economy: LIVE estimates 1955–1976. One-period forecasts at 1977

	(1)	(2)	(3)	(4)	(5)
CPNCF	36735	277	278	281	470
DXML	2.92	0.07	0.07	0.07	0.07
IFIT	6949	206	209	209	268
LI	7735	67	70	66	148
MT	13806	293	288	312	391
PCL	3.02	0.03	0.03	0.03	0.04
VAP	55818	460	449	487	599
XT	16971	519	522	541	603

Glossary

CPNCF = Private consumption
DXML = Price deflator for exports
IFIT = Private investment
LI = Employees in industrial sector
MT = Imports of goods and services
PCL = Price deflator of private consumption
VAP = Gross output of private sector
XT = Exports of goods and services

13.5.3 IBM model of United Kingdom

The model analysed in this section is the model of the United Kingdom, developed by the IBM Economics Department. It is a quarterly model, with 120 equations, 21 of which are stochastic, and includes 32 exogenous variables; there are 68 structural estimated coefficients. The start of the sample period varies from 1956 II to 1969 I but always ends at 1975 IV. Estimation has been performed by means of the limited information instrumental variables efficient method (LIVE) (Table 13.3).

For the experiments with analytic simulation and Monte Carlo on coefficients, the complete covariance matrix of the structural coefficients has been used.

Table 13.3 IBM model of United Kingdom: LIVE estimates. One-period forecasts at 1976 I

	(1)	(2)	(3)	(4)	(5)
BI	2.37	0.05	0.05	0.05	0.07
CPI	108	0.57	0.65	0.59	1.40
EM	22.7	0.03	0.04	0.03	0.09
GNP	26.7	0.14	0.15	0.14	0.33
GNPC	28.9	0.21	0.23	0.22	0.40
IM	7.33	0.05	0.05	0.05	0.20
XIP	102.0	0.87	1.00	0.89	1.80

Glossary

BI = Private fixed investment
CPI = Consumer price index
EM = Private sector employees
GNP = Gross national product
GNPC = GNP in current prices
IM = Imports
XIP = Index of industrial production

13.5.4 Bonn model 10 of Germany (real sector)

The submodel, for the real economy, of the Bonn Forecasting System n. 10, used for these experiments, consists of 136 equations, 59 of which are stochastic; it includes 39 exogenous variables and 163 estimated coefficients (data are annual). For most of the equations, the estimation period is 1960–1977. For a detailed description of the model, reference should be made to Krelle (1976) and to Conrad and Kohnert (1979).

The model has been re-estimated by means of limited information instrumental variables efficient method (LIVE) (Table 13.4).

As the estimated covariance matrix of structural coefficients could not be triangularized, experiments with Monte Carlo on coefficients have been performed assuming the matrix to be block diagonal.

Analytic simulation on coefficients has been performed both with the complete covariance matrix and with the block diagonal matrix; as the results did not change significantly, at least for most variables, only results obtained with the complete matrix are displayed in column 2.

13.5.5 Klein–Goldberger model: 2SLS–8PC estimates

The model on which the experiments have been performed is the revised Klein–Goldberger model described in Klein (1969). It is nonlinear and consists of 16 stochastic and 4 definitional equations, with 54 estimated coefficients; data are

Table 13.4 Bonn forecasting system n. 10 for Germany (real sector): LIVE estimates. One-period forecasts at 1978

	(1)	(2)	(3)	(4)	(5)
BP'BPGS	29.1	3.4	3.4	3.5	6.6
C'PR	463.0	2.3	2.4	2.8	4.3
M'GSNO	347.0	3.6	3.5	3.8	6.8
P'C	1.54	0.004	0.004	0.004	0.01
WR'P	18.6	0.14	0.14	0.13	0.22
U'DIR	1.33	0.24	0.25	0.23	0.39
T	510.0	5.7	5.7	5.0	11
FW	1.70	0.10	0.10	0.10	0.17
YDP'P	734.0	4.3	4.9	5.5	6.1

Glossary

BP'BPGS = Bal. of paym. goods and services
C'PR = Private consumption
M'GSNO = Imports of goods and services
P'C = Price index of consumption
WR'P = Wage rate private
U'DIR = Unemployed persons
T = Total tax payment
FW = Foreign workers
YDP'P = Gross domestic product private

annual and the sample period is divided into two parts: 1929–1941 and 1947–1964 (Table 13.5).

Estimation has been performed by means of 2SLS with 8 principal components, as in Klein (1969); forecasts are related to 1965.

13.6 COUNTEREXAMPLES

This section is concerned with the numerical results obtained on three models, one of which is again Klein-I estimated in two different ways.

The results obtained in Section 13.5 still hold for the analytic simulation method; they hold for stochastic simulation and re-estimation in all cases except one: they do not hold at all for the Monte Carlo on coefficients method. With Monte Carlo on coefficients the sample variances did not converge as the number of replications increased; outliers caused, from time to time, abnormal fluctuations in the experimental results. This effect is demonstrated by inserting, in the tables, more columns of results, indicated by 4/1, 4/2, etc., with the indication of the numbers of replications to which they refer.

The same problem has occurred in one case with stochastic simulation and re-estimation and also in this case the effect of outliers has been demonstrated by inserting columns 3/1, 3/2, etc., with the indication of the number of replications to which they refer.

Table 13.5 Klein–Goldberger revised model 2SLS–8PC estimates. One-period forecasts at 1965

	(1)	(2)	(3)	(4)	(5)
C_d	56.5	1.1	1.2	1.1	2.4
C_n	304	1.5	1.6	1.5	3.7
R	22.9	0.58	0.56	0.57	1.2
H	7.60	0.10	0.10	0.10	0.25
I_m	29.9	0.56	0.55	0.54	1.1
X	534	3.6	3.7	3.6	8.4
$h.100$	102	0.78	0.88	0.81	2.6
W	313	1.9	2.0	1.9	4.6
w	5.51	0.02	0.02	0.02	0.07
r	4.86	0.13	0.12	0.13	0.36
I	46.7	1.1	1.0	1.1	2.4
D	59.1	0.70	0.71	0.70	1.3
r_s	4.63	0.15	0.14	0.16	0.35
P_c	43.7	3.0	3.6	3.1	6.9
N_w	68.0	0.48	0.61	0.50	1.1
Y	375	2.6	2.7	2.6	5.9
p	1.22	0.014	0.018	0.015	0.04
S_c	3.61	2.8	3.4	2.9	6.6
Π	88.2	2.9	3.3	2.9	6.5
Π_r	33.9	0.35	0.45	0.38	0.86

Glossary

When not otherwise specified the variable is expressed in billions of 1954 dollars

C_d = Consumption of durables
C_n = Consumption of nondurables and services
R = Residential construction
H = Stock of inventories
I_m = Imports
X = Gross national product
h = Index of hours worked per week, 1954 = 1.
W = Wages and salaries
w = Annual earnings, thousands of dollars
r = Average yield on corporate bonds, percent
I = Investments in plant and equipment
D = Capital consumption allowances
r_s = Yield on prime commercial paper, percent
P_c = Corporate profits
N_w = Wage and salary workers, millions
Y = Personal disposable income
p = Implicit GNP deflator, 1954 = 1
S_c = Corporate savings
$\Pi - P_c$ = Proprietors' income
Π_r = Rental income and net interest

One of the experiments is based on ordinary least squares estimates. In this case not all the assumptions concerning consistency of the estimates still hold. From a purely technical point of view, however, the three methods can be applied without any change. The statistical properties of the results will be completely unpredictable, but this does not mean that they cannot be of practical use.

13.6.1 Bonn model 5 of Germany

The model used in these experiments is the Bonn University Model 5, described in Krelle (1974) and Quinke (1978). It consists of 126 equations, 50 of which are stochastic, with 20 exogenous variables; the estimation period is 1960–1975 for most equations, but some equations have been estimated on 1960–1977; the first year outside the sample period is, therefore, 1978; data are annual (Table 13.6).

The re-estimation of the model has created some difficulties, giving rise to some convergence problems in the solution of the model inside the sample estimation period. LIVE estimates have been performed, but they led to some unacceptable values of a few coefficients and to unreasonable forecasts at 1978. It was, therefore, decided to maintain the model in its original form, with ordinary least squares estimates.

Monte Carlo on coefficients has been performed using a block-diagonal covariance matrix for the structural coefficients.

Stochastic simulation and re-estimation has been performed replicating OLS estimates.

Analytic simulation on coefficients has been first performed using the block-diagonal covariance matrix for the coefficients, then has been repeated with a complete matrix obtained with the same formula used for instrumental variables, but with the historical values of endogenous variables instead of the instruments. The results slightly changed; those obtained with the full matrix were closer to those obtained with stochastic simulation and re-estimation, so those displayed in column 2 are referred to the complete matrix, whatever the statistical properties of such a matrix may be.

13.6.2 Klein-I model: FIML estimates

The Klein-I model has been estimated by means of full information maximum likelihood (Table 13.7). The estimated coefficients and standard errors can be found, for example, in Hausman (1974).

13.6.3 Klein-I model: LIVE estimates 1921–1939

For this experiment the Klein-I model has been re-estimated by means of instrumental variables on a sample period shortened two years (Table 13.8).

Table 13.6 Model 5 of Bonn University for Germany: OLS estimates. One-period forecasts at 1978

	(1)	(2)	(3)	370 repl. (4/1)	380 repl. (4/2)	1000 repl. (4/3)	(5)
YDP	653.0	16.0	13.0	28.0	162.0	102.0	11.0
Y'PP	277.0	21.0	15.0	22.0	626.0	386.0	14.0
C'PNO	715.0	17.0	11.0	21.0	369.0	228.0	9.5
I'PN	239.0	19.0	15.0	33.0	901.0	556.0	14.0
T	508.0	12.0	12.0	19.0	413.0	255.0	14.0
GS'GD	168.0	1.9	1.7	1.8	1.80	1.80	1.9
HW	45.0	1.0	0.70	1.5	8.60	5.40	0.67
M'GSNO	326.0	7.8	6.4	10.0	171.0	106.0	8.3
X'GSNO	345.0	8.0	8.9	8.0	8.10	8.40	5.3
BP'GS	18.3	8.2	7.2	10.0	170.0	105.0	10.0

Glossary

YDP = Gross domestic product
Y'PP = Profit income private
C'PNO = Private consumption
I'PN = Gross private investment
T = Total tax payments
GS'GD = Gov. demand goods and services
HW = Hours of work
M'GSNO = Imports of goods and services
X'GSNO = Exports of goods and services
BP'GS = Bal. of paym. goods and services

Table 13.7 Klein-I model: FIML estimates 1921–1941. One-period forecasts at 1948

	(1)	(2)	(3)	380 repl. (4/1)	390 repl. (4/2)	500 repl. (4/3)	1000 repl. (4/4)	(5)
C	76.5	1.4	1.3	1.7	9.2	8.2	6.1	2.3
I	6.27	1.0	1.0	1.2	6.8	6.1	4.5	1.9
W_1	58.2	1.4	1.3	1.5	5.8	5.2	3.9	2.2
Y	91.0	2.3	2.2	2.7	16	14	11	4.2
P	24.1	1.2	1.2	1.6	10	9.2	6.8	2.2
K	204	1.0	1.0	1.2	6.8	6.1	4.5	1.9

Table 13.8 Klein-I model: LIVE estimates 1921–1939. One-period forecasts at 1940

	(1)	(2)	(3)	310 repl. (4/1)	320 repl. (4/2)	440 repl. (4/3)	1000 repl. (4/4)	(5)
C	65.6	1.0	1.1	1.3	2.0	2.7	2.3	2.0
I	2.97	0.67	0.64	0.98	1.4	2.6	2.4	1.5
W_1	45.9	0.80	0.84	0.95	1.3	1.9	1.7	1.8
Y	74.3	1.6	1.6	2.2	3.3	5.2	4.6	3.4
P	20.4	1.1	1.0	1.5	2.2	3.5	3.0	1.9
K	204	0.67	0.64	0.98	1.4	2.6	2.4	1.5

13.6.4 Klein–Goldberger model: 2SLS–4PC estimates

For this experiment the Klein–Goldberger model has been estimated by means of 2SLS with 4 principal components, as in Klein (1969) (Table 13.9).

Table 13.9 Klein-Goldberger revised: model 2SLS–4PC estimates. One-period forecasts at 1965

	(1)	(2)	10 repl. (3/1)	50 repl. (3/2)	100 repl. (3/3)	40 repl. (4/1)	200 repl. (4/2)	1000 repl. (4/3)	(5)
C_d	55.3	1.1	0.72	6.4	4.6	1.1	1.4	16.0	2.4
C_n	303.0	1.5	1.5	6.1	4.5	1.4	2.2	15.0	3.6
R	22.4	0.55	0.54	1.5	1.2	0.48	0.58	2.9	1.2
H	7.55	0.10	0.06	0.59	0.42	0.08	0.15	1.4	0.25
I_m	30.4	0.70	0.71	35.0	25.0	0.77	6.5	87.0	1.1
X	530.0	3.5	3.4	54.0	39.0	3.6	11.0	136.0	8.5
$h.100$	102.0	0.83	1.4	29.0	21.0	1.1	4.3	50.0	2.3
W	311.0	2.0	1.9	25.0	18.0	1.9	4.5	67.0	4.8
w	5.52	0.02	0.02	0.82	0.59	0.03	0.21	1.1	0.08
r	4.89	0.14	0.17	0.14	0.13	0.13	0.15	0.14	0.36
I	46.7	1.1	1.2	1.0	1.0	1.1	1.1	1.1	2.4
D	59.1	0.70	0.85	0.84	0.72	0.69	0.72	0.70	1.3
r_s	4.63	0.15	0.19	0.14	0.14	0.18	0.15	0.15	0.35
P_c	42.0	3.5	5.3	14.0	11.0	5.3	6.1	76.0	6.1
N_w	67.9	0.71	1.0	36.0	26.0	1.3	6.5	51.0	1.4
Y	369	2.6	1.9	35.0	25.0	2.6	7.1	68.0	6.1
p	1.22	0.022	0.035	6.2	4.4	0.043	0.52	5.0	0.036
S_c	1.90	3.6	5.3	18.0	14.0	5.7	7.5	75.0	6.0
Π	86.2	3.2	4.8	9.7	7.6	4.4	4.0	75.0	5.8
Π_r	33.8	0.57	0.83	6.4	4.7	0.95	1.9	1.8	1.1

13.6.5 Comments

The Klein-I model, being linear and sufficiently manageable, can be used to try to explain the abnormal fluctuations in the results obtained, in Section 13.6, with Monte Carlo on coefficients. It seems quite reasonable to believe that a similar explanation can be extended to the other models.

The structural form of the model is:

$$\begin{aligned}
C &= a_1 + a_2 P + a_3 P_{-1} + a_4 (W_1 + W_2) + u_1 \\
I &= a_5 + a_6 P + a_7 P_{-1} + a_8 K_{-1} + u_2 \\
W_1 &= a_9 + a_{10}(Y + T - W_2) + a_{11}(P + W_1 + T)_{-1} + a_{12} t + u_3 \\
Y &= C + I + G - T \\
P &= Y - W_1 - W_2 \\
K &= K_{-1} + I.
\end{aligned}$$

By substitution into the three stochastic equations, the three identities can be eliminated, obtaining:

$$\begin{aligned}
&C - a_1 - a_2(C + I - W_1 - W_2 - T + G) - a_3 P_{-1} - a_4(W_1 + W_2) = u_1 \\
&I - a_5 - a_6(C + I - W_1 - W_2 - T + G) - a_7 P_{-1} - a_8 K_{-1} = u_2 \\
&W_1 - a_9 - a_{10}(C + I - W_2 + G) - a_{11}(P + W_1 + T)_{-1} - a_{12} t = u_3.
\end{aligned}$$

In the notation of equation (2.2), the matrix A is

$$A = \begin{bmatrix} 1 - a_2 & -a_2 & a_2 - a_4 \\ -a_6 & 1 - a_6 & a_6 \\ -a_{10} & -a_{10} & 1 \end{bmatrix}.$$

The inverse of the matrix A, involved in the reduced form equations (3.2) (and therefore, in forecasts), has the denominator of each element equal to the determinant of A, which is

$$D = 1 - a_2 - a_6 + a_2 . a_{10} - a_4 . a_{10} + a_6 . a_{10}.$$

Performing Monte Carlo on coefficients, assuming for the coefficients a multinormal distribution with zero mean and covariance matrix equal to that of FIML estimates (as well as FIML estimates of the coefficients), produces first of all a control value of the determinant equal to 1.6, then a distribution of the determinant with mean, approximately, 1.6 (practically equal to the control value) and standard error, approximately, 0.62; values of this determinant between plus and minus 1/5 of its control value occur approximately in 1.7% of cases. If the numerators of the elements of the inverse of A and of B were all constants (and this is clearly not the case, but can be supposed for a while), there would be 1.7% replications that would produce forecasts larger, in absolute value, than 5 times the control forecasts. A smaller percentage would produce forecasts at least 10 times larger, 20 times larger, and so on. It is clear that these outliers produce a kind of instability in the Monte Carlo process, so that there is no warranty about convergence by increasing the number of replications. The standard error and the value 1.7% have been computed using the asymptotic normal approximation to the distribution of the determinant, then they have been confirmed by means of Monte Carlo with 10^5 replications.

The same can be said for the model estimated by LIVE on the period 1921–1939. In this case the control value of the determinant is 0.67 and its approximate standard error is 0.22; approximately 0.8% of the values fall between plus and minus 1/5 of the control value. As above, the standard error and the value 0.8% have been computed by means of a normal approximation to the distribution of the determinant and then have been confirmed by means of Monte Carlo with 10^5 replications.

If, as in Section 13.5.1, LIVE estimates are performed on the period 1921–1941, the control value of the determinant is 0.66; using a normal approximation, the standard error of the determinant would be 0.16 and only 0.04% of the values would be expected to fall between plus and minus 1/5 of the control value (again, Monte Carlo with 10^5 replications confirms the value 0.04%); the probability of encountering outliers is, therefore, so small (or at least so much smaller than in the previous two cases) as to exclude, in practice, problems of instability in the convergence of Monte Carlo.

This exemplifies and, in some sense, explains with numerical evidence the presence or absence of dangerous outliers in the experiments with Monte Carlo on coefficients. The same examples can be used to show why, in the same cases, no outlier has ever produced trouble in the experiments with stochastic simulation and re-estimation. For the Klein-I model, estimated by LIVE on the sample period 1921–1939, 10^4 replications of stochastic simulation and re-estimation have been performed, each time computing the determinant of the matrix $\boldsymbol{A}$. The results, as far as moments of the first two orders are concerned, are almost the same as those obtained with Monte Carlo on coefficients or with the asymptotic normal approximation; however, the distribution of the determinant was strongly skewed (Figure 13.1), with the left tail much shorter than the right tail, so that no value of the determinant was ever less than 1/5 of the control value.

We can reasonably presume that something similar must happen for the other estimates of the Klein-I model and for Bonn's model 5, even if, since the latter is nonlinear, the transformations from the structural form to the reduced form cannot be followed explicitly; but it clearly does not happen for the Klein–Goldberger model estimated by means of 2SLS with 4 principal components. Among all the experiments described in this paper, only this case demonstrates evidence that the nonconvergence risk involved in stochastic simulation and re-estimation method is actual and not purely theoretical; however, the entire set of experiments suggests that such a risk seems to be smaller than in the case of Monte Carlo on coefficients.

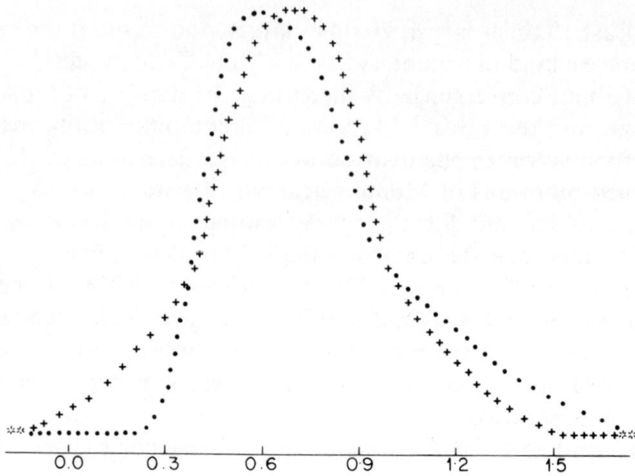

Figure 13.1 Klein-I model: LIVE estimates 1921–1939. Probability density of the determinant of matrix *A*. + Monte Carlo on coefficients; • stochastic simulation and re-estimation

13.7 ANALYTIC SIMULATION VERSUS MONTE CARLO ON COEFFICIENTS

It has been pointed out in Section 13.4 that the basic conceptual difference between analytic simulation and Monte Carlo on coefficients lies in the choice of the stage of the computation where asymptotic estimates are considered as approximating the corresponding small sample estimates; the effects of this different choice can be dramatic, as in the examples of Section 13.6.

The two methods are also computationally quite different. However, it is possible to introduce a slight modification into the Monte Carlo method which makes it exactly equivalent to the analytic simulation method (and, in fact, leads to identical results, apart from the sampling variability). This modified Monte Carlo is derived from the method described and applied, for different purposes (standard errors of dynamic multipliers), in Bianchi *et al.* (1979). It is proposed again simply because it shows a kind of logical connection between the two methods.

This Monte Carlo method is carefully designed to take into account explicitly that the normality of the estimated coefficients is asymptotic; the procedure is the following (recall that $\hat{\mathbf{a}}$ and $\hat{\mathbf{y}}_h$ are kept fixed over all the experiment).

1. A tentative value n (greater than 1) is fixed: for example $n = 10$.
2. A vector $\tilde{\mathbf{a}}$ of pseudo-random numbers with multivariate normal distribution, mean equal to $\hat{\mathbf{a}}$ and covariance matrix equal to $\hat{\mathbf{\Psi}}/nT$, is generated.
3. The elements of $\tilde{\mathbf{a}}$ are inserted into the model and the model is solved in the forecast period h, producing $\tilde{\mathbf{y}}_h$.

4. The vector of differences $(\tilde{\mathbf{y}}_h - \hat{\mathbf{y}}_h)$ is computed.
5. Remultiplying by the scaling factor $\sqrt{n}$, we compute $\sqrt{n}(\tilde{\mathbf{y}}_h - \hat{\mathbf{y}}_h)$.
6. The steps from 2 to 5 are repeated a certain number of times (for example 1000); each time a new vector $\sqrt{n}(\tilde{\mathbf{y}}_h - \hat{\mathbf{y}}_h)$ is computed.
7. The sample variances (or the covariance matrix) can now be computed for the elements of $\sqrt{n}(\tilde{\mathbf{y}}_h - \hat{\mathbf{y}}_h)$; they are a first approximation to the estimated asymptotic variances of the component of the forecast errors under consideration.
8. After the process has been performed for the first time, n must be increased (for example, by a factor of 10) and a new iteration must be started from step 2; in the other cases, the sample variances obtained in the last iteration must be compared with those of the previous one; if significant differences are found, a new iteration must be started from step 2, after increasing n (for example, again by a factor of 10).

The process is stopped when no differences are found in the first three or four significant digits of the sample variances in two consecutive iterations. To avoid the problem of differences caused by the sampling variability, it is warmly recommended that the same set of pseudo-random numbers are used for each iteration.

The role of the scaling, and final re-scaling, by a value $\sqrt{n}$ should be clear at this point. The above experiment with $n = 1$ is nothing but the Monte Carlo on coefficients method described in Section 13.4.2. A large (and increasing, in theory, to infinite) value of n simulates the behaviour of an increasing sample size (T); it generates a narrow and collapsing distribution of the generated pseudo-random numbers $\tilde{\mathbf{a}}$ around $\hat{\mathbf{a}}$ (as asymptotically the distribution of $\hat{\mathbf{a}}$ collapses around $\mathbf{a}$); for $\tilde{\mathbf{y}}_h$, this generates a distribution collapsing around $\hat{\mathbf{y}}_h$ (as asymptotically the distribution of $\hat{\mathbf{y}}_h$ collapses around $\bar{\mathbf{y}}_h$); finally the collapsed differences $(\tilde{\mathbf{y}}_h - \hat{\mathbf{y}}_h)$ are re-scaled by $\sqrt{n}$ (as the covariance matrix to be estimated is that of the asymptotic distribution of $\sqrt{T}\,(\hat{\mathbf{y}}_h - \bar{\mathbf{y}}_h)$, divided by the actual value of the sample period length T). Moreover, a large value of n generates pseudo-random numbers with a very narrow distribution, thus avoiding in practice the instability effects due to outliers.

Numerical results obtained with this method do not need to be displayed; they are, in fact, equal to those obtained by means of analytic simulation on coefficients, apart from small differences due to the sampling variability of the Monte Carlo method.

13.8 CONCLUSIONS

This paper has been mainly concerned with empirical comparisons of three methods of analysing the effects of coefficient estimation errors, on forecasts produced by structural econometric models.

The experiments have been designed to include a sufficiently wide and representative set of real-world models. However, it has been pointed out that the methods present not only technical, but also conceptual, differences, so that we cannot conclude with precise criteria for ranking among the three methods. We shall, therefore, confine ourselves to these concluding remarks.

1. From a purely technical point of view, all methods can be applied to macroeconomic models of practical interest.
2. The applicability of analytic simulation strictly depends on the assumption of asymptotic normality of estimated coefficients; in practice, however, the method can be applied also when this assumption is violated and the results seem to be 'numerically' reasonable, even if with unpredictable statistical properties.
3. Monte Carlo on coefficients is not confined to the assumption of coefficient normality. Its correct application, however, would require the knowledge of the distribution of estimated coefficients and the technical availability of a pseudo-random numbers generator from such a distribution. If, in the absence of this information, which usually involves overwhelming difficulties, a normal distribution is adopted, problems like those discussed in Section 13.6 can be encountered.
4. Analytic simulation requires the model to be solved as many times as the number of structural estimated coefficients; furthermore, to compute derivatives with sufficient precision, it needs a computational accuracy much greater than in the usual simulation experiments. Therefore, it could be more efficient to use Monte Carlo for models with more than 40 or 50 coefficients; if outliers do not affect the stability of the Monte Carlo process, in fact, 40 or 50 replications (with fewer problems of accuracy) are usually enough to provide a sufficient approximation to the desired standard errors.
5. Stochastic simulation and re-estimation is computationally the most inefficient method. However, it does not need, among input data, the covariance matrix of all the structural coefficients, thus avoiding the cumbersome problems of its estimation and storing and the problem of its triangularization, which is required by Monte Carlo on coefficients; furthermore, it avoids the problem of storing the matrix of partial derivatives (usually large), which is required by analytic simulation.
6. The method discussed in Section 13.7 can be of some interest for the experimenter; it is, in fact, technically similar to Monte Carlo on coefficients, but conceptually equivalent to analytic simulation.
7. The main problem in applying stochastic simulation and re-estimation or Monte Carlo on coefficients is, in any case, the possible instability in the convergence process due to outliers; in practice stochastic simulation and re-estimation seems to be less sensitive than the other to the presence of outliers. In any case the experimenter cannot simply prefix a number of replications to

be performed and then take uncritically the final results; the experimenter, on the contrary, should carefully take into account intermediate results as well.

8. An alternative empirical way of detecting the presence of outliers could be the comparison of the standard errors due to the structural coefficients with the standard errors due to the structural disturbances (the so called 'reduced form' standard errors); it seems reasonable, when forecasting in the first period outside the sample estimation period, to expect two standard errors with the same size, or the error due to structural disturbances slightly larger than the other; when, on the contrary, the error due to coefficients is larger than the other (2, 3, 4 times or more, as in Tables 13.6–13.9), problems of outliers have probably occurred.
9. When problems of instability in the convergence process have not been encountered, the three methods always produced similar results, thus suggesting a kind of empirical equivalence of the methods themselves.

NOTES

[1] The authors gratefully acknowledge helpful comments and criticisms from John Bradley, Ray C. Fair, Lawrence R. Klein, Jacques Mairesse, Joel L. Prakken, and Peter K. Schoenfeld, but retain sole responsibility for any errors.

[2] Reference can be made, for example, to Goldberger *et al.* (1961), Denton and Kuiper (1965), Feldstein (1971), Schink (1971), Haitovsky and Wallace (1972), Cooper and Fischer (1974), Schmidt (1974), Oliver (1979), Bianchi and Calzolari (1980), and Fair (1980).

[3] It is perhaps worth mentioning that these means and variances are sometimes referred to as deterministic simulation bias and reduced form variances, respectively.

REFERENCES

Amemiya, T. (1977). 'The maximum likelihood and the nonlinear three-stage least squares in the general nonlinear simultaneous equation model.' *Econometrica*, **45,** 955–968.

Bianchi, C., and Calzolari, G. (1980). 'The one-period forecast errors in nonlinear econometric models.' *International Economic Review*, **21,** 201–208.

Bianchi, C., Calzolari, G., and Corsi, P. (1979). 'A Monte Carlo approach to compute the asymptotic standard errors of dynamic multipliers.' *Economics Letters*, **2,** 161–164.

Bianchi, C., Calzolari, G., and Corsi, P. (1981). 'Standard errors of multipliers and forecasts from structural coefficients with block-diagonal covariance matrix.' In J. M. L. Janssen, L. F. Pau, and A. J. Straszak, (Eds), *Dynamic Modelling and Control of National Economies* (IFAC), Pergamon, Oxford, pp. 311–316.

Brundy, J. M., and Jorgenson, D. W. (1971). 'Efficient estimation of simultaneous equations by instrumental variables.' *Review of Economics and Statistics*, **53,** 207–224.

Christ, C. F. (1966). *Econometric Models and Methods*, Wiley, New York.

Conrad, K., and Kohnert, P. (1979). 'Economic activity, interest rates and the exchange rate in the Bonn forecasting system no. 10.' Universität Bonn, Institut für Gesellschafts- und Wirtschaftswissenschaften, Wirtschaftstheoretische Abteilung, discussion paper.

Cooper, J. P., and Fischer, S. (1974). 'Monetary and fiscal policy in the fully stochastic St. Louis econometric model.' *Journal of Money, Credit, and Banking*, **6**, 1–22.

Denton, F. T., and Kuiper, J. (1965). 'The effects of measurement errors on parameter estimates and forecasts.' *Review of Economics and Statistics*, **47**, 198–206.

Dhrymes, P. J. (1970). *Econometrics: Statistical Foundations and Applications*, Harper & Row, New York.

Dhrymes, P. J. (1973). 'Restricted and unrestricted reduced forms: Asymptotic distribution and relative efficiency.' *Econometrica*, **41**, 119–134.

Fair, R. C. (1980). 'Estimating the expected predictive accuracy of econometric models.' *International Economic Review*, **21**, 355–378.

Feldstein, M. S. (1971). 'The error of forecast in econometric models when the forecast-period exogenous variables are stochastic.' *Econometrica*, **39**, 55–60.

Gallant, A. R. (1977). 'Three-stage least-squares estimation for a system of simultaneous, nonlinear, implicit equations.' *Journal of Econometrics*, **5**, 71–88.

Goldberger, A. S., Nagar, A. L., and Odeh, H. S. (1961). 'The covariance matrices of reduced-form coefficients and of forecasts for a structural econometric model.' *Econometrica*, **29**, 556–573.

Haitovsky, Y., and Wallace, N. (1972). 'A study of discretionary and nondiscretionary monetary and fiscal policies in the context of stochastic macroeconometric models.' In V. Zarnowitz (Ed.). *The Business Cycle Today*, National Bureau of Economic Research, New York, pp. 261–309.

Hatanaka, M. (1978). 'On the efficient estimation methods for the macro-economic models nonlinear in variables.' *Journal of Econometrics*, **8**, 323–356.

Hausman, J. A. (1974). 'Full information instrumental variables estimation of simultaneous equations systems.' *Annals of Economic and Social Measurement*, **3**, 641–652.

Klein, L. R. (1950). *Economic Fluctuations in the United States, 1921–1941*, Cowles Commission Monograph 11, Wiley, New York.

Klein, L. R. (1969). 'Estimation of interdependent systems in macroeconometrics.' *Econometrica*, **37**, 171–192.

Krelle, W. (1974). *Erfahrungen mit einem Öekonometrischen Prognosemodell für die Bundesrepublik Deutschland*, Verlag Anton Hain, Meisenheim/Glan.

Krelle, W. (1976). 'Das Bonner Prognosemodell 10. Teil I, Reales Modell.' Universität Bonn, Institut für Gesellschafts- und Wirtschaftswissenschaften, Wirtschaftstheoretische Abteilung, discussion paper.

Mariano, R. S. (1980). 'Analytical small sample distribution theory in econometrics: The simultaneous equations case.' Université Catholique de Louvain. Center for Operations Research & Econometrics, discussion paper.

McCarthy, M. D. (1972a). 'Some notes on the generation of pseudo-structural errors for use in stochastic simulation studies.' In B. G. Hickman (Ed.), *Econometric Models of Cyclical Behavior*, National Bureau of Economic Research, Studies in Income and Wealth no. 36, New York, pp. 185–191.

McCarthy, M. D. (1972b). 'A note on the forecasting properties of two-stage least squares restricted reduced forms: The finite sample case.' *International Economic Review*, **13**, 757–761.

Nagar, A. L. (1969). 'Stoichastic simulation of the brookings econometric model.' In J. S. Duesenberry, G. Fromm, L. R. Klein, and E. Kuh (Eds), *The Brookings Model: Some Further Results*, North-Holland, Amsterdam, pp. 425–456.

Nissen, D. H. (1968). 'A note on the variance of a matrix.' *Econometrica*, **36**, 603–604.

Oliver, F. R. (1979). 'Rebased and revised data: Their effects on econometric estimates.' *Economics Letters*, **4**, 355–359.

Quinke, H. (1978). 'Bonner Modell 5.5, Variablen, Gleichungen, Daten 1965–1977, Prognosen 1978–1985, Zusammenstellung.' Universität Bonn, Institut für Gesellschafts- und Wirtschaftswissenschaften, Wirtschaftstheoretische Abteilung, discussion paper.

Rao, C. R. (1965). *Linear Statistical Inference and its Applications*, Wiley, New York.

Sargan, J. D. (1976). 'The existence of the moments of estimated reduced form coefficients.' London School of Economics and Political Science, discussion paper A6.

Sartori, F. (1978). 'Caratteristiche e struttura del modello.' In *Un Modello Econometrico dell'Economia Italiana: Caratteristiche e Impiego, Ispequaderni*, **1,** 9–36.

Schink, G. R. (1971). 'Small sample estimates of the variance covariance matrix of forecast error for large econometric models: The stochastic simulation technique.' University of Pennsylvania, Ph.D. dissertation.

Schmidt, P. (1976). 'The asymptotic distribution of forecasts in the dynamic simulation of an econometric model.' *Econometrica*, **42,** 303–309.

Schmidt, P. (1976). *Econometrics*, Dekker, New York.

Theil, H. (1971). *Principles of Econometrics*, Wiley, New York.

Discussion

J. MAIRESSE
I.N.S.E.E., Paris

The paper by Carlo Bianchi and Giorgio Calzolari is an interesting and useful piece of research. It was a pleasure to have been asked to read it with particular care.

The paper compares three alternative methods of assessing the uncertainty of forecasts resulting from errors in estimated coefficients for nine 'real-world' models. I shall restrict myself to three of the many comments that this stimulating paper suggests. In as much as these comments sound somewhat critical, they should, in all fairness, be considered as suggestions for future analysis, since the authors have been extremely clear and modest in defining the exact scope and ambition of their present work.

I wish also to stress that the paper rests on numerous computations and experimentations, involving first-class expertise and know-how in computers and numerical analysis, which is kept discreetly in the background. One might expect such performance from researchers in an IBM centre, but one still must be thankful to them for avoiding any ostensible display of their comparative advantage.

My first comment addresses the fact that the paper deals only with one-period forecasts. It will have to be extended to cope with multi-period forecasts, since we are generally interested in a set of forecasts for a succession of years in the case of annual models, and in a set of forecasts for at least four quarters in the case of quarterly models. But this is not a trivial extension once lagged endogenous variables enter into the model, as they will. Three of the maintained hypotheses in the present work will have to be deleted: the hypothesis that the forecast errors can be decomposed into two independent terms pertaining respectively to the structural disturbances and to the errors in the estimated coefficients; the hypothesis of certain knowledge of the predetermined variables; and the hypothesis of the independence over time of the structural disturbances.

My second comment relates to the exclusive focus of the authors on the computation of the matrix of variances and covariances of the model forecasts. This is all very well when the sample size is large and the distribution of the forecasts is approximately normal. Unfortunately, a problem may arise in small samples, however, since the true variances of some of the estimated coefficients, hence of the forecasts themselves, may not exist in the sense that they may be infinite. In these cases the 'estimated variances' of the forecasts are bound to be large; but over and above that, they are meaningless.

For this reason, it is particularly advisable in small samples to consider the whole distributions of the forecasts, and not only their standard errors. In practice one could plot the simulated small-sample distributions of the forecasts of the main endogenous variables, or compute, say, the quartiles of these distributions. (The graph given in Section 13.6.5 of the paper is a good example).

My third comment concerns the existence of so-called 'outliers' in the simulations and the possibility of nonconvergence of the methods. These difficulties also derive from the infinite variance of some of the estimated coefficients.

The problem of the possible nonexistence of finite moments for the small-sample distribution of estimated coefficients or forecasts cannot be avoided. It is a true problem. The real issue is how frequently it happens in 'real-world' models. Based on the experiments performed in the paper the occurrence is apparently not unusual. It is evident in the presence of four so-called 'counterexamples' out of a total of nine examples; in these counterexamples the standard errors of the forecasts of all the major endogenous variables are indeed largely affected.

The issue has a significant bearing on the conclusions of the paper about the relative performance of the three methods in question. Apart from very important considerations of calculation costs and practical feasibility, the authors seem to rank the three methods on the basis of the presence or absence of 'outliers' and instabilities in the simulation exercises. Based on the same criteria, however, I would be tempted to make the opposite ranking. That is, if such difficulties reflect the genuine problem of the infinite variance of some of the estimated coefficients and forecasts, then it may be more of a defect than an advantage for a method to conceal its occurrence.

Actually it is easy to see why the 'Analytical simulation on coefficients' method avoids difficulties of convergence, whereas the 'Monte Carlo on coefficients' method does not. Suppose $\hat{a}$ is a small-sample estimate of a coefficient a, with a true standard error $\sigma_{\hat{a}}$ which is infinite. Then the computed estimated standard error $\hat{\sigma}_{\hat{a}}$ will be of course a finite number, though probably large. The analytical method performs the computations of the estimated standard error $\hat{\sigma}_{\hat{y}}$ of the forecast $\hat{\mathbf{y}}$ on the basis of only small finite differences $\Delta\hat{a}$, which are not related to the magnitude of $\hat{\sigma}_{\hat{a}}$. On the contrary, however, the Monte Carlo method relies on $\hat{\sigma}_{\hat{a}}$ to generate the set of pseudo-random $\tilde{a}$ used in computing the pseudo-forecasts $\tilde{\mathbf{y}}$, on the basis of which the estimated standard error $\hat{\sigma}_{\hat{\mathbf{y}}}$ is finally derived.

But the 'Stochastic simulation and re-estimation' method has the advantage over the previous two of completely avoiding use of $\hat{\sigma}_{\hat{a}}$. The method directly simulates the small-sample distribution of $\hat{a}$ by generating a pseudo-sample of observations $\tilde{\mathbf{y}}$ and re-estimating the model.

Hence, to the extent that the problem of infinite variance matters, my ranking of the methods would be: first 'Stochastic simulation and re-estimation' though very expensive; last 'Analytical simulation on coefficients', though much more economical.

Let me end on a final suggestion for future research. Simulation methods are very good and useful, but whenever possible fully analytical methods can provide more insight and understanding in the case of a difficult problem. It would be worthwhile to consider some very simple textbook models, and work out explicitly the small-sample distributions of the forecasts in these examples. This might be possible using various approximations to the small-sample distributions, as in recent work on the small-sample properties of estimators and tests.

Evaluating the Reliability of Macro-economic Models
Edited by G. C. Chow and P. Corsi

CHAPTER 14

Use of Macro-economic Studies in Preparation of the French VIIIth Plan

A. GAURON
Commissariat Général du Plan, Paris
H. GUILLAUME
Ecole Centrale de Paris
J. MAURICE
Commissariat Général du Plan, Paris
J. C. MILLERON
Commissariat Général du Plan, Paris

This paper describes the macro-economic work done with the assistance of the INSEE model DMS (see Fouquet *et al.*, 1978; Guillaume, 1978; INSEE Programs Department, 1980) in preparation of the VIIIth Plan.

As a preliminary, it is necessary briefly to recapitulate some institutional characteristics of French planning.

Preparation of the French VIIIth Plan for the period 1981–1985 took from October 1979 to September 1980. It involved on a consulting basis commissions of representatives of trade associations and unions, and senior civil servants and experts. The commissions' reports are submitted to the Planning Agency before drafting of the Plan which, after consideration by the Government, is voted by the Parliament.

Of the commissions, the Development Commission, chaired by the Planning Commissioner, plays an important part, as it synthesizes the preparatory work and examines the macro-economic consistency of the medium-term economic policy measures.

The quantitative studies are designed to provide a quantified ascertainment of past trends of the French economy and of the situation at the start of the Plan, and to explore the future prospects and the economic policy options. But, in preceding Plans, the macro-economic studies were traditionally focused on development of a single central normative forecast binding on the Government and Parliament.

Preparation of the VIIIth Plan involved a rethinking of the quantitative study methods and use of macro-economic models. The Development Commission's work was noteworthy for:

— abandonment of a single forecast in favour of development of several medium-term scenarios;
— development of a systematic method of exploration of the economic policies which are the most efficient for reducing unemployment during the VIIIth Plan. From the technical standpoint, this involved testing on the DMS model the macro-economic impact (calculation of multipliers) of the elementary economic policy programs (analytic variants) specified by the Development Commission, and determining the optimal combination thereof by linear programming techniques, the objective function being maximization of employment.

The advantage of this approach is obviously not its theoretical contribution, but the fact that it is a large-scale experiment (both in the size of the model — 1500 equations — and in the number of variants studied — nearly 90) in response to a request by the non-economist members of the Development Commission, formalizing their thinking.

Use of the DMS model will be analysed from this standpoint. Reference is made to Gauron and Maurice (1980) and Maarek (1980) for fuller explanation.

14.1 THE SCENARIO METHOD IN THE MEDIUM-TERM QUANTITATIVE WORK

This is not a new method, being commonly used in long-term forecasting in which the uncertainty of future prospects requires study of several trend assumptions considered more or less probable. Until the VIIIth Plan, it was rarely used in medium-term work.

To start the work of the VIIIth Plan commissions, four scenarios were developed in the summer of 1979[1] by crossing two international environmental assumptions and two economic policy assumptions (adjustment policy and structural adaptation policy).

The principal assumptions of the starting scenarios are described in Table 14.1. The principal results are shown in Table 14.2.

In all four scenarios, there is a sharp slowing in the French economy's growth rate from the pre-1974 trend, and loss of the positive growth differential of the French economy *vis-à-vis* its principal trading partners. Combined with France's population trend (entry of many young people into the job market between 1980 and 1985), these trends result in significant period-end unemployment (2 to 2.4 million unemployed in 1985).[2]

But the Development Commission, followed by other VIIIth Plan commissions and committees, forthwith demonstrated the limitations of such scenarios, which reflect all the principal macro-economic magnitudes and the results of all the assumptions, without enabling the specific effect of each to be assessed. Hence, if one or more results are unacceptable, how can they be improved? Of all the assumptions, which must be changed, and how? Empirical

Table 14.1 Starting scenarios: the assumptions

International environmental assumptions (increase on an annual average— % per year)

	Favourable	Unfavourable
World inflation		
—in world currency	4.3	4.9
—in francs	6.3	6.9
Depreciation of the actual franc exchange rage (DMS indicator)	1.9	1.9
Depreciation of the dollar	0.5	1.9
Real price of oil (in excess of inflation)	0	7.0
Foreign gross domestic product, in volume (DMS indicator)	3.6	2.7

Economic policy assumptions

Average annual changes (1980–1985)	Adjustment	Structural adaptation
Energy saving (millions of TOE/year)	3	4
Average workweek reduction per year	30 minutes	One hour
Annual welfare contribution increase	0.8 point	0.4 point
Average annual increase		
1. *Industry*		
Workweek reduction	1.5 % pa	2.8 % pa
Reduction in time of use of capital	1.4 % pa	1.0 % pa
2. *Government expenditures*		
Investments (volume)	2.0 % pa	2.0 % pa
Consumption (volume)	3.0 % pa	3.0 % pa
Employment	1.2 % pa	2.45 % pa
Per capita employed purchasing power	1.5 % pa	0.5 % pa
3. *Public enterprises*		
Capital expenditures (volume)	−1.0 % pa	+1.8 % pa

Table 14.2 Principal results of the starting scenarios

			ECONOMIC POLICIES			
			ADJUSTMENT International environment		STRUCTURAL ADAPTATION International environment	
	PAST TRENDS		Favourable	Adverse	Favourable	Adverse
Uses	1960–74	1974–78	1978–85	1978–85	1978–85	1978–85
Market price gross domestic product	5.9	2.9	2.9	2.5	3.2	2.7
Imports	11.3	5.4	6.1	4.5	6.7	5.1
Supply (volume % per year)						
Net domestic consumption, noncommercial government sectors	5.0	6.5	3.6	3.6	3.6	3.6
Household consumption	5.5	4.1	3.6	3.1	3.8	3.4
Total gross fixed capital formation:	7.1	0.3	1.4	0.8	1.9	1.2
By companies, quasi-companies and proprietorships	6.4	0.4	1.9	0.8	2.3	1.7
By government agencies	6.1	2.2	1.5	1.5	1.7	1.7
By credit institutions and insurance companies	15.4	−0.1	0	−0.8	0.1	−0.7
By households	8.3	−0.8	0.7	0.8	1.5	1.5
Inventory changes (billions of francs)	14.1	8.5	12.3	10.4	13.2	11.3
Exports	10.3	5.7	5.6	4.3	5.9	4.6
Prices and *purchasing power* (% per year)						
Household consumer prices	4.6	9.7	7.1	7.3	7.1	7.3
Average annual wage purchasing power	4.2	2.5	2.5	2.1	2.2	1.8
Employment (net changes, thousand per year)						
Total	98.5	−22.2	−96.2	−131.1	4.2	−33.1
Industrial	80.5	−120.9	−127.1	147.3	−51.6	−73.5
1985 financing needs (*% of GDP*)						
Nation			−0.1	0.4	−0.1	0.2
Government agencies			1.2	2.4	1.1	2.1

change of given data one by one would be a process of tedious and uncertain groping. Certain results could be improved but others would probably be worsened. And there is no guarantee that the proposed changes would be the most efficient. The scenario method, helpful as a starting point, thus does not make it possible to proceed to the next stage: fixing of goals and of the means best calculated to attain them.

The Development Commission and other commissions requested adoption of employment as goal, and determination of the conditions under which it would be possible to improve it in the VIIIth Plan, from the prospects revealed by the starting scenarios.

14.2 EXPLORATION OF EFFICIENT POLICIES FOR INCREASING EMPLOYMENT

Compared with the early models of the 1950's, which had only 60 equations or so, the current models tend toward giantism. Using large models and faced with especially uncertain environments, determination of economic policies which, if not optimal, are at least satisfactory, by direct simulation is extremely laborious.

The method described below was developed for purposes of the VIIIth Plan to circumvent these problems. The method has two phases:

- as systematic an analysis as possible of the variant effects of the DMS model for each economic policy program (analytic variants). One of the significant results of these analyses is that, in the variation range considered for the control variables, the DMS model's reactions are linear.
- an attempt, by means of linear programming techniques, to combine such programs (complex variant) to increase employment as much as possible in a system of constraints relating to the program variables or the results (foreign trade and public finance equilibria).

14.2.1 Definition of the analytic variants

The analytic variants are defined in relation to a reference scenario which is the starting scenario combining an adverse external environment and a regulatory economic policy. The policy instruments used are listed in Table 14.3.

This table also describes the assumptions made as to the amplitude of fluctuations of the economic policy instruments

$$(a_t^{\min} \leqslant a_t \leqslant a_t^{\max})$$

in relation to the reference scenario. The set of these assumptions defines, so to speak, the maximum intensity of the sacrifices the country would agree to in order to improve the economic and social situation in relation to the outlook described in the starting scenario. The more vigorous the programs, the wider the latitude

Table 14.3 Assumptions as to the brackets* applicable to the economic policy programs envisaged in the complex variants

	Symbol***	*A* VARIANTS moderate latitudes floor	*A* VARIANTS moderate latitudes ceiling	*B* VARIANTS wider latitudes floor	*B* VARIANTS wider latitudes ceiling	*C* VARIANTS wider latitudes + workweek
(a) *Social expenditures***						
Health consumption	⌐⌐⌐	−0.55% pa(1)	0	−1.1% pa	0	same latitudes as *B* variants
Family benefits	⌐⌐⌐	−0.40% pa	+0.40% pa	−2.4% pa	+0.8% pa	
Old age benefits	⌐⌐⌐	−0.95% pa	+0.95% pa	−1.9% pa	+1.9% pa	
(b) *Welfare contributions*						
Employees' (no ceiling)	⌐⌐⌐	−0.4 point/pa	0	−0.4 pt/pa	0	
Employers' (no ceiling)	⌐⌐⌐	−0.4 pt/pa	0	−0.8 pt/pa	0	
Employers' (ceiling) to CNAF	⌐⌐⌐	−1 point from 1981	0	−3 points from 1981	0	
(c) *Government spending* (*APU*)						
APU staff(2)	⌐⌐⌐	0	+0.5% pa	0	+1.0% pa	
APU pay per capita	⌐⌐⌐	−0.5% pa	+0.5% pa	−1.0% pa	+1.0% pa	
APU consumption	⌐⌐⌐	−0.5% pa	+0.5% pa	−1.0% pa	+1.0% pa	
APU GFFC(3)	⌐⌐⌐	−1.0% pa	+1.0% pa	−2.9% pa	+2.0% pa	
Equipment subsidies(4) to following sectors:						
—AAI	⌐	−0.6 BnF (81)	+1.0 BnF (81)	−0.6 BnF (81)	+1.0 BnF (81)	
—Intermediate goods	⌐	−0.8 BnF (81)	+1.0 BnF (81)	−0.8 BnF (81)	+2.0 BnF (81)	
—Capital goods	⌐	−1.0 BnF (81)	+1.0 BnF (81)	−1.0 BnF (81)	+2.0 BnF (81)	
—Consumer goods	⌐	−0.4 BnF (81)	+1.0 BnF (81)	−0.4 BnF (81)	+3.0 BnF (81)	
—Construction/public works	⌐	−0.4 BnF (81)	+1.0 BnF (81)	−0.4 BnF (81)	+1.0 BnF (81)	
—Services	⌐	−1.0 BnF (81)	+1.0 BnF (81)	−1.0 BnF (81)	+1.0 BnF (81)	
—Trade	⌐	−0.4 BnF (81)	+1.0 BnF (81)	−0.4 BnF (81)	+1.0 BnF (81)	
(d) *Government receipts*						
Personal income tax	⌐⌐	−0.7% pa	+0.7% pa	−0.7% pa	+1.4% pa	
Corporate income tax	⌐	−2 BnF (81)	+2 BnF (81)	−4 BnF (81)	+4 BnF (81)	
TVA on energy	⌐	+0	+45.0%	0	+89.0%	
Other TVA on:(5)	⌐					
—farm products	⌐	−5.0%	+5.0%	−10.0%	+10.0%	
—AAI	⌐	"	"	"	"	

—transport	⌐	"	"	"	"	Same latitudes as *B* variants
—services	⌐					
(e) *Public enterprises*						
GFFC[3]	⌐⌐	0	+6 BnF (81) in 85	0	+12 BnF (81) in 85	
Energy rates	⌐⌐	0	+1.0% pa	0	+1.0% pa	
Trans.–Telecom. rates	⌐⌐	0	+0.05% pa		+2.0% pa	
(f) *Energy saving*						
Housing	⌐⌐	0	+0.10 pa	0	+0.30 pa	
Tertiary	⌐⌐	0	+0.15 pa	0	+0.60 pa	
Industry	⌐⌐	0	+0.15 pa	0	+0.60 pa	
Transport	⌐⌐	0	+0.05 pa	0	+0.20 pa	
(g) *Housing*						
Public units constructed	⌐	0	+12 500 pa	0	+25 000 pa	
Household investments	⌐	0	+1.3 BnF (80)	0	+5.4 BnF (80)	
(h) *Wage and nonwage income*						
Hourly earnings:		0	+1.4% pa	1.4% pa	+1.4% pa	
—continuing increase	⌐⌐	−0.45% (80 + 81)	0	−0.90% (80 + 81)	0	
—freeze then increase	⌐⌐	+0.36% (82–85)	0	+0.72% (82–85)	0	
—self-employed income	⌐⌐	+0.5% pa	0	−2.0% pa	0	
—mark-up coefficients	⌐	1.0%	0	−5.0% pa	0	
(i) Employment-workweek						
—workforce (immigrants)	⌐⌐	0	0	−50 000 (85)	0	
—workweek[6]	⌐⌐	0	0	0	0	−36 min pa

* In relation to the reference scenario.

** The order of the measures is technical only and not indicative of priorities.

*** A staircase corresponds to a progressive measure applied every year. A step corresponds to a measure applied the first year and kept constant thereafter.

(1) pa = per annum.

(2) The ratio of public administrations (APU) staff to consumption increases 1% pa–0.28% pa.

(3) Gross formation of fixed capital.

(4) Only equipment subsidies are considered, the variants having shown that operating subsidies are less efficient. The floors are so calculated that, in relation to 1978, the equipment subsidies granted to the sectors do not become negative.

(5) For each product, the apparent tax on value added (TVA) rate is multiplied by a number between 0.95 and 1.05.

(6) The reference account entails a downtrend of 30 minutes per annum.

for action and the larger the field accessible by means of the linear combinations of analytic variants, thus providing more substantial prospects of improvement.

Three sets of assumptions were made for the latitudes:

— case A of narrow latitudes:
— case B of wider latitudes;
— case C, with the same latitudes as in B but coupled with the assumption of negotiation of accelerated worktime reduction in exchange for pay moderation and more shift work.

The DMS model simulations enable the impact matrix to be determined, i.e. the matrix which describes the effect of the analytic variants on the result variables. If $\mathbf{a}^t$ describes the column vector giving the intensity fluctuations of the economic policy instruments in year t in relation to the reference scenario, the linearity of the model results for each year in:

$$\Delta \mathbf{r}_t^\theta = (\boldsymbol{m}_t^\theta)\mathbf{a}^t$$

where $\Delta \mathbf{r}_t^\theta$ is a vector giving the fluctuations of the result variables in year $\theta (\theta \geqslant t)$, and $\boldsymbol{m}_t^\theta$ is the impact matrix in year θ for an economic decision applied in year t.

14.2.2 Development of the complex variants

These are determined by the method of linear optimization (Figure 14.1). The goal adopted by the Development Commission is maximization of the total employment variation during the VIIIth Plan or, rather, which amounts to the same thing, the annual variation in total employment during the Plan. The constraints relate respectively to:

— the latitudes of action on the economic policy instruments (see Section 14.2.1);
— the constraints on the result variables. Two key variables are constrained: the nation's financing capacity limit *vis-à-vis* the reference scenario ranges from 0 to −10, −20, −40 billion 1980 francs per year, then is no longer limited (free).

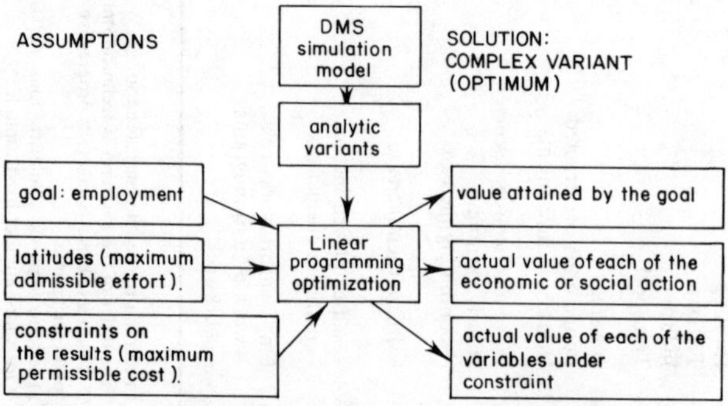

Figure 14.1. Diagram of the complex variants method

Likewise, the average annual fluctuation in public agency financing capacity rises from 0 to -30 billion francs, then is no longer limited (free).

By crossing these two constraints, 15 cases are obtained, each corresponding to a complex variant.

14.2.3 The results of the complex variants

Table 14.4 shows the principal results.

For each of these complex variants, the values to be given to the various program variables are calculated by the algorithm on the basis of the contribution of each to attainment of the goal and respecting the constraints; such optimum values are almost all, as anticipated, either at the upper or the lower limit; only one or two, serving for adjustment, are inside their latitude.

Stress must be laid in this connection, for each complex variant, on the fact that the optimum combination corresponding to the program variables forms a whole and is a sort of package: if one program were withdrawn from the package or if another program were given a value other than its optimum value, the results and the optimum value of the other program variables would be more or less affected. Hence, it is not possible to pick and choose on the basis of preferences without distorting the exercise.

On given latitudes, when the transition is made from one complex variant to the next, on the assumption of a larger trade deficit, one or more program variants 'swing', i.e. shift from their lower (or upper) limit position toward their upper (or lower) limit position. The new adjustment variable(s) incidentally appear precisely as 'swinging'. In fact, some program variables never change direction, i.e. must always stay at the limit they reach on the most restrictive trade deficit assumption. They are those which have a large job content and a small import content (or a favourable effect on competitiveness). It is thus always advantageous to increase energy conservation, promote productive investment and business profitability[3] (slowing of nominal wage gains, stabilization of employer welfare contributions, government aids to industry), and support economic activity by public spending, by the housing agencies or housing of families, or by certain community consumptions (hospital care, public jobs, etc.).

When the external debt condition is progressively relaxed, the other program variables swing, one after another, in ascending 'import content–job content' ratio order. They include the various measures affecting household consumption (welfare benefits, government agency pay, income tax, etc.). At the outside, if the trade deficit were no longer constraining (as a simple 'case of school'), all the programme variables could be applied favourably to employment, irrespective of the external cost.[4] In these circumstances, if the curve of increase[5] of employment is drawn on the basis of tolerance of added external debt[5] (Figure 14.2) its concave side is down: the yields are diminishing, since decreasingly advantageous (to employment) and/or increasingly costly (in debt) measures are being applied.

Table 14.4 Principal fluctuation results in relation to the reference account

Group A: Moderate effort variants having limited effects on employment (long time working trend)

Name of variant	A01	A01	AL1	AL2	AL4	A0L	A3L	ALL
Financing capacity								
—gov't agencies, billion 1980 F per year	+4	*0*	−10	−24	−51	0	−30	−56
—nation, billion 1980 F per year	0	*−10*	*−10*	*−20*	*−40*	−11	−32	−49
Net annual wage purchasing power per capita in % per year	+0.07	+0.40	+0.22	+0.74	+0.92	+0.33	+0.33	+0.89
1985:								
—jobs, thousands	+215	+275	+295	+365	+495	+275	+420	+530
—job seekers, thousands	−81	−105	−113	−136	−186	−103	−157	−197
Annual market price GDP growth (% per year)	+0.16	+0.28	+0.34	+0.52	+0.85	+0.29	+0.65	+0.92
Average annual % of change in volume in:								
—household consumption (% per year)	−0.03	+0.07	+0.15	+0.47	+0.94	+0.09	+0.64	+0.38
—business capital spending (% per year)	+0.95	+1.74	+1.69	+2.05	+3.00	+1.72	+2.76	+3.50
Consumer prices (% per year)	−0.15	−0.40	−0.50	−0.56	−0.86	−0.41	−0.76	−0.36

Group B: same as Group A

Name of variant	B00	B01	BL1	BL2	B34	BL4	B0L	B3L	BLL	B00-bis	BL1-bis	BL2-bis
Financing capacity												
— gov't agencies, billion 1980 F per year	6	*0*	−8	−23	*−30*	*−50*	*0*	*−30*	−102	13	−7	−22
— nation, billion 1980 F per year	0	*−10*	*−10*	*−20*	*−40*	*−40*	−21	−42	−90	*0*	*−10*	*−20*

— jobs, thousands	+535	+605	+620	+700	+800	+840	+645	+800	+1115	+480	+595	+690
— job seekers, thousands	−239	−265	−271	−304	−335	−254	−276	−332	−453	−202	−260	−305
Annual market price GDP growth (% per year)	+0.39	+0.53	+0.58	+0.76	+1.01	+1.10	+0.65	+1.00	+1.78	+0.38	+0.60	+0.76
Average annual % of change in volume in:												
— household consumption (% per year)	−0.67	−0.52	−0.43	−0.24	+0.20	+0.27	−0.34	+0.22	+1.17	−0.16	−0.12	−0.10
— business capital spending (% per year)	+3.63	+4.44	+4.36	+5.10	+6.12	+6.00	+6.12	+6.09	+8.40	+2.36	+3.74	+4.75
Consumer prices (% per year)	−1.6	−1.8	−1.8	−2.2	−2.3	−2.6	−2.0	−2.3	−3.0	−0.7	−1.4	−2.9

Group C: Assumptions for negotiation of accelerated reduction in work time against slowed purchasing power and expansion of shift work

Name of variant	C00	CL1	CL2	CL4	CLL	C00 (2)
Financing capacity						
— gov't agencies, billion 1980 F per year	−8	−21	−36	−65	−89	+6
— nation, billion 1980 F per year	0	−10	−20	−40	−70	0
Net annual wage purchasing power per capita in % per year	−1.94	−1.60	−1.27	−1.09	−1.06	0
1985:						
— jobs, thousands	+1215	+1290	+1360	+1500	+1645	+1110
— job seekers, thousands	−587	−612	−638	−689	−740	−506
Annual market price GDP growth (% per year)	−0.33	+0.50	+0.67	+1.02	+1.37	+0.30
Average annual % of change in volume in:						
— household consumption (% per year)	−1.18	−0.90	−0.66	−0.15	+0.26	−0.20
— business capital spending (% per year)	+5.04	+5.50	+5.96	+6.82	+8.40	+2.30
Consumer prices (% per year)	−2.3	−2.5	−2.7	−3.0	−3.1	−0.4

The magnitudes printed in italic are those limiting the breadth of the programs considered.

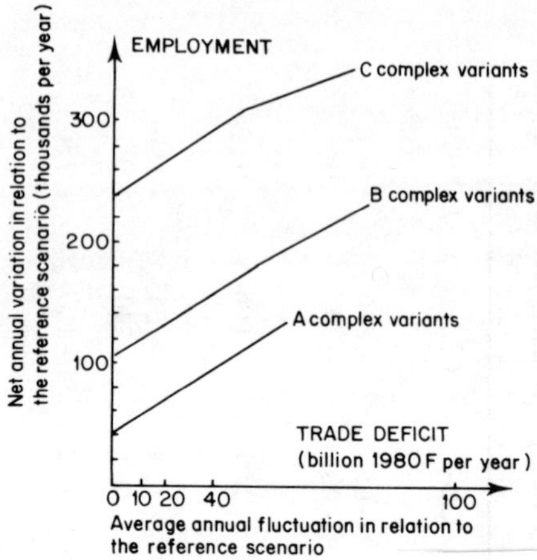

Figure 14.2 Increase of employment in the complex variants. A, complex variants with narrow latitudes; B, complex variants with widened latitudes; C, B latitudes plus assumption of worktime reduction (with moderation of wages and expansion of shift work).

For the same reasons, when on given latitudes the external debt tolerance rises, the apparent elasticity of imports in relation to the GDP[5] increases as shown in the following table.

Apparent elasticity of imports $\frac{\Delta IM/IM}{\Delta GDP/GDP}$	Tolerated additional trade deficit billion 1980 Francs per year			
	0	+10	+20	+40
A latitudes	1.25	1.65	1.77	1.82
B latitudes	1.05	1.38	1.58	1.64

The two foregoing determinations simply show that relations such as trade deficit–growth, growth–employment, or imports–growth are linear neither in level nor in growth rate; they depend on the nature and intensity of the economic policy followed. In these circumstances, elementary estimates by 'rule of three' which are all too often encountered are to be taken with a grain of salt; they can only supply an opening magnitude at best.

Similarly, the trade deficit and public deficit are not linked by one to one correspondence, but are nonetheless not independent of each other either. In the exercises carried out, it is rare for the constraints relative to both deficits to be saturated. To mobilize given additional external debt, it is necessary to be able to increase the level of economic activity, and for that purpose to increase 'autonomous demand' or more generally to implement economic policy programs taking more or less public funds: consequently, too strict a limitation of the goverment-agency deficit would prevent full advantage being taken of the assumed external tolerance. Conversely, the public deficit cannot rise too high on pain of applying measures too costly in imports[6] and overrunning the trade deficit limit fixed. The following table gives the upper limit of the additional trade deficit compatible with a given additional trade deficit.[5]

Unit: Billion 1980 francs per year on an annual 1981–1985 average

Additional trade deficit	0	10	20	40
Additional public deficit				
—A latitudes	−4	10	24	51
—B latitudes	−6	8	23	50

The aforesaid diminishing yields have another effect. On given latitudes, the more relaxed the trade deficit constraint, the greater the tendency of the deficit to increase adversely in time:

— If the constraint is rather low, the optimum combination of economic policy programs, according to DMS, promotes investment, net consumption; imports tend to capital goods and build up the productive plant; they are temporary and even thereafter promote expanded exports (exportable surplus effect, and enhanced competitiveness). So the trade deficit tends gradually to be overcome.

— If the constraint is not so low, the optimum combination allows for more consumption, reducing the exportable surplus and generating imports tending to permanency: the trade deficit is not reduced and even tends to increase as a result of interest charges.

The exercises thus demonstrate a limit which the trade deficit should never overrun, on pain of a vicious circle. Due to the correspondence with the public deficit, the latter should never increase to an unreasonable extent.

On given trade and public deficits, the other avenues to be explored with a view to increasing employment consist of increasing the internal effort, i.e. widening the latitudes. The increase derives from the fact that the most labour-intensive and/or most import sparing (or most competitive adverse) programs can be applied on a larger scale. Figure 14.2 enables the increased employment in the case of type B or C latitudes to be compared with the increase in the type A latitudes. The differences are substantial; the exercises confirm that internal efforts—if socially and politically acceptable—are not devoid of effects on employment. In particular, the type C complex variants produce results far superior to the other complex variants. They tend to show that accelerated worktime reduction, under strict conditions of wage moderation and maintenance of the time of use of equipment, could be a key factor in increasing employment. But they also raise a crucial question of the limits of the exercise; what is the real meaning of macro-economic calculations in a question as complex as worktime reduction, involving an infinite variety of micro-economic, technical, social, and political factors? This example demonstrates—if need be—that quantitative studies are a powerful tool for exploring economic and social policies, but are not sufficient to guarantee the plausibility or even the simple 'feasibility' thereof.

Finally, the method is apt for study of different scenarios of an international environment. This approach was used to assess the effects of new world prospects attendant on the oil price increases decided on by OPEC in Caracas and those which have ensued. The new international environmental assumptions are given in Table 14.5. The employment results are shown by curves E_D and E_F in Figure 14.3, reflecting a large loss in relation to the reference scenario: 100 000 jobs per year in the case of the new unfavourable international environmental scenario.

14.3 CONCLUSION

The quantitative studies made in connection with the VIIIth Plan were characterized by extensive use of the scenario method and the method of optimum complex variants. The latter method was used for systematic

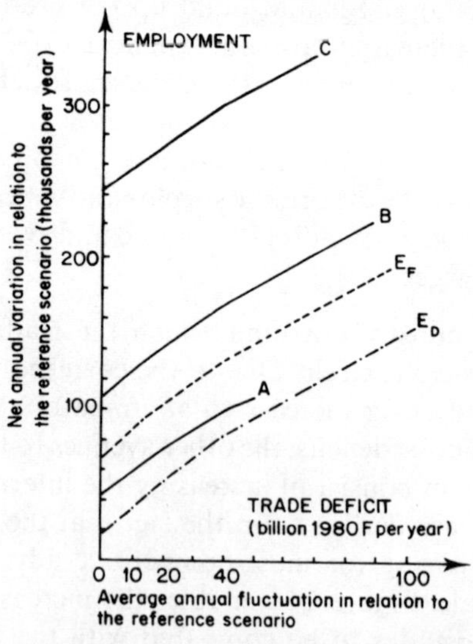

Figure 14.3 Effect on employment of worsening of the international environment. A, complex variants with narrow latitudes; B, complex variants with widened latitudes; C, B latitudes plus assumption of accelerated worktime reduction; E_F, B latitudes plus new favourable international environmental scenario; E_D, B latitudes plus new unfavourable international environmental scenario

Table 14.5 International environmental assumptions

1. The price of oil (% per barrel)

	1980	1981	1982	1983	1984	1985
Old assumptions (summer 1979)						
—favourable real price + 0%	21.5	23.0	24.5	26.2	28.0	29.9
—unfavourable* real price + 7%	22.5	26.2	30.5	35.5	41.3	48.2
New assumptions (spring 1980)						
—favourable real price + 2%	31.0	35.0	38.6	42.8	47.3	52.1
—unfavourable real price + 7%	31.0	36.6	42.8	49.8	58.1	67.5

* Assumptions of the October 1979 starting scenarios and complex variants A, B, and C.

2. Growth and inflation of the trading partners

	foreign GDP growth—% per annum	foreign GDP price increase % per annum
Old assumptions (summer 1979)		
—favourable case	3.6	5.8
—unfavourable case*	2.7	6.9
New assumptions (spring 1980)		
—favourable case	2.4	7.7
—unfavourable case	2.2 2.0	7.9 8.1

*Assumptions of the October 1979 starting scenarios and complex variants A, B, and C.
Source: *Economie et Statistique*, No. 115, for the old assumptions, and Report of the administrative group chaired by D. Lallier, Deputy Director, Forecasting Bureau, for the new assumptions.

exploration, from the macro-economic point of view, of an aggregate of economic policies based on the assumption of increase of employment as a priority goal. It has the advantage of clearly correlating:

- —the improvement of the target function (here, employment);
- —the assumptions relative to the efforts made, in terms of economic policy programs and changes in certain behaviour or certain institutional rules;
- —the assumptions relative to the constraints affecting the results, i.e. the maximum costs considered permissible, in terms of increase in debt or limitation of purchasing power for example.

It is of course not incumbent on the technician, but on labour, management, and the authorities to arbitrate between the expected improvement, the nature and extent of the programs to be deployed, and the acceptable amount of the costs involved. The technician's role resembles, to use W. Leontief's comparison, that of a cook: it consists of preparing various dishes and showing the menu, listing the dishes and prices to the consumers for them to make a selection. It is a sort of menu of this type that an endeavour has been made to present by use of the method of optimum complex variants.

NOTES

[1] Disregarding the effects of the second oil shock, examined in the second part of the text.
[2] This diagnosis is aggravated by the oil shock and persisting inflationary pressure higher than initially forecast.
[3] Due to the significant role of profit in investment functions according to the DMS model.
[4] In this case the latitudes would themselves determine the extreme value of the trade deficit, which could not be exceeded except by widening the latitudes.
[5] In relation to the reference scenario.
[6] Or overly impairing competitiveness.

REFERENCES

Fouquet, D., Charpin, J. M., Guillaume, H., Muet, P. A., and Vallet, D. (1978). '*DMS = Dynamic Multisector Model*.' Les Collections de l'INSEE. **64–65,** INSEE, Paris.

Gauron, A., and Maurice, J. (1980). 'Economic policies for the VIIIth Plan: An exploration of all the possibles.' *Revue Economique*, **31,** 894–921.

Guillaume, H. (1978). 'Analysis of the DMS economic policy multipliers.' *Annales de l'INSEE*, **32,** 57–106.

Maarek, G. (1980). 'Macroeconomic models and linear programming.' *Rèvue Economique*, **31,** 982–998.

INSEE Programs Department (1980). 'A representation of the French economy: The DMS model.' *Rèvue Economique*, **31,** 930–981.

Discussion

M. TIVEGNA[1]
Confederation of Italian industry (Confindustria), Roma

1 INTRODUCTION

The exposure to the very interesting technical work which lies beneath the French planning effort is a welcome opportunity to devote some time to one of the most remarkable planning practices and procedures in Western Europe.

Given the nature of our meeting and the fact that the paper I am discussing is based on deviations from one unreported control scenario, I will not get into commenting on parameters and structure of the French economy in relation to the results of the paper. I believe it will be more fruitful from my standpoint to raise a few issues pertaining to the use of macro-models in public and private bodies whose main function is to make decisions or comment upon decisions. I hope I will be able to catch some of the loose ends that applied econometricians typically face in their daily practice. In so doing, my purpose will be to stimulate further comments on the paper I am discussing and, hopefully, on some of my remarks as they originate from applied work.

2 SUMMARY OF GAURON *ET AL.*'S PAPER

By explicit indication of the authors, the main innovation which originates from the quantitative work supporting the French Eighth Plan is represented by the 'abandonment of a single nominative forecast in favour of development of several medium-term scenarios'. Also noteworthy is their effort to combine standard multiplier analysis and optimal control techniques to put together a 'menu' (as they call it) of alternative policy options to maximize employment, over the 1980–85 planning horizon, under the usual public sector budget and balance of payments constraints.

The procedure which has been adopted is outlined in Figure 14.1. It seems to consist of preliminary simulations of elementary policy proposals (what the authors call analytic variants) to assess their impact on the endogenous variables, followed by several control experiments to maximize total employment variation using policy packages (complex variants, as the authors call them) as instruments. In the final stage of the work the model is solved for some of the optimal packages. In so doing the background quantitative work described in the paper responds 'to a request by the non-economist members of the Development Commission, formalizing their thinking'.

The main finding of the policy exercises is that worktime reduction — 'under strict conditions of wage moderation' and keeping constant the average life of capital stock — is a very powerful tool for increasing employment over the planning horizon. The relationship between balance of payments and government deficit (in its various definitions) shows the familiar Keynesian pattern due to the structure of DMS.

3 SHORT-TERM ECONOMIC POLICIES AND STRUCTURE

The French planning procedures allow for a large participation of the Trade Unions, various Trade Associations, and other concerned parties in the construction of the Plan. This is probably the most correct procedure as it can result in a reference scheme that is built 'together with' and not 'against' the organized groups whose behaviour can determine the success or failure of the plan.

All these organized groups frequently have definite opinions on industrial relations and economic development and must normally respond to their constituencies.

A deep-rooted opinion, quite popular among some of the most influential Trade Union movements in several Western European countries—and notably in France and Italy—implies that some specific policy measures, of both long- and short-term nature, could *at the same time* influence the final outcome *and* the transmission mechanisms that lead to it. In model terms, movements in the sole exogenous variables could influence simultaneously both parameters and endogenous variables.

Typical examples of this attitude consist of the asking for higher wages together with Trade Union control over those production arrangements that can lead to higher productivity of labour and/or lower input content per unit of output. Other examples could be recalled consisting basically of all those instances where Trade Union control over flows of private investment or public expenditure is claimed to be conducive to a better economic performance.

The above-mentioned situations originate from a bargaining process between Trade Unions, Employers Associations, and/or government agencies. Therefore they are frequently based on totally unrigorous foundations on all sides. Any attempt to build an underlying quantitative structure to the behaviour of all economic agents, especially over the long-term, would be, then, highly welcome.

In order to foster as broad a consensus as possible, at the planning stage, some attempts should be made to run several scenarios embodying the basic beliefs of all concerned parties on the parameter response to the proposed policy measures. This could be done through some kind of sensitivity analysis on key parameters whose values could either be supplied on a 'revealed preference' basis or correctly estimated through some external (to the model) scientific investigation.

I will state my point more precisely with an example drawn from the 'wage–price–productivity nexus' referred to a specific industry. On a highly simplified basis this nexus could be represented by the following system of relationships:

$$\begin{aligned} PQ &= a_0 + a_1 \left(\frac{\overline{W/E}}{Q/E} \right) + a_2 \overline{PINP} \\ Q &= \overline{D} \\ E &= F^{-1}(Q, \overline{K}) \end{aligned} \tag{1}$$

where

PQ: Price of output
W: Wage bill
E: Manhours
Q: Output at constant prices
$PINP$: Price of inputs
D: Demand for Q at constant prices
K: Capital stock.

The bar indicates exogenous variables and $F^{-1}(.)$ is an inverted production relationship.

In the bargaining (or planning) process between the 'partenaires sociales', the Trade Unions could claim to be able to exert some influence over both labour productivity and a more rational use of production inputs. If the model were estimated as in (1), it would be convenient to code and simulate it as:

$$PQ = a_0(t) + a_1\left[\frac{\overline{W/E}}{\gamma(t)(Q/E)}\right] + \tilde{a}_2\left(\frac{INP}{Q}\right).\overline{PINP}$$
$$Q = \overline{D} \qquad (2)$$
$$E = \delta(t)F^{-1}(Q, \overline{K})$$

where INP represents total inputs at constant prices and $a_0(t)$, $\gamma(t)$, and $\delta(t)$ would be time-varying parameters proposed by the interested parties along with values for INP/Q.[2]

Another way to approach the same basic issue of parameter response to policy measures, or to particular behaviour of policy-makers, Trade Unions, or Trade Associations, would be to code in the model several policy reaction functions— or 'contractual' functions—which would make some allowance for the effects of this behaviour.

With respect to the previous example, the basic set of relationships (1) could be coded:

$$PQ = a_0 + a_1\left(\frac{\overline{W/E}}{Q/E}\right) + \tilde{a}_2\,\overline{PINP}$$
$$\frac{Q}{E} = b_1\left(\frac{\overline{W}}{E}\right) + B(L)\overline{I} \qquad (3)$$
$$Q = \overline{D}$$
$$E = \left(1\Big/\frac{Q}{E}\right).Q$$

where I is investment in plant and equipment at constant prices and $B(L)$ is a lag operator. In (3) productivity (output per manhour), wage rates, and employment would come out from an agreement reached at the planning table according to the parameters b_1 and $B(L)$. This set of relationships would formalize an agreement between the so-called 'social partners' (partenaires sociales in France, 'parti sociali' in Italy) on productivity, wages, work hours, and specific forms of investment in plant and equipment which would make the above-mentioned relations possible.

All these relations would of course be possible only at a sectoral level where output and production processes are quite homogeneous.

Another typical example of a situation where these types of functions could be plugged into the model is represented by the announcements, frequently made by Governments and Central Banks in recent years, that monetary policy will be responsive to wage–price moderation. Warnings of this kind have been issued quite frequently in Italy in the last few years as a way to keep expectations on the exchange rate and inflation under control. Long-term planning models can hardly make some allowance for this type of expectations and so it would be useful to somehow include these factors.

4 THE USE OF ECONOMETRIC MODELS IN POLICY MAKING: SOME CONCLUSIONS

Starting from the mid-sixties, the use of macro-econometric models in government and industry has expanded very quickly. But the attitudes of decision-makers on the use of models to propose policy measures, or to assess their impact, still differ quite substantially, ranging from total devotion to computer printouts to the use of these same printouts just as a public relation tool.

Model-builders, on their part, frequently resent the futility of their work which—it must be said—is one of the most time-consuming tasks in professional economics. What they most resent is the 'political noise' that all too often creeps into the various 'optimal' economic policy trajectories produced by their models. The authors of the paper under discussion have undertaken a far-reaching effort to provide their policy-makers with a very rich set of alternatives and constraints to choose from. Even though they propose 'optimal packages' to be accepted as a whole, they allow for differential paths in the exogenous ('environmental', as they call it) variables. Besides that, the control algorithm they are using should make it possible to switch to different policies in case some optimal policies cannot be implemented over time.

The suggestions I put forward in this paper can make the various vested and opposed interests of a free and democratic society closer to the planning effort.

In the recent past, one important Trade Union and a few Employers Associations (including Confindustria) in Italy have built econometric models—or some 'econometric arguments'—and made experimental use of them. Nothing has shown up so far at the bargaining table and maybe never will. Some of my more 'literate' colleagues maintain that when you get at 'the real thing' you must use other arguments. Nevertheless, I believe that the various forms of factual background information which goes along with the use of econometric models have considerably—and fruitfully—reduced the width of the bargaining area and made the 'old opponents' more aware of their common interests.

'What is the real meaning of macro-economic calculations in a question as complex as worktime reduction, involving an infinite variety of micro-economic, technical, social, and political factors? This example demonstrates—if need be—that quantitative studies are a powerful tool for exploring economic and social policies, but are not sufficient to guarantee the plausibility or even the simple feasibility thereof.' This is what the authors say: I believe that the preparatory work for the French Eighth Plan, and some of the amendments I have suggested, can substantially increase the area of consensus in policy-making, thereby laying down the path for a higher, more balanced economic growth.

NOTES

[1] The opinions expressed by the author do not necessarily represent the positions of Confindustria on the matters herein discussed.

[2] It could be possible, of course, to model productivity, Q/E. In this case, it would just be necessary to modify the parameters of the equation if past experience were considered inappropriate to explain future performance.

Author Index

Subject Index